MAGAZINE

The Guide to Retail Business Planning

*The complete handbook
for creating a winning plan
for any retail business*

Warren G. Purdy

INC. BUSINESS RESOURCES

Boston, Massachusetts

The Guide to Retail Business Planning
The Complete Handbook for Creating
a Winning Plan for Any Retail Business

Published by *Inc.* Business Resources, a division of *Inc.* magazine.
Copyright © 1997 Goldhirsh Group, Inc.
Boston, Mass.

Editorial Director: Bradford W. Ketchum, Jr.
Managing Editor: Sarah J. Fernberger
Book and Cover Designer: Cynthia M. Davis
Cover Photo-Collage Artist: Jeff Bryce

Library of Congress Catalog Card No.: 97-072581

ISBN: 1-880394-31-6

First Edition

Printed in the United States of America.

1 2 3 4 5 6 7 8 9 10

Visit *Inc.* Online at www.inc.com.

DEDICATION

To My Mom and Dad,
Frederic and Eleanor Purdy

ACKNOWLEDGMENTS

With any undertaking of this size, many people's help and support are essential to bring it to a successful conclusion. *The Guide to Retail Business Planning* is no exception. In fact, because so much of our material was generated from outside sources, we relied heavily on many people who gave generously of their time and expertise, and I want to extend my sincere thanks to all of them.

Several individuals and institutions in particular deserve special mention. Tom Misner, research associate and partner-in-crime on the book, has done yeoman's work, writing, updating data, ferreting out hard-to-find information, and searching for case examples to blend into the book. Tom's perseverance was remarkable considering that his first child, Benjamin, arrived smack in the middle of the process! Bradford W. Ketchum, Jr., editorial director, and Sarah J. Fernberger, managing editor, at *Inc.* Business Resources, provided all the support, guidance, encouragement, and insight so necessary to make this book possible. Cindy Davis also deserves special thanks for her expert layout and design work, as well as Jacqueline Lapidus and Audra Mulhearn for their excellent copy editing.

I am also indebted to Rebecca Black, Deirdre and Michael Robinson, and Ken Hawk, the entrepreneurs who so graciously allowed us to publish their plans so that others might learn from their experiences, and to others who provided quotes and excerpts. Our expert panel consisted of Laura Crossen, CPA, Michael Fram, CPA, and Marcella Mosier, all from Ernst & Young LLP; David Aloise, executive director of small business banking for BankBoston, N.A., and Don Rielly at the Massachusetts Small Business Development Center at Boston College. They deserve special thanks for reviewing and evaluating the business plans selected for inclusion in the book. Don's book, *A Guide to Planning and Financing Your Business in Massachusetts,* also served as an important resource.

A number of individuals and trade associations also provided us with significant amounts of information. These include: Bruce Van Kleeck at the National Retail Federation; Nancy Womac at the International Franchise Association; Christina Duffney and Edward Pfeiffer at the Direct Marketing Association; Howard Bassuk at the Franchise Network; Kevin Yeanoplos at Moran, Quick, and Yeanoplos; Francie Smith at the Data Base Marketing Resource Center; Bob Purvin at the American Association of Franchisees and Dealers; Larry Henning of the American Bar Association; Scott Small, CPA with MacDonald Page and Company; and Michael Tubrity at the International Council of Shopping Centers.

Many thanks to Sam Males, director of the Nevada SBDC, and Bradford W. Ketchum III at *Inc.* Business Resources, who shared the vision for this joint publication, and to a number of Small Business Development Centers that nominated business plans from Georgia, Idaho, Louisiana, Massachusetts, Nevada, and Pennsylvania. In addition, I express my appreciation to Mary Ellen Beck, director of the State University of New York SBDC Research Network, and to her staff, for their advice and for access to their research center and its substantial holdings.

I also thank four colleagues at the University of Southern Maine: Professors Carter Manny and John Sanders, for their reviews of the legal and financial sections of the book; Janice Tisdale, director of Business Information Services at the Maine SBDC, and Zip Kellogg of Reference Services, for their help with secondary resources.

Finally, thanks to my wife Leanne, who again spent long hours during her interminable commute to Boston reviewing my chapter drafts prior to submission to the eagle-eyed editing staff at *Inc.*

Warren G. Purdy
Rye, New Hampshire
September 1997

CONTENTS

INTRODUCTION

WHY A BUSINESS PLAN?

Ask successful small-business founders, bankers, and consultants what are the most important factors contributing to the long-run viability of a small business, and they will give you consistent answers. Among the factors they cite most often are management skills and business planning.

It is important to understand these observations as you contemplate starting a business, because most people who start one do not succeed. Studies show that **80%** of businesses fail within the first five years of operation. Most businesses that fail generally lack a formal, written plan to help guide them through their initial years. The good news is that you can learn basic planning skills to help avoid this pitfall.

Poor planning and unskilled management are significant causes of business failure and are closely related. Most people go into a business based on a specialized skill or interest that they have. You decide to open a craft shop or kitchen-appliance store because you are an accomplished artist or a skilled appliance repairperson. Without a comprehensive business plan, you might carry the largest merchandise supply in town and still fail because you have inadequate working capital, no rational promotion strategy, and a recordkeeping system of the shoebox variety.

The planning process will force you to consider all aspects of your prospective retail operation, helping to reduce the number of mistakes business founders and owners usually make. How much money should you tie up in inventory? Should you locate downtown or in the suburbs, or sell products via direct mail? Are you capable of handling your bookkeeping, or do you need an accountant? Your detailed business plan will address these questions before you are caught scrambling for the answers.

A well-researched and documented business plan will significantly increase your chances of success. A carefully thought-out plan will force you to take a hard look at your business on paper before you even order your first ream of letterhead. You'll find it easier to obtain financing for your dream, staff your business effectively, and attract customers. This planning guide will enable you to approach the task of launching your business with enthusiasm and confidence.

Why the Retail Industry?

Retail operations in the United States generated $2.34 trillion in sales from more than 1.5 million establishments in 1995. From 1994 to 1995 the sector as a whole grew at a rate of approximately 5% and represents the second-largest industry in our economy after the service industry.

Retailing has experienced more changes during the past decade than it did in the preceding generations. Although one can argue that retailing is still a domain of small business (that is, approximately 75% of all retail stores have annual sales of less than $1 million), in recent years slightly more than 80% of all sales were generated by stores with sales above $1 million. In addition, the growth of discount retailers has increased at a rate, some experts claim, three times that of the industry. This is due primarily to companies like Wal-Mart (which has been credited with creating one out of every 16 new jobs in the United States in 1994) and to an increase in wholesale membership clubs, factory-outlet malls, and category-killer stores such as Toys "R" Us and Circuit City.

Although these trends may raise alarms about the well-being of the smaller store, retailing today still presents significant opportunities, provided you recognize that the market has fundamentally changed and you develop your strategies accordingly. This planning guide will address issues you'll need to consider, such as competitive return and credit policies, variable pricing, compatible product lines, and store hours. Kenneth Stone, an expert on the impact of discount giants on local retailers, discusses the phenomenon further in his book *Competing with the Retail Giants*, which is recommended reading for all retail entrepreneurs.

Social/Demographic Factors

In addition to adopting new strategies to help level the playing field for smaller retailers, you can count on a number of socioeconomic factors that bode well for the future. These include:

The aging of the U.S. population. There are more people over 65 years old than teenagers in the United States. Baby Boomers, who are now approaching or over 50, are traveling for pleasure and enjoying more leisure activities. This fundamental change in the population will have profound effects on the demand for retail business of all kinds.

High retirement rates. Nearly two million people are retiring each year, and by 2000, that number will grow to three million a year. By 2030, Americans over 65 will outnumber all children under 18. Americans can now expect to spend up to one-third of their lives in retirement. This shift in the population represents a great opportunity for retailers, who can attract this market by offering higher levels of service and more specialized product lines than their mass-merchandising counterparts.

Mail, phone, and online sales. The explosive growth of credit and credit card use, plus purchases of products by mail, phone, and computer, have created new, direct, and convenient distribution channels to which buyers are flocking.

Concern for health and fitness. Heightened interest in maintaining health and fitness has inspired growth in the specialty food, apparel, and educational sectors.

Multicultural society. An increasingly varied population from many parts of the world is creating new demand for a wider range of products.

These factors, among others, offer new market potential for the retail industry. Smaller retailers should be in a good position to capitalize on these changes. Consumers with more specific tastes, higher levels of disposable income, and more leisure time can be expected to sustain new retail businesses tailored to their needs.

Why This Planning Guide?

Whether you plan to start a business from scratch, enter a franchise agreement, or buy an existing store, there is no substitute for personally developing a business plan. Don't rely on the slick presentation of a potential franchiser, or the bare financial statements and some very convincing jawboning offered by the seller of a business, or a plan that you have paid a consultant to write.

The reasons for writing your own plan are simple. This is *your* business, an enterprise that you will live with day and night for years to come. Your financial security will be dependent on your business's success. It is too important to leave to third parties.

Although information and assistance from others may be essential to the development of your plan, they should not be a substitute for it. You have to be convinced your plan will work because, in the final analysis, you will have to make it work (even if you can call on your investors for a cash infusion when your payroll comes up short or that unforgiving bank wants another loan payment). You'll need to study your market, foresee growth, and develop ongoing relationships with suppliers and customers.

This planning guide was created because of a specific need in the marketplace—the need for a resource that combines specific *information* on how to write a business plan, a *directory* enabling you to identify and find the resources you will need to complete your plan, and *actual business plans* that have been used to launch successful enterprises.

This guide is designed to integrate all of the information you will need to lead you through the process of designing a plan that will work for you.

To help you research and write your retail-business plan—and to make this guide as user friendly as possible—we have placed reference guides throughout the book so that you can find the information you need quickly and easily.

Three symbols are used:

IS> p. 181   *Inc.Sheets*—The "IS" symbol refers to the page number of an *Inc.Sheet* that can help you gather the information you need or perform the described exercise.

R> p. 225   *Resource*—The "R" symbol refers to the page number of the corresponding resource in Section V, Resource Directory.

B> p. 292   *Bibliography*—The "B" symbol refers to the page number in the Bibliography where you can find further reading on the topic at hand.

Section I

Developing a Business Plan

WRITING YOUR PLAN

This section illustrates how to develop a business plan for the retail industry. It is designed so that you can easily identify the types of information that should be included in each part of your plan. Although individual business plans differ in style and organization, all of the elements covered here are necessary to develop a comprehensive plan for your business.

As you will quickly see when you begin to work on your own plan, you'll want a lot of information that you don't have at your fingertips. This is when the Resource Directory in Section V will be most useful. Every category of information or data identified in this planning section refers you to a specific part of the Resource Directory, where you will find a list of sources to help answer your questions.

As you are writing out your plan, you should refer to Section III, which includes three real-life business plans developed by inspired entrepreneurs like yourself. Fully tested, these plans will prove useful as you develop your own approach and style in writing your business plan.

And finally, use the *Inc.Sheets*—do-it-yourself worksheets—in Section IV to guide you each step of the way to creating a successful blueprint for your retail business.

THE EXECUTIVE SUMMARY

OVERVIEW

The Executive Summary, by definition, should appear at the front of your business plan. Don't assume, however, that just because it is a summary, it's supposed to be written after the plan has been completed and then inserted at the beginning. Although many business owners may have done this, we suggest that you take a slightly different approach.

The Executive Summary represents your vision for your business. If you don't have a clear vision up front, you can't expect anyone else to see it. That's why a great deal of the content in this section should be well thought out beforehand—not after the fact. Write a two- to three-page draft of your Executive Summary first, as best you can. It can always be revised or corrected for accuracy once your entire business plan has been completed.

The Executive Summary could be the most important part of your plan, particularly if you are looking for external sources of debt or equity. If potential lenders or investors are evaluating your plan, the Executive Summary is the first and sometimes the only thing they really read. Why? Because most people evaluating your plan probably have a stack of others they are reviewing, and if you don't capture their imagination and enthusiasm at the beginning, your proposal may end up in the reject pile before it has been fully evaluated.

Compare this to the process of buying a book. If you know the author, you might purchase it without a second look. If, on the other hand, the author is new to you, you will most likely read the reviews on the cover and take a look at the introduction, then make your purchase decision.

If you are starting a franchise, the franchisor may provide you with a "boilerplate" plan from which you can adapt certain sections for your trading area. Otherwise, you will need to include some specifics about the franchisor in your Executive Summary. This information should include the name and address of the franchising company; size in terms of sales and number of franchisees; history and duration of the parent business; and terms of the franchise agreement. For more information on franchising, see Section II.

THE BASICS

What, Why, Whom, When, Where

This is the essence of the Executive Summary. The reader needs to know in concise and unambiguous terms:

What are you planning to do?
> *(describe your business)*
> Start a table-tennis and billiards retail store, offering a complete line of tables, paddles, high-performance balls, and accessories. We will also offer lessons and reconditioning services…

Why are you planning to do it?
> *(explain your business)*
> Table tennis (or ping-pong) is the second most popular sport in the world, played by more than 18.2 million Americans in 1996…

Whom are you planning to do it for?
> *(identify your customers)*
> Primary market will be the greater Nashua, N.H., area with secondary markets including the entire United States and Canada via mail-order sales. Our goal is to offer high-quality merchandise to amateurs and professionals alike…

When are you planning to do it?
> *(timetable, schedules)*
> Store hours will be from 9 a.m. to 7 p.m., Monday through Friday, and 9 a.m. to 5 p.m. on Saturday. Table-tennis and billiards

lessons will be offered in the evenings throughout the week…

Where do you plan to do it?
(specific site selection)
Our fixed-base location will be on Route 101, just two miles from Nashua, in the Pheasant Lane Mall. Other stores in the mall include May's department store, JCPenney, Payless Drug, and General Nutrition Center. The mall is the region's largest, and generates a traffic flow of more than 7,000 customers daily…

IS▶ p. 183

MISSION STATEMENT

Our goal is to offer carts, kiosks, and trailers that are inexpensive, innovative, and customized to be used as alternatives to traditional storefront points of distribution. We are dedicated to providing our customers with the highest quality products and services available. Our aim is to have successful, long-term relationships with our customers and to have the reputation of being the most innovative and technology-driven company in our industry. Our development goals are to maximize shareholder value, double sales in each of the next three years, and to be profitable after the first year.

Matthew Steele
21st Century Carts & Kiosks Inc.
Lovingston, Va.

Mission Statement

A mission statement in its simplest form is a statement of your company's purpose, values, vision, and goals. The statement does not have to be lengthy but should answer basic questions, including: What business is your company in? What products and services do you provide? What are your strengths and competitive advantages? Who are your target markets/customers? What are the basic beliefs and values of your company?

A well thought-out and articulate mission statement is a very important component of your business plan, as it will enable you to communicate clearly and concisely exactly who you are and why you are in business. If your mission statement is effective, it will also become a living document that will change over time, adapting to your evolving markets and stakeholders including employees, customers, suppliers, and stockholders. Your mission statement should be placed either at the front of your plan, right after the Table of Contents, or included as part of your Executive Summary.

IS▶ p. 185 **B▶ p. 294**

Management Team

The Executive Summary should describe briefly the background and experience of the owner/managers. In addition, if you plan to have a board of directors or advisers, or if you are using consultants, their backgrounds should also be highlighted. Identify their most relevant experience. Include complete résumés in the Management section or appendices of your business plan.

Objectives

Although you specifically outlined earlier what you intend to do in your business, you need to mention both your intermediate and your longer-term goals here. For example, in your table-tennis and billiards business, you may plan at some point to develop a customer-based newsletter, or host tournaments and guest demonstrations. Significant plans for the future should be mentioned.

Investment

If you intend to use your business plan to help secure financing or equity investors (stockholders), the Executive Summary should include the types of capital and amounts you hope to raise. As with other parts of this section, you don't have to provide every detail here, just enough to enable the reader to get the big picture in terms of your financial needs. In addition, you should mention whether you already have equity investors or large potential customers interested in or committed to the business, unless you have a compelling reason to keep the information confidential.

B▶ p. 292

PITFALLS

The major problems with most Executive Summaries is that they are too long, lack focus, and fail to garner the enthusiasm of the reader. This section of your plan should be a few pages long, at most (not including your mission statement). Even better, try to get it on one or two pages, with just enough room for a page number at the bottom. Remember, everything in this section will be explained in detail in some other part of the plan, so *focus on the opportunities* that your business presents.

SOME ADVICE

"Attention to detail is important. I'm a form person as well as a content person. If I see poor wording, bad spelling, and lousy punctuation, it suggests that the writer does things sloppily. If the Executive Summary—something that's pretty important—is sloppy, maybe the business will be run that way, too. I'll read the whole plan, but my expectations will be much lower."

Holly Thomas
Vice President
First Union National Bank of Florida
Tampa, Fla.

EXCERPT

Tinder Box Gourmet

EXECUTIVE SUMMARY

The following plan outlines the organization and operation of Tinder Box Gourmet Shop, which will be operated by Jay Schmitt. The business plan serves as an initial operating guide and financial proposal.

The enclosed plan includes a description of the Tinder Box franchise, products and services, market analysis, strategies, and programs. Management and financial analysis will also be covered.

Tinder Box Gourmet Shop is a new retail store offering tobacco products and wine and beer service. The business is a franchise operation through Tinder Box International of Philadelphia. This business is a sole proprietorship to be operated by Jay Schmitt.

Tinder Box International was founded in 1928 and has conducted its business in its present corporate form since its incorporation in 1961. Tinder Box International, or "TBI," has granted franchises for its stores since 1965 and currently has 107 franchised stores operating in 28 states. TBI does not operate any company-owned stores.

Generally TBI stores are located in shopping centers or shopping malls servicing geographic areas having populations between 50,000 and over 1,000,000. This store is to be located in such a shopping area at Mayberry Landing on Mayberry and McCarran in Reno, Nev. (Appendix G).

The average sales for these stores in 1994...

Source: Tinder Box Gourmet

DESCRIPTION OF BUSINESS

OVERVIEW

Generally speaking, it may not be necessary to include a Description of Business section in your business plan. If you have provided enough information in the Executive Summary so that your reader has a clear sense of the "What, Why, Whom, When, and Where" of your business, a Description of Business section would be redundant.

However, there are some important exceptions to this rule. If you need to elaborate on certain aspects of your business that cannot easily be discussed in full detail in the Executive Summary, a Description of Business section is essential. For example, if you are purchasing an existing business, you can include important information about the *background* of the business in this section. If the products you are planning to provide are unique or unusual in the market, or if you will be starting a business that has complex product offerings to multiple target markets, you can use the Description of Business section to give readers of your plan a full understanding of *innovative or complex features* of your business. If you are purchasing a franchise, this section is essential to give details about the franchisor, the terms of the franchise agreement, and the product line.

To see if you really need to include a Description of Business section, have a couple of friends or colleagues read your Executive Summary. If they have only a few questions when they are finished, you might need to add just a few details or some clarification to the Summary to accommodate them. If, on the other hand, your reviewers have a large number of questions, you probably need to have a Description of Business section as part of your plan.

IS> p.186

THE BASICS

A Description of Business expands on the information contained in your Executive Summary and provides further detail regarding your business. Here are some of the situations in which you may find it useful to include a Description of Business section.

Buying an Existing Business

If you are planning to purchase an existing business, this section is a good place to include its business history: when it was founded, how it was financed, how it was organized, how successful it has been, and why the current owner wants to sell. In addition, you should explain how you plan to carry out the transition from the current owner's management to yours in a way that maximizes customer goodwill. Often, this is accomplished by the current owner providing services (such as working along with you) after you have purchased the business, for a fixed length of time on a contract-for-services basis.

In a separate section of the plan, you will need to provide a business valuation and numerous financial records, such as the last several years' tax returns. Check with your accountant and refer to the appropriate resources for specific business valuation techniques.

B> p. 292

A Different Drummer

If your type of product either is new to the marketplace or deviates significantly from the way comparable products are being offered and/or distributed by competitors, it is probably wise to provide additional detail to ensure that those evaluating your plan don't simply discard it as just "one more business doing the same old thing."

For an example of a business that may need a substantial explanation in addition to what is provided in the Executive Summary, let's look at

Ostriches Online, a full-service ostrich and ostrich-product broker with offices in Illinois, Singapore, Brazil, and the United Kingdom. Owner Steve Warrington sells ostriches for domestic farm use, ostrich meat (a red meat low in cholesterol), feathers, eggs (for both hatching and consumption), and leather. His company maintains ostrich farms in the United States and abroad, and it regularly imports and exports the birds and their products. In addition, Steve sells a software package for ostrich-farm management. Ostriches Online has a Web site (http://www.ostricheson line.com) with extensive information relative to the business and an easy-to-use interface.

Steve has found a niche in the marketplace for Ostriches Online, and his business is booming. Because the nature of his business is clearly innovative and unconventional, Steve included a Description of Business section in his plan.

Unusual Offerings

If your business has numerous or unusual product offerings, a variety of distribution strategies, and multiple target markets, a Description of Business section can be used to describe them in detail.

An example of a business offering an unusual product is Griller's World (http://virtual.chat tanooga.net/grill), makers of high-end, indoor electric grills. These grills are targeted primarily to RV and boat owners, as well as urban apartment dwellers who cannot, by law, have open-flame grills. Small, but highly efficient, these electric grills employ a unique grid construction. By utilizing extremely dense steel materials, they keep the heat transfer rate high, and the meat retains its natural juices, providing a tender, healthy, flavorful meal. While it does have a retail location, Griller's World sells its products primarily at trade shows, over the Internet, and through catalog sales.

Because of the characteristics of its target markets and the product itself, which sets it apart from traditional barbecue grills, Griller's World would want to include a Description of Business section in its plan.

B▶ p. 294

Another example of a unique enterprise is The Ultimate Gift Company. For a small fee, The Ultimate Gift Company will officially name a star in the sky for your loved ones. Your star dedication gift set includes a personalized certificate with the star's coordinates, newly designated name, and dedication date, and a map that shows the star's exact location in the sky. While this is not a difficult concept to grasp, it is clearly a unique idea that may need some explanation in this section.

PITFALLS

Balance

You need to strike a balance between what the reader of your business plan "needs to know" and unnecessary or incomprehensible detail. In the example of The Ultimate Gift Company, it would be wise to substantiate how it can exclusively dedicate a star (for instance, which astronomical societies will recognize the dedication), but it needn't go into detail about stellar cartography or the methods used to locate stars.

Expert Knowledge

Don't assume that those evaluating your plan have high levels of expertise about your proposed business. There is nothing worse than a plan that's filled with jargon such as "feed-to-weight ratio," "thermo-conductive material," or "galactic center point." If the readers of your proposal don't have a clear understanding of what you are trying to do because they don't understand the language you are using, there is a high probability that your business plan will not be taken seriously.

Redundancy

Be sure not to let your Description of Business simply repeat the information in your Executive Summary. It needs to be complete, but succinct and to the point. If your Description of Business section is redundant, consider eliminating it and adding pertinent details to your Executive Summary.

Henry's Lawn and Garden Center
DESCRIPTION OF BUSINESS

The key to the development and growth of our customer base will be an innovative presentation of premium products/services targeted to the unmet needs of the region's gardeners. The lawn and garden industry in Maine is highly seasonal, peaking in the late spring, summer, and early fall. The late fall, winter, and early spring seasons are slow, relying mainly upon winter storm-related products (i.e., snowblowers, shovels, etc.) to carry them through the season. We intend to smooth out the seasonality curve by offering the region's gardeners opportunities to continue their hobbies throughout the year.

The business will offer five major categories of products and services:

❑ Lawn and Garden Products

❑ Educational/Greenhouse Programs

❑ Plant Question Telephone Hot Line

❑ Customer-Specific Promotions

❑ Season-Specific Promotions

Following is a brief description of the positioning for each:

Lawn and Garden Products: Given the affluent nature of the market, coupled with the large number of home starts, premium garden and garden-related home decorative products will be a major element in our offering. Research of garden centers beyond our region has found that those retailing lawn and garden products targeted to the more selective clients maintained higher customer loyalty. Although low-cost planters will be available, our focus will be on the premium accessory items that the selective new home-owner currently finds in the upscale lawn and garden catalogues. New home owners spend a great deal of money decorating their homes, and understand the value of money; as a result they are looking for quality items that are both attractive and durable.

Garden tools and equipment will also be sold but will be primarily limited to hand-operated equipment. Power equipment such as mowers and tillers can be purchased from a variety of area businesses, many of which have buying power that allows them to sell at sharp discounts that our operation will not be able to match. Therefore, power equipment sales will be limited to specialized high-end tools for the selective gardener.

Educational/Greenhouse Programs: One of our methods of attracting new customers and compensating for the business seasonality will be our offering a series of educational programs and seminars on garden-ing-related topics. The programs, ranging from one-night seminars to three-week classes, will be held in conjunction with the local adult education programs. They will be promoted...

Source: Henry's Lawn and Garden Center

SOME ADVICE

"A flower shop is a flower shop is a flower shop. The issue at hand is what specific niche, product, or hook you will use to keep your customers coming back. What is it that will make your business more successful than the flower shop across the street? Use your Description of Business section to illustrate how your shop is going to differentiate itself from similar businesses in your trading area."

Glenn Yamada, Vice President, Commercial Banking
Seafirst (Seattle First National Bank)
Seattle, Wash.

THE MARKET

OVERVIEW

The Market section of your business plan is extremely important. In this part of your plan you must convince potential lenders and investors—that is, stakeholders in the outcome—that there is enough potential demand for your product to justify yet another business entering the marketplace. The skepticism that bankers and investors often express about new ventures is based on their knowledge of the very high failure rates of small businesses. Therefore, your ability to describe your market and its potential is probably the most important tool you have to help relieve their concerns.

What is this thing called marketing? Most people would respond with answers like "advertising, sales, and communications." Each of those answers would be correct, but only in part. Marketing is a comprehensive activity that includes determining:

❑ what **products to provide** and to whom

❑ how to **price** those products

❑ how to **promote** those products

❑ how to **sell and deliver** them.

Marketing activity per se is critical because it integrates most of the fundamental business activities. Therefore, each of these functions should be explained in detail in your business plan.

The Market section of the plan should address these specific issues: overall market size, growth potential, segmentation, and target market strategies. The Executive Summary and Description of Business sections have already presented a good overall view of the products you intend to sell and how you plan to merchandise them. Pricing and promotional strategy will be detailed in separate sections of the plan.

As you begin to write the Market section, remember that although this is a significant part of your business plan, it is not a full-blown marketing strategy. What's the difference? Marketing strategies tend to be far more tactical in nature, and their

higher levels of specificity are simply not necessary here. In your business plan you want to give enough detail to assure the readers that there is a good, well-documented potential market for your product, but not with so much information as to overwhelm them. Include a few charts and tables that indicate in general how you plan to market your business, but do not quote specific strategies or dollar amounts. A good Market section can be written in three or four pages.

R▸ p. 262, 264

RESEARCH

Once you are familiar with this book's concept of a good business plan, begin gathering the information that you will need to develop your own. The prospect of doing this may be distressing to you for a number of reasons. Perhaps you haven't been inside a library in years and wouldn't know where to start once you got there. Perhaps you think research is really the domain of people with very thick glasses and too much education. Perhaps you think you are beginning to understand the types of information necessary to develop your plan but don't have the skills to go about accessing those information sources yourself. Don't worry! This guide is designed to enable you to find the information you need.

Research is a process of gathering and analyzing data. The gathering part should not be too difficult but will take some time. Much of the "searching" for potential sources of information (e.g., magazine articles) in libraries is now done by computer. In addition, most libraries, particularly those associated with Small Business Development Centers, will have professional reference staffs to assist you.

IS▸ p. 187   **R▸ p. 235, 251**
B▸ p. 294

Define Information Needs

Figure out what information/data you are looking for before you take your first step into a library or start to do a search from your home computer.

Develop a very specific list of questions (information needs) that you want answered. Don't make the mistake that most people do, of simply going to the library with the goal of developing a business plan for, say, an art gallery, and start looking in reference guides and magazines under "A" for art, or "G" for gallery. The number of titles available will overwhelm you unless you are prepared to narrow your search to specific topics.

The best way to start the research process is to create a file folder for each topic identified in your Table of Contents. Then, in each file, make a list of the questions you need to answer (information required) to complete that section of your plan. This method will force you to stay focused, keep on schedule, identify areas where you may need help, and keep fishing expeditions where they belong—by a river with a fly rod.

You can start this process right now by generating your questions, chapter by chapter, as you read this guide. Finally, this structured system of gathering information will allow you to optimize use of your time. As you are researching a question for your Market section, for example, you may read an article that includes some data that you need for your financial projections. You can immediately place the article in the appropriate folder to revisit at a later time. Remember, the process of writing a business plan is not linear. You will constantly be discovering information that you can set aside to use at a later time or that will help you refine data already gathered.

IS> p. 187

Data Collection

There are basically two types of data. The lion's share of the information you will be gathering for your business plan will come from *secondary sources*. These are materials that already exist, predominantly in written form—and your job is to find them. (The Reference Section of this guide will direct you to rich sources of secondary information.)

The other type of data comes from *primary sources*. This is information not available in written form, or at least you may be unable to find it. Therefore, you have to create it, using methods such as interviews, questionnaires, observation, and focus groups. Secondary data take much less time, are less expensive to collect, and are generally more reliable for your purposes. You will, however, need to gather some information firsthand when you begin to evaluate your competition and start looking for a location.

R> p. 230, 245, 246, 267

THE BASICS

The Market section of your business plan should include information on the following topics:

How Big Is the Pie?

The first thing that must be established with regard to your prospective market is just how large it is. Remember that although you may (and hopefully do) know a lot about the market size characteristics for your industry, you can assume that the reader of your business plan knows very little. Start with the big picture, the national or regional market. Then provide information about your local market, if you can find it. In many cases, localized data may not be available, so you'll need to conduct some primary research.

In our example of the table-tennis and billiards store, you know that demand for its products will be generated by a nationwide growth of interest in table tennis and billiards, Americans' increased propensity for indoor leisure activities, and greater disposable-income levels. Potential customers might include preteens, teenagers, school and community groups, retired people, sports bars, and summer camps. Therefore, the way to start the analysis would be to determine the size of each of these markets. These statistics can be obtained using sources identified in the Resource Section.

R> p. 230, 232, 233

Trend Analysis

Related to the size of the market are the industry's growth trends. Often you'll find trend data in the same resources you used to establish market size, but in other cases, you'll have to investigate further. It is very important to collect information that is as credible as possible, because the future market potential for your business is an area that most stakeholders will evaluate very carefully.

IS> p. 188

It is simply not enough to say that there are a lot of these types of businesses out there already as justification for offering another one. The argument that "because similar businesses are doing well, there must be room for one more" won't hold water. Consider any number of businesses, such as baseball/trading-card stores or family-owned drug stores and hardware stores, which at one time were fast-growth industries but now are stagnant, if not in significant decline.

The best way to find trend data for specific retail businesses is to search in the periodical indices, trade associations, and franchise literature. Remember that you don't want to overwhelm your readers with factoids, just convince them that your business has a high probability of success.

R> p.252, 254, 258

Segmentation

Now that you have established that there is a large market with positive growth trends for your proposed business on a national/regional basis, you must break down these data to reflect the conditions of the market you plan to serve, i.e., your **target market.** The process by which very large and somewhat homogeneous markets are reduced to smaller target markets is called **market segmentation.**

The purpose of segmenting your market carefully is to ensure that the target market that you have identified is indeed accessible and large enough to sustain your overall operation. How do you do it? There are many ways to break down markets by characteristics: age, sex, ethnic group, education, family size, income, business type, geographic location, and so on. Your job is to find the characteristics that are most important for identifying your **potential customer base,** and then measure them. For example, if you are starting a business that sells luggage and other travel goods, you would probably segment your market by age, gender, income, and occupation.

IS> p. 189   **B> p. 294**

Your Slice

The ultimate aim of the business plan is to convince your reader that the large and growing market you have identified really exists where you intend to do business. Although it would be nice to figure this out now (and perhaps finish your plan in record time), you should first take a look at your competition, then return to this most important issue in a separate section of the plan entitled "Market Share," which deals specifically with this topic. You could also complete your competitive analysis, then return to the Market section of your plan and include the evaluation of your market share here.

IS> p. 190

OTHER FACTORS

Product Cycle

While you are looking for trends that influence your industry, you should also look for trends that are affecting the products you plan to carry. This is easier for some businesses than for others. Toy stores around the country could not keep "Tickle-Me-Elmo" in stock during the 1996 holiday season, and "Beanie Babies" were in such demand in 1997 that they had to be rationed. No one, even the toys' manufacturers, could have predicted this meteoric rise to fame. Other items, such as pagers and cellular phones, have enjoyed a consistent increase in sales over a period of several years.

IS> p. 191   **B> p. 294**

It is important to look at your product mix in terms of its life cycle. A retail store that consists entirely of fad items will probably not be in business long, unless the owner has incredible market foresight. The Boston Consulting Group created a common method of categorizing products. Its matrix divides products into four categories that can help determine a profitable product mix.

Star. A star is a product or service that maintains high levels of income despite increasing competition. Stars usually require a high infusion of cash for advertising, distribution, and product refinements, but these costs are almost always offset by high profit margins and the capture of a large market share.

Cash Cow. A cash cow has a loyal following, sells steadily, and therefore requires little cash for advertising and customer-retention programs.

Likewise, it requires little in the way of new development, and simply provides high income in a stable market.

Question Mark. This is an unknown producer in an unsure market. Question marks require considerable investment in marketing programs to entice the consumer to buy, while facing keen competition. Businesses must carefully analyze the return on investment for question marks.

Dog. Dogs have been in the marketplace for an extended period of time, yet continue to produce lackluster sales and less-than-desirable income. No amount of advertising or marketing effort can turn a dog into a star or a cash cow. It is possible to market a dog in a highly specialized niche, but the risk generally outweighs potential returns.

The Boston Consulting Group Matrix

RELATIVE MARKET SHARE

		High	Low
INDUSTRY GROWTH RATE	High	Star	Question Mark
	Low	Cash Cow	Dog

You must carry enough "stars" and "cash cows" to cover potential losses from "question marks" and "dogs." Issues related to product mix should be covered in the Executive Summary and/or Description of Business sections of your plan.

Diversification

Diversification allows your business to avoid being too dependent on one product line. Imagine that Joan owns a natural-food store that carries a large line of jams, jellies, condiments, and other "spreadables." These products have developed quite a following over the years, and Joan's major supplier, Nature's Secret, has provided the bulk of her inventory. Nature's Secret Jam has been a "cash cow," providing steady income for her business. Unfortunately, a recent death in the family that owns this company has forced Nature's Secret to close its only manufacturing facility and stop production of its entire product line. If Joan is not well diversified, this could be a significant problem for her business. Fortunately, Joan planned

ahead and identified two other suppliers of comparable products. She also intends to add a line of organic baked goods and handwoven table linens to her product mix. The keys to diversification are a good product mix and alternative sources of supply for your product lines.

Seasonality

With many retail products, seasonal demand will affect your sales to some extent. Snowblowers, for example, are only in demand in the fall and winter months (70% of all retail sales occur in October, November, and December). Similarly, you would be hard pressed to sell a lawnmower in North Dakota in January. Even calculators and notebooks experience a temporary rise in sales as students return to school in the fall.

The most common ways of offsetting the seasonal nature of these types of products is to choose your product lines carefully so as to even out your sales. Reduce your inventory of bicycles after the Christmas season, having stocked up on ski equipment in the fall. As spring approaches, let your inventory of skis, poles, and goggles decline, and rebuild your supply of racing bikes, helmets, and water bottles. A good business plan will clearly detail additional products and marketing techniques that will offset any seasonality in the product line.

PITFALLS

The most significant problems you may encounter while developing a case for your market probably fall into one of these categories.

Unbridled Optimism

Don't overstate your case. Be sure that the market data you are using actually reflect demand for your products as closely as possible. For example, if you're planning to open a lawn-and-garden business that sells rototillers and fertilizer, don't simply use data showing that the average household with a certain income level spends so many dollars on lawn-and-garden supplies per year. Research a little further to see if you can find a breakout of sales of specific garden machines and supplies in your area, by type, material, and quality.

Stale Data

Be sure that your references are as up-to-date as possible. For example, the U.S. Census is conducted only once every 10 years, so the farther you are from the first year in each decade, the less reliable the data become. Not to worry, though—not only are portions of the census updated more frequently, there are simple techniques you can use to update it yourself. For example, you might have a figure that is three or four years old regarding the population in your target market area. Although that number alone might be a bit stale, it may become useful when combined with the state or municipal government's estimates of population growth rates and demographic changes over that period.

Too Little Documentation

Provide very specific references to give the reader confidence that credible sources were used to support your findings. In some cases, you may rely on footnotes. In other cases, you may want to include specific pieces of information, such as trade association studies or articles from business magazines, as appendices.

EXCERPT

Soccer Seventeen
THE MARKET

INDUSTRY INFORMATION

Professional soccer in the U.S. began in the early 1930s. However, it failed to catch on, and major efforts to bring the game into national television in the 1960s and 1970s were plagued with low ratings and poor attendance. Recently, however, soccer has become extremely popular with young Americans. The number of elementary and secondary schools with soccer teams has increased from 2,000 in 1970 to more than 6,500 in 1994, according to John Rooney, coauthor of *Atlas of American Sport. American Demographics* magazine explains that there are more than half a million Americans over the age of six playing soccer in 1992 in Pennsylvania alone.

Today, soccer has become a common occurrence in communities large and small across America. In fact, soccer now leads all team sports as the number one supervised activity for youths 18 and under, according to Sandy Briggs, executive director for the Soccer Industry Council of America. The United States Amateur Soccer Administration says that U.S. soccer registration for adults 19 and over has increased from 103,735 in 1985 to 175,046 in 1995, a 69% increase.

Key findings from a *1995 Survey of National Soccer Participation*, published by the Soccer Industry Council of America, indicate the following:

Total Participants (U.S. Population, 6 years and older, at least once/year)	18,231,000	100%
Under 18	13,384,000	73%
18 and over	4,847,000	39%
Frequent Participants (25 or more days/year)	7,618,000	42%
"Core" Participants (52 or more days/year)	**3,531,000**	**19%**
Aficionados (Soccer is favorite activity)	3,465,000	19%

Source: Soccer Seventeen

SOME ADVICE

"We have been advertising on the Internet for some time now, and it has begun to pay off. Internet sales account for about 5% of our business and have brought us into new markets that we couldn't have tapped before. We now sell our products in Russia, Norway, and several other foreign countries. The Internet has effectively leveled the playing field. Consumers don't know if we are a 20-story department store or working out of a small basement office. Size is no longer important."

Ed Malkin
Marmel Gifts & Toys Online
Farmington Hills, Mich.

THE COMPETITION

OVERVIEW

A well thought-out and logically presented competitive analysis is a critical component of your business plan. Although planning experts readily agree on the types of information that should be included in the examination of your competitive environment, often the process of gathering it is more difficult than meets the eye.

Keep in mind that every business has competition, and if you think that you've found one without any, you're wrong! For example, the competition for your "Megaman" clothing shop is not just other big-and-tall shops. You will face competition from major department stores in your area that have men's plus size departments or catalog sales, mail-order companies that specialize in oversize apparel, even local tailors who alter and custom make clothing to order. Your competitors include every business that sells similar products in your target market. Even though your market may be underserved, there is always competition.

The goal of the competitive analysis is to demonstrate that you have a thorough knowledge of *who and where* your competitors are, as well as their relative *strengths and weaknesses*. Once you have accomplished this, you will be able to carve out a market niche for your business, then estimate its size. That there will be competition is a given. How you differentiate your business will be the key to its success.

THE BASICS

The Competition section of your business plan should include the following:

Where Is Your Competition?

To analyze your competition, it is important to define your selling area in unambiguous terms. The best way is literally to take a map and plot the area where you plan to concentrate your business. This process will help define your customer base, help identify competition, and be an important factor in the development of your promotional strategy.

For example, consider Renae Morse, a kite shop manager with several years of experience. Renae would like to open her own kite store, Blue Sky Kites, near Anaheim, Calif. On the basis of her customer profile, local traffic patterns, and nearby attractions, Renae determines that most of her business will come from within a 10-mile radius of her store. Using a map of the Anaheim area, Renae draws a circle with a 10-mile radius around her store location. The majority of her customers, she supposes, will reside within this circle.

Next, Renae draws another circle with a 20-mile radius surrounding the first circle. If other kite stores have similar customer profiles and traffic patterns, this larger circle should encompass most of her competition. Remember, however, that these competitors must have similar markets—that is, even if Kite World, a huge discount megastore, lies outside Renae's competitive circle, it is likely to draw considerable business away from her by offering lower prices and a larger selection. In that case, she would need to modify the shape of her "circle" to show the impact of Kite World on her competitive analysis. Similarly, the presence of major highways (easing or limiting access), retail neighbors, and other attractions (malls, restaurants, and tourist stops) can have an impact on the competitive circle.

For some types of retail businesses, defining the market and the competition will be a more difficult task than Renae Morse's. Consider, for example, an entrepreneur whose mail-order business specializes in the "under-$10" gadget market. The vast majority of her products appeal to an exceptionally wide audience, both geographically and demographically. Her competition is ubiquitous; it comes from other mail-order catalogs, large discount-chain retailers, and small local businesses. She cannot possibly define the competition in every market where she sends a catalog.

Instead, she describes her competitors in general terms, and focuses on what competitive advantages she may have over the local marketers such as product selection, distribution channels, shop-at-home convenience, and lower prices.

IS▸ p. 192   **R▸ p. 255, 261**

B▸ p. 292

Who Is Your Competition?

Revisit the basic description of your business as it appears at the beginning of your plan. Make sure you have identified all of the tangible and intangible characteristics that must go into a comprehensive explanation of what customer needs your business expects to satisfy. You may find that you need to add or delete some items. Remember that business plan development is a fluid process. You will end up making many changes to your plan before you have a final version.

Now that you are focused on customer needs, you can begin the process of identifying your competition. Put yourself in the position of a potential customer who is searching to satisfy a need. Let's say you're looking for art supplies for a variety of media. You need paint brushes, canvas, an easel, a drafting board, and mechanical pencils. Check out the competition as a prospective customer would.

R▸ p. 257

General Resources for Identifying Competition

Yellow Pages. The telephone book is an excellent and convenient source for retail businesses. Some of your competitors may not be found there, however, because they started their business after the directory was published, are not listed under a category you're looking for, or use a residential number for the business.

Local Papers. Local newspapers are a rich resource for identifying competition through an examination of display advertising and inserts. Some of your competitors may not advertise there, however, because they may feel that it is too expensive and/or they use other media more extensively.

Trade Associations. Professionals and many other types of businesses belong to trade or professional associations. If there is one for your type, contact the group's offices to see what information is available. This may require contacting a national trade association to access the local chapter.

Internet. Even if you have no current plans to conduct business electronically, be sure to search for potential competitors online.

CABWA (Competitive Analysis by Walking Around). Many small businesses' primary means of promotion is by word-of-mouth. The best way to identify folks who don't advertise and to ensure that you haven't missed others is to literally walk/drive around your trading area. In addition, check local bulletin boards, lampposts, and even doorknobs for posters, sale flyers, or discount offers your competitors may be spreading around the neighborhood. Also, ads in local publications (like high school yearbooks or community concert programs) cost less than newspaper ads, making them good sources for local competitive information.

Licensing. Most businesses are required to have a license or permit to operate, and chances are that such licenses are a matter of public record. You can request a list of names and addresses from the state or local authority that issues these permits.

R▸ p. 231, 256, 260

SWOT Analysis (Strengths, Weaknesses, Opportunities, Threats)

Once you have discovered who your competitors are and where they are located, develop a detailed and comprehensive profile for each one. The goal here is to identify competitive gaps and weaknesses and then modify your product mix to exploit them.

You may find that as you begin to call or visit your competition to get information about their products and prices, the people answering the phone lack the appropriate product knowledge, or the sales clerks seem too busy to talk to you. Even worse, they may be in a large store with numerous departments, which may involve running around or waiting on hold for phone transfers to get you to the right person (assuming you don't get disconnected).

Although this may impede your research, think of how their current and prospective customers must feel! A clear weakness of your competitors is the difficulty prospective customers experience when seeking information or buying a product. Knowing this should prompt you to provide enough trained staff to handle customer inquiries and volume appropriately.

The first step of your SWOT analysis is to make a list of what you consider to be all of the relevant attributes of your business. These would include:

❑ What specific products will you sell?

❑ To whom will you sell these products?

❑ Where will you be located?

❑ What geographic area will you serve?

❑ How will you price your products?

❑ What will be your hours of operation?

❑ What will be your credit policy?

❑ How will you promote your products?

❑ What types of guarantees or assurances will you offer?

❑ What follow-up service will you provide?

❑ Other differentiators (to be added as you evaluate your competition)

At this point, you'll be ready to contact your competitors and compare what *they* say they do to what *you* plan to do. In most cases this is easily accomplished over the phone, under the guise of being a prospective customer. During this "conversation," get as many questions answered as possible. Also look for product features and opportunities you hadn't considered.

For example, while conducting one such "interview," Anne discovered that a potential competitor for her toy store was offering customers a punch card to record each purchase of Thomas or Brio model railroad cars. After buying 10 cars the customer was entitled to one free. Anne decided to offer frequent shoppers a discount program that would be based on the total amount of purchases and that would apply to all merchandise in the store, which she felt would give her a significant advantage over her competitor.

These interviews may uncover significant opportunities for your business. It is also important to ask potential competitors to send you any promotional material they may have. To facilitate this process, develop a competitive grid. Use the one that follows, created to evaluate competition in the nail salon and day spa industry, as a model.

IS▶ p. 194

Competitors' Analysis

NAME OF SALON	# OF HAIR TECHS	# OF NAIL TECHS	TANNING?	WAXING?	RETAIL	CLIENTELE SERVED	OTHER COMMENTS
A Unique Experience Salon and Day Spa	2 FT	2 PT	Yes	Yes	Full lines of hair, nail, skin, and tanning products	All	See attached business plan and brochure.
The Perfect Place	2 FT 1 PT	1 PT	Yes	Yes	Limited hair care	All	Been in business approx. 5 years. Just moved to new location, but has lost key techs recently.
Magic Mirror	6 FT	None	Yes	Yes	Good	All	Good selection of hair care products, but no nail or skin care products offered. Varied ages and types of techs with established client base.
Makin Waves	1 FT	None	No	Yes	Limited	All	One-person shop. Limited services offered.
Judy's Salon	6 FT	None	Yes	Yes	Limited Matrix & Nexxus	All	Established salon.
Barbara's Beauty Salon	1 FT	None	No	Yes	Limited	All	Established salon, but limited retail products.
Downtown Beauty	2 FT	None	No	Yes	Good	All	Merle Norman dealer for Cordele area and has established customers from this. Retail product line is main draw.
Fay's Beauty Shop	1 FT	None	No	Yes	None	Older clientele	Established salon for older ladies. Offers no additional services aside from hair care.
First Impressions	1 FT 1 PT	1 apprentice	No	Yes	Limited	All	Small shop, limited client base.
Kay's Beauty Salon	1 FT	None	No	Yes	Limited	Older clientele	Established salon for older ladies. Offers no additional services aside from hair care.
A Perfect 10	None	2 FT 1 PT	Yes	Yes	Limited nail care and tanning	All	Nail and tanning salon only. Established client base, but higher prices.

Source: A Unique Experience Salon and Day Spa

Such a grid enables you to look at your competition side by side with your own business, and enhances your ability to identify gaps in what they sell. Once you have gathered this information, you will be in a position to fine-tune your product offerings and begin to evaluate your potential market share. Time spent on this evaluation is well invested, because lack of thoroughness can have a compounding effect as you begin to forecast sales later on in your business plan.

The Retail Giants (a.k.a. Discount Retailers, Wholesale Membership Clubs, Factory Outlet Malls, and Category-Killer Stores)

Competing with these stores is difficult for small retailers. Because of their economies of scale, self-service approach, and warehouse-style inventory, they can offer their products at substantial discounts to the consumer.

As an entrepreneur, you must realize that planning for this competition is essential to the success of your business. Evaluate competitive strengths and weaknesses carefully, and attempt to offer something truly unique to your customers. Shop the competition; evaluate their advertisements; talk to other retailers and potential customers; read books and articles on the subject; and compare prices on a variety of products.

Consumers generally base decisions about where they shop on the prices of only a few items. For example, you may need to take a "loss" on tissue paper because the chain gift shop down the street offers it for less. (Note: In some states it is illegal to sell products for less than cost.) Make up for it in sales of handmade gift boxes or picture frames that your competition doesn't carry. If you find a niche in the marketplace, you can reduce the overall competition for your products and services.

B▶ p. 294

For example, Toys "R" Us stores are generally located in heavily populated areas near malls or other major attractions. Let's say you are opening a small toy store, The Toy Chest, in the same city as an existing Toys "R" Us. Look at how you might compete with this category-killer.

Toys "R" Us	The Toy Chest
Mall location	Downtown location catering to businesspeople and working families
Warehouse style	Personalized service in separate departments
Low prices	High-quality products that don't feel mass-produced; focus on safety and durability
Wide assortment of products	Good vendor relationships; overnight order fulfillment for any non-stock items

Do not discount customer service as a viable competitive strength. According to an article in *The New York Times,* a recent survey by the Yankelovich partners revealed that respondents ranked department and discount stores 11th and 12th respectively in customer service, out of a list of 20 consumer businesses—well behind the U.S. Postal Service, restaurants, and local telephone companies. This clearly suggests that one way virtually every small business can compete effectively is by providing personalized, high-contact customer service.

PITFALLS

Initial Product Offering Too Broad

Proposing too many products will leave your business unfocused, with the risk of facing bigger or more specialized competitors in the marketplace.

Name and Brand Recognition

In general, people are willing to travel farther to Ben & Jerry's than to Puck's Frozen Dairy Barn. This is a problem for most small businesses starting out. In the early stages of your business life, you will have to rely more heavily on effective pricing strategies, good marketing, location, and other competitive advantages in order to compete with established businesses or national franchises.

Underestimating Competition

Failure to identify all relevant competitors will lead to false assumptions in market share and pricing, which could have devastating effects.

Overestimating Your Competitive Strength

Making too-optimistic projections about your new store and customers' reaction to it, compared with the attractions your competition offers, can lead to the downfall of an otherwise great idea.

Failure to Modify Your Plan

If you neglect to make adequate changes to your initial plan, based on findings in your competitive analysis, your business may be doomed before you begin.

These potential problems can all be avoided by being attentive to detail and flexible as you conduct your analysis. On the one hand, be sure to identify and document your competition as it exists; on the other, look for opportunities and take advantage of them where possible.

SOME ADVICE

"People aren't stupid. If you're doing something right and it works, then sooner or later they're going to figure it out and come after you. Can your people respond? Can you keep innovating? Can you stay ahead? These are the real questions you should be dealing with."

Ken Hendricks, Founder and CEO
ABC Supply Co.
Beloit, Wis.

Sparkle Paint Company
COMPETITION

The Baltimore paint market is estimated at $15 million per year (including retail, commercial, and industrial paint products). The paint market is being serviced by four primary types of business. Each type of business provides its customer with a different level of service and attracts its particular customers because of the type of service it provides.

Large department store businesses such as Sears, Wal-Mart, and Montgomery Ward offer their customers generic, premixed paint products with very little customization or paint tinting available. Customers shopping at these businesses generally are retail customers that have basic painting needs.

Home-improvement centers and lumber stores such as Home Depot, Scotty's, Lowe's, and locally owned lumber stores sell moderately priced paint primarily to retail customers. These businesses generally do not have commercial customers. However, their sales are generally dominated by sales to retail customers. These customers purchase from these businesses because of moderate prices, convenient locations, accessibility of nonpaint merchandise, and the wide variety of paint colors.

Company-owned or independently owned and licensed paint stores such as Porter Paints, Benjamin Moore, Sherwin-Williams, and Glidden Paints cater primarily to commercial painters who demand a high-quality paint product combined with strong product knowledge and a high level of service. These stores generally have a retail customer base ranging from 20%-40% of their total sales. In addition to carrying a variety of paint products, they also supply painting-related supplies, along with decorating products such as wallpaper, window coverings, and possibly carpet. Sales volume in these types of stores ranges from $300,000 to over $1,000,000 in annual sales.

National paint companies without local company stores or licensed dealers have well-trained sales forces in the Baltimore area calling primarily on large industrial accounts. Sales generated in this manner relate primarily to large contract jobs. The contracts generally specify the exact type of paint to be used and usually are price sensitive.

The segment of the paint market in which SPC will compete will be the company-owned or independently owned licensed paint-dealer store segment. These stores are servicing over 100 commercial painting companies in the Greater Baltimore area. The following is a list of the paint stores competing in this segment in the Greater Baltimore area:

Store Name	Estimated Sales Volume	No. of Employees	No. of Estimated Sales Reps
Glidden Paints	$2,200,000	8	2
Sherwin-Williams East	$1,800,000	5	3
Sherwin-Williams South	$1,000,000	3	None
Capital Paint and Decorating (Benjamin Moore)	$900,000	3	None
C and D Paint Company	$750,000	6	2
Color Expressions	$500,000	4	1
Bright Idea Paints	$400,000	2	None
Working Man	$250,000	2	None

Source: Sparkle Paint Co., Baltimore, Md.

DETERMINING MARKET SHARE

OVERVIEW

Market-share analysis gives credibility to your sales projections. It should draw on and be consistent with the information presented in the Market and Competition sections, so that it is clear your entire business plan is based on the same fundamental assumptions.

One of the most serious shortcomings of business plans is a lack of strong connection between the sections on demand and competition and the rationale used to support sales projections. The Market section presents data demonstrating a strong national, regional, and local demand for your merchandise. The Competition section contends that there is a viable niche for your business. But the Financial section of the plan, with its cash-flow forecasts, makes little or no attempt to quantify the share of the market the business intends to capture, let alone establish a rationale for it. This problem is exacerbated by the use of electronic spreadsheets.

Changing sales forecasts, to make the bottom line look good, can be done so effortlessly that it is easy to lose sight of the fact that strong underlying assumptions are necessary to support them. In addition, the computer printout itself looks so professional that sometimes it obscures the fact that the supporting data are inaccurate or inconsistent. To avoid this problem, support your sales projections with a cogent and thorough market-share analysis.

Determining market share may sound like a complicated task, but it is not. All you are doing is documenting what share of the potential sales in your target market is reasonable for you to capture. This is not a highly scientific process with sophisticated formulas that produces a definitive answer. It is an evaluation in which you look at a combination of factors, many of which you have already discovered in the marketplace, to arrive at logical expectations about sales.

Keep in mind that it's not like repairing a Swiss watch, where one small mistake can render the watch useless. Rather, you are developing estimates that will vary according to the methods you use and the assumptions you make. Try to see the big picture, and don't expect that the different techniques you learn to use will yield exactly the same answers.

At the outset, determining your market share may seem a discouraging prospect. You may be wondering how your small business can hope to steal market share from retail giants such as Wal-Mart, Kmart, Target, and other regional chain stores that dominate the market with their low prices and massive economies of scale. It will take time to find and exploit their weak spots and to develop a niche that will enable your business to succeed, but it can be done. Armed with your competitive analysis, you can make plans to gain market share based on your strengths.

You have several options as to where to put your market-share information. Either you can use a separate section of your plan, or you can place this information in another area, such as the Market section, or as a long footnote to your cash-flow analysis. The important thing is to have it in your business plan and to present it in a compelling fashion.

R▶ p. 236

THE BASICS

While looking at a display case carrying his chicken dogs in a supermarket, Frank Perdue once commented, "I suppose it would be unreasonable to have the whole area." He was referring to the fact that his competition was also holding shelf space. Market-share information enables you to estimate more accurately the amount of business you can capture.

Although there is no definitive formula to compute market share, several techniques can be employed to help you estimate it. Combined, the factors you've analyzed will contribute to a logical basis for your sales projections. Each business situation differs somewhat in terms of characteristics and data availability. Therefore, individual business plans will not all look the same. The important thing to remember is that your general analytical tools can be adapted to meet the needs of your particular situation.

Here are three basic methods that can be used to estimate future sales.

Average Competitor Sales

One way to develop your sales projections is to argue that you have used sales levels reflecting those of your competition. In fact, you'll want to project your sales at lower levels than theirs, even though your merchandise may be of a higher quality with more features at a lower price.

B▸ p. 294

Let's say you are proposing to start a sporting goods store. Here is the formula for establishing the average sales level of your competitors. Generally this calculation is made using statewide data.

$$\text{Average Sales Per Business} = \frac{\text{Retail Sales}}{\text{Number of Establishments}}$$

IS▸ p. 196

Sales data. Your state bureau of taxation has information available on sales tax paid, by business category. This is a matter of public record, so you should just have to call the bureau to obtain it. From tax amounts you can calculate sales amounts. In states that have no sales taxes, you can gather tax information from a state(s) with similar characteristics (e.g., size, population, population density) and use that for your projections.

Number of establishments. There are many potential sources for this information, including *Census of Retail Trade, County Business Patterns,* the Yellow Pages, and state-specific retail directories.

R▸ p. 232, 233

Other. If your industry has a good trade association, it probably compiles industry or membership studies that contain sales data. The problem is persuading the association to share the information with you. For example, there might be an industry report that sells for $100. See if you can get a free copy of the previous study or permission to photocopy the specific information you need from the current one. Remember, you are a potential future member, so if you are polite and patient, you can usually get what you need.

How to use this information. As you begin to project sales, the average sales figure for your type of business is a good place to start. Usually it is wise to make your projections slightly lower than your average competitor's sales figures, because your estimates will look more conservative and attainable.

a. Total retail sales for sporting goods stores in Minneapolis	=	$22,581,000
b. Total number of sporting goods stores in Minneapolis	=	33
c. Average sales per establishment (a ÷ b) ($22,581,000 ÷ 33)	=	$684,273
d. Projected sales for your store (estimate from your financial statements)	=	$400,000

Average Customer Base

Another important factor that should be considered when developing your market-share analysis is the underlying population required to support the average business in your industry. Generally this calculation is also based upon statewide data. You can approximate the average customer base as follows:

$$\text{Average Number of People per Business} = \frac{\text{Population}}{\text{Number of Establishments}}$$

Number of establishments. Same sources as for competitors' sales.

Population. Bureau of the Census.

IS▸ p. 196

How to use this information. These data can be used to respond to the question, "Don't we already have enough sporting goods stores in the area?" Perform the same analysis as above, but for your own trading area. That is, divide your target population by the number of competitors you identify in your trading area. If the result in potential customers per store is significantly higher than the state average, that indicates there is room for another competitor.

e. Total number of sporting goods stores in Minnesota	=	556
f. Total population of Minnesota	=	4,375,099
g. State average number of people per sporting goods store	=	7,868
h. Total number of sporting goods stores in Minneapolis	=	33
i. Total population of Minneapolis	=	943,981
j. Average number of people per sporting goods store (i ÷ h) (943,981 ÷ 33)	=	28,605

Conclusion: There appears to be room in the Minneapolis area for another sporting goods store.

Sources: Census of Retail Trade,
Sourcebook of Zip Code Demographics

R▶ p. 232, 234, 252, 254

Industry Sales per Square Foot

As you are gathering market-share data for your business, you will undoubtedly find trade data representing average sales per square foot in the industry. These data can be useful when combined with other information you are gathering (much as you would use comparative financial ratios to help test your assumptions about operating costs). Be careful, however, not just to take the industry data and multiply by the number of square feet in your proposed location. Using that logic, you would find yourself in a very large store with lots of inventory and probably not enough customers to enable you to survive the first month of operation.

Sales Projections Using National or Regional Demand Data

Some entrepreneurs will find it difficult to access all of the data necessary to complete the type of analysis described on pages 29-30. Another technique you can use is to gather consumption or spending data on a regional or national basis, then shrink them to fit your target market area.

IS▶ p. 197

The first step will be to develop a customer profile. Let's say you are interested in starting Bird Brains, a business that specializes in everything for the amateur and professional bird-watcher, ranging from binoculars and field guides to birdhouses and seed, and artwork depicting birds. As you begin to search for data on your business, you find a lot of information on birds, bird-watching, and binoculars, but little on your local market. In that case, start doing key word searches at your local library (or on the Internet), and dig up volumes of information from sources including:

❏ *American Demographics*, "Golden Wings"
❏ *Audubon*, "Field Guide for America: Roger Tory Peterson Taught This Country to See Its Birds—and Much More"
❏ *Brandweek,* "Bird-Feeding Enterprise Finds Flocks of Followers*"*
❏ *Business Week*, "The Cardinal Rules of Bird Feeding," "It's High Time for Bird Watching"
❏ *Forbes*, "Avian Nation"
❏ *Library Journal*, "Sowing a Wildlife Garden Resource"
❏ *Nation's Business*, "Bird-Watcher Boutique"
❏ *New Statesman*, "Stand Still, Look Up and Marvel; You Don't Need Agility or Even Good Eyesight to Be a Bird-Watcher, Just Patience"
❏ *Sports Illustrated*, "Armed Combat (Bird Watching)"
❏ *State Legislatures*, "A Bird in the Hand"

R▶ p. 234, 243, 244, 248
B▶ p. 293

From the information contained in these articles, among others, you will be able to develop a customer profile.

Bird Brains' customer profile. Average age: 53. Equal numbers of men and women; 62% have family incomes over $50,000; 70% have attended college. Of a total of more than 51 million American bird-watchers, 8 million will travel across state lines to see a particular species of bird.

Armed with this profile, you will be able to measure the potential for your total market by determining how many people who live in your target area fit this profile, using statistics on age, income, and education. Then you can review your competitive data and estimate your market share.

IS> p. 197

Market saturation. There are several ways of calculating how saturated your target market is with similar merchandise. Using the most current census data, adjusted for local conditions, and expenditure data from the U.S. Census of Retail Trade, you can determine approximately how much each consumer in your trading area spends on your type of merchandise. In addition, you can compare expenditures in different trading areas to help determine the best place to locate your store. The following calculation, known as the Index of Retail Saturation, is a common way to measure your local market in terms of your competitors.

$$\text{Index}^1 = \frac{C^1 \times RE^1}{RF^1}$$

Where:

Index^1 = Index of Retail Saturation for area 1

C^1 = Number of customers in area 1

(Source: U.S. Census, CACI)

RE^1 = Retail expenditures per consumer in area 1

(Source: U.S. Census of Retail Trade)

RF^1 = Retail facilities in area 1

Sources: Observation, Yellow Pages, *and* County Business Patterns

IS> p. 199

Example

CALCULATING MARKET SATURATION

Jim and Bill are planning to open a furniture store in Burlington, Vt. They have been involved in furniture design and construction for years and are very familiar with the market in the area. Their bankers, however, are not so familiar with what appeals to the furniture-buying public. For their business plan, they would like to indicate the current market saturation levels for Burlington as a means to convince the bankers that their area is currently underserved by quality furniture stores.

Through some research, Jim and Bill find that, according to the 1990 United States Bureau of the Census report, 58,690 people live in the greater Burlington area (including the surrounding towns). The Census of Retail Trade says that the total expenditure in the furniture-store category for Burlington was $3,612,000 in 1992 (when the last census was taken). Dividing this figure by the number of people in the target market, they get average expenditure per person on furniture.

$3,612,000 / 58,690 = $61.54 per person

They know from their own observations that there are 11 furniture stores in their trading area with a total of 19,500 square feet of selling space. By using the formula for the Index of Retail Saturation, they easily plug in the numbers for their area:

$$\text{Index} = \frac{58,690 \times \$61.54}{19,500}$$

$$= \$185.22$$

Using this formula, Jim and Bill can evaluate different locations (St. Johnsbury, Vt., Montreal, and Manchester, N.H.) using the same formula and compare them. In general, the higher the Index, the lower the competition level, and the higher the chance of success for your business.

PITFALLS

Unrealistic Market-Share Projections

Make your sales and market-share projections conservative. It is usually a good idea to make two projections: one at the level that you think you can reasonably achieve and the other at a level closer to your break-even point. (For break-even analysis, see pages 46-47.)

Sales Projections Exceed Capacity

Be careful not to show sales levels that cannot be maintained with the resources indicated in your business plan. For example, if you are planning to start a hardware store, make sure you plan for enough weekend and seasonal help to meet your projected demand. If you are unable to provide adequate customer service, your customers will go elsewhere (and never return to your store).

Target Market Too Broad

Do not try to be all things to all people. Segment your market and differentiate your services. You can always expand your business later. For example, if you start a pizza and sandwich restaurant, think very carefully before adding take-out ice cream. Do you have adequate parking for both businesses to survive? Can your staff handle large crowds on busy Friday and Saturday nights? Can you clearly separate areas for beer sales from areas for ice cream? How will your underage ice-cream clientele react to the pub atmosphere in your pizza restaurant? What about demand in the winter?

It is important to keep your business endeavors complementary to one another. Perhaps adding a pool hall to your pizza restaurant might be a better match, or a miniature golf course to your ice-cream business.

Profitability

Be sure that your target market is large enough to be profitable. For example, if you plan on opening a headstone business with the intention of servicing a few local funeral homes and cemeteries, you may have to expand your area of operations by 10 or 20 miles to reach a large enough customer base to operate profitably.

SOME ADVICE

"It is always a bright day in the life cycle of a retailer when conservative projections exceed the minimum necessary for success. Avoid wishful thinking and possibly gloomy business performance that can occur by overestimating market potential. Thorough market research and competitive analysis will help ensure against any supposition and guesswork that could cost you your business."

Ed Gray
Senior Vice President, Corporate Business Banking
AmSouth Bank
Birmingham, Ala.

Henry's Lawn & Garden Center

PROJECTED MARKET PENETRATION

Our business will strive to gain customers in both retail and wholesale lawn and garden supply markets. The recent favorable demographic trends, coupled with the opportunity presented by an unfilled premium product's niche, make us confident that we are in a very good position to rapidly acquire a viable and profitable share of the local market.

Following are key variables relevant to our estimation of our potential market:

1994 Maine lawn and garden sales	$122,000,000
Maine population	1,240,000
Number of lawn and garden stores in Maine	79
Local market population	70,000

Using the above information, the characteristics for the lawn and garden market in our target market area can be projected as follows:

Average Maine resident lawn and garden expenditures	$98.00
Average sales per lawn and garden store	$1,544,000
Population served per lawn and garden store	15,755
Projected local market dollar sales	$6,860,000

Given that, on average, there is one lawn and garden store per 15,755 people, we can calculate what the local market can bear:

South Portland, Scarborough, Cape Elizabeth population	70,000
Statewide average population served per store	15,755
Potential number of stores supported by the local population	4.4

Since only three lawn and garden stores are in operation in this area, our calculations suggest that the market is not saturated and should be able to easily support an additional store. This information, coupled with the continued increases in population and new housing starts, indicates that there is clearly an opportunity to make inroads into the region.

Another method of evaluating our potential in the market is to calculate a break-even analysis to determine what percentage of the market's population we would have to capture in order to succeed. The following break-even projections are based upon the cost assumptions found in the financial section of this business plan and the calculated per capita sales estimates...

Source: Henry's Lawn and Garden Center

LOCATION

OVERVIEW

The location of your business is crucial to its eventual success or failure. As you contemplate where to locate your business, analyze such basic factors as proximity to your target market and where your competition is located. In addition, be sure to evaluate your alternatives in the light of changing factors in the retail environment, such as the growth of discount warehouse shopping clubs like BJ's and Sam's, an ever-increasing number of franchises, the proliferation of network marketing, and advances in telecommunications and computer technologies, which have had a serious impact on a small business's ability to compete via direct marketing channels.

Don't assume that just because your competitors have selected a particular type of location, you should make a similar decision. Keep an open mind. Don't just accept how things have always been done. Remember that as times change, so do the ways in which products can be delivered most efficiently.

B> p. 294

Consider the home computer market. Barely 10 years ago, if you wanted to purchase a computer for use at home, you visited a computer store downtown that sold a limited variety of PCs and relied on the resident geek to guide you through the selection process. Then you might wait from four to six weeks to receive your new computer. Today, you can order a new computer over the phone or via the Internet 24 hours a day, seven days a week, and have it delivered to your home the next day. Or, you can buy it at a wholesale club, where a wide variety of models are available at discount prices.

To survive in this market, small retailers must substantially differentiate themselves (with top-notch personal service, expertise, training, and so on) from these new forms of competition. Be creative in finding new ways to get your merchandise into the hands of your potential customers faster, cheaper, and more efficiently.

THE BASICS

What Type of Business Are You In?

The first step in determining what location would be most appropriate for your business is understanding how your customer will perceive or classify your merchandise. Traditionally, for consumer products, the following classifications are used.

IS> p. 200   R> p. 250

Convenience Goods. Includes products such as toilet paper, basic canned foods, snack foods, milk, soft drinks, and possibly beer. With convenience goods, the consumer feels that he/she has all the knowledge necessary to make the purchase decision and will not need to ask a store clerk which toilet paper is the softest or which beer has the least aftertaste. Generally price and quality will not be compared, as the consumer is looking to buy at a location close to home or work, expending as little time and effort as possible.

Major location consideration: Convenience stores need to be located as close as possible to the target population.

Shopping goods. These include such items as clothing, furniture, and jewelry. When purchasing these types of products consumers compare quality and price, because they are not familiar with every competitive product feature. They may visit several stores before making a selection. Consumers are likely to spend a considerable amount of time shopping and may be willing to travel some distance to look for these products.

> **Note:** This guide assumes that you intend to rent or lease your location. If you plan to buy the property, you will need to go through a thorough business valuation process. There are numerous references on this subject. Consult your accountant or business adviser for assistance with a valuation analysis.

Major location consideration: Stores that carry shopping goods should be located in close proximity to their competition, because their customers will want to do comparison shopping. If you locate off the beaten path, chances are that most potential customers will find what they are looking for before getting back into their cars to search you out.

Specialty goods. For these items, customers are willing to spend considerable time finding your store to avail themselves of particular brands (such as a Rolex watch) or the staff's expertise (as in a rare coin and stamp shop).

There is often a gray area between shopping and specialty goods. In the past, expensive 35mm SLR cameras were considered specialty goods. That is, camera buyers were willing to go out of their way to seek the experience of a camera store owner/staff to assist in the purchasing decision. Today, however, most cameras of this type are sold at large discount stores, such as Service Merchandise, where the consumer is willing to trade off expertise for price. The same could be said for automobiles sold in auto malls and jewelry sold at JC Penney.

The point is, if you intend to offer specialty goods in the classic sense, you will have to differentiate your store with features such as superior customer service, technical expertise, and customization, because you won't be able to compete on a price basis with volume or discount competitors.

Major location consideration: Because your potential customers will be willing to make an effort to seek out your expertise and/or brand selection, you can choose a location away from a central shopping district and off the "main drag," thus decreasing your rent/lease expense considerably. Use common sense here. Selling specialty goods doesn't mean that you have to look for out-of-the-way locations; rather, evaluate those near but not necessarily in the middle of other retailing activities or population centers.

Estimating Your Trading Area

Prior to selecting a specific location for your business, you need to determine your trading area—that is, the geographic area from which you expect to attract potential customers. Remember, you have already analyzed whether there is a good potential market for your store in the Market Share section of your plan, and you've also learned how to classify your store in this section. Now you will need to look at a few additional variables as you compare alternative locations for your business.

IS> p. 203

The actual size of your trading area will be affected by such previously discussed factors as number of competitors, type of products sold, and so on. One conventional method for estimating your trading area for shopping and specialty goods is to draw a circle around your potential location(s), with a 15-mile radius for an urban area and up to a 50-mile radius for rural markets.

Next, divide this trading area into primary, secondary, and fringe zones. The primary zone (a three- to five-mile radius, or a drive 10 minutes or less from your location) will usually encompass 60% to 65% of your customer base. The secondary zone, which is usually not more than a 20-minute drive, will include approximately 20% of your potential customers, and the fringe zone, which can extend up to 50 miles in a rural area, will include most of the rest.

Once you have broken down your trading area, you can find the demographic characteristics of people living there, which will be critical as you begin the process of projecting sales.

Remember, estimating the size of your trading area is just that—estimating! There are many other variables that will affect the size and shape of a trading area, including natural borders such as a major highway or river, numbers of competitors, population density, and the like. You can use this analysis to help make better decisions about potential locations, but they are not precise measurements.

Convenience * Specialty

LOCATION ALTERNATIVES

Shopping Centers (Malls)

Mall locations can provide attractive opportunities for most types of retail businesses. Malls today claim from 50% to 60% of all retail space and have grown in numbers from about 2,000 in 1957 to more than 42,000 today. With 5.1 billion square feet of leasable space, shopping centers garnered $973.6 billion in retail sales in 1996 and provided employment for more than 10 million people. Approximately 80% of all Americans shop at a mall at least once a month. In some malls you can attend college, get married, or even give birth to your baby!

Malls offer the general advantages of parking, a variety of stores for customers to do comparison shopping, and significant group advertising and promotion power. On the downside, mall-location operating expenses can be quite high, and there are many rules and regulations, such as required hours of operation, that must be obeyed.

Within a shopping center itself, you have several options for your business location. You may rent or lease a store location from the mall's management agency, or you may opt to rent a variety of smaller sales locations such as carts, kiosks, or tall wall units.

These venues are in the mall's common areas. They can provide a small but efficient way to market specialty goods. A cart is highly flexible, is usually on wheels, and can be moved from location to location within the mall. A kiosk is usually stationary and offers some of the conveniences of a store location, such as telephone service and electrical power. A tall wall unit is a new concept in retail sales. Large 7- to 10-foot shelves on a common area wall serve as a selling space and do not impede the central traffic flow.

Central Business District

Central Business Districts (CBDs) are found in downtown metropolitan areas. They feature such amenities as mass transit, tourism, and heavy foot traffic, but have drawbacks such as little room for expansion, lack of parking, and high rents. Unless your business is specifically suited for a down-town location, it may be more advantageous to locate in a suburban area.

Co-location

As the term suggests, co-location refers to two or more businesses sharing the same location. Generally the businesses that enter such arrangements are *complementary*, such as a sandwich deli (for example, D'Angelo's) and an ice cream store (such as Chips Ice Cream). *Competitive* businesses are most likely to co-locate in a shopping center and take advantage of comparison shoppers. Occasionally, however, two competitive small businesses, such as a jeweler and a leather-goods shop, may co-locate in a single building. Both businesses are going after the same "accessory" dollar, but offer products different enough from each other to survive on their own.

Co-location arrangements serve two purposes. First, they can significantly reduce overhead. Second, they can increase sales potential because customers for each business are highly probable ones for the other businesses occupying the shared location.

Virtual Retailer (a.k.a. Direct Marketing)

With the network of contractor services available today, it is possible to develop your business with broad offerings but low overhead, including location expense.

R▶ p. 261   B▶ p. 292

Write-Off Executive Writing Supplies sells a variety of personalized writing implements including mechanical pencils, pens, highlighters, and markers. Most of the product line is targeted toward the upscale market and garners a higher selling price thanks to high-quality components, professional engraving, and executive-style gift packaging. Write-Off maintains separate toll-free sales and service numbers, as well as different mail addresses for shipping, receiving, sales, and administration. The company has a site on the Web through which you can order products or get information on replacement parts. It has a fancy brochure, business cards with phone and fax numbers, an E-mail address, and a Yellow Pages listing.

College town => (handwritten)

Eight Major Types of Malls

According to the International Council of Shopping Centers (ICSC), there are eight major types of malls.

Neighborhood Center. This center is designed to provide convenience shopping for the day-to-day needs of consumers in the immediate neighborhood. According to ICSC's SCORE publication, roughly half of these centers are anchored by a supermarket, while about a third have a drugstore anchor. These anchors are supported by smaller stores offering drugs, sundries, snacks, and personal services. A neighborhood center is usually configured as a straight-line strip with no enclosed walkway or mall area, although a canopy may connect the storefronts.

Community Center. A community center typically offers a wider range of apparel and other soft goods than the neighborhood center. Among the more common anchors are supermarkets, super drugstores, and discount department stores. Community-center tenants sometimes include off-price retailers selling such items as apparel, home improvement/furnishings, toys, electronics, or sporting goods. The center is usually configured as a strip, in a straight line, "L" or a "U" shape. Of the eight center types, community centers encompass the widest range of formats. For example, certain centers that are anchored by a large discount department store refer to themselves as discount centers. Others with a high percentage of square footage allocated to off-price retailers can be termed off-price centers.

Regional Center. This center type provides general merchandise (a large percentage of which is apparel), and services in full depth and variety. Its main attractions are its anchors: traditional, mass-merchant, or discount department stores or fashion specialty stores. A typical regional center is usually enclosed, with an inward orientation of stores connected by a common walkway, and parking surrounds the outside perimeter.

Superregional Center. Similar to a regional center, but because of its larger size, a superregional center has more anchors, a broader selection of merchandise, and also draws from a larger population base. As with regional centers, the typical configuration is an enclosed mall, frequently with multiple levels.

Fashion/Specialty Center. A center composed mainly of upscale apparel shops, boutiques, and craft shops carrying selected fashion or unique merchandise of high quality and price. These centers need not be anchored, although sometimes restaurants or entertainment can provide the draw of anchors. The physical design of the center is very sophisticated, emphasizing a rich decor and high-quality landscaping. These centers are usually found in trade areas having high-income levels.

• Stuyvesant (handwritten)
• Newton (handwritten)

Power Center. A center dominated by several large anchors, including discount department stores, off-price stores, warehouse clubs, or "category-killers," i.e., stores that offer tremendous selection in a particular merchandise category at low prices. Some of these anchors can be freestanding (unconnected). The center has only a minimum number of small specialty tenants.

Theme/Festival Center. This center typically employs a unifying theme that is carried out by the individual shops in their architectural design and, to an extent, in their merchandise. The biggest appeal of this center is to tourists; it can be anchored by restaurants and entertainment facilities. The center is generally located in an urban area, tends to be adapted from an older, sometimes historic, building, and can be part of a mixed-use project.

Outlet Center. Usually located in a rural or occasionally in a tourist location, an outlet center consists mostly of manufacturers' outlet stores selling their own brands at a discount. An outlet center typically is not anchored. A strip configuration is most common, although some are enclosed malls, and others can be arranged in a "village" cluster.

Source: ICSC Shopping Center Definitions

On first glance, you might think this is a fairly large company. There is a good chance, however, that it is a virtual one. That is, the owners of Write-Off may be two people who rely on a whole cadre of other small businesses and access to technology to perform many functions.

In this case, the owners probably handle product sales, but outsource most (if not all) of the manufacturing and shipping functions. Both of the owners perform the same administrative tasks, but the separate sales and service phone lines allow the owners to answer the phone in the appropriate manner (e.g., if a call comes in on the sales line, an owner could answer "Sarah Lewis, sales," and if a call comes in on the service line, the same person could answer "Customer service, Sarah speaking"). The separate mailing addresses add to the illusion of size. In fact, a business like Write-Off might be operated out of a home office, even though the official address is an office suite (which is nothing more than a mailbox service).

Another example is Ken Yunker, who sells his Concours Carnauba Paste Wax to car collectors, car club members, and others who want their cars to appear to be in showroom condition. While Ken markets his high-end product primarily at car shows and via direct marketing, virtually every other aspect of his business, ranging from order taking to warehousing and shipping, is handled by independent contractors. In fact, Ken works out of his home office and has a booth set up for retail sales when he goes on the road to sell at trade shows, car shows, and rallies.

OTHER FACTORS AFFECTING LOCATION

Whatever you decide concerning location, the following factors should be considered, if applicable. It will be helpful to construct an evaluation grid in order to compare the attributes of the different locations you are contemplating.

Costs

As you compare location alternatives, estimate costs carefully. Remember that your expenses may include not only your monthly lease payments but also leasehold improvements, lease and security deposits, utilities, and other possible assessments. One way to determine whether you are paying too much for your location is to compare your costs with those of other, similar businesses. You can look up your business type and compare, on a percentage-of-sales basis, what similar businesses pay for rent.

Leases

A lease is basically an agreement to rent a property (location) for a specified period of time and use it as if you were the owner. A lease arrangement

may be your only viable option, since buying a property is often financially out of reach and may not be a wise investment. The two biggest downsides are, one, all of your monthly payments have no residual value, and two, at the end of the term of your lease, the cost may be increased to an amount that your business can't sustain.

Prior to entering into a lease agreement, you should evaluate certain factors, such as renewal options and liability issues, which should be discussed thoroughly with your attorney. There are several common types of leases.

Straight lease. The straight lease, the simplest type, states that the lessee will pay the lessor a fixed amount of rent per month for a fixed period of time. A graduated straight lease, which is used more commonly, sets your rent at a modest level, for example, $750 per month for the first two years, then moves to a larger amount, say $1,100 per month, for the remaining three years in the lease.

Net lease. A frequently used form of lease agreement, the net lease obliges the lessee to pay a lower rent and also some or all of the real-estate taxes. A net-net lease requires the lessee to pay the property insurance as well. A triple-net lease includes rent, real-estate taxes, insurance, maintenance, and utility expenses.

Percentage lease. In a percentage lease, often used for mall locations, rent is based on your retail sales and will vary each month. The percentage lease is usually a fair way of determining rent, because it is realistic for both retailer and landlord in terms of inflation and income. Percentage leases can also have a specified maximum that, in effect, puts a ceiling on the amount of rent paid. This method rewards successful retailers by enabling them to keep the percentage of sales that exceeds the maximum rent. Conversely, leases can have a specified minimum, which requires a certain sum to be paid for rent, regardless of how low sales levels are. Finally, a sliding scale can be applied to a percentage lease. With a sliding scale, the retailer pays a certain percentage for the first increment of sales, and then a different percentage for the next increment. For example, the lease agreement may state that the amount of rent paid is 5% of sales on the first $100,000, and 3.5% for all sales above $100,000.

Traffic Patterns

If foot or vehicular traffic is important to sustain your business, it is necessary to determine what the traffic volume is, and at what times. Your state Department of Transportation is an excellent source for traffic counts, but, in general, the data will need further analysis.

Consider a discount outdoor supply and canoe outlet located in the heart of Denver's financial district that recently went out of business. Its business plan included a traffic and market analysis, which established that there was an ample number of outdoor enthusiasts in town to support the store. The problem was that although plenty of tire-kickers came in to browse, the store's sales yield was very low—particularly on bulky, high-margin items. In retrospect, it seems clear that while potential customers were attracted to the store, they were buying many big-ticket items at locations more convenient for weekend shopping, where parking was easier and merchandise could more easily be taken home.

Potential customer traffic is indeed something that you should evaluate, preferably firsthand. Go to the proposed location(s). If it's foot traffic that you are documenting, record information such as volume (number, density, timing) and characteristics of the passersby. Interview some of them. If you are analyzing vehicle traffic patterns, try to determine whether there are special circumstances, such as those in our example, then revise your estimates accordingly.

IS▶ p. 201   **R▶ p. 238**

Parking

Is the parking adequate? The answer to this question is affected by many variables, such as the length of time your customer is likely to spend at your business, your expected customer flow, whether customers need to be able to take purchases home in their cars, and whether you will reasonably be able to restrict a parking area just for your customers. Here, again, there is no substitute for on-site analysis.

Permits and Licenses

Make a list of all the permits and licenses that are required for your particular business. Not only are there some that might surprise you, they may also differ from location to location. For example, if you have a storefront location, don't just go out and buy a fancy (and expensive) sign. You may find that there are local regulations restricting the size of your sign and how it can be displayed. In addition, certain types of businesses, such as those dealing with food and toxic waste, need both state and federal permits. If you have any doubt, the best place to check is your local Small Business Development Center, Chamber of Commerce, trade association, or appropriate state agency.

Expansion

Will the location accommodate your business two, three, or five years down the road, relative to your growth projections? If not, where could you potentially relocate, and how would such a move affect your customer base?

Zoning Restrictions

Be sure to check with local government authorities (e.g., town hall) to ensure that the location you are considering is zoned for your particular type of business. Even if you are considering a home office, don't make the assumption that it is allowed until you've checked at the town hall. For example, a young couple started an Amway business in their home that involved a great deal of shipping and receiving. At first the occasional UPS truck went unnoticed. However, as the business quickly grew, more and larger trucks appeared in the neighborhood on a regular basis. Local residents began to complain about the new traffic, and the business was forced to move to a new location that was properly zoned for the amount of trucking that was required.

Home-Based Business

If you operate your business out of your home, as in the case of a direct marketer, you can usually deduct a percentage of your utilities, insurance, and maintenance, and depreciate the portion of your home that you are using exclusively and regularly for business purposes. The IRS has very strict rules governing home office expenses, spelled out in Publication #587 (right).

Network Marketing

Network marketing is not a business in itself. Rather, it is a method of distributing a variety of products or services to the consumer. Network marketing seeks to eliminate the wholesaler and deliver the merchandise directly from manufacturer to end-user. A network marketer sets up the sale and sends the order to the manufacturer. The manufacturer fills the order without going through intermediaries, effectively using you as its sales force.

Network marketing typically builds from one distributor to another, each sharing part of the sales from new clients (generally referred to as "downline"). Funds that would have gone to pay for advertising, overhead, and staff retention go instead to pay commissions to distributors.

As in any business, you must be cautious before entering into a network marketing agreement. In the past, network marketing schemes have cost would-be businesspeople their life savings and ruined otherwise productive businesses. One should take note that some networks are little more than Ponzi schemes, where nothing is actually sold, and most of the money is made by investors at the top of the pyramid. Presently, however, network marketing is legitimately used by very large and reputable companies and is considerably less risky, thanks to government regulations and public awareness.

Publication #587

Use tests. Whether you are an employee or self-employed, you generally cannot deduct expenses for the business use of your home. But you can take a limited deduction for its business use if you use part of your home exclusively and regularly:

1) as the principal place of business for any trade or business in which you engage;

2) as a place to meet or deal with patients, clients, or customers in the normal course of your trade or business; or

3) in connection with your trade or business, if you are using a separate structure that is not attached to your house or residence.

Employee use. Even if you meet the exclusive and regular use tests, you cannot take any deduction for the business use of your home if you are an employee and either of the following situations apply to you:

1) The business use of your home is not for the convenience of your employer. Whether your home's business use is for your employer's convenience depends on all the facts and circumstances. However, business use is not considered for your employer's convenience merely because it is appropriate and helpful.

2) You rent all or part of your home to your employer and use the rented portion to perform services as an employee.

Trade or business use. You must use your home in connection with a trade or business to take a deduction for its business use. If you use your home for a profit-seeking activity that is not a trade or business, you cannot take a deduction for its use.

Source: Internal Revenue Service Publication #587

FOOTPRINT

Be sure to include a floor plan for your business in the Location section, along with a map that shows the street location; proximity to competitors, suppliers, and complementary businesses; major thoroughfares; and public transportation.

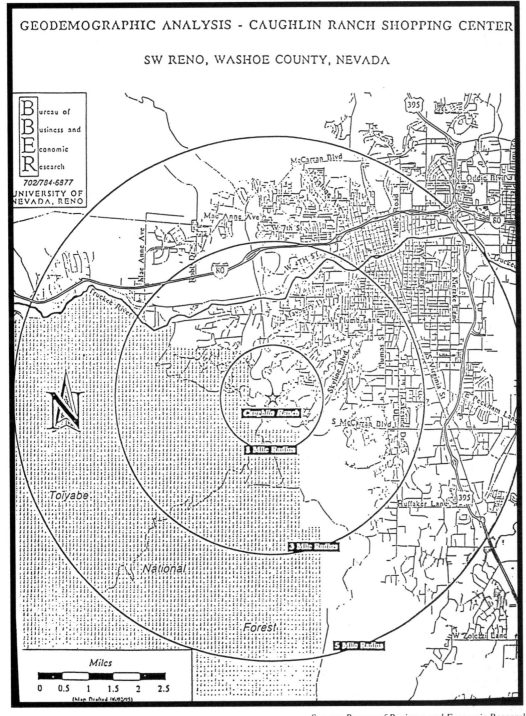

Source: Bureau of Business and Economic Research, Univ. of Nevada, Reno

Store Layout and Design

An important part of the location section of your business plan will be a layout map of your proposed store (or your expansion). By showing what your retail location will look like, you give the reader a "hands-on" feel for your business. The type of layout you use will depend largely on the products you are selling. Whether you design a free-flow, grid, or loop layout, be sure to identify the locations of product displays, checkout stands, and storage areas.

IS▶ p. 204

Three common types of layout include:

Grid. This layout is commonly used by people in grocery, convenience, and drug stores. Evenly spaced rows of shelving provide maximum product display and stocking, with minimal wasted space. This layout is not the most eye-catching, but it provides quick access to a large variety of merchandise. Because the racks are similar in construction, fixture and maintenance costs are generally low.

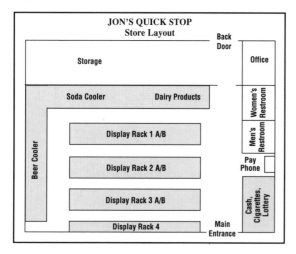

Free-form. A free-form layout contains a mixture of shelves, displays, and fixtures (rounders, four-ways, straight racks, and gondolas) in an asymmetrical pattern throughout the store. The intent is to create a home-like atmosphere for shopping, without high-pressure sales. This style of layout is most successfully used by small boutiques and specialty shops, where consumers spend a large percentage of their time browsing. The downside of a free-form layout is increased custom-fixture

costs, increased theft opportunities, and, because customers often need assistance to locate merchandise, increased staffing costs.

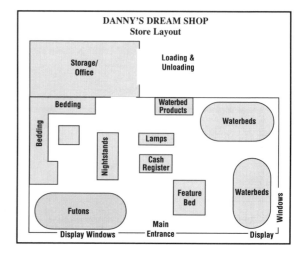

Loop (racetrack). Loop designs are typically employed by large department stores with several departments or boutiques. Aware of the consumer's need to feel comfortable while shopping, large retailers divide their store into smaller departments, each featuring its own small-business atmosphere. These individualized boutiques are indicated by a change in carpet, wall decor, or display amenities. The purpose of the loop is to pull the consumer from department to department, and encourage impulse purchases along the way. Typically, high-traffic draw departments are placed in the rear of the store, so as to require the shopper to traverse the entire store before reaching his or her destination.

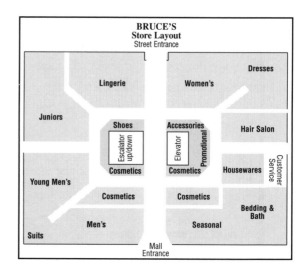

PITFALLS

Underestimated Costs

Identify and project accurately all relevant costs associated with each location. For example, if you are renting a property that was previously either a retail location for another type of merchandise or not a retail location at all, make sure to include the costs for all leasehold improvements that need to be made to create the atmosphere best suited to merchandising your products.

Location Costs Too High

If your location costs as a percentage of sales are significantly higher than industry averages, evaluate the situation carefully. Local market conditions could justify this, but if not, your higher overhead will have a direct effect on profitability.

Better Locations Available

Evaluate a number of alternative locations to make sure that you are getting not only an economical situation that you can afford, but also the location that best suits your business in terms of image, efficiency, type of merchandise offered, and cost-effectiveness.

SOME ADVICE

"For most retail businesses, location is often the most critical element for success. Being essentially a direct marketer, we have very little walk-in business, so a high-traffic location is not that important to us. We are in an industrial park that has low rent and plenty of space. Occasionally customers visit our location, but only when they are specifically seeking us out. It is more important for us to have low overhead and high accessibility to distribution channels than it is to have a fancy store downtown."

J. David Traywick
Griller's World
Ringgold, Ga.

PRICING

OVERVIEW

At first glance, setting prices appears to be a simple task. **What is price?** The value the market places on a product. **How is it determined?** By calculating the costs of providing the product and then adding a profit margin.

In actuality, establishing prices can be quite complex. It will be one of the most important decisions you make, since it will be a key determinant in whether your business is profitable. While pricing certainly involves an analysis of costs and profit margins, a number of other factors will ultimately have significant effects on your decision. These include *elasticity of demand,* which measures the relationship between changes in prices and the quantity of demand for your products or for items that are close substitutes.

For example, if you are going to provide a product that has no close substitutes—say, by opening the only video store in your town (if there is still a town without one), the pricing environment will be relatively inelastic. That is, for a certain level of demand, you can charge relatively high prices. However, if you plan to open your area's third children's clothing and toy store, the demand will be relatively elastic, meaning that you may need to offer your products at lower prices to attract customers from your competitors (particularly if one of your rivals is a large, discount mass merchandiser such as Wal-Mart).

The best way to consider the price of your product is from the consumers' perspective. Your customer doesn't care about your cost basis or profit margin. What customers are looking for is good comparative value within the context of what they can afford to pay and what you and your competition have to offer.

Your company *image* has a significant effect on the prices that you will be able to charge. Consider the Hitching Post, which is located in a small but heavily visited tourist town on Long Island, N.Y. This store sells premium-priced, brand-name men's clothing and accessories. It also has a line of clothes that carries the store's own private label. The Hitching Post does not try to compete on a price basis with numerous competitors located in fairly close proximity. What the owners do is differentiate their store by offering unmatched personal service, a product line of very high quality, and store layout and design that create an atmosphere conducive to a feeling of exclusivity. Customers of the Hitching Post feel special because they are all treated that way.

B> p. 294

Intangibles often have the biggest effect on your customers' perception of value and, accordingly, on their purchase decisions. The quality of your warranty, friendly service, and follow-up add value to your offering, and many people may be willing to pay extra for them. The importance of these factors and their relationship to price cannot be overstated.

The logical development of your pricing strategy is very important for another reason. Those who may evaluate your business plan will be keenly aware of the problems smaller retailers face from the predatory pricing strategies of the large mass-merchandisers. Therefore, you must show how your pricing strategy, along with other elements of the marketing mix, will enable you to compete effectively in the marketplace.

IS> p. 205

WHAT PRICING OPTIONS ARE AVAILABLE?

In the long run, all pricing, by definition, has to be *competitive*. In most mature markets, you will find products offered at different price levels (high, moderate, low) reflecting varying degrees of consumer demand, ability and willingness of customers to pay, and the retailers' ability to differentiate their offerings. Your store will fall into one of those categories.

In establishing your introductory pricing strategy, you should also consider two other alternatives.

Penetration Pricing

This strategy involves pricing your merchandise at a level below that of your competition. Your goal is twofold: to get customers to switch from your competitors because they perceive that you can give them better value, and to attract customers who have never used such products before or use them infrequently because of the price barrier. This strategy works most effectively for businesses that can achieve economies with increases in volume.

Consider Dover Marine, a discount supply store that carries specialized product lines for the boating enthusiast. Dover Marine has everything from life preservers to fish finders. It has established itself as a discount retailer and attracts customers from a wide geographic area by offering low prices, variety, and an exceptional selection of merchandise. The owners are able to do this because they buy in quantities large enough to take advantage of discounts. Dover Marine also has a catalog from which you can order almost any boating equipment within a very short turn-around time, whereas the local Wal-Mart carries relatively few items and has virtually no control over when out-of-stock items will arrive.

You must be very careful when implementing this type of pricing structure, for two reasons.

First, you must be confident that you can achieve your financial goals at these lower price levels. Don't think that if your projected sales levels don't come to fruition, you can always solve the problem by simply increasing the price. At that point, faced with higher prices, your newfound customers may revert to their former sources of supplies, or those new to the market may find they cannot afford to continue to use the products they bought from you.

Second, your competitors have the ability to interfere with your pricing strategy in the short run, assuming they don't want to lower their own prices over the long term. For example, they could mail discount coupons to their customers or advertise a special offer to attract new customers. Both of these techniques are inexpensive and can be implemented rapidly.

Premium Pricing

Premium pricing, as the name suggests, is a strategy whereby you price your merchandise at the high end of the market. You are trying to attract customers who are willing to pay more for what they consider to be superior merchandise; who assume that higher price, by definition, means higher quality; or who get some ego gratification from selecting your product.

Look at G-Willikers in Portsmouth, N.H., a children's toy and clothing store that carries premium-brand merchandise. It targets upscale buyers and those who are looking for gifts for special occasions. It does not attempt to compete with the Wal-Marts of the world. G-Willikers can maintain relatively high price points by carrying excellent product lines, providing solid customer service, and building a good reputation within the business community.

The upside of this strategy is more profitable sales. The downside is a mirror image of the penetration strategy. That is, if you are forced to lower prices because you misread consumer demand or new competitors entered the market, you may find that your old customers don't come back and that new ones fail to appear, since you no longer differentiate your products by linking price to higher quality.

B▶ p. 294

THE BASICS

Here are the steps and considerations fundamental to establishing your introductory pricing strategy.

How Low Can You Go?

The first step in determining price is to *calculate your costs*. Then, *establish the return* you are looking for in quantitative terms. For start-ups, the return is most often expressed as the amount of salary you will require for yourself over the short term. As your business grows, you can expect earnings to increase as well, but in the formative years, when you are establishing yourself, plan to take only a modest amount from the business. If you are more successful than you planned, all the better. This approach will help ensure a viable business and, potentially, more funds for advertising and promotion. As your business grows, you may expand your pricing objectives to include maintaining or improving market share, price stability, or preventing competition.

Pricing involves determining your *break-even point* (BEP). The BEP is the point at which your total costs are equal to your total revenue. At sales levels below the BEP, you will have a loss, and above the BEP, a profit. For your purposes it is best to calculate BEP in two ways: 1) the dollar amount of sales necessary to cover all your costs (the break-even quantity) and 2) the number of customers necessary to achieve break-even.

The following formula will enable you to determine the dollar amount of sales you will need to achieve break-even. Sales consists of total revenue generated from your day-to-day income. Then you can estimate the number of customers you need, and compare that number to your estimated market share information. These calculations should indicate how likely you are to achieve the minimum level of sales required in your first year.

IS▶ p. 206

BREAK-EVEN QUANTITY (Sales)

$$\text{BEQ (sales)} = \frac{FC}{P - VC}$$

BEQ (sales) = dollar amount of sales necessary to break even

FC = fixed costs for one year

P = price that you will charge for a single product or group of products (i.e., estimated sale per customer, which may include several items)

VC = direct or variable costs related to each product

To complete your break-even analysis, you will have to make a lot of assumptions, any one of which could have a substantial effect on its outcome. That, however, is the nature of this type of analysis. It is advisable to calculate your BEQ under a number of different conditions and select the one that seems most reasonable.

Example

CALCULATING BREAK-EVEN

On several vacation trips to Mexico, Fred and Diane noticed that the ceramic giftware and sterling silver jewelry they saw was being sold in the United States for five times the store price in Mexico. They had always wanted to start their own business, so they decided to look at the feasibility of starting an import boutique in Chicago, their hometown. Their store, to be called The Mexican Connection, would be located in a local destination mall that has numerous specialty stores as tenants. As a first step they hired a local agent in Mexico and visited a number of small "factories" that produced merchandise they wanted to carry. Their agent felt that it would cost approximately 50% of their purchase price to cover import costs, including fees, duties, and transportation.

CALCULATING FIXED COSTS

Fixed costs, often referred to as *overhead*, are costs that do not change in the short run as the number of your customers increases or decreases. Fixed costs include items such as rent, insurance, utilities, owner's salary, and vehicles. All these costs should be calculated on an annual basis. (For retail businesses, most costs are considered fixed because it is difficult to allocate items like advertising or utilities to a specific product or department.)

IS▶ p. 213   R▶ p. 229, 264, 271

For The Mexican Connection, Fred and Diane researched other costs related to starting their business, including those associated with Diane working full time, employing a salesperson during the week, and Fred helping out on weekends. Their fixed costs included:

Salaries	$48,000	(a)
Rent	12,000	
Advertising	3,500	
Insurance	1,500	
Utilities	2,200	
Store Fixtures & Equipment	1,800	(b)
Total Fixed Costs	**$ 69,000**	

(a) This figure includes a full-time salary of $25,000 for Diane, a salary of $18,000 for a full-time salesperson, and a part-time salary of $5,000 for Fred.

(b) This represents one year's worth of payment on a bank loan of $8,000 for store fixtures.

These calculations show that they would have to generate $69,000 in sales in the first year to cover fixed costs.

ESTIMATING VARIABLE COSTS

Variable costs are costs that change as the volume of your business increases or decreases. For most small retail businesses, variable costs simply include your direct costs for inventory and any freight or storage costs you may incur. Because Fred and Diane intend to price on an average of four times their costs, their variable costs will be 25¢ for each dollar's worth of products sold.

PRICING THE GOODS

After you determine your fixed and variable costs, you will need to calculate your *contribution margin.* The contribution margin is the amount left over after variable costs are deducted from the sales price. The remainder, or contribution margin, is what is available to help cover fixed costs and eventually generate a profit, once your break-even level has been achieved.

$$\text{Contribution Margin} = \text{Sales} - \text{VC}$$
OR
$$\text{Contribution Margin} = \text{Price} - \text{VC}$$
(for an individual product)

On the basis of some comparison shopping, Fred and Diane still felt it was reasonable to price on an average level of four times their costs (including shipping, fees, and the like). That is, if they buy a hand-made vase in Guadalajara for $2, plus $1 in other costs, they plan to sell that vase for $12 in their shop. Or, for the average product they sell, their direct costs will be equal to 25% of the price, resulting in a contribution margin of 75%. Now, Fred and Diane can figure their break-even sales using the formula below:

$$\text{Break-Even Sales} = \frac{\text{Total Fixed Costs}}{\text{Contribution Margin} \text{ (as a \% of Sales)}}$$

$$\text{Break-Even Sales} = \frac{\$69,000}{75\%} = \$92,000$$

This means that in one year, Diane and Fred must sell $92,000 worth of goods to cover their costs and break even. With sales above $92,000, The Mexican Connection will make a profit. With sales below $92,000, the store will lose money.

HOW MANY CUSTOMERS DO YOU NEED?

You may also want to calculate how many customers you must have to break even. On the basis of more market research, Diane anticipates that customer purchases will average $25. She can now determine how many customers they need to break even.

$$\text{Number of customers needed to break even} = \frac{\text{Break-Even Sales}}{\text{Estimated Average Purchase per Customer}}$$

$$= \frac{\$92,000}{\$25}$$

$$= 3,680 \text{ customers per year}$$

If there are 307 business days in the year (6 days per week multiplied by 52 weeks per year, minus 5 holidays per year), then the store will need an average of:

$$\text{Customers per day} = \frac{3,680}{307}$$

$$= 11.98$$

By this calculation, The Mexican Connection will need 12 customers per day at an average purchase amount of $25 per customer to break even. Remember: This number represents an average, which may change significantly, based on factors such as changes in competition, increased costs, seasonality, and increasing or decreasing average sales per customer.

PRICING METHODS

Now that you have a good understanding, albeit based on many assumptions, of the levels of sales and number of customers you will need to cover costs, plus some general notion of your pricing alternatives, you will need to develop a pricing *strategy*.

Keystoning

Probably the most common method small retailers use to determine prices is keystoning. It is a simple method whereby you double the cost of any item you are considering purchasing, and then ask "Can I sell this for double my cost?"

For example, while on a buying trip to the New England Products Trade Show, Jane Doubleday came across some unusual wall clocks that the manufacturer was selling for $45, plus $5 shipping apiece. Jane liked the clocks very much and felt she could sell them for $100 in her store, so she ordered 10 clocks. Later in the day she spotted some beautiful stackable coffee tables that were wholesaling for $120 for a set of four. She did not think that they would sell in the $240 range in her store, so she passed.

As you can see, keystoning is a very practical method. It will work as long as the margin will pay for your overhead and remain consistent with your profit goals. It can also be adapted (as in The Mexican Connection) to situations where you feel that multiples of the standard markup are achievable, or lowered in cases where you feel that individual items need to be priced more competitively.

Calculating Standard Markup

Markup is a term you will often hear used when reading about or discussing pricing. It simply refers to the amount added to the wholesale price to determine the retail price. The markup can be viewed in two ways, which sometimes creates a bit of confusion.

For most retailers the markup percentage (or margin) is (usually) determined on the sales price. In our clock example, if Jane bought the clock for $50 and is selling it for $100, her markup is 50%. After all, 50% of $100 is $50. The other way to determine markup is on the basis of wholesale price. Most of you would probably say that Jane had 100% markup (or markon). However, the first method sounds better to retailers and their customers, which is why it is used most frequently.

B▶ p. 294

Whether you plan to keystone or use some other margin, the following formula will enable you to calculate the sales price easily under any condition:

$$\text{Selling price} = \frac{\text{Cost of Item}}{100 - \text{Markup Percentage}} \times 100\%$$

For example, let's say Jane wants to offer her new clocks at lower than 50% markup to attract customers, but from experience does not want to set her margin below 35%. Her selling price would be calculated as follows:

$$\text{Selling price} = \frac{\$50}{100 - 35\%} \times 100\%$$
$$= \$76.92$$
Or approximately: $77

MSRP

Typically, a manufacturer will provide a retailer with a *manufacturer's suggested retail price* (MSRP). This price is based on the total cost of manufacture and delivery to the retailer, profit to the manufacturer, and a standard profit margin to the retailer for the particular type of product.

For example, say the total cost to manufacture, package, and ship a particular model of vacuum cleaner is $100 (which includes research and development, materials, plant expenses, salaries of production, sales, and administration personnel, and so on). The manufacturer adds its profit margin to the price, wholesaling the unit to retailers for $150. Knowing that the typical retail markup (based on selling price) for vacuums is 40%, the manufacturer will suggest a retail (list) price of $250.

Most smaller retailers will not actually sell the unit for this price, however, because the overhead costs as computed by the manufacturer are often significantly understated for smaller retailers;

therefore, by using them you will not be able to achieve an acceptable profit margin. The MSRP can be used as a benchmark and, in some situations, as an effective promotional tool. For example, the retailer's advertising can say, "We are offering these new, lightweight, powerful vacuums at 15% below the manufacturer's suggested retail price."

Price Lining

Price lining refers to offering products at a limited number of price points, or zones. Price points are a small number of specific prices (generally one to four) at which you might sell your merchandise. For example, an automotive warehouse might sell three types of car batteries for $39.99, $49.99, and $59.99. Customers can choose which battery they want on the basis of perceived value caused by the price differential. Other attributes (like length of life, cranking power, and so on) will generally have less effect on the customer than price.

For example, in Jane's clock shop, she may offer 10 different wall clocks in each of three price zones. For the budget conscious, she has clocks from $15 to $35. For those with a fatter wallet, Jane carries more elaborate clocks in the $50 to $75 range. And for those who want the ultimate in handcarved elegance, she has a selection of wall clocks for $150 to $250. This helps Jane to departmentalize her inventory and make her buying decisions appropriately based on sales in each zone.

In addition, if you priced each product strictly on its cost, pretty soon you would have an unmanageable system, difficult for you and confusing for the customer. Take, for example, Mrs. Fields' Cookies. It is clearly more expensive to produce a White Chunk Macadamia-Nut cookie than it is to produce a simple sugar cookie, yet both are sold for the same price. Maintaining separate break-even points (and separate prices) would be confusing for the bookkeeper, the salesperson, and the customer. By aggregating the costs of production for all cookies (taking into consideration the demand for each kind), Mrs. Fields can calculate an average cost and charge one price per cookie.

Variable Pricing

As Ken Stone points out, no matter what pricing method or combinations thereof you use, unless you have a product line that is truly unique, you will be faced with price competition from "category-killer" stores, discount merchandisers, membership warehouse clubs, and the like. Therefore, in most cases, it would be prudent to modify your pricing strategy for price-sensitive items that your large competitors also carry.

For example, a grocery store that finds itself competing with a new warehouse club, such as BJ's or Costco, should price its eggs, bread, and milk in line with the competition. The reality, however, is that many items carried by these new titans of retailing are not in fact discounted. Consumers assume they are getting a good deal on all the items in their shopping basket, since other price-sensitive products carried by the discounter are priced lower than the competition's. One effective strategy is to monitor your warehouse competitor's pricing on frequently purchased items and try to price yours at comparable levels. That way, customers shopping in your store won't simply assume that *all* your prices are higher than the warehouse competitor's tags.

OTHER FACTORS AFFECTING PRICE

You will have to consider factors other than direct and fixed costs when calculating price.

Credit Cards

Currently, credit purchases make up nearly a third of all retail sales, and that number is expected to increase to one-half by 2000. In other words, consumer credit accounted for more than $76 billion in 1996 alone. Customers are carrying less cash and are relying on retailers to accept a multitude of plastic alternatives.

In order to accept credit cards, a business must make formal arrangements with the card issuer. For example, if you intend to accept VISA at your store, you sign a contract with VISA allowing you to do so. When a customer purchases items from your store using his or her VISA card, VISA will bill the customer for the sale, and deposit funds in your account on the same day as the sale, less a percentage commission. This percentage ranges from 2% to 6% of each sale, depending on the volume of business you do with the credit card issuer.

If you plan to offer credit services to your customers, it is important to remember that you must account properly for those costs in your financial projections and your pricing strategy. For example, if you expect to sell 50% of the merchandise by credit card, you will have to increase prices 2% to 3% to maintain your profit margins.

Credit-card sales are a must for most businesses and can obviously work to your advantage. By accepting credit cards, you can usually expect larger sales and lower collection costs, since the card issuer will handle the collection of the debt for you.

Shipping and Handling

Shipping and handling costs can be one of the highest components in your cost of goods sold, second only to the cost of the product itself. Therefore, negotiation of the terms of shipping between vendor and retailer are vitally important when calculating costs. Shipping terms define not only who pays for transportation of the items between certain points, but also when legal ownership of the merchandise actually changes hands. Any shipping and handling costs must be accurately reflected in the price you charge for your merchandise.

Discounts and Allowances

You may be able to avail yourself of many types of discounts, which can have a dramatic effect on your costs. For example, most suppliers will offer cash discounts for paying bills on time. It is common for a vendor to give you a 2% discount if you pay your bills within 10 days. Another example is quantity discounts. Suppliers may offer discounts based on the quantity you buy, so it's often helpful to group your orders so as to take advantage of these savings. Distributors will usually require a minimum purchase (such as a dozen or a case) to get the discount, so planning carefully in this regard is important.

Returns

A good returns policy is essential for you to be competitive. Most large retailers are moving or have moved to "no questions asked" policies, which is a very effective marketing tool. Make sure your return policies are well thought out and understood by your customers and suppliers alike. For example, if a customer returns merchandise because it is defective or because he or she just didn't like it, under what conditions will the manufacturers take it back (will they offer credit, who will pay for shipping, what on-site services are provided)? If your returns policy and projected costs associated with it have not been thought out and accounted for carefully, it can have a dramatic effect on your profitability.

PITFALLS

A number of factors can have a negative impact on your overall pricing strategy.

Underestimating Costs

Failure to identify and estimate all relevant costs accurately will have a significant effect on the performance of your business.

Competition

You need to identify all relevant competitors and their pricing policies. Failure to do so, and to adjust your pricing strategy accordingly, may result in overestimating market share and lead you into pricing errors that could be fatal to your business.

Substitute Awareness Effect

If any substitutes for your products are available, your customers will become more price sensitive. In today's market of too many stores, many alternatives are available for a given product, driving competition up and prices down. While you can use this phenomenon to your advantage and steal business from your competitors, they can use it against you in the same way. It is imperative that you carefully evaluate your prices against those of substitute products in your trading area. For example, if you are opening a bagel shop, you must be aware of the pricing strategy used by the local donut shop(s) and convenience stores/gas stations. While each shop may offer different products, if they are accepted by consumers as substitutes for each other, you may not be able to charge a premium simply for offering the only bagel in town.

SOME ADVICE

"With all of the competition that has developed in our industry over the past decade, the country-club-based pro shop can't afford to match prices with the discounters. We must sell value, which in most cases translates to superior service (both before and after the sale) that most customers are willing to pay a premium for. We also have differentiated our product line to include our own distinctive private-label merchandise and other articles not easily found elsewhere."

Jim Sheerin
PGA Master Golf Professional
Abenaqui Country Club
Rye, N.H.

EXCERPT

> ### Let's Make Music
> *High-end audio and video equipment*
>
> **Inventory, Pricing, and Warranties.** The profit margin on the products we sell ranges from 38% to 50%. There is an established manufacturer's recommended selling price that we will adhere to the majority of the time. My pricing structure is to discount a product only when a "system" is being purchased, or to meet a competitor's price. A few customers will call out-of-town retailers to find products at a 10% to 15% discount. We will rarely meet this price since Let's Make Music offers services that an out-of-town retailer cannot, such as immediate repairs and loaner equipment should a product fail. Most of these customers can be convinced to purchase their equipment from us. Because most of our product lines are exclusive (Thiel, Mark Levinson, Proceed, Conrad-Johnson, and Linn), discounting is rarely an issue. If a customer does ask for a discount, we will explain that the products that we have chosen to represent are a value at the price set by the manufacturer. We have evaluated all the products available and represent these because of their value-to-cost ratio. When a customer realizes our customer service policies are also included, like full trade-up allowance, in-home installation, and the best service technician, then a discount is usually not an issue. The average "system discount" in the industry is 5%. I will turn to this only to close a sale. As you can see, the margin of 40% chosen to use in the cash-flow analysis is a bit low. We will probably be in the 42% to 43% category, but chose 40% to be conservative.

Source: Let's Make Music

PROMOTION

OVERVIEW

Promotion is any form of communication that informs your potential customers that you have products available to them, convinces them your products meet their needs, and persuades them to purchase what you're selling. As a retailer, you create the message that you want to convey to current and potential customers, select the medium (television, radio, newspaper, Internet) to be used to carry your message, and then send it.

The first step in developing a promotional strategy is to create a list of goals you expect to achieve. They should be clearly stated in quantitative terms wherever possible. Each aspect of your promotional campaign should be measured against these objectives. For example, if you decide to use a certain amount of radio advertising—let's say a package that provides 30 spots per week—you can check its effectiveness by determining to what extent it meets your goals in terms of customer reach and frequency.

Evaluating the effectiveness of the various components of your promotional strategy is an important but often difficult task. A comprehensive statement of your **goals** should include the following.

IS> p. 207

Establish and/or expand your customer base. How does the proposed strategy ensure that potential customers will become aware of your products? How many new customers will be reached?

Differentiate your products. How does the promotional activity make your store and products look unique, different from those offered by your competitors? After all, in today's marketplace you would be hard pressed to find a product, or at least a close substitute, that isn't available to your customer from a competitor as well as from you.

Therefore, you must emphasize factors such as price, hours of operation, selection, quality, and personalized customer service to differentiate your business. If you do this effectively, you will actually change the shape of your demand curve, making it more inelastic, thus making your merchandise less price-sensitive.

Influence people to become customers. Does the promotional activity provide an incentive for the prospective customer to purchase? For example, ads reading "Giant end-of-season sale on all outboard engines! Start next spring on a new Mercury" or "Two-for-one on all in-stock recliners" may help achieve this goal.

Build goodwill. Does this promotional technique build your reputation as a good citizen and establish a positive image for your business that people will remember? Contributions such as support of community fund-raising activities, buying Little League uniforms for local teams, and donating to public television auctions fall into this category.

Goals in hand, your next step is to create a comprehensive promotional plan. Assume that most customers you want to attract to your store will have numerous alternatives or substitutes available to them. That's why the most important factor contributing to your business success will be your ability to inform customers and prospects about your offerings and differentiate them from those of your competitors.

THE BASICS

This section focuses on promotional mix and several other factors that influence the development of a well-rounded promotional strategy. Before you begin to evaluate your promotional alternatives, consider these three factors.

IS> p. 208

Reach. This refers to the number of people who will actually see or hear your promotional message. For example, an advertisement in the local newspaper will reach subscribers and their families or roommates, as well as people who buy the paper at the newsstand.

Reach is important because you want your promotional material to get to your target market but not too far beyond it. If you have a convenience store, you might decide not to advertise in the county newspaper because there would be no point in paying to reach a large number of people who are outside your geographic target market. The local paper, however, might be a very appropriate venue to place a coupon for an Italian sandwich two-for-one offer.

Frequency. This is the number of times you think your potential customers need to be exposed to your message for it to be effective. For example, if you think that radio would be a good way to promote your toy store, your customers will probably have to hear your ad several times for it to generate a response. Radio listeners who are concentrating on driving a car may not be paying particular attention to the message and may not remember your address or telephone number.

CPM. CPM stands for dollar cost per thousand potential customers reached by a particular advertisement. It is a valuable tool to use as part of your analysis of how to allocate your advertising budget. To compute CPM, simply take the cost of the promotional activity and divide it by the number of people reached. For example, if you pay $2,500 to place an ad in a specialty model-train magazine that has a circulation of 375,000 to promote your mail-order business, your CPM would be $6.67. You can then compare that figure to the CPMs of your other promotional alternatives.

Cost per thousand is a good analytical tool. However, just because one promotional activity has the lowest CPM, it is not necessarily the best alternative. Other factors to consider are the medium's focus on your target market and your overall costs.

The Promotional Mix

The promotional mix includes five basic ways to communicate about your products: advertising, sales promotion, personal selling, publicity, and public relations. The promotional mix is a blend of these options. Which ones you choose depends on factors such as available funds, competition, and stage of your business life cycle.

Although when starting your business you will probably not employ all of these methods, it is very important to be aware of the different tools available as your business grows or a particular circumstance arises, such as a request to support a fund-raising drive for your local hospital. Your strategy should not be created by happenstance. It should result from an analysis of your alternatives, weighed against your promotional goals.

Advertising

Advertising, as Carol Schroeder points out in her book *Specialty Shop Retailing,* "doesn't cost—it pays." It is important to think of advertising costs as an investment, which should pay some dividends in the short term but whose real benefits will accrue over time. Advertising includes all paid promotional activities that are used to communicate to your target market about your product.

IS▶ p. 209   B▶ p. 294

ADVERTISING ALTERNATIVES

Literature	Print Advertising	Direct Mail
Brochures	Newspapers	Newsletters
Flyers	Buyers' guides	Catalogs
Leaflets	Magazines	Brochures
Circulars	Specialty publications	Coupons
		Sales letters
		Cooperative Direct Marketing (e.g., Super-Coups)

Broadcast	Outdoor Advertising	Other
Television	Billboards	Internet postings
Cable TV	Signs	Web pages
Radio	Banners	CD-ROMs
		Co-op advertising

As you evaluate your advertising expenditures in the context of reach, frequency, and CPM, you also need to be aware of the general characteristics of each medium. Specific advertising rates, circulation figures, and readership, viewer, or listener demographics can be obtained by contacting prospective newspapers, magazines, radio stations, or other media directly. A general overview follows.

Literature. Brochures and flyers can be easy and inexpensive to produce and change. They can also be used for multiple purposes. For example, you could use the same flyer you hand out at the student union to promote your discount textbook-store for direct mail to previous customers, whose names you've collected and entered into your database, reminding them about your specialty pricing and open-ended return policy. Or, you could take the brochure that you use as a direct-mail piece for your cheese factory/retail store and distribute it to local motels and restaurants for them to place in their display racks along with information for tourists about local attractions.

Print advertising. More small-business advertising dollars are spent on *newspapers* than on any other medium. Newspapers are timely, widely read, have low CPMs, and are flexible, in that ads generally require short lead times. Their major downside is that their life span is brief. People generally read the paper and throw it away on the same day (with the exception of large-circulation Sunday newspapers such as *The New York Times,* the *Boston Globe,* and the *San Francisco Examiner,* which people tend to keep and read throughout the week).

Specialty *magazines,* such as *Fly Rod and Reel,* have grown exponentially over the last decade. There are more than 10,000 in print on subjects ranging from needlepoint to paint ball. These magazines are good venues for many types of retail businesses, from sporting equipment and hobbies to fine jewelry. These publications tend to be highly focused, so there is little wasted circulation. The ads tend to have a long shelf life, as most readers save the magazines for reference. Each time readers consult the magazine or show it

to a friend, there is a high probability that they will see your ad again, increasing frequency of exposure. Specialty magazines tend to be far less expensive than their larger-circulation counterparts. However, there is usually a substantial time lag before getting your ad into print.

Buyer's guides and specialty publications, such as local promotional maps, tourist guides, and paper place mats, are also alternatives worth evaluating.

Direct mail. Direct mail (DM), also becoming known as *database marketing,* has been the fastest-growing component of the promotional mix over the past decade. A significant part of this growth can be traced to the fact that many small businesses now have access to DM services that were formerly the domain of larger companies. Even the smallest retailer can afford this form of promotion because the tools needed to use it are readily available, usually at modest cost. You can usually rent mailing lists for between $50 and $60 per thousand names, and there are fulfillment services that do everything from stuffing, labeling, and mailing to taking orders.

B> p. 292

The best place to start building a database, however, is with your own customers. Although this may sound quite obvious, in a comprehensive study of retailers conducted by Arthur Andersen & Co. and the Illinois Retail Association, reported in *Small Business Survival,* 53% of merchants in Illinois admitted that they either didn't maintain customer data or, if they did, they didn't use them!

Building a database is not a difficult task, but it takes persistence. You and your staff must gather data from your customers on a routine basis. This information should include not only name, address, zip code, and phone number, but also what types of merchandise they purchase, how much they spend, and how frequently they visit your store.

There are simple techniques for collecting the basic demographic data, such as asking customers to sign up for your mailing list so that you can apprise them of sales and special events. Once you have the basic information (name, address, and phone number), you can enter it into a database program available with most software suites, such as Microsoft Office or Lotus Smart Suite. Once your customer name is in the database, you can add sales and other information to develop a more sophisticated customer profile.

Direct mail is successful because it is the most selective advertising technique. With little wasted circulation, DM can be very cost-effective. For example, if you ran a business such as Great Bay Golf and Ski selling discounted equipment, clothing, and supplies, you could rent mailing lists from any number of specialty magazines serving readers with these interests, such as *Senior Golfer* or *Ski*. Because your store is located on the border between Massachusetts and New Hampshire, you would probably only want to rent names with selected zip codes, then send these potential customers a brochure promoting your highly discounted products.

Many retailers argue that the most cost-effective method of communicating and maintaining a good rapport with customers is via *newsletters*. They are relatively inexpensive and are excellent vehicles to keep your customers up-to-date on what's going on in your store, including new products, sales, and new staff. The same software package that you're using to build a database will most likely have a program that creates a newsletter right on your desktop, with little skill other than typing required on your part.

Catalogs can also be an effective means of promoting your products. Although your own catalog can be an expensive proposition, multivendor and single-supplier catalogs are less expensive options that may be worth evaluating as you develop and expand your promotional strategy.

The downside of direct mail is that there is so much of it that it is hard to get your prospects to open your envelope rather than simply tossing it away. Don't despair! Start small and keep it personal. Hand-stamped mail, test lists, and follow-up are just a few of the techniques that can have a dramatic effect on your response rates.

There are also companies, such as Val-Pak and Super-Coups, that mail packets of coupons from several different businesses to all residents within specific zip codes. These types of services may be

a cost-effective DM alternative. If direct mail looks like a good option for you, because your target audience is clearly identifiable and reachable, there are several good publications, and professional help is available.

Broadcasting. In terms of dollars spent on advertising, *radio* weighs in at around 13%, which places it third in terms of total advertising dollars spent. Radio has a low CPM, is flexible, and can target customer groups. Its disadvantage is that it leaves only an audio impression, and multiple exposures are needed for a radio spot to be effective. In addition, audiences vary a great deal, depending on the time of day your advertisement is aired. "Trip" or "drive" times are expensive. Packaged plans are often a good idea because they provide a variety of exposures.

Cable TV (CATV) is becoming a popular medium for small-business advertising. Unlike its network cousins, cable's local programming enables you to target specific markets, using color and sound, at costs that will fit most promotional budgets. As CATV expands to systems with hundreds of channels, many programs become akin to specialty magazines. You can promote your products, as in the case of Newell's Custom Rod and Fly Shop, on highly targeted fishing programs to which large numbers of potential mail-order customers are tuned in. In addition, local programming can be a very effective way for almost any retailer to get a message out to customers within its trading area.

Outdoor billboards, signage, and banners.
These can be important parts of a promotional mix. If you depend on customers coming to your place of business (such as a tire warehouse), a billboard message not only alerts them to your existence, product lines, and directions to where you are located, but also stimulates demand by reminding drivers, your potential customers, while they are actually in their vehicles. For those who often travel the same roads, billboards and signs generate frequency of exposure, which can boost patronage.

Signage is important for businesses that depend on customer traffic. The sign makes a statement about your business and is often your customer's first exposure to your store. Banners are effective in drawing attention to your place of business and promoting sales. They are a must for trade shows or other types of special events. A stationery store, for example, would need banners and other booth signage if it exhibited wedding invitations at a bridal show. Local and/or state regulations often limit the use of billboards and signs, so be sure to check with the appropriate authorities. If you locate your shop in a mall, the leasing agent will inform you of any restrictions that apply.

Electronic commerce. Selling products over the Internet, and particularly the World Wide Web, is becoming a cost-effective way to reach a large number of potential customers. Businesses ranging from apple orchards to zipper supply houses are using this medium very successfully. The Internet has given small retailers the ability to advertise and sell to thousands of people worldwide every day, at low cost, and with little maintenance. A good example is Crafts Etc. Ltd., an Oklahoma City company that advertises more than 9,000 products in dozens of categories, which can be ordered over the Internet for next-day delivery.

R▶ p. 243   B▶ p. 292, 294

If you intend to promote your business on the Internet, there are many things you should be aware of, including these three "rules of thumb" on the Net.

❏ *Only put useful content on your Web site.* Since you are asking your customers to pay for the information they are receiving from you (in terms of download time), they will not be happy if they must spend a great deal of time on the computer to get a cursory overview of your business.

❏ *Limit the graphics used in your home page.* While they look great, graphics can take a long time to download, causing frustration for your customers. Images of products you sell are more useful than merely decorative graphics.

❏ *Include valuable links to other Web sites.* A link (often called a "hyperlink") can direct the customer to other places of interest with the click

of a mouse. If your hours vary from season to season, include a link to a listing of your hours. You can update your hours monthly, so that your customers will know when you are open. Another link might connect them to your sales department for up-to-the-minute price quotes, or another can offer a calendar that shows upcoming events.

It is important to keep online time to a minimum, providing the maximum amount of information. Net customers can be very loyal if you provide them with useful, desirable products for a small investment of time and effort.

Sales Promotion

Sales promotion refers to "demand-stimulating" activities such as displaying at trade shows and giving away coupons or premiums that motivate potential customers to visit your store or Web site, take a catalog, or get on your mailing list. Sales promotion activities should be developed to augment your advertising strategy.

Trade shows and expositions. Virtually every industry sponsors events, most often at multiple locations around the country. If you sell high-fashion stage apparel, you might attend music conventions, clothing trade shows, or beauty pageants, which would have costumers, accessory retailers, and cosmetics manufacturers displaying their wares. Trade shows and expos are a cost-effective way to reach highly targeted markets.

Premiums. You can have giveaways, such as pens, wallet-sized tipping charts, or key rings, imprinted with your company name to hand out or mail to customers and prospects. These low-cost items are effective because they repeatedly expose your company name, not only to your customer but, with certain items like a hat or bumper sticker, to other potential customers as well.

Coupons. Coupons offering price discounts, two-for-one bargains, or free introduction to your products can be a cost-effective way to attract sales. The same coupons can be used simultaneously in many places, such as direct mailings and newspaper ads.

Publicity. Publicity is generally free exposure that communicates valuable information about your company and your product. It can be effective because it is presented by a third party and is thus perceived as unbiased. Although you don't usually have to pay for it, you will have to spend some time and money generating it. For example, you will want to send press releases or other materials to local newspapers, most of which run regular articles on new businesses. It is interesting to note that only 56% of the retailers in the Illinois study had relationships with local news media. Don't let yourself fall into the other 44%. Here is an article that recently appeared in the Portsmouth (N.H.) *Herald,* which exemplifies what a little publicity can do for business.

Article from the Portsmouth (N.H.) *Herald,* April 29, 1997

Service Speaks Volumes:
Small-Town Feel Mixes with a Big Store's Diversity

By Richard Fabrizio, *Herald* Correspondent

There's nothing small about the plans of the Little Professor Book Center located at 103 Congress Street in Portsmouth.

Led by the Weisbrots, a husband-and-wife team, the Little Professor hopes to provide more than just books to the Portsmouth community.

"We want to progress to the point where we are giving back to the community," said Trish Weisbrot. "A lot of what we are doing is part and parcel of our overall concept, which is to create a feeling of family and fun for our customers. We want people to know this is a place where they can come and receive special, personal service. That's where we think we can have an edge over the large bookstore chains."

"We're here because it's fun for us," added Howie, her husband. "We have worked to create a place where people can come and have a good time along with us."

Previous residents of Vermont, Mrs. Weisbrot is a former teacher. Mr. Weisbrot was a longtime film producer. Together they said their arrival in Portsmouth was a matter of fate.

After retiring from their respective careers, both agreed that they wanted and needed to do something to keep themselves busy. According to Trish, it didn't take long to find a new purpose. Based on their mutual love of books, the pair began looking for the opportunity to purchase a bookstore. The Weisbrots contacted a realtor, who quickly found a Little Professor store for sale in Dover. After meeting with the owners of that store, they visited the Little Professor store in Portsmouth to gather more information about the franchise arrangements. Unexpectedly, the Weisbrots said they found themselves negotiating to purchase that store instead, which they officially took over in October, 1995.

"Given the set of coincidences, we thought this had to be it," said Trish. "In a matter of eight months of searching we found a great store and a great area. It was like it was predestined."

Mrs. Weisbrot said she and her husband are joined by a daughter, Lesley, and together the three have slowly shaped a new concept of the store. Lesley is deaf. As a result, the store offers a special section and service for hearing impaired customers. Additionally, the store holds a reading club, "Just for Kids Club" for first grade students. Demand for the club is so strong Trish said she is looking to expand it for the fall. She said the club is particularly rewarding to her because first grade is where reading starts. Also the Little Professor created "The Book Angel Tree" aimed at raising money and collecting donated books for the Rockingham Community Action's Gift Reading Program. Mrs. Weisbrot said Little Professor, along with the help of various community members, has contributed over 130 books since the campaign's inception.

Another way that the Weisbrots are positioning the store to serve its community is by promoting local authors, said Trish. Through a variety of book signings and poetry readings, Trish said she hopes the store can produce increased exposure for the many talented writers in the Seacoast area. This past Saturday, the store hosted a book-signing and reading by Charles Simic, a University of New Hampshire professor and poet.

Additionally, the Weisbrots host discussion groups on the third Wednesday of each month. The groups provide the opportunity to discuss a preselected book of the month in a relaxed environment. Recently reviewed books were Julia

(continued)

Service Speaks Volumes
(continued)
Alvarez's "In the Time of Butterflies," and "Hotel du Lac" authored by Anita Brookner.

The Weisbrots are actively working with the Heart of Portsmouth Merchants Association to promote businesses on upper Congress Street. Efforts include the raising of flags along the sidewalks and a summer concert series, said Trish. Along with Brewer, Cook, and Baker and Franklin Block Opticians, the Little Professor will again host an outdoor musical series this summer each Wednesday at noon.

Despite all the promotional activities the heart of the business remains its library of books, said the Weisbrots. Although the relative size of the store limits the depth of its inventory, Trish said she believes the Little Professor offers a wider selection. Knowledge of not only the materials in the store but of the many others in print affords another drawing point, said Trish.

"Because of the way we have developed the store it has a more homey feel," she said. "We know people by their first names and can and do get them materials more quickly. We offer the more unusual books and if it is in print, we can get it."

"We bend over backwards to please our customers. It's all part of our ambiance."

The Little Professor Book Center is open Monday to Saturday, 9:30 a.m. to 6:00 p.m., and from noon to 4:00 p.m. Sunday.

How many ads would you have to have placed to get this kind of impact? Remember: This article was free!

Public Relations

This outreach effort is designed primarily to influence the opinion of noncustomer groups. Public relations can have a significant impact on your business. For example, if you are opening a gift shop specializing in environmentally friendly products, it pays to invest time supporting politically active environmental groups, sympathetic legislators, and industry innovators to help ensure that issues related to the environment remain high on the public agenda.

Customer Service

According to Timothy Hatten in *Small Business: Entrepreneurship and Beyond,* "Satisfying the customer is not a means to achieve a goal, it *is* the goal." A strong commitment to customer service should be made evident in every business plan. A good customer-service program can be a key selling point for any business and serve as a major factor in justifying repeat sales projections.

Customer service includes everything the customer sees, hears, and feels from the moment he or she walks into the store (or calls on the telephone), and long after leaving it. The store's cleanliness and decor, the appearance, friendliness, and knowledge of the salespeople, security in the parking lot, and post-sale service add up to the customer's image of your business.

With huge retailers like Wal-Mart and Kmart providing high-customer-contact policies to satisfy the purchaser's needs for service, the small business retailer must employ the same tactics to compete. Services such as personal notes to customers when special inventory arrives, individual in-store attention, accurate billing, good return policies—even simple telephone etiquette—will stimulate favorable word-of-mouth and help your business compete with the giants. Customers will often pay more for your products and offer you repeat business if they receive good service.

Personal Selling

Face-to-face customer contact is the most powerful form of promotion because it is flexible and enables you to match the customer's needs to specific attributes of your products. Whether your customer is most interested in the on-time reliability of delivery from your office-supply company or needs some encouragement as to how a new Easter bonnet looks, you can focus your sales pitch on that feature, offering to refer him or her to other customers for references on the dependability of your delivery service or helping to find the hat that is most becoming.

Although some people have natural selling skills, most sales staff need some training, and it is well worth the effort. On a recent golfing excursion, three friends had the opportunity to observe how lack of attention to selling and customer service directly impacts revenue. They went to a large golf retailer that is part of a well-known national chain. Each of them was in the market to purchase items ranging from clubs and a new golf bag to balls and a glove. In fact, the trio had been at the same store a year earlier and are still paying off their charge cards to prove it. This year, however, the salespeople wouldn't give them the time of day, and their attitude bordered on rudeness when the golfers asked questions. The golfers ended up buying very little, and the store will surely be scratched from next year's shopping spree.

Be sure that your employees are familiar with your merchandise and understand that their only mission is to help customers satisfy their needs. Achieving this awareness is not free, however. The cost includes the time you, the owner, spend on training, which may include seminars, self-paced instructional materials, and monitoring. In addition, good salespeople will probably be more expensive to hire and retain. If your business requires salespeople, consider providing them with results-based compensation, in the form of commissions or a share of the equity, to offset costs.

OTHER CONSIDERATIONS

Evaluation
One of the most difficult aspects of designing an overall promotional strategy is determining how to measure its effectiveness, particularly if you have more than one activity going on simultaneously, such as a radio promotion and a newspaper ad. In the *Small Business Survival* study, 50% of retailers said they "just know" how effective their ads are. This led them to contemplate the well-known line from John Wanamaker: "I know only half of my advertising is working. The problem is, I don't know which half."

There are several methods you can use to determine how each medium is drawing and, therefore, which is most cost-effective. Your print advertising, for example, can include a special offer that must be presented or mentioned when someone calls or comes in for service. If you are

using several different print outlets, you can add a different fictitious department or box number to your address in each ad to see where the responses are coming from.

On radio, a very good strategy is asking listeners to "mention this ad," which normally generates results. In addition, as part of every customer contact, whether by phone or in person, you should gather data on how the customer found out about your store.

Even if you use all these techniques and more, you won't get perfect data. Some customers won't remember, some will inadvertently give the wrong information, or you may forget to collect the data. The point here is to collect as much as you can, usually at the cash register and, on a regular basis, add it to your ever-growing database. At a minimum, this will reduce your uncertainty about how you are spending your advertising dollars.

Packaging
Your packaging can serve as a great form of advertising, and it doesn't need to be too expensive. Consider the Murphy Goode winery in California's Alexander Valley. At its retail shop, it packs all its merchandise in glossy white bags with a self-adhesive Murphy Goode label. It can use the label for a wide variety of package sizes, thus reducing costs while still providing a useful and distinctive bag for customers to carry throughout their wine country visit.

Guerrilla Marketing
Unconventional methods can be used, usually at low cost, to reach potential customers. Unusual, eye-catching techniques, such as having people dressed as TV or cartoon characters hand out fliers or samples on a beach or having them parachute into a high-school football championship half-time celebration, are examples of guerrilla marketing. Guerrilla marketing has proved to be very successful, and is a strategy that should be seriously considered as you develop your plan of attack.

Budgeting

How much money to spend on promotional activity poses a constant problem. Although there are no hard and fast rules, some guidelines suggest that up to 10% of net sales should be earmarked for promotion during the first year. Comparisons can also be found in *Financial Studies of the Small Business* and in the Appendix to determine what other, similar retailers are spending as a percentage of sales.

R▶ p. 240

Remember that these figures will reflect average expenditures, and that your expenses in the first year will probably be significantly higher. You must promote your store, and although promotion is expensive, it is as important as (if not more than) all other expenses. Don't look at it as money that you can afford to spend only after all other bills, including your salary, have been paid. If you do that, eventually all you will have are bills to pay.

Evaluate your promotional options relative to your competition and your customer base. Let the budget follow the plan. Use financial and trade association data to compare your proposed expenditures with other businesses in your industry, remembering that start-up and location factors will have a substantial effect on the numbers. Consult a local ad agency, a Small Business Development Center counselor, and other marketing professionals for their advice.

Cooperative Advertising

One way to reduce advertising expenses is cost-sharing arrangements. These are very common and fall into two basic categories. First, *vertical co-op advertising* links you with your suppliers, who agree to share advertising costs up to a certain dollar amount (anywhere from 50% to 100%) if you feature their products in your ads. For example, a regional soda distributor may cosponsor festival events (such as "Old Home Days" or holiday parades) with a local retailer of the soda, giving the retailer more exposure than he would otherwise have been able to afford. Another example: Your brand-name supplier of plumbing fixtures pays for your shop's newspaper ads featuring its new faucet.

Second, *horizontal co-op advertising* allows you to advertise jointly with noncompetitive businesses. For example, if you sell furniture, you might find an art store or a bed-and-bath shop with which you could pool resources to purchase larger and/or more frequent ads. In a mall, all of the businesses may pool their resources to place an ad in the local newspaper that mentions the individual stores. Even if the ad attracts customers to a particular store, chances are they will stop at several other stores and make purchases at more than one. Cooperative advertising is an excellent and, in most cases, a necessary technique to leverage advertising dollars.

PITFALLS

Common mistakes that new businesses make in developing and executing a promotional strategy include:

Underestimating Costs

Do not assume that you can leave promotional strategy at the bottom of your list in business planning. Make sure you have provided for an adequate budget allocation at the level required to sustain your sales projections.

Differentiation

Use promotion to adequately differentiate your store from your competitors. Be careful not to stimulate a general need for the type of products you sell with no compelling reason to purchase them from you, thereby creating a potential sale for your competitor.

Lack of Research

"Gut feel" is an unreliable guide for deciding how to promote your products. Spend adequate time conducting an analysis to find out which promotional techniques most effectively meet your goals, quantifying results as much as possible.

EXCERPT

Simple Elegance Bridal Boutique

PROMOTIONAL ACTIVITIES

After a few weeks of business operations, a grand opening is planned. There will be a daily drawing for door prizes and a grand prize drawing for a wedding outfit or a honeymoon trip. Promotional flyers offering a first-purchase discount will be distributed at this time.

An advertising budget of $2,200 has been allocated for our grand opening. Of these dollars, 40% will be used in newspaper advertising, 20% for flyers and promotional material, and 40% for direct mail advertising. We plan to arrange advertising cooperatives with clothing manufacturers and local travel bureaus. In addition, we anticipate contacting manufacturers' sales reps, as they will on occasion contribute promotional items to be used for grand openings.

We plan to market our location by holding bridal shows at area malls and country clubs. Flyers will be distributed to the Junior and Senior classes at area high schools, announcing the arrival of our new prom and winter formals. In addition we will also offer a student discount on gown purchases and tuxedo rentals.

Private showings will be held at the shop promoting our newest bridal, prom, and winter formals. Radio, newspapers, special bridal guides, and bridal magazines are some of the media in which we have planned to advertise.

Source: Simple Elegance Bridal Boutique

SOME ADVICE

"In order to provide high-quality customer service, you must be experienced in all phases of your business. We have spent considerable time on the phone with our customers doing informal surveys about their experiences with our products, staff, and company. Find out what the customers want, what they like, and what they don't. In mail order, telephone etiquette and feedback are key."

Richard Rosen
By Nature
Miami, Fla.

FORMS OF OWNERSHIP

OVERVIEW

Analysis of your business's legal form of ownership should be undertaken from a broad perspective. The first question to ask is not "How do I incorporate?" but rather, "What are my organizational options, and which one of them best meets my needs?"

To determine the most appropriate legal structure for your business, consider issues such as capital requirements, business succession, legal liability, taxation, decision-making authority, and control. Many of these issues will be addressed in various sections of your business plan, and therefore no decisions should be made on ownership status until the appropriate sections of the plan have been completed.

Once you have gathered the relevant information, an attorney and an accountant should be consulted for advice on your options in light of your particular situation. When selecting an attorney, choose one with experience in new ventures. Don't assume that your brother-in-law, the divorce lawyer, is the fellow to call. He is probably not the right choice, nor are other lawyers whose practices are not business-oriented.

If you do not know a lawyer who fits your needs, ask a successful small-business owner, banker, or accountant for a referral. Each state also supports a Lawyer Referral Service, which can provide you with the name and location of a lawyer in the specialty you seek. In return for a listing with the service, many of these lawyers provide a reduced rate to the client, or a free initial meeting. Contact your state bar association for the telephone number of your state's referral service. In addition, if you are considering a franchise operation, select an attorney who has extensive experience with this highly specialized form of business.

Your legal form of ownership does not have to be presented in a separate section in your business plan. The form you selected and your rationale for it should be included in the Introduction or Management section.

IS▶ p. 210   B▶ p. 293, 294

THE BASICS

Following are descriptions of the three fundamental forms of ownership and their relative advantages and disadvantages.

Sole Proprietorships

A sole proprietorship is a business that is owned and operated by one person. No legal distinction exists between you as an individual and your business entity. Many proprietorships function on a DBA (doing business as) basis, such as a local lobster pound owned by Mike Trafton, DBA The Lobster Pot. DBA status enables your business to use any name you like, as long as it has been properly registered and does not infringe on someone else's trademark or trade name. The DBA allows you to create a separate "image" for your business that is appropriate to the products you will sell, but which is not associated with your personal name.

Proprietorships can have employees and, in fact, some are quite large. Over 75% of all businesses operate as sole proprietorships, according to the U.S. Small Business Administration.

Advantages of Proprietorships

❏ **Costs.** Start-up costs tend to be low. Once you've registered your name and secured any necessary licenses and permits, you'll be able to solicit your first customers.

❏ **Control.** As a proprietor, you have complete control over all business decisions. You are free to hire and fire within the labor laws, and decisions can be made quickly.

❏ **Profits.** The owner keeps all profits net of applicable federal, state, and local taxes.

❏ **Flexibility.** You can decide to close your business as easily as you started it. There are no forms or costs other than to pay off your suppliers and any debt you may have incurred.

Disadvantages of Proprietorships

❏ **Unlimited liability.** As a sole proprietor, you make all of your assets available to satisfy a creditor or a plaintiff in a legal action.

❏ **Less available capital.** All financing is based on your personal financial statement, business record, and character. You do not have the ability to raise equity.

❏ **Limited scope of management.** As your business grows, it will probably need a professional management and sales staff. It may be difficult to hire and retain this staff as a sole proprietor, if you are unable to offer equity in lieu of salary.

❏ **Business life.** If you become disabled, retire, or die, usually the business will cease to exist unless it is inherited by someone who is ready and able to continue it. This disadvantage has many implications, not the least of which is its effect on your customers. The more they depend on your products, the less comfortable they may become with your status as sole proprietor.

Partnerships

A partnership is a form of organization in which two or more individuals conduct business as co-owners. Partnerships can have any number of partners; however, while service businesses can include hundreds or even thousands of partners, most retail businesses have only two or three. As with a proprietorship, a partnership does not exist as a legal entity separate from its owners. There are two types: *general partnerships,* by far the most common form of partnership, and *limited partnerships.* Partnerships can be formed by a simple handshake. However, a detailed partnership agreement, signed by all partners, is highly

recommended. A sample partnership agreement can be found in Appendix B on page 281.

Advantages of a General Partnership

❏ **Capital availability.** Partners contribute capital to the business, providing for a potentially larger resource base than proprietorship offers. As the business grows and more partners are added, your capital base will expand.

❏ **Continuity.** If one of the partners becomes disabled, retires, or dies, the business can continue, although a new partnership must be created.

❏ **Taxation.** Partners can agree to divide profits any way they see fit, typically based on pro rata share of ownership. However, if there is no agreement, they share profits equally. Each partner pays income tax on his or her share of the profits at the individual's tax rate.

❏ **Growth potential.** The ability to add new partners to the business provides the opportunity to recruit new expertise and build management infrastructure.

Disadvantages of a General Partnership

❏ **Liability.** Generally each partner is responsible for the business debts of the partnership. There is unlimited joint liability, which may mean that if one partner has more substantial personal assets than the others do, he or she could end up paying more to satisfy a debt or claim, even though the partnership shares were equal. This would occur, however, only after each partner's assets have been depleted.

❏ **Divided authority.** In a partnership, by definition, you have less authority and control than in a proprietorship. As your business grows and partners are added, your authority and control may continue to be diluted.

❏ **Capital.** Although capital becomes available as partners are added, you still do not have the ability to sell shares of your business to investors.

Limited Partnership

Designed to attract investors, this type of partnership includes at least one general partner and a number of limited partners. The limited partners are passive investors. They have no say in management issues and no role in running the business. Their legal liability is limited to the amount they have invested in their partnership share. The laws regulating limited partnerships, including the number of limited partners you can have, vary from state to state, so you must check with your state attorney general's or secretary of state's office for the rules and regulations. Limited partners also get tax advantages, so consult both your attorney and your accountant.

Corporations

The corporation is a state-chartered organization owned by shareholders. Shareholders elect a board of directors who are ultimately responsible for the management of the business. The corporation is a separate legal entity and, as such, it can make products and provide services to customers, own and sell property, sue, and be sued. The corporate form of ownership was developed to reduce the number of problems and disadvantages associated with partnerships and proprietorships.

To create a corporation, you must file a Certificate of Incorporation or Corporate Charter with the secretary of state's office. You can obtain information, including forms that may be required, by contacting that office in your state.

There are two forms of for-profit corporation: the *C corporation* and the *S corporation* (so-called because it is defined under subchapter S of the Internal Revenue Code). Although for most start-ups the S corporation (also known as the "Sub S") is the most appropriate, this is an area where professional advice from your lawyer and accountant is imperative. An example of a corporate charter can be found in Appendix A on page 278.

Advantages of the C Corporation

❑ **Limited liability.** Stockholders' liability is limited to the amount they have invested in the company. If the company fails, creditors cannot attach the personal assets of stockholders. There are exceptions to this rule in certain areas of taxation and fraud. If any corporation fails to pay withholding taxes or is involved in some type of fraudulent activity, the "corporate veil" can be pierced, and individual stockholders may be held liable. Although this situation doesn't occur frequently, it is something you should be aware of, particularly in the S corporation.

❑ **Access to capital.** The corporation can raise money directly through the sale of stock (equity) and bond (debt) offerings. The corporation can also borrow from commercial sources, using corporate assets to secure the loan. However, with a small corporation, most commercial lenders will require the major stockholder(s) to guarantee the loan personally.

❑ **Perpetual life.** Because the corporation is a separate legal entity, its existence will not be affected by the retirement, injury, or death of any stockholder. That is not to say that when the president of a closely held company dies suddenly, the business won't have some problems. One of the problems it won't have, however, is losing its legal identity and standing.

❑ **Transfer of ownership.** The transfer of ownership in the corporation is simple. The number of shares owned determines the percentage of ownership. These shares can be traded or sold, assuming there is a market for them, with little effort.

❑ **Ability to attract management.** Often business growth is stymied in a proprietorship or partnership by the inability to attract specialized management expertise and build general management infrastructure, because these organizations cannot pay market-level salaries or add additional partners. The corporation has the ability to use stock options as a powerful incentive to attract such managerial talent.

Disadvantages of the C Corporation

❑ **Taxation.** Corporate income taxes are paid prior to the distribution of any dividends to stockholders. Once these dividends have been received, they are again taxed as part of the individual stockholder's income. In other words, the profits have been taxed twice.

❏ **Government regulation and paperwork.**
Certain government reports, forms, and other paperwork must be filed and/or monitored regularly. This places a particular burden on small enterprises and can create a considerable hidden cost of doing business.

❏ **Costs.** Paperwork and other initial costs, including legal and filing fees, can be significant. They can amount to thousands of dollars, depending on the complexity of the incorporation and the amount of work you are willing to do yourself.

The S Corporation

Created in 1958, this has become a very popular form of ownership for small business. The Sub S retains most of the advantages of incorporation, including limited liability, but eliminates the disadvantage of double taxation. All profits, as in the partnership, are distributed on a pro rata basis to the stockholders and are then taxed at each individual's income tax rates.

Disadvantages of the S corporation include taxes on many fringe benefits; limits on retirement benefits, which are treated more favorably in the C corporation; and limitations on the number of stockholders. In addition, the tax benefits of the Sub S will change, for better or worse, with changes in corporate and individual tax rates. Some states do not recognize the S corporation for state tax purposes. All of these issues should be discussed with your lawyer and accountant.

To qualify as an S corporation, your business must meet these legal requirements:

❏ It must be an independently owned and managed domestic corporation.
❏ It may have no more than 35 stockholders.
❏ It must have only one class of stock.
❏ It may have no stockholders who are nonresident aliens.
❏ It cannot be a financial institution that takes deposits and makes loans.

❏ It cannot be in the insurance business, taxed under Sub-Chapter L of the IRS Code.
❏ It cannot have received tax credits for doing business in the United States.

Limited Liability Company

The limited liability company (LLC) is a state-chartered organization that may offer the best of both worlds in terms of structure for small businesses. An LLC allows for the reduced personal liability of a corporation, but with the tax advantages of a partnership, although not all LLCs qualify for partnership federal income-tax treatment. Its partnership approach enables the company to act as a reporting agent and not as a taxable organization, therefore eliminating the "double taxation" of a C corporation (where corporate profits are taxed, and then taxed again as income to the owners/shareholders when the dividends are distributed), yet allows for an unlimited number of partners. There are also no restrictions on member nationality (as there are with an S corporation).

Conversely, the corporate aspect of the LLC lies in its ability to eliminate personal liability for the firm's debts and enjoy perpetual life. As with most small businesses, however, no matter what form of organization you use, bankers are typically not risk takers and may still require the major partners of a new business to personally guarantee any loans made to their concern. Finally, unlike a Sub S, an LLC can issue several different types of stock (thus allowing for unequal shares of company assets). This gives the company greater access to capital.

First established in Wyoming in 1977, the LLC form of organization took the country by storm. By early 1997, approximately 48 states had their own versions of Limited Liability Company laws and/or Limited Liability Partnership laws. The American Bar Association has reviewed a document written by the National Conference of Commissioners on Uniform State Laws (NCCUSL), proposing a Uniform Limited Liability Company Act.

However, nationwide acceptance of this legislation is still several years away. Since each state differs somewhat in the regulations used to govern an LLC, resolution of a taxation or liability claim could be difficult and costly if a dispute should arise between businesses in different states. Likewise, the tax and liability benefits associated with an LLC will vary from state to state. Again, it is imperative that you contact a qualified attorney if you are considering this form of organization.

PITFALLS

Lack of Adequate Analysis

The form of ownership you select is a critical decision. Take time to consider your alternatives carefully, to make sure that your decision will provide the best combination of flexibility, protection, and income at your business's current stage of development.

Lack of Professional Advice

The tax and liability consequences of your choice of ownership structure are potentially enormous. Many of the issues you have to evaluate to make your decision require the advice of a lawyer and an accountant. Although there are costs associated with their services, in many cases they will provide these services on a fixed-fee basis. Good preparation prior to meeting with your advisers can reduce your costs significantly, in terms of both time and money.

Failure to Review Legal Structure

As your business grows, you should evaluate your form of ownership on a periodic basis. You may find that the business you started five years ago as a partnership, which made sense at the time, would now be better off as a limited liability company.

SOME ADVICE

"The limited liability company and the limited liability partnership are fast becoming entities of choice for closely held retail businesses. Each combines the key advantages of a corporation with those of a partnership. Members of LLCs, like shareholders in traditional corporations, enjoy limited personal liability but gain the greater flexibility of a partnership in areas such as management and income distribution."

Joel I. Cherwin, Senior Partner
Cherwin, Glickman, & Theise, LLP
Boston, Mass.

COMPARING ORGANIZATIONAL STRUCTURES

Attribute	S Corp	C Corp	Partnership	Proprietorship	LLC
Liability protection	Yes	Yes	No	No	Yes
Member restrictions	Yes	No	No	Yes	No
Double taxation	No	Yes	No	No	No
Transfer of shares	Yes	Yes	No	No	No
High cost of start-up	Yes	Yes	No	No	Yes/No*
Easy access to capital	Yes	Yes	Yes/No	No	Yes

* Can be high, particularly in states that have only recently adopted LLC regulations.

Sources: Business Week *and* Inc. *magazine*

MANAGEMENT AND PERSONNEL

OVERVIEW

How will you staff and manage your business? These are critical issues that require planning and creative thinking. Usually, in a start-up situation, you have limited resources available. Therefore you have to be as creative as possible to attract the qualified personnel you need, at the salaries you can afford to pay.

From a management viewpoint, how you organize your business will also be important to your business success and the job satisfaction of your employees. Carefully think through your own contribution to the business, in the short run and longer term, as well as the role that you may want external consultants and others to play.

The Management and Personnel section of your business plan must make those evaluating your plan confident that you have the ability to hire and manage the team needed to make your business a success. The section can be short and concise.

The reader should already be well aware of what your business is trying to accomplish. The purpose here is to show how you expect to garner the human resources to do it. You must demonstrate that you will build a team, leveraging all of the appropriate resources available to you, and that you have thought out your staffing needs in detail. Additional information, such as complete résumés of your managers and job descriptions for key personnel, should be presented in your appendices.

IS> p. 211   R> p. 262, 271
B> p. 293

THE BASICS

Although initially you may be relying on some people for pro bono assistance or on others, including yourself, for "sweat equity," you should fully evaluate the staffing needs of your business, as well as the management configuration you will use. The following areas relating to management and personnel should be covered in your plan.

Management

Short one-paragraph profiles, or biographies, should be included for yourself, partners, and any others who will have management responsibility. The profiles should highlight experiences that are directly related to the work at hand.

For example, if you were planning to open a furniture store that is part of a national chain, you would want to include your work experience in other furniture stores, as well as your completion of a franchise training program. You might also list any seminars or conferences you have attended on topics such as interior design, period architecture, business management, or marketing. If none of your full-time management team has direct experience, be sure that other individuals closely associated with your business, such as consultants or advisers, do. Include a full résumé for each of these individuals in the appendices.

Key Personnel

A short bio should also be included for any key members of your staff who are not in management positions. Let's say that your sister, who used to manage a La-Z-Boy shop in another state, plans to work as a part-time salesperson in your furniture store while she raises a family. Her considerable experience should be mentioned in a key-person profile, even though she will not take an active role in the management of your store.

Professional Advisers

Your business should have established a relationship with an attorney, accountant, and insurance adviser as you developed your plan. These individuals are key members of your team; their bios should also be included in this section.

Staff

Although you may have some ideas about particular individuals whom you may want to hire to work in your business, this section should include descriptions of the jobs that need to be performed, salary and benefit levels, and any special requirements or qualifications.

For example, if you were staffing your upscale California-style bar and grill, you would need several trained bartenders, waitstaff, and at least one accredited chef for your kitchen (or someone with a strong local following). These individuals would need to have a certain amount of training and experience, be willing to work specific hours at a certain salary and benefit level, and, for the bartenders and waitstaff, have excellent people skills. The descriptions in this section should resemble well-written want ads, and there should be one for each position.

Consultants

If you plan to use consultants, include their bios. Consultants bring expertise to the business that your management team (in many cases, a team of one) may not possess. Consultants' experience and credentials can make a difference to a potential banker or investor.

For example, if you are starting a paint and wallpaper store, you might find a retired painting contractor to advise you on product lines, customer-service programs (such as job-site delivery and volume discounts), contractor relations, and training programs. A well-known and respected member of the professional community can also help generate business through his/her extensive network of contacts. These contacts can be a key sales factor for your business plan. Any counselors, such as those associated with Small Business Development Centers, should also be mentioned in your plan.

Boards of Directors/Advisers

No matter how small your business, consider establishing a board of directors or advisers. This board can be instrumental in offering advice as you develop and grow your business. Except in the case of a corporation where the bylaws will

govern, the structure of your board can be informal and flexible. The board is a low- or no-cost resource that can add significantly to your overall management capabilities, assuming you have selected individuals with substantial backgrounds and experience. Bios of these individuals should also be included in the plan.

Organizational Chart

If your business employs several people, or has a variety of product offerings, include an organizational chart. The chart should show how you plan to organize your human resources to reach your goals. It should indicate areas of responsibility of individuals within the organization and who reports to whom. For example, in a bookstore, the chart would indicate who is responsible for various sections (reference, card and gift, children's books), who does the purchasing, who organizes book fairs and special events, and so on.

B▶ p. 293

Staffing Plan

Briefly describe your future professional and staff personnel needs, making sure that the description reflects the business growth projections that appear in other sections of your plan. If your employees will need any kind of training or certification, you will have to hire personnel with these qualifications or provide the necessary training. Hiring trained staff can be more costly, but training them yourself can cause delays in productivity and efficiency. It is a tradeoff that you must weigh carefully prior to hiring anyone.

Salary and Benefits

Explain your philosophy regarding the work environment and company culture you intend to create and how you plan to compensate and reward employees. Your long-term goal may be to provide a wide range of fringe benefits, including health insurance, retirement benefits, and incentive saving plans. In the short term, however, you may be able to offer only a few benefits like life insurance or paid vacation time, and build from there as your business grows.

Benefits can also include intangibles. It is sometimes not enough to pay your employees more than the competition does. It has been clearly documented that employee satisfaction in all aspects of the job has a direct effect on your business image. Constant and consistent evaluation, reward systems, employee involvement/ empowerment, and good leadership combine to create an enjoyable and successful work environment.

PITFALLS

Estimate of Personnel Needs

Overestimating your human resources needs will dramatically affect the bottom line—you'll have higher working-capital requirements. On the other hand, underestimating personnel needs will inhibit your ability to sell merchandise efficiently. Map out your staffing requirements as carefully as possible, and consult your advisers to test your assumptions.

Compensation Package

Your compensation package must be adequate to attract and retain employees. Your employees' satisfaction should come second only to that of your customers. In the long run, your ability to offer a comprehensive and competitive benefit plan will help attract high-quality workers and reduce turnover.

Chain of Command

Employees, particularly in closely held or family-run businesses, need a clear understanding of whom they report to and what they are responsible for. Often employees find themselves answering to more than one boss, which can be very frustrating and can lead to confusion and inefficiency.

Management

You want an adequate degree of supervision in your business, but not too much. Your employees should have a clear sense of their superior's duties and responsibilities. They should not feel that there are too many people watching the work being done and not enough doing it.

SOME ADVICE

"In a start-up business, performance-based incentives can be the key to attracting good entry-level personnel as well as experienced staff who are ready to make a career change. These incentives can include profit-sharing plans or substantial salary increases, but be prepared to pay up. Don't let promises made at your Grand Opening come back to haunt your bottom line."

Mike Choe
President
LA Shirts
Culver City, Calif.

EXCERPT

The Titusville Dairy Queen store will be owned by Dale and Caroline Santini. Dale Santini will supervise the operations of the business, and Caroline will perform accounting functions. They will have one operations manager and two shift managers who will supervise the staff.

Dale Santini is currently employed by Allstate Insurance Company as an agency manager. He has been employed in that capacity for six years, and before that he was an agent for three years. He is responsible for 24 agents and manages in excess of $24 million worth of premium. Dale Santini will not only serve as president of the corporation, he will also supervise the operations managers of the business. Dale will attend a comprehensive training school provided by International Dairy Queen. The school trains prospective owners and managers in all the facets of a Dairy Queen Brazier Store. Once it is opened, Interstate Dairy Queen will provide management people for 28 in-store days.

Caroline Santini is employed in the business office of the Titusville Area School District. Her responsibilities are in the tax and revenue areas, and she will serve as the secretary/treasurer of the Titusville store. Caroline Santini will be responsible for payroll, accounts receivable, accounts payable, and royalties. Both Caroline and Dale will maintain their current positions and therefore will not withdraw any money from the business during the first three years of operations.

There will be one operations manager and two shift managers who will supervise the staff during the assigned shift period. The operations manager will be responsible for the daily operations of the business and will receive an annual salary of $17,000. He will report directly to Mr. Santini for all equipment repairs that need to be made and any problems that may occur…

FINANCIAL INFORMATION

OVERVIEW

The Financial Information section of your business plan creates a picture of how you expect your business to perform in quantitative terms, based on market assessments that you make as you develop the plan. This picture will be drawn using financial statements, which are simply standard formats used to present financial information. Most of your statements will be developed on a pro forma basis, which means that you are projecting data, such as future revenues and expenses, using assumptions you have made and can defend.

Complete, accurate, and well-documented financial information is crucial for a number of reasons. For example, if you are using the plan to apply for commercial financing, loan officers usually focus their attention on the numbers. That is, after reading the Executive Summary and the Market overview, they proceed directly to your financial information. This is understandable because loan officers are experts at—and most comfortable with—dealing with financial information, as opposed to marketing data or promotional strategy.

Once they have a basic understanding of the type of business you plan to enter, they review your financial information and develop a preliminary assessment as to whether they would be willing to finance you. If the answer is yes, they go back and read through your entire business plan in detail.

Accurate financial information is also very important because it establishes the basic framework you will use to monitor and control your business and report information to the government (e.g., for tax purposes), bankers, investors, and other stakeholders.

Although it is wise not to become too dependent on electronic spreadsheets, when used properly they can make your job a lot easier. As you begin to gather and record information for your financial statements, you will want to be able to update them and sometimes change your assumptions. Spreadsheet software enables you to do this with little effort and the highest degree of mathematical accuracy. In addition, a manual "one-write" type of checking system, an electronic checkbook program, or a computerized accounting package are inexpensive and efficient ways to organize your records, both for generating financial statements and for tax purposes.

Finally, be sure to document all of the assumptions you use as a basis for your projections in this section of your plan. Don't simply present statements without explanation. There should be a bright line that links the data presented in the Market, Market Share, and Competitive Analysis sections of your plan to the projections you make in the Financial Information section. When in doubt as to whether you have made it clear enough, restate your assumptions as notes to your cash-flow or income statements and/or refer the reader to the appropriate section(s) of your plan for more detail. Of all possible flaws in the presentation of a business plan, lack of clear connection between assumptions and financial projections ranks among the most serious, yet it's one that can be easily fixed.

R▶ p. 273 **B▶ p. 292**

Note: If you intend to use your business plan to secure financing, most banks will require:

- ❑ three balance sheets (start date, end of Year 1, and end of Year 2),
- ❑ one cash-flow statement (monthly for the first year),
- ❑ two income statements (annually for Year 1 and Year 2).

THE BASICS

The financial and other related statements described in this chapter should be included in your business plan.

For purposes of illustration, we will use Susan's House of Style, an imaginary women's apparel store in Akron. The business is owned by Susan Rausch, a former buyer for Macy's and Nordstrom. Susan plans to offer upscale merchandise for the professional woman, at midlevel prices. She intends to carry a seasonal variety of dresses, skirt and blouse ensembles, women's suits, and accessories. Eventually, she would like to carry outerwear as well.

Susan has done a significant amount of research on the local Akron market and found that her store will fill a niche that is currently underserved. A location analysis revealed that the site best suited for her target customer is in the heart of the city, at the corner of 10th Street and Broadway. Unfortunately, Susan's House of Style will have to pay a high price for rent, but she expects to be able to recover the cost through heavy traffic flow.

Susan will employ two additional part-time clerks. Her store will be open from 10 a.m. to 6 p.m. Monday through Thursday, 10 a.m. to 7 p.m. on Friday, and 8 a.m. to 12 p.m. on Saturday. Like most downtown businesses, hers will be closed on Sundays. Through careful analysis, Susan estimates her total financing needs to be $58,700 (see "Start-Up Cost Estimate," page 73), 25% of which ($14,675) she will contribute herself as owner's equity.

Susan's House of Style is a start-up business; therefore all its statements will be developed on a pro forma basis, that is, in advance. If you are already in business, you will be generating the same types of statements, but most of the information/data will come from your actual business records. Even if you are working with a consultant while developing your business plan, it is very important for you to understand how your own projections are made and to agree with them. They will form the basis of your financing needs and your salary level, which may be with you long after your friendly adviser leaves to sow other seeds.

The best way to complete this section is to use the *Inc.Sheets* in Section IV for each of the following statements. Fill in the information as you locate or develop it. Many of the statements are interdependent, so you will probably be working on them concurrently.

Capital Assets List

This list should include a description and cost for each item of machinery, equipment, display furniture, and other physical assets you must purchase to start your business. An accountant would consider these items, along with other assets, as "tangible long-lived assets," meaning that they have physical properties and last longer than one year. The list should be detailed; however, you can combine similar articles of low unit value, such as glassware and place settings in a restaurant business or display fixtures in an apparel store. High-ticket items, such as computers or vehicles, should be footnoted to provide a quote from your supplier. The capital equipment list will be used to help determine the amount of fixed-asset financing you will require.

IS> p. 212

Susan's House of Style Inc.

CAPITAL ASSET LIST, JANUARY 1997

ITEM DESCRIPTION	QTY.	UNIT COST	COST	TOTAL
Equipment (Register & Computer)[1]				
Cash register	2	$1,300	$2,600	
Compaq computer 166MHz w/CD-ROM	1	1,800	1,800	
17" color monitor	1	600	600	
Color ink-jet printer	1	400	400	
MS Office 97 software	1	800	800	
Subtotal				$6,200
Equipment (Other)				
Safe	1	750	750	
AT&T telephone system[2]	2	600	1,200	
Tag machine	2	60	120	
Subtotal				2,070
Store Fixtures				
4' Rounders	6	200	1,200	
3' Four-ways	6	150	900	
6' Wall rack sections	10	150	1,500	
Accent track lighting (2 lights each)	10	75	750	
Chairs (dressing room area)	4	75	300	
Antique display table	1	1,500	1,500	
Floor-length triple mirror	2	250	500	
Fast-track shelving system (display area)	2	1,300	2,600	
Open shelving system (stock area)	4µ	200	800	
Steamer rack	1	600	600	
Subtotal				10,650
Furniture				
Office desk	1	350	350	
Desk chair	1	175	175	
File cabinet	2	200	400	
Subtotal				925
TOTAL				**$19,845**

[1]CompUSA, 1555 Mall Blvd., Akron
[2]Staples, 925 Mall Blvd., Akron

Start-Up Costs

This statement estimates the amount of money you will need to launch and maintain your business until sales receipts can cover operating expenses and debt service. In addition, you need to project all monthly expenses such as utilities and salaries; prepaid expenses such as insurance; and one-time expenses like your Grand Opening event. Once these have been calculated, you should "build in a cushion" to provide for some margin of error if sales do not materialize as quickly as you expect. Often this margin will be an amount equal to two or three times your monthly operating expenses, employees' salaries, and your salary (draw). This statement will also be used to estimate working capital needs.

On the basis of your projected sales levels, you can estimate how much starting inventory you will need by looking at industry inventory turnover figures and sales-to-inventory ratios in *Financial Studies of the Small Business*. For example, you find that in the apparel industry, the ratio of sales to inventory is 2.9 in your expected sales category ($10,000 to $250,000). This indicates that if you project sales of $43,500, you will need $15,000 in inventory.

Depending on the type of business you are planning, it may be necessary to provide more detail for your opening inventory entry. For some businesses, like a lawn-and-garden retailer that sells high-ticket machinery, a thorough listing of your inventory may be helpful. For others that may deal with scores of products in several categories, a lump figure will suffice. In our example of a women's apparel shop, you may opt to give a single figure for inventory in your start-up cost estimate and footnote it to an appendix, which details sources of supply and specific starting inventory.

IS> p. 213   R> p. 228

Susan's House of Style Inc.

START-UP COST ESTIMATE, JANUARY 1997

PRE-START-UP

ITEM	Estimate
Capital Assets	$19,845
Leasehold Improvements	3,500
Beginning Inventory (see note below)	5,000
Subtotal	**$38,345**

ADDITIONAL START-UP COSTS

Deposits with Public Utilities	$200
Legal and Other Professional Services	350
Licenses & Permits	225
Advertising & Promotion	2,000
Prepaid Insurance	300
Hangers, Tags, Size Rings	300
Other Expenses	200
Subtotal	**$3,575**

WORKING CAPITAL

ITEM	Est. Cost Per Month	# Months Coverage	Total Estimated Cost
Salary of Owner	$1,500	2	$3,000
Other Salaries/Wages/Fees	1,500	2	3,000
Payroll Taxes	630	2	1,260
Rent	900	3	2,700
Advertising	650	2	1,300
Supplies	95	3	190
Telephone	125	3	375
Other Utilities	325	3	975
Insurance	510	3	1,530
Debt Service	450	3	1,350
Maintenance	150	2	300
Legal and Other Professional Fees	300	2	600
Miscellaneous	100	2	200
Subtotal			**$16,780**

TOTAL FROM PRE-START-UP	$38,345
TOTAL ADDITIONAL START-UP COSTS & WORKING CAPITAL	$20,355
TOTAL ESTIMATED START-UP	**$58,700**

Sources and Uses of Cash Statement

This statement indicates how you plan to secure funds to start your business and how you intend to spend them. Both your sources and uses should be categorized. For example, if you plan to borrow money to purchase a building, a truck, and equipment, these loans should be listed as separate items because the interest rates and repayment terms will be different for each. For the purposes of this analysis, 25% owner equity/investment is assumed. Your sources of cash must always equal your uses. If they don't, you probably haven't calculated your equity properly.

IS> p. 214   B> p. 292

Susan's House of Style Inc.

SOURCES AND USES OF CASH, JANUARY 1997

SOURCES

Owner's investment	$14,675
Loans	
Working capital (a)	16,780
Capital equipment (b)	
Computer & register equipment (b)	
Leasehold improvement (b)	
Opening inventory (b)	27,245
Total Sources	**$58,700**

USES

Working capital (c)	$16,780
Additional start-up costs (d)	3,575
Purchase register & computer equipment (e)	6,200
Purchase capital assets (f)	13,645
Leasehold improvements (g)	3,500
Opening inventory (h)	15,000
TOTAL USES	**$58,700**

Notes:

(a) Working capital loan to be repaid in 12 months, per loan agreement in Appendix F
(b) Combined commercial loan through All-City Bank, per loan agreement in Appendix F
(c) See "Working Capital" from Start-Up Cost Estimate
(d) See "Additional Start-Up Costs" from Start-Up Cost Estimate
(e) See "Equipment (Register & Computer)" on Capital Asset List
(f) See "Equipment (Other), Store Fixtures, and Furniture" on Capital Asset List
(g) See "Leasehold Improvements" on Start-up Cost Estimate
(h) See "Beginning Inventory" on Start-Up Cost Estimate

Balance Sheet

The balance sheet answers the question, "What is the financial condition of your company on a particular date?" It lists what your company owns (its assets) and what it owes (its debts). The balance sheet also reflects net worth, or total owner's equity, which is the amount left over after the total debts are subtracted from the total assets.

The formula for the balance sheet is:

Assets = Liabilities + Equity

Assets are what your business owns (cash, supplies, accounts receivable, equipment, land, buildings). These are the investments your business has made to generate revenue. *Liabilities* are debts your business owes (accounts payable, loans, mortgages, installment debt, and so on). *Equity* represents the claims against business assets by the owner(s) of that business. This amount includes the owners' investments plus any profits that have been retained by the business (in the case of a corporation these are called "retained earnings"). If your business is incorporated, the *owner's equity* is referred to as *stockholders' equity*.

IS> p. 215   R> p. 247

If you are in a start-up phase, your balance sheet will be constructed on a pro forma basis, meaning that you have to project what your assets and liabilities will look like on the day you start your business. These figures can be derived from your Sources and Uses of Cash statement. For example, if you are transferring ownership of a car to the business, it should be listed as an asset on your company's balance sheet. If your business is already in operation, gather the actual amounts for each category as of the day you plan to generate the statement.

Susan's House of Style Inc.

BALANCE SHEET, SEPTEMBER 1, 1997

ASSETS		LIABILITIES	
Current Assets		**Current Liabilities**	
Cash (on hand and in banks)	$ 20,355	Accounts payable	$ 0
Accounts receivable	0	Current portion of long-term debt	11,000
Notes receivable	0	Notes payable	0
Inventory	15,000	Taxes payable	0
Other current assets	0	Accrued payroll	0
		Other liabilities	0
Total Current Assets	**$ 35,355**	**Total Current Liabilities**	**$ 11,000**
Fixed Assets		**Long-Term Liabilities**	
Leasehold improvements	$ 3,500	Notes payable (bank)	$ 44,025
Equipment	8,270	Less current portion	(11,000)
Furniture/fixtures	11,575		
Less accumulated depreciation	(0)	**Total Long-Term Liabilities**	**$ 33,025**
Total Fixed Assets	**$ 23,345**	**Stockholders' Equity**	
		Capital stock	$ 14,675
Total Assets	**$ 58,700**	Current earnings	0
		Total Equity	**$ 14,675**
		Total Liabilities & Equity	**$ 58,700**

Income Statement

The income statement, also known as the profit and loss statement or simply the P&L, is the record of your business's financial activities over a period of time. The income statement, usually prepared on an annual basis, documents your revenue and expenses and establishes whether a gain or loss has occurred during that period.

As with the balance sheet, a start-up business must project or estimate the numbers to be used on the pro forma income statement. All these figures, with the exception of depreciation, can be obtained from your cash-flow projections, which will be covered in the next section of this chapter.

The amount of depreciation (i.e., the part of an asset's dollar value written off as an expense over its useful life) to include on the income statement will be determined by the number of depreciable assets your business owns and the method you use to depreciate them. The Internal Revenue Service has a depreciation schedule for all property purchased for business use. Most businesses use straight-line depreciation, which is simply the total cost of the item, less any salvage value, divided by the number of years in its useful life. For example, an automobile with a five-year life span, an $11,500 initial price tag, and a $1,500 salvage value will be depreciated by 20% (or $2,000) each year, starting in Year 1, until its value equals $1,500 (its estimated residual value) in Year 5.

Another method of depreciating tangible property for tax purposes is the Modified Accelerated Cost Recovery System, or "MACRS," which was introduced in 1986. For more information on MACRS and its specific applications, consult your accountant.

In addition, most small businesses are allowed under IRS regulations to expense (write off)

$17,500 worth of depreciable assets (not including real estate) purchased in the current tax year. In 1997, the IRS placed this deduction (known as a Section 179 deduction) on an indexed scale, which means that it will grow to more than $25,000 in the coming years. For more information on depreciation, consult IRS publication #946, or ask your accountant.

The formula used for *income* is:

$$\text{Revenues} - \text{Operating Expenses} = \text{Income}$$

Revenues are the total sales revenue less any sales returns, discounts, or allowances. Operating expenses include items such as rent, advertising, salaries, insurance, and other day-to-day operating costs. In the case of restaurants, food and beverage inventory can also be considered as Cost of Goods Sold (See Appendix D, page 288, for a typical income statement from a restaurant business). In the case of a C corporation, income taxes are an additional expense, which is listed separately in the Income Statement.

IS> p. 216   R> p. 247   B> p. 292

Basic Structure of the Income Statement

It may be helpful to think of the Income Statement as a series of simple calculations:

	Net Sales
−	Cost of Goods Sold
=	Gross Profit
−	Operating Expense
=	Earnings Before Income Taxes
+	Other Revenue (Expenses)
=	Net Income (Income Before Taxes)

Susan's House of Style Inc.

INCOME STATEMENT FOR YEAR ENDING DECEMBER 31, 1997

GROSS SALES		$225,000
Less: Returns & Allowances		9,000
NET SALES		$216,000
COST OF GOODS SOLD		$118,000
GROSS PROFIT		$98,000
OPERATING EXPENSES		
Salaries & Wages	$36,000	
Accounting/Legal	3,000	
Rent	10,800	
Maintenance	1,800	
Utilities	3,900	
Telephone	1,500	
Office Supplies	1,140	
Marketing & Advertising	6,000	
Interest	832	
Depreciation	4,200	
Insurance	6,000	
Travel	500	
Miscellaneous	1,200	
TOTAL OPERATING EXPENSES		$76,872
INCOME FROM OPERATIONS		$21,128
OTHER REVENUE (EXPENSES)		
Interest Earned on Investments		$1,350
NET INCOME		$22,478

Cash-Flow Statement

The cash-flow statement is the most important financial management tool you have. It documents all cash transactions (income and expenses) that occur from month to month. It is like your personal checkbook, where you post your deposits and then draw checks against them. As with your checkbook, if you spend more than you take in, your check bounces.

The reason this statement is so useful is that it forces you not only to analyze your sources of income and expenses but to do it on a cash basis. That is, you may sell products to a customer over the course of a month (for example, a lumberyard that sells primarily to contractors), but because your customer wants to be billed you may not receive the payment (cash) for 30 to 45 days, or maybe longer. During this same period, you will probably have to pay your workers on a weekly basis. Where does the money come from? Cash received from customers who have been billed for sales in previous months? A working capital loan from the bank? Or money you may have to invest in the business?

What if your business has seasonal peaks and valleys? Your cash-flow statement will reflect them and indicate the amount of cash reserve you must retain from the peak periods to enable you to survive the slow times. In other words, it enables you to project your cash needs and prepare in advance for times when you might need to borrow money, change your billing terms, or pay your suppliers.

Cash-flow statements are developed on a 12-month basis, but should be adjusted each month to reflect the actual cash in and cash out during that period. The difference between your cash-flow projection and what actually happened is called a variance. As you calculate these variances over time, you will notice trends that will enable you to adjust your cash flows more accurately in the future.

IS> p. 217

Layout of the Cash-Flow Statement

SOURCES OF CASH	USES OF CASH
Cash Flow from Operations	Cash Outflow from Operations
+ Cash Flow from Investments	+ Cash Outflow from Investments
+ Cash Flow from Financing	+ Cash Outflow from Financing
Total Cash Available in the Current Period	Total Cash Used in the Current Period

The difference between *total sources* and *total uses* is the *net cash flow* in the current period.

Note: The cash-flow statement on the following page represents the first quarter operations *only* for Susan's House of Style. The actual cash-flow statement would continue through month 12.

Susan's House of Style

MONTHLY CASH-FLOW PROJECTION

Month	Pre-Start-Up Position		1		2		3	
	Estimate	Actual	Estimate	Actual	Estimate	Actual	Estimate	Actual
1. CASH ON HAND (Beginning of Month)	14,675.00	14,675.00	14,625.00	16,689.00	11,109.00	10,527.00	5,993.00	6,267.00
2. CASH RECEIPTS								
(a) Cash Sales	0.00	0.00	5,000.00	6,800.00	6,500.00	7,316.00	8,000.00	8,523.00
(b) Collections from Credit Accounts	0.00	0.00	0.00	0.00	150.00	130.00	350.00	380.00
(c) Loan or Other Cash Injection (Specify)	44,025.00	44,025.00	0.00	0.00	0.00	0.00	0.00	0.00
3. TOTAL CASH RECEIPTS (2a + 2b + 2c = 3)	44,025.00	44,025.00	5,000.00	6,800.00	6,650.00	7,446.00	8,350.00	8,903.00
4. TOTAL CASH AVAILABLE (Before cash out) (1 + 3)	58,700.00	58,700.00	19,625.00	23,489.00	17,759.00	17,973.00	14,343.00	15,170.00
5. CASH PAID OUT								
(a) Purchases (Merchandise)	15,000.00	15,000.00	0.00	3,000.00	4,000.00	4,000.00	5,000.00	4,700.00
(b) Gross Wages (Excludes Withdrawals)	0.00	0.00	3,000.00	2,500.00	3,000.00	3,000.00	3,000.00	3,000.00
(c) Payroll Expenses (Taxes, etc.)	0.00	0.00	630.00	400.00	630.00	630.00	630.00	630.00
(d) Outside Services	750.00	750.00	250.00	225.00	250.00	150.00	250.00	150.00
(e) Supplies (Office and Operating)	95.00	110.00	100.00	145.00	100.00	92.00	100.00	63.00
(f) Repairs and Maintenance	3,500.00	3,762.00	150.00	0.00	0.00	0.00	0.00	0.00
(g) Advertising	1,000.00	987.00	1,000.00	1,063.00	750.00	739.00	750.00	800.00
(h) Car, Delivery, and Travel	0.00	0.00	0.00	0.00	0.00	0.00	0.00	0.00
(i) Accounting and Legal	500.00	500.00	400.00	342.00	200.00	200.00	200.00	185.00
(j) Rent	900.00	900.00	900.00	900.00	900.00	900.00	900.00	900.00
(k) Telephone	75.00	83.00	75.00	61.00	75.00	79.00	75.00	72.00
(l) Utilities	500.00	680.00	285.00	316.00	285.00	308.00	285.00	276.00
(m) Insurance	510.00	510.00	510.00	510.00	510.00	510.00	510.00	510.00
(n) Taxes (Real Estate, etc.)	0.00	0.00	0.00	0.00	0.00	0.00	0.00	0.00
(o) Interest	0.00	0.00	66.00	66.00	66.00	66.00	66.00	76.00
(p) Other Expenses (Specify)								
Construction Party	250.00	362.00	0.00	0.00	0.00	0.00	0.00	0.00
(q) Miscellaneous (Unspecified)	150.00	98.00	100.00	154.00	100.00	147.00	100.00	103.00
(r) Subtotal	23,230.00	23,742.00	7,466.00	9,682.00	10,866.00	10,821.00	11,866.00	11,465.00
(s) Loan Principal Payment	0.00	0.00	850.00	850.00	850.00	850.00	850.00	840.00
(t) Capital Purchases (Specify)								
Equipment (register & computer)	6,200.00	4,799.00	0.00	1,300.00	0.00	0.00	0.00	0.00
Equipment (other)	2,070.00	1,986.00	0.00	0.00	0.00	0.00	0.00	0.00
Store Fixtures	10,650.00	10,854.00	0.00	0.00	0.00	0.00	0.00	0.00
Furniture	925.00	0.00	0.00	936.00	0.00	0.00	0.00	0.00
(u) Other Start-up Costs	500.00	630.00	200.00	194.00	50.00	35.00	0.00	0.00
(v) Reserve and/or Escrow (Specify)	0.00	0.00	0.00	0.00	0.00	0.00	0.00	0.00
(w) Owner's Withdrawal	500.00	0.00	0.00	0.00	0.00	0.00	0.00	0.00
6. TOTAL CASH PAID OUT (Total 5a thru 5w)	44,075.00	42,011.00	8,516.00	12,962.00	11,766.00	11,706.00	12,716.00	12,305.00
7. CASH POSITION (End of Month) (4 minus 6)	14,625.00	16,689.00	11,109.00	10,527.00	5,993.00	6,267.00	1,627.00	2,865.00
ESSENTIAL OPERATING DATA (Non-cash flow information)								
A. Sales Volume (Dollars)	0.00	0.00	5,000.00	6,800.00	6,650.00	7,446.00	8,350.00	8,903.00
B. Accounts Receivable (End of Month)	0.00	0.00	150.00	247.00	350.00	523.00	600.00	980.00
C. Bad Debt (End of Month)	0.00	0.00	0.00	0.00	0.00	0.00	0.00	0.00
D. Inventory on Hand (End of Month)	15,000.00	15,000.00	13,350.00	14,106.00	15,911.50	17,454.32	19,698.82	21,460.83
E. Accounts Payable (End of Month)	0.00	0.00	0.00	0.00	0.00	0.00	0.00	150.00
F. Depreciation	0.00	0.00	350.00	350.00	350.00	350.00	350.00	350.00

PITFALLS

Failure to Update Records

It is critical to keep your financial records as up-to-date as possible. For example, as you compare your projected cash sales to actual ones in your cash-flow analysis, it doesn't do any good if you don't update the rest of your cash flow based on this information. *Therefore, you must update your income and cash-flow statements no less than once a month, and sales receipts should be calculated every day.*

Failure to Document Assumptions

Every financial assumption, from your projected sales levels to your utility bills, needs to be documented. Most expense documentation can be provided as footnotes to your cash-flow statement. This will indicate to anyone evaluating your plan that you haven't just pulled numbers from thin air. In the case of your sales projections, detail your methodology in the Market Share or Pricing sections of the plan, and reference the location in the footnote.

Too Much Optimism

Keep your projections and estimates conservative. It is always better to err on the conservative side, and possibly borrow a little more money initially, than to run out of working capital because you have failed to achieve unrealistic sales forecasts. If this situation does occur, it will be difficult to borrow additional funds from the bank.

SOME ADVICE

"All financial information for a new business should be well documented. Information used to develop these projections should be researched from reliable primary and secondary resources. This will limit any unforeseen cash 'drains' that could have a negative impact on your business. This is a dynamic process; the financial projection data will prove invaluable when comparing your estimates to the actual results."

John Sanders, CPA, CMA
Portland, Maine

INSURANCE

OVERVIEW

Business insurance protects your business against losses from fire, employee injury, lawsuits, automobile accidents, or other occurrences beyond your control. Although all of these events will probably not happen to you, you can't afford to take the risks.

Insurance has also taken on new dimensions in response to record numbers of lawsuits over issues of liability and alleged malpractice. The cases range from a pet groomer being sued because the owner didn't like his pet's "do" to a multimillion-dollar award to a McDonald's customer because the coffee was too hot! Or take the example of a New Hampshire man who, while on assignment out of town, was having a few drinks with his supervisor. A fight broke out, and the supervisor hit the employee with a two-by-four. A court decided the man was entitled to workers' compensation for his injuries.

All businesses need adequate insurance coverage. You must identify the potential risks in your business, then evaluate your insurance options in the context of those risks and how much you can afford to pay. Insurance against some risks, such as workers' compensation, is mandatory, while other items, such as fidelity bonding, may be desirable but not required. Some risks, such as shoplifting, are uninsurable.

Most insurance brokers can be helpful in assessing your needs and alternatives. It is important, however, that you evaluate your needs as thoroughly as possible prior to consulting a broker so that you will be an educated buyer. This can save you considerable time and money.

It is also important to review your insurance needs on a regular basis. An increase in the value of your assets and the possibility of finding lower premiums in a competitive insurance market are two good reasons to do this annually. Many small-business trade and professional associations offer their members discounted group insurance programs. After you have discussed your needs with an insurance professional, contact a few of these organizations to see what alternative insurance programs they provide.

IS▶ p. 220, 221 **R▶ p. 250, 271** **B▶ p. 293**

THE BASICS

Insurance needs can be broken down into three categories: 1) mandatory, 2) essential, and 3) desirable.

Mandatory Insurance

Workers' compensation insurance. If you plan to hire employees on either a full-time or part-time basis, workers' compensation insurance must be secured before your workers start their jobs. Rates for workers' comp are based on the degree of risk associated with the particular job. A hazardous-material handler will have a relatively high rate, while a bookkeeper will have a much lower one. Workers' comp can add significantly to your cost of doing business. The following practices can help reduce costs and potential liability.

❑ Review your job classifications to make sure that each one is included in the least costly category.

❑ As your business grows, contact your insurance broker when new employees are hired. Failure to do so will require back premium payments when the insurance company audits your business.

❑ If you use subcontractors, obtain a certificate of insurance from them. If they are not insured, you may end up paying the insurance premium on their payrolls.

> **Note:** Few business plans need a separate section on insurance. Unless your business is unusual and involves high risk, it is probably best to include this information either as an appendix or clearly detailed as a footnote to your cash-flow statement.

❏ Separate regular pay from overtime pay. Premiums are based on regular pay; overtime pay is excluded.

❏ Keep your work environment as safe as possible and maintain records of any claims made by your employees. Your rates will be adjusted on the basis of an "experience modification factor" which is computed each year, based on your loss history over the three preceding years.

Vehicle insurance. You may be legally liable when employees or subcontractors use your vehicle or their own on your behalf. If you are using vehicles to deliver merchandise, make sure that they are covered under your policy. A rider may have to be added to the policy to cover merchandise and personal property. It is imperative to carry adequate coverage for both liability and property damage. Although insurance can be expensive, there are several ways to reduce premiums, such as increasing your deductibles and buying fleet coverage if you use several vehicles.

Essential Insurance

Fire insurance. Fire insurance is essential, unless you are renting or leasing a property that has coverage. In that case, you should check the policy carefully to make sure that the coverage is adequate. If there is a coinsurance clause in your policy, which may reduce the premium, be sure that you understand the implications. For example, if you insure your property for 75% of its value, in the event of a fire you will be responsible for covering 25% of the cost to rebuild.

You may also want to insure against perils such as theft, vandalism, explosion, wind, and smoke. The need for, and costs of, such insurance should be discussed with your broker.

Liability insurance. Liability insurance protects your business from potential losses caused by accidents suffered by others when using your products or property. This liability usually extends to both your employees and subcontractors.

In recent years the number of civil lawsuits has been staggering. According to the U.S. Administrative Office of the Courts, in 1993 nearly 20 mil-

lion civil cases were filed in state and federal courts, and that number could reach as high as 30 million today, with median awards ranging from $40,000 to $625,000. Therefore, it is very important to assess your potential liability and discuss it in detail with your insurance broker before selecting coverage.

Although premiums have increased dramatically for most businesses, usually you can secure an umbrella policy, which provides inclusive coverage for vehicles, liability claims, and personal injury claims, for a single premium. Separate policies must be obtained for workers' compensation, fire, or theft. Even for a small enterprise with low risk factors, liability insurance of $1 million would not be considered high in most cases.

Key-person insurance. If you are in a business that depends on an individual(s) whose skills would be difficult to replace in the short to intermediate term, you should carry life and disability insurance on that person. This policy would be owned by, and payable to, the company and would provide funds needed to operate the business in the short term until the individual is replaced. Key-person coverage is also important as your company grows, to make sure that it has the cash to settle a deceased partner's estate (or a stockholder's estate in a closely held corporation).

Title insurance. If you own real estate, title insurance will protect you against potential claims questioning the validity of your title. Such coverage is generally inexpensive.

Desirable Insurance

Group health insurance. Although it's the subject of great national debate, at this point no employer is required to carry health insurance. However, if you do and you have 20 or more part-time or full-time employees, your plan must satisfy a number of requirements, including provisions for continuing coverage if your employee leaves. Continued coverage is required under the Federal COBRA Act, which states that an employee who was covered under a group policy is entitled to health insurance for a period of 18 months after he or she leaves the company (provided such employees apply for the coverage within 60 days of termination). The insurance is normally provided at a higher rate to the former employee, however, and the company is under no obligation to pay any premiums on the employee's behalf. The company is required to maintain the former employee's records throughout the duration of the coverage.

Your ability to provide health insurance benefits can offer significant recruiting advantages and help reduce employee turnover. Group policies tend to be significantly less expensive than individual contracts. This possibility should be reviewed in detail with your insurance agent.

Group life insurance. If you offer all employees group life insurance and cover the premiums, you can deduct up to $5,000 annually as a business expense, and the value of the insurance is not taxable as income for the employees. Check with your insurance agent to determine the costs and the minimum number of employees required to qualify for the group rate.

Disability insurance. You can purchase low-premium insurance to cover an employee's income for short periods of disability due to a nonwork-related injury.

Business interruption insurance. This insurance provides income when your business is unable to operate owing to certain circumstances, such as a fire. The premiums for this type of insurance tend to be quite high. Sometimes because of inability to pay bills and payroll, by the time payment is made on a claim, an owner may have been forced out of operation.

Fidelity bonding. A fidelity bond protects your business against financial losses caused by a dishonest employee. For example, if you have salespeople who go into customers' homes to demonstrate your products, a fidelity bond covers any losses that may be incurred if an employee is found to have stolen from the homeowner. Obtaining fidelity bond insurance can be difficult for start-up businesses, however, as the underwriter typically looks at a firm's reputation, years in business, and employee-screening methods to determine eligibility.

Employee dishonesty. Employee dishonesty insurance differs from fidelity bonding in that there is no third party involved. For example, if the manager of your jewelry store steals items from the display cases, employee dishonesty insurance can protect you (the business owner) against those losses. The insurance company usually handles all the legal proceedings against the thief for you as well. In most cases, however, for employee dishonesty insurance to pay off, there must be a conviction in a court of law.

Special forms coverage. Special forms coverage is an individually tailored policy covering many items that are otherwise excluded from your insurance. For example, fire, theft, and flood are called "named perils," and are generally covered under other parts of your policy. But what about food spoilage for a restaurant, or loss of records due to computer failure? These items would be covered under a special forms policy, which provides replacement costs for lost or damaged inventory or operational materials. Generally sold "à la carte," special forms can be very inexpensive for only a few covered items, or very costly if it includes many riders.

PITFALLS

Underestimating Insurance Needs

Be sure that you have double-checked your insurance plans and consulted with at least one professional for advice. One adverse liability judgment can easily wipe out your business and personal assets.

The Corporate Veil

Don't get the mistaken impression that just because you are incorporated, you can afford to carry less liability insurance. In some situations, you may find that you can be held personally responsible for claims against your company.

The Fringe Benefit Effect

Insurance can be as powerful a motivator as salary increases, and sometimes more so. Insurance helps satisfy your employees' safety needs and can have a substantial effect on job performance and turnover.

SOME ADVICE

"We determined what coverage we needed by weighing projected costs and revenue against family obligations and our respective debt. Initially, we left our insurance strategy rather vague in the business plan, but now we make it specific every year to try to pinpoint what percentage of our expenses will be insurance costs. And every year or so, we get two or three quotes on the coverage we need to make sure we're getting the best price."

Nathan Ryske, President
Ryske's
(restaurant & catering)
Kalamazoo, Mich.

Section II

Franchising

When you choose to go into business for yourself, you have three options. You can start a business from scratch, buy an existing business, or enter into a franchising agreement. No matter which alternative you choose, you will have to do the same type of analysis to ensure that your prospective business will be viable. This chapter looks specifically at franchising and suggests some techniques that will be helpful in evaluating franchising opportunities. It also directs you to resources that will be invaluable to you if you decide to pursue franchising as an option. Remember that you still need a business plan for your franchise. It should contain all of the elements discussed throughout the *Guide*.

B> p. 292

OVERVIEW

What Is a Franchise?

A franchise is a legal agreement between a franchisor (the seller) and the franchisee (the buyer) in which the franchisor grants to the franchisee the rights and licenses to sell products and/or services developed by the franchisor, in accordance with terms and conditions specified by the franchisor. There are three general categories of franchises.

❏ **Format franchise,** in which the franchisor furnishes a complete and comprehensive system for operating the business. Every aspect of the business, ranging from signage requirements and accounting systems to product ingredients (even how much the milkshake should weigh!), is specified and/or provided by the franchisor. Franchises such as McDonald's, The Maids, and Jiffy Lube fall into this category.

❏ **Product-distribution franchises,** where you buy the right to resell products via exclusive distribution systems, as in the case of Coca-Cola bottlers or Texaco gas stations. Conventional distributors may handle several lines of competing products, whereas franchised distributors handle only the products of the franchisor company.

❏ **Trade-name franchises,** where your business is identified with a trade name such as TrueValue or Color Tile. In this type of franchise, you conduct business under the given trade name but are not restricted from distributing other products that do not carry the manufacturer's brand.

It should be noted that when you enter into a franchise agreement, you are not really buying a business. You are only buying rights to conduct the business under a franchise agreement for a limited period of time—usually for 10, 15, or 20 years—with renewal options.

R▶ p. 261

Franchising Today

Although many people think that franchising is a relatively new phenomenon, it has actually been around for a long time. Its history in the United States can be traced back to the early 1860s, when Singer Sewing Machine Company granted distribution rights for its products. Over the next half-century many businesses followed the pattern, including those in the automotive, soft drink, retail, drug, and restaurant industries. Franchising was viewed by many companies as the most practical way to expand their distribution systems on a national basis.

Today, franchises are the most rapidly growing kind of business in the country. More than 5,000 franchising opportunities are available in almost every business category, ranging from health-care products to wine shops, and this number continues to grow. According to the International Franchise Association (IFA), franchising accounts for more than $800 billion in sales annually—two fifths of all retail sales—and employs more than eight million people. Approximately 41% of all retail sales are made through retail establishments, and one out of every 12 business establishments is a franchise business. The IFA estimates that by the end of the decade, over 50% of all retail sales will be generated by franchises.

THE BASICS

Who Should Consider Franchising?

Although franchising isn't for everyone, every new retailer should probably consider it, for at least two reasons. First, most franchises are less risky than their new start-up counterparts, and a great deal of support and guidance is generally available from the franchisor. Second, even if you are sure that you want to buy an existing business or start a new one from scratch, franchisors can be a tremendous source of market data.

Let's say you want to open a giftware boutique specializing in costume jewelry. To get you to sign up, a potential franchisor would have to convince you that there is, indeed, a market for such products in the location you are considering. The most persuasive argument would probably take the form of industry and trade data that you might find very useful as you develop the Market section of your business plan.

However, franchises have other characteristics that may make them less appealing. One, you must be willing to give up a great deal of control. Running most franchises is akin to being the divisional or district manager in a large corporation. That is, you will have responsibility in such areas as staffing, scheduling, maintenance, and financial reporting but little freedom in the areas of product development, pricing, and promotion. Two, franchises may require a substantial financial commitment in the form of fees and royalty payments. In addition, as stated above, you are not buying the business, only the rights to it for a period of time.

According to data in a DePaul University/ Francorp Franchise Marketing and Sales survey, the average franchise buyer has former corporate experience and significant financial wherewithal. The average franchise buyer is 40 years old and has a net worth of about $329,000. About 42% are husband-and-wife teams, 20% are women, 11% belong to minority groups, and more than one third came to franchising out of the corporate ranks. The June 1996 edition of *Franchise Times* adds that a typical franchise owner has an annual income of between $50,000 and $299,000 (reported mean is $127,000). Eighty-seven percent of franchisees are college-educated.

If you don't fit this profile, don't despair. Many franchises can be started with modest investments—like Laser Charge, a printer-toner recharging chain that requires a total investment of between $4,900 and $6,900—although virtually all of them require some capital.

IS▷ p. 222 **R▷ p. 242**

What Are the Advantages and Disadvantages of Franchising?

Following are some key benefits and drawbacks associated with entering into a franchise agreement. Although this list is not exhaustive, it contains the major factors that should be evaluated before you make a decision.

Advantages

❑ **Training.** Most franchisors offer training that will be invaluable to start, maintain, and grow your business. In the case of most format franchises, it will be very detailed, covering topics from hiring employees to recordkeeping. A good training program will enable you to gain thorough knowledge of all aspects of the business without having had years of experience in the field.

❑ **Proven Products and Methods.** Good franchises will significantly reduce most business risks because of their experience and know-how. They have done it over and over again and have learned what works and what doesn't. In addition, you are able to build on the franchisor's reputation and goodwill.

❑ **Low Risk of Failure.** While the business failure rate for start-ups averages around 80%, the failure rate for franchises averages less than 5%.

❑ **Collective Buying Power.** Not only can the franchisor achieve tremendous economies of scale in purchasing, but such companies are able to amass large amounts of money to fund national and regional advertising campaigns.

❑ **Financing.** In many cases, franchisors will make financing options available.

Disadvantages

❑ **Fees.** Virtually all franchises require payment of a fee, plus royalty payments based on sales.

❑ **Other Costs.** Franchisees will also be responsible for the cost of equipment, merchandise, supplies, rental and lease rates, and required participation in promotional and other support services.

❑ **Loss of Independence.** Although as a franchisee you manage the day-to-day operation of your business, most franchisors have strict guidelines and regulations that must be adhered to.

❑ **Limited Expansion Possibilities.** While many small retailers own multiple units of a particular franchise and/or multiple franchises, your ability to expand rests with the franchisor.

❑ **Work, Work, Work.** Any retail business will require a significant commitment of time and effort, and franchising is certainly not unique in this respect. Some of your time will be devoted to activities related to the franchisor's requirements, such as special reporting or strict hours of operation. However, you may be able to find a part-time franchise opportunity.

How to Identify Franchising Opportunities

The process of identifying franchise opportunities is identical to that of finding any business opportunity. Although most franchisors provide you with substantial amounts of information to create your business plan, and some even offer you a plan off the shelf, it is still very important that you do some research yourself to validate the company's claims.

Normally an entrepreneur chooses to start a business in an area in which he/she has prior experience or a strong interest. If that is the case, and you've chosen the type of business that you're interested in, you should begin the process of identifying and quantifying the market, using techniques found in the Market section of this *Guide,* page 16.

If you haven't yet identified the specific type of business you are interested in, you can use magazine articles (identified through online searches at the library) and publications such as the *Industrial Outlook* or the *Franchise Annual* to pinpoint sectors of the economy with high growth potential.

Factors Affecting Your Selection of a Franchise Opportunity

Once you have identified a specific business area that you want to pursue, it is a good idea to calculate the constraints that might affect your choice of a particular franchise. These factors include:

❑ How much money are you willing to invest?

❑ How much income do you want to make?

❑ How much risk are you willing to take?

❑ Where do you prefer to locate your business?

❑ Do you want to work full or part time?

❑ Do you want a home-based operation?

❑ Do you expect to hire employees?

❑ How long do you want to be in business?

Once you complete your needs assessment, the best overall source for identifying franchises is the *Franchise Annual,* published by Info Press. This guide provides descriptions of over 3,000 franchises including product lines, years in business,

years in franchising, size, fee structures (as well as financial assistance programs, if any), and whom to contact for more information about them. Although the *Franchise Annual* may not address all of the specific "constraints" that you have identified, the contact person for the individual franchises will.

How to Evaluate a Franchise Opportunity

During your evaluation process you should assess the competition, as well as the market for your type of business; study the Uniform Franchise Offering Circular; interview other franchisees doing business with the company; and, of course, have all your questions and concerns addressed by the franchisor. Be sure to refer to your *Inc.Sheets,* which contain lists of questions you should be asking during the course of your evaluation.

Throughout this process you should consult both an attorney and an accountant. Be sure that each of these individuals is well versed in business and corporate law and experienced in dealing with franchises. This is a highly specialized field requiring in-depth knowledge related specifically to the franchise industry.

Uniform Franchise Offering Circular (UFOC)

The Federal Trade Commission and all states have been using the same Uniform Franchise Offering Circular (UFOC) since 1995. All prospective franchisees must be provided with this document at least 10 days prior to signing any contract or paying any money. Some states may require broader disclosure, but at a minimum, the UFOC will address the topics below. Examine this document thoroughly. Each of these items should be reviewed carefully with your legal and/or tax advisers, as it contains information fundamental to evaluating the franchise offering. (A more detailed review of the UFOC can be found in *The Franchise Bible.*)

Following are highlights of each of the 23 disclosure items listed in the *Business Franchise Guide Report,* No. 161, "Revisions to the Uniform Franchise Offering Circular," published by Commerce Clearing House in Chicago. While this is not a complete representation of the document, it is provided to give you a basic idea of what should be included in all offering circulars. Review the actual document in detail as you explore a specific franchise.

1. The Franchisor, Its Predecessors, and Affiliates

Disclose in summary form:

A. The name of the franchisor, its predecessors, and affiliates

B. The name under which the franchisor does or intends to do business

C. The principal business address of the franchisor, its predecessors and affiliates, and the franchisor's agent for service of process

D. The business form of the franchisor

E. The franchisor's business and the franchises to be offered in this state

F. The prior business experience of the franchisor, its predecessors and affiliates.

2. Business Experience

List by name and position the directors, trustees and/or general partners, the principal officers, and other executives or subfranchisors who will have management responsibility relating to the franchises offered by this offering circular.

3. Litigation

Disclose whether the franchisor, its predecessors, a person identified in Item 2, or an affiliate offering franchises under the franchisor's principal trademark:

A. Has an administrative, criminal, or material civil action pending against that person alleging a violation of a franchise, antitrust or securities law, fraud, unfair or deceptive practices, or comparable allegations

B. Has during the 10-year period immediately before the date of the offering circular been convicted of a felony

C. Is subject to a currently effective injunctive or restrictive order or decree relating to the franchise.

4. Bankruptcy

State whether the franchisor, its affiliate, its predecessor, officers, or general partners during the 10-year period immediately before the date of the offering circular (a) filed as debtor; (b) obtained a discharge of its debts under the bankruptcy code; or (c) was a principal officer of a company that filed as a debtor.

5. Initial Franchise Fee

Disclose the initial franchise fee and state the conditions when this fee is refundable.

6. Other Fees

Disclose other recurring or isolated fees or payments that the franchisee must pay to the franchisor or its affiliates or that the franchisor or its affiliates impose or collect in whole or in part on behalf of a third party. Include the formula used to compute these other fees and payments. If any fee is refundable, state when each fee or payment is refundable.

7. Initial Investment

Disclose the following expenditures stating to whom the payments are made, when payments are due, and whether each payment is refundable.

A. Real property, whether purchased or leased

B. Equipment, fixtures, other fixed assets, construction, remodeling, and leasehold improvements and decorating

C. Inventory required to begin operations

D. Security deposits, utility deposits, business licenses, other prepaid expenses

E. Additional funds required by the franchisee before operations begin and during the initial phase of the franchise

F. Other payments that the franchisee must make to begin operations.

8. Restrictions on Sources of Products and Services

Disclose franchisee obligations to purchase or lease from the franchisor or its designee, or from supplier approved by the franchisor or under the franchisor's specification. For each obligation disclose:

A. The goods, services, supplies, fixtures, equipment, inventory, computer hardware and software, or real estate relating to establishing or operating the franchised business

B. The manner in which the franchisor issues and modifies specifications or grants and revokes approval to suppliers

C. Whether, and for what categories of goods and services, the franchisor or its affiliates are approved suppliers or the only suppliers

D. Whether, and if so, the precise basis by which the franchisor or its affiliates will or may derive revenue or other material consideration as a result of required purchases or leases

E. The estimated proportion of these required purchases and leases to all purchases and leases by the franchisee of goods and services in establishing and operating the franchised business

F. The existence of purchasing or distribution cooperatives.

9. Franchisee's Obligations

Disclose the principal obligations of the franchisee under the franchise and other agreements after the signing of these agreements.

10. Financing

Disclose the terms and conditions of each financing arrangement that the franchisor, its agent, or affiliate(s) offers directly or indirectly to the franchisee.

11. Franchisor's Obligations

Disclose the following:

A. The obligations that the franchisor will perform before the franchise business opens

B. The obligations to be met by the franchisor during the operation of the franchise business

C. The methods used by the franchisor to select the location of the franchisee's business

D. The typical length of time between the signing of the franchise agreement or the first payment of consideration for the franchise and the opening of the franchisee's business

E. The training program of the franchisor as of the franchisor's last fiscal year end or a more recent date.

12. Territory

Describe any exclusive territory granted the franchisee. Disclose whether:

A. The franchisor has an established or may establish another franchisee who may also use the franchisor's trademark

B. The franchisor has established or may establish a company-owned outlet or other channels of distribution using the franchisor's trademark

C. The franchisor or its affiliate has established or may establish other franchises or company-owned outlets or another channel of distribution selling or leasing similar products or services under a different trademark

D. Continuation of the franchisee's territorial exclusivity depends on achievement of a certain sales volume, market penetration, or other contingency, and under what circumstances the franchisee's territory may be altered.

13. Trademarks

Disclose the principal trademarks to be licensed to the franchisee including:

A. Whether the principal trademarks are registered with the United States Patent and Trademark Office

B. Currently effective material determination of the Patent and Trademark Office

C. Agreements currently in effect that significantly limit the rights of the franchisor to use or license the use of trademarks in a manner material to the franchise

D. Whether the franchisor must protect the franchisee's right to use the principal trademarks and must protect the franchisee against claims of infringement or unfair competition

E. Whether the franchisor actually knows of either superior prior rights or infringing uses that could materially affect the franchisee's use of the principal trademarks.

14. Patents, Copyrights, and Proprietary Information

If the franchisor owns rights in patents or copyrights that are material to the franchise, describe these patents and copyrights and their relationship to the franchise.

15. Obligation to Participate in the Actual Operation of the Franchise Business

Disclose the franchisee's obligation to participate personally in the direct operation of the franchise business and whether the franchisor recommends participation.

16. Restrictions on What the Franchisee May Sell

Disclose restrictions or conditions imposed by the franchisor on the goods or services that the franchisee may sell or that may limit the customers to whom the franchisee may sell goods or services.

17. Renewal, Termination, Transfer, and Dispute Resolution

Summarize the provisions of the franchise and other agreements dealing with termination, renewal, transfer, dispute resolution, and other important aspects of the franchise relationship.

18. Public Figures

Disclose the following:
  A. Compensation or other benefit given or promised to a public figure
  B. The extent to which the public figure is involved in the actual management or control of the franchisor
  C. The total investment of the public figure in the franchisor.

19. Earnings Claims

  A. An earnings claim made in connection with an offer of a franchise must be included in full in the offering circular and must have a reasonable basis at the time it is made.

  B. An earnings claim shall include a description of its factual basis and the material assumptions underlying its preparation and presentation.

20. List of Outlets

Disclose the following:
  A. The number of franchises of a type substantially similar to those offered and the number of franchisor-owned or operated outlets
  B. The names of all the franchisees and the addresses and telephone numbers of all their outlets
  C. The estimated number of franchises to be sold during the one-year period after the close of the franchisor's most recent fiscal year.

21. Financial Statements

Prepare financial statements in accordance with generally accepted accounting principles. These statements must be audited by an independent certified public accountant. Include the following financial statements:
  A. The franchisor's balance sheets for the last two fiscal year-ends before the application date. In addition, include statements of operations, of stockholders' equity, and of cash flows for each of the franchisor's last three fiscal years.
  B. Affiliated company statements
  C. Consolidated and separate statements.

22. Contracts

Attach a copy of all agreements proposed for use or in use in this state regarding the offering of a franchise, including the franchise agreement, leases, options, and purchase agreements.

23. Receipt

The last page of the offering circular is a detachable document acknowledging receipt of the offering circular by the prospective franchisee. It must contain the following statement in bold type:

FRANCHISING

This offering circular summarizes certain provisions of the franchise agreement and other information in plain language. Read this offering circular and all agreements carefully.

If _____ offers you a franchise, _____ must provide this offering circular to you by the earliest of:

1) The first personal meeting to discuss our franchise; or
2) Ten business days before the signing of a binding agreement; or
3) Ten business days before a payment to _____.

You must also receive a franchise agreement containing all material terms at least five business days before you sign a franchise agreement.

If _____ does not deliver this offering circular on time or if it contains a false or misleading statement, or a material omission, a violation of Federal and State law may have occurred and should be reported to the Federal Trade Commission, Washington, DC 20580 and (STATE AGENCY). (ANY ADDITIONAL STATE DISCLOSURE TIME OR REQUIRED STATUTORY LANGUAGE)

Competition

Once you have selected a particular industry, be sure to look at competing franchises, as you may find one that better meets your goals and objectives. A franchise exposition may be the best place to gather information about franchises and get a good overall view of the industry. The *1997 TradeShows & Exhibits Schedule* lists dates and locations for a variety of events.

Other Franchisees

For answers to your questions about a particular franchisor, talk with other franchisees in the system. The franchisor is required to provide you with a list of all its franchisees, including their addresses and phone numbers.

Call a number of these retailers in different geographic locations to ask specific questions about their experience with the franchising company and the business itself. In most cases you'll find them very willing to help you. After all, they were in the same position when they were starting their businesses.

Be sure to do your homework before you make these contacts. It is a good idea to prepare a list of questions in advance. (Sample questions can be found on page 222.) It is usually best to set up a "phone appointment" in advance, as these interviews can be quite time consuming.

The Franchisor

You and your advisers will undoubtedly have questions, based on your analysis of a particular franchise opportunity, for the franchisor. Any reputable franchisor will understand that this is part of a normal evaluation process and will want to be sure that you have evaluated the business carefully. If at any time you feel you are pressured into signing an agreement, that usually indicates that you should proceed with caution, if at all.

PITFALLS

Earnings Claims

Be sure that the franchisor's earnings claims are accompanied by written substantiation. The Federal Trade Commission requires this disclosure. Don't believe a franchisor if it says that it is not allowed to make earnings claims.

Fees and Royalties

The main sources of income for a franchisor are fees and royalties. The franchise fee represents your initial investment to purchase the franchise, while the royalty is based on a percentage of sales and is paid to the franchisor on an ongoing basis.

In most cases, for an established business, you would want most of the franchisor's income to come from royalties. Dependence on royalties gives the franchisor a strong vested interest in keeping franchisee sales growing. The franchisor will have a stake in constantly improving the product(s), running successful promotional campaigns, and keeping training programs up-to-date. If, on the other hand, most of its money comes from initial investment fees, the company is likely to be more interested in prospecting for new franchisees.

Pressure Tactics

Be very wary of any franchise salesperson who puts pressure on you to sign an agreement.

Evaluating a franchise opportunity should be a deliberative process, and any reputable company will understand that and expect you to take your time. There are very few circumstances under which you will "lose the last territory in your area if you don't sign up by tomorrow."

Training and Support

Training and follow-up support are two of the biggest advantages of buying a franchise. It is very important for you to evaluate these services as thoroughly as possible. Don't simply rely on the franchisor's brochures or what is written in the UFOC. This is where interviews with current franchisees will be invaluable.

EXCERPT

Wild Birds Unlimited Inc.

"We bring people and nature together and we do it with excellence."

Wild Birds Unlimited Inc. was established as a franchisor in 1983. Since that time it has firmly established its name in the United States and Canada. It has received annual nationwide acclaim as one of the companies in the "Annual Franchise 500" since 1987. In addition, it was recognized as one of the top 200 franchises by *Entrepreneur* magazine in 1996 and was ranked 33rd as the best franchise in the country in *Success* magazine's "Franchise Gold 100" in 1995. (See exhibit B for Honors and Recognitions)

Wild Birds Unlimited has had steady growth over the past three years, with franchise income growing over 67% between 1993 and 1995. The number of franchise stores has increased from 121 in 1993 to 192 in 1995 and currently numbers 215. New franchises are opened each year while a small number close each year, indicating that the stores are experiencing financial success and satisfaction with the franchisor.

Wild Birds Unlimited franchise stores have increased their gross income over the past six years. In 1988, first-year franchise average gross sales were $100,229. In 1994 first-year franchises averaged a gross of $188,384. This is an increase of 53% and may indicate increasing popularity of the stores and increasing interest in bird-watching as a hobby.

Wild Birds Unlimited has established strategic alliances with Cornell University, the National Wildlife Federation, and the Nature Conservancy. The institutions provide the franchisor with additional credibility and nationwide exposure.

- ■ The National Wildlife Federation alliance provides Wild Birds Unlimited with the exclusive rights to sell the "backyard habitat program." This is an information packet, which explains various types of habitats that a bird-watcher can create in order to attract certain birds. A Wild Birds Unlimited customer can write to the National Wildlife Federation and receive a packet with a list of required supplies, and the Wild Birds Unlimited store is responsible for providing the customer with the necessary items and education.

- ■ Alliances with the Nature Conservancy and Cornell University provide Wild Birds Unlimited with additional publicity. Wild Birds Unlimited's name is included on all press releases and promotional material when each institution sponsors fundraising activities related to birding.

Wild Birds Unlimited provides assistance to its franchisees in all aspects of the business including...

Source: Wild Birds Unlimited Inc.

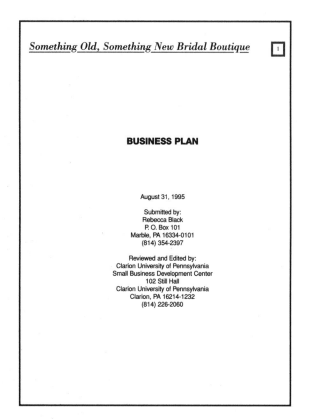

Something Old, Something New Bridal Boutique   1

BUSINESS PLAN

August 31, 1995

Submitted by:
Rebecca Black
P. O. Box 101
Marble, PA 16334-0101
(814) 354-2397

Reviewed and Edited by:
Clarion University of Pennsylvania
Small Business Development Center
102 Still Hall
Clarion University of Pennsylvania
Clarion, PA 16214-1232
(814) 226-2060

Something Old, Something New Bridal Boutique

FINANCING PROPOSAL

FUTURE ENDEAVORS, INCORPORATED

d/b/a
LEARNING EXPRESS
NASHUA, NEW HAMPSHIRE

Submitted to:
Small Business Administration

Prepared by:
Deirdre Robinson
Michael Robinson
November 23, 1996

Learning Express

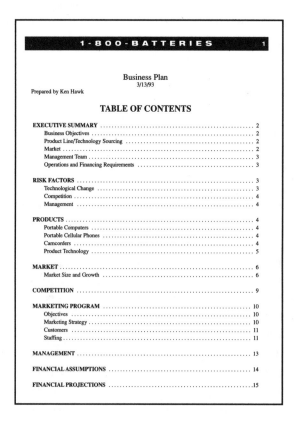

1-800-BATTERIES   1

Business Plan
3/13/93

Prepared by Ken Hawk

TABLE OF CONTENTS

1-800-BATTERIES

Section III

Sample Business Plans

In this section you'll find two fully documented business plans and one preliminary, or venture, plan. The first plan is for a traditional storefront retailer, and the second is for a franchise business. The third plan, developed for a direct marketing business, is a venture plan. It is the type of document you would send to potential investors or venture capitalists. It thoroughly explains your business concept and highlights certain parts of your strategy without going into the comprehensive detail that one would expect to find in a complete business plan.

Because we have yet to see a perfect business plan, we asked a panel of experts to comment on the strengths of the individual plans and on areas that could be improved. We have also included some brief biographical information about the founder(s) of these businesses.

Each plan was developed for a real business by individuals who have generously allowed us to publish them in the hope that their hard work might benefit you as you create your business plan. No changes have been made to the plans, including the financial data, but due to space availability the number of appendices had to be limited. We want to again thank Rebecca Black of Something Old, Something New Bridal Boutique; Deirdre and Michael Robinson of Future Endeavors, DBA Learning Express; and Ken Hawk of 1-800-BATTERIES, for their kind contributions.

These examples will provide you with a great deal of insight into how business data and information can be used and communicated effectively. They will be invaluable tools as you develop and write your own business plan.

Something Old, Something New Bridal Boutique

Company:	Something Old, Something New Bridal Boutique
Entrepreneur:	Rebecca Black
Location:	Wentling Corners, Pa.
Business Description:	Bridal Shop
Opening Date:	November 13, 1995
Starting Capital:	$63,000
1996 Sales:	n/a
Owner's Equity:	$13,000
Employees:	2 (including owner)
Education:	High school diploma in Cosmetology
	Business and Communications courses
	Computer operator course
	Diploma in Barber Operator and Manager/Teacher courses

*"I really enjoy the bridal business.
It's fun. Helping people create an event
that is one of the most important moments
in their lives makes you feel good." —Rebecca Black*

Rebecca Black always knew she would own her own business, but since she had a background in cosmetology and barber training, she thought it might be a hair salon. Then, in 1991, she planned her own wedding, including flowers, apparel, and decorations. Family and friends marveled at the beautiful event and began hiring her to plan their weddings.

Previously, Rebecca had been working for various hair salons in the area. With the birth of her second child, she sought a job where the hours were not too long so that she could spend more time with her family. Rebecca went to work for a local hospital pharmacy and had little desire to leave her job there. She continued doing family weddings, however, and became very familiar with the bridal market in her area and the wedding industry in general.

When a bridal shop in her hometown came up for sale, Rebecca saw a niche in the market that she could fill. Research went into overdrive, and with the help of the local SBDC, Rebecca developed a business plan in just three months. Her counselor, Jeanne Haas, helped Rebecca with questions to ask in her research and what to look for in starting her business. Rebecca called a lot of local competitors and became a self-proclaimed "bridal detective." Her sister-in-law, who had been in the wedding business herself, was an invaluable help in getting the store off the ground.

Rather than buy the existing business (and the poor reputation that went along with it), Rebecca chose to locate across town, in a newly renovated shop with low rent and good landlords. Her husband made some leasehold improvements, and she continued to do research and contact suppliers. On November 13, 1995, Something Old, Something New opened for business.

"The business plan process is very educational. When you do research for a business plan, there are things you don't think of, and that's where your consultants come in. It really lets you know what to expect and what you need to do. It makes you look at how you are going to run things. It gives you goals."

SECTION

Executive Summary: This section is well presented, concise, and provides enough information to let the reader know the purpose of the business. Bringing some information on the competitive environment to the front could make it even stronger.

Description of Business: Contains all required elements of legal form of organization, location, and type of business. Hours should probably include "by appointment."

Market: Clearly presented demographics, target markets, and analysis. Use of matrices is particularly helpful to illustrate the data. The owner may have identified too many markets, however, trying to "be everything to everyone."

Competition: Very thorough review of competitor's strengths and weaknesses. Again, use of matrices provides an excellent illustration.

Market Share: Although this is a very competitive market, little information is given about how the business plans to obtain 7% of the market in the first year. Market-share figures may not have been available at the time of the writing, but should be included as soon as possible.

Location: Adequately covered for this business. Additional information might include traffic counts, nearby cities that might provide competition, and so on.

Pricing: Pricing strategy is in line with the market, and the pricing policies are well documented. It is clear this business should be able to cover its costs.

Promotion: A well-considered promotional plan should help to stabilize nonpeak season. This section has clearly mapped out the promotional strategy.

Form of Ownership: The plan does not waste any time on this section. The form of ownership is clearly covered in two sentences.

Management and Personnel: There is a good list of outside consultants, but is there enough staff to provide the superior customer service the owner is striving for? Résumés of management and advisers would be a good addition.

Financial Information: What is included is adequate, but here is where the plan may want to take a few extra steps. Provide projected balance sheets, and reorder the statements from newest to oldest, with all notes and explanations appearing at the end of the financial section.

Insurance: For a business such as this, an insurance section is not necessary. However, basic coverage and amounts should be mentioned somewhere in the plan, perhaps as a footnote to the cash-flow statement.

Overall Comments: Clearly an excellent plan, with complete, concise, and simple coverage of most required ingredients. Repairs for minor problems (see Market Share and Financial Information) would make this plan one of the best we've seen.

BUSINESS PLAN

August 31, 1995

Submitted by:
Rebecca Black
P. O. Box 101
Marble, PA 16334-0101
(814) 354-2397

Reviewed and Edited by:
Clarion University of Pennsylvania
Small Business Development Center
102 Still Hall
Clarion University of Pennsylvania
Clarion, PA 16214-1232
(814) 226-2060

EXECUTIVE SUMMARY

The Company

Something Old, Something New Bridal Boutique will be a start-up retail bridal shop specializing in bridal gowns, bridal party wear, tuxedo rental, flower arrangements, bridal event miscellaneous rentals, and bridal consulting. The business will be located off Exit 7 of I-80 at the Route 338/State Route (SR) 3007 intersection in Wentling Corners, Pennsylvania. Something Old, Something New Bridal Boutique will be a sole proprietorship owned and operated by Rebecca Black, of Marble, Pennsylvania.

The Company Mission

Ms. Black's mission is to establish Something Old, Something New Bridal Boutique as a premier bridal shop committed to providing the highest quality bridal merchandise at fair market prices. The company's products and services will reflect Ms. Black's belief that, as a specialty business creating a once-in-a-lifetime event, her customers will be able to secure all their wedding needs in one place.

Products and Services

Something Old, Something New Bridal Boutique will offer a variety of bridal and attendant attire, tuxedo rental, bridal consulting, flower arrangements, wedding ceremony and reception miscellaneous items for rent, miscellaneous wedding supplies, and, beginning in the second year, rental of formal dresses. The store will offer a selection of bridal gowns, veils, shoes, gloves, jewelry, lingerie, and miscellaneous items for the bride for her big day. In the attendant-wear line, Something Old, Something New Bridal Boutique will offer gowns and dresses in a variety of styles and price ranges. In addition to bridal and attendant wear, Something Old, Something New Bridal Boutique will offer a selection of clothing for the mother of the bride, including dresses and suits in a variety of styles and price ranges, as well as jewelry, shoes, hats, and gloves for the mother of the bride to wear on her daughter's special day. Something Old, Something New Bridal Boutique will also offer tuxedo rental for the male members of the bridal party. Flower arrangements, wedding invitations, wedding favors, ceremony and reception decorations, gifts, and accessories will also be offered. The store will provide rental of various items to make the reception hall a delight to the eye, items such as topiary trees, altar arrangements, lattice arbors, vases, etc. See Appendix J for a complete listing of rental items. Something Old, Something New Bridal Boutique will also offer a selection of party dresses for various social occasions, such as proms, sorority functions, holidays, etc. In addition, Ms. Black will offer her services as a bridal consultant, providing a variety of consulting packages to the bride. A final unique offering, beginning the second year, will be the rental of party dresses for any occasion.

Something Old, Something New Bridal Boutique of Wentling Corners will be open six days a week, Monday through Saturday. Hours will be from 10 a.m. to 6 p.m. Monday, Wednesday, and Friday; 10 a.m. to 9 p.m. on Tuesday and Thursday; and 8 a.m. to 4 p.m. on Saturday.

Company Location

Something Old, Something New Bridal Boutique will be located on SR 3007, Wentling Corners, Pennsylvania. The businesses located to the northeast of the bridal shop are the Wolf's Camping Resort, the Wolf's Den Restaurant, the Wolf's Den Bed and Breakfast, Wolf's Mini-Storage, a Pennzoil gasoline station, Don Hartzell Auto Sales, and Good Tire Service Inc. Located to the south of the bridal shop are the following businesses: BJ's Eatery, Frye's Garage, Kerle Tire Service, Mt. Joy Lanes, and two offices for Clarion Riverhill Gas. To the west of the bridal shop are located Countryside Crafts & Countryside Quilts and Tharan Custom Contracting Inc. Exit 7 of I-80 is located less than one quarter mile from Something Old, Something New Bridal Boutique.

There is storefront parking at Something Old, Something New Bridal Boutique. There is also additional parking located in front of the adjacent businesses. This commercially zoned property is located in Wentling Corners in a 40-ft by 50-ft building. The location affords easy visibility for travelers on either side of SR 3007, which is the access road to I-80 at Exit 7.

Marketing and Sales Strategy

Something Old, Something New Bridal Boutique will quickly develop a reputation for quality merchandise and service, which will help to expand the customer base for the new store. In addition, one of the shop's employees, Rebecca Black, sister-in-law of the owner, has six years of experience in bridal shop operations. The sister-in-law will be referred to as Becky Black hereinafter, to avoid confusion. In addition to assisting Rebecca Black in day-to-day operations, Becky Black will provide assistance to the company during the annual buying trip, better assuring a proper mix of inventory items. Becky Black, the employee, has agreed to fill in for Rebecca Black, the owner, for vacations and emergencies.

Promotional efforts will include advertising in local publications, Yellow Page advertisements, promotional letters in response to engagement announcements, "monthly specials," fashion shows, advertising in school publications, and cross-promotional advertising with appropriate bridal industry vendors. These efforts will combine to inform the public that Something Old, Something New Bridal Boutique will deliver superior products and services. Something Old, Something New Bridal Boutique will be promoted as a complete bridal store.

A combination of newspaper and radio advertising will be used, with repetition being the key to advertising success. Available services will be advertised to keep the name of Something Old, Something New Bridal Boutique in the public's eye. Special methods of promotion, such as fashion shows, will be planned regularly. Ms. Black has provided wedding consulting services in the past, including consulting on flowers, decorations, clothing patterns, and colors of attire. She also is an excellent seamstress and has created a number of dresses for various weddings. She, personally, will do some of the tailoring for the shop.

The Competition

Something Old, Something New Bridal Boutique has several closely located competitors, including her foremost local competitor, Jeanne's Bridal Shop of Van. Ms. Black will be purchasing the assets of what would have been another primary competitor — Cloud Nine, which is located in Clarion. Several florist shops in Knox and Clarion offer primary competition for the floral arranging segment of the business. These shops include Vickers Florist and Gehres Gift & Flower Shop, both located in Knox; and The Flower Center, Flowers N' Bows, Wilshire's Flowers & Gifts, and Phillips Flowers, all located in Clarion. Competition for the sale of invitations will come from Matthew's Hallmark with locations in Clarion and the Cranberry Mall, Banker's Supply House of Clarion, and Knox Printing of Knox. Competitors for the rental of reception items will be Clarion Candy Company and Scott Rental, both of Shippenville, and Grand Rental Station of Cranberry. Competition for the sale of party supplies will come from Clarion Candy Company of Shippenville and Jo-Ann Fabrics and Plan-A-Party of Clarion. Competition for tuxedo rental will come from various dry cleaning establishments, such as Town and Country Cleaners of Clarion and Brockville, as well as from a number of clothing stores, such as Wear Else and Crooks Clothing, both of Clarion. There are no competitors for the bridal consulting services.

Management

Something Old, Something New Bridal Boutique will be owned and operated by Rebecca Black. Ms. Black will be responsible for the development of the business and will serve as the day-to-day manager, developing operational policy and initiating personnel policy. Her husband, Benjamin Black, a professional contractor, will oversee leasehold renovations and general building maintenance. Ms. Black will handle the bookkeeping and banking duties for the store. Something Old, Something New Bridal Boutique will employ one full-time person. A second individual will be employed on a part-time basis, working approximately 20 hours per week. These individuals will assist in clerical, sales, and general labor duties.

Financials

For the year ending October 31, 1996, Something Old, Something New Bridal Boutique projects net income to be $20,411, with an ending cash balance of $5,000. The net income and ending cash balance for the year ending October 31, 1997 are projected to be $29,209 and $16,360, respectively. For the year ending October 31, 1998, net income is projected to be $41,511, with an ending cash balance of $33,697. Break-even sales for the three years ending October 31, 1996, 1997, & 1998 are $108,785, $113,489, and $122,177, respectively.

Funds Sought and Utilization

Rebecca Black is seeking a commercial loan of $50,000. To this amount, she will be adding $13,000 in equity funds. The application of funding will be as follows: Inventory - $27,300; Furniture and Fixtures - $8,443; Leasehold Improvements - $16,713; Alarm System - $300, Supplies Inventory - $1,000; Rental Inventory - $1,000; Gifts Inventory - $300; Computer System - $3,350; and Working Capital - $4,594.

Table of Contents

*Note: Appendices omitted because of space constraints.

COMPANY DESCRIPTION

Something Old, Something New Bridal Boutique, to be located in Wentling Corners, will be a retail bridal shop that will be owned and operated by Rebecca Black of Marble, Pennsylvania. The bridal shop will specialize in bridal and formal attire, floral arrangements, rental of items for wedding ceremonies and receptions, bridal consulting services, tuxedo rental, and the sale of miscellaneous wedding items.

The Company's Mission

Something Old, Something New Bridal Boutique will be committed to providing high quality products and services at acceptable market prices. All services will reflect creativity and management's pride in her products. Rebecca Black will establish excellent word-of-mouth advertising by providing personalized attention in a professional, yet friendly manner to each customer. The staff of Something Old, Something New Bridal Boutique will be well trained and professional. Something Old, Something New Bridal Boutique will continually strive to improve responsiveness to the needs and concerns of its customers through the development of new products and services.

Management will also continuously review current product offerings. Ms. Black will promote the ability of the store to offer all the products and services needed for life's most special occasions, and they will all be available in one location. This will engender less hassle and less anxiety for the bride and her family.

Company Location

Something Old, Something New Bridal Boutique of Wentling Corners is to be located at Exit 7 off I-80, an exit that is referred to as the Knox Exit, Knox being located approximately three miles away. The store faces northeast. The business is adjacent to a warehouse for Kerle Tire Service and two offices for Clarion Riverhill Gas. The businesses that are located immediately across the road from Something Old, Something New Bridal Boutique are Wolf's Camping Resort, the Wolf's Den Restaurant, the Wolf's Den Bed and Breakfast, Wolf's Mini-Storage, a Pennzoil gasoline station, Don Hartzell Auto Sales, and Good Tire Service Inc. Located on the same side of the road as Something Old, Something, New Bridal Boutique are B J's Eatery, Frye's Garage, Kerle Tire Service, Mt. Joy Lanes, Countryside Crafts & Countryside Quilts, and Tharan Custom Contracting Inc.

This commercially zoned property is located in Wentling Corners in a 40-ft by 50-ft building. Adequate parking is provided in front of the building. The business's location also affords easy visibility for travelers on SR 3007, the access road to I-80. Travelers on Route 338 will locate Something Old, Something New Bridal Boutique via signage constructed at the intersection.

There are two major routes, Rt. 338 and SR 3007, coming into Wentling Corners. State Route 3007 accesses I-80 less than one-quarter mile off Route 338. Besides the Knox vicinity, which includes Wentling Corners, business will be generated from the major population areas in Clarion, Venango, and Forest Counties. These areas include, but are not limited to: Clarion, Fryburg, Shippenville, Strattanville, Foxburg, Sligo, Rimersburg, New Bethlehem, Pleasantville, Oil City, Franklin, Sugarcreek, Kennerdale, Emlenton, Clintonville, Polk, Tionesta, Cooksburg, and Marienville. Secondary market areas will include Jefferson, Northern Butler, and Armstrong Counties.

The building provides over 1,800 square feet of space for the business. The business space will be divided into a retail area of 1,050 square feet; a work area of 473 square feet for seamstress activities; two dressing rooms, each 56 square feet; and an office area of 80 square feet. Storage will be provided in the work area.

The building is a 22-year-old pole-building structure, which Ms. Black plans to face in brick. It is owned by Robert L. and Vivian L. Russell of 4023 SE 26th Street, Okeechobee, FL 34974. Monthly rental will be a total of $400 per month. However, the Russells will repay Ms. Black for the extensive renovations to the building by allowing a $200 per month rental reduction, until the entire leasehold improvements of $16,713 have been repaid, which will be approximately a seven-year period of time.

Mr. Black will renovate the interior of the building by installing drywall; new electrical and plumbing systems; a rest room; central air; new doors and windows; and completing surface finishing, such as wallpaper and paint. See the construction bid in Appendix I.

The companies providing utilities to the property are North Penn Gas Co. of Venus, Penelec of Oil City, and Alltel of Brookville. Monthly charges for each of the utilities are found in the financial statements. Water and sewage are provided from the private systems owned by the landlord, and the charge for each is incorporated into the monthly rental charge.

A list of Furniture & Fixtures and Inventory that will be purchased with the loan proceeds for Something Old, Something New Bridal Boutique can be found in Appendix B. This equipment includes office furniture, display cases and fixtures, mannequins, and a multitude of other items.

Legal Status and Ownership

Something Old, Something New Bridal Boutique of Wentling Corners will be owned and operated as a sole proprietorship of Rebecca Black. Ms. Black will take an active role in the day-to-day management of the business and will be responsible for supervising personnel, ordering inventory and supplies, and all other aspects of the business.

Financial Development

The total start-up project cost for Something Old, Something New Bridal Boutique is $63,000. Funding for the start-up business will come from Commercial Lending—$50,000. Ms. Black will contribute $13,000 in cash equity to the project. The application of the sources of funds will be as follows: Inventory—$27,300; Furniture & Fixtures—$8,443; Leasehold Improvements—$16,713; Alarm System—$300; Supplies Inventory—$1,000; Rental Inventory—$1,000; Gifts Inventory—$300; Computer System—$3,350; and Working Capital—$4,594. See Appendix B for a complete listing of Furniture & Fixtures and Inventory items to be purchased, Appendix I for a complete listing of Renovation expenditures, and Appendix J for a complete listing of items to be purchased for rental. The total project amount will provide sufficient funding to successfully establish and maintain a retail bridal shop business through its inception period. The total project sum will be sufficient to finance the acquisition of the business assets and the start-up phase so that Something Old, Something New Bridal Boutique can establish itself as an ongoing, profitable enterprise.

Please refer to the Sources and Applications of Funds Statement on page 29. Net income is projected to be $20,411, $29,209, and $41,511 for the three years ending October 31, 1996, 1997, and 1998, respectively, based on net sales of $143,380, $166,042, and $199,952 in each of these respective years. Break-even sales were calculated to be $108,785, $113,489, and $122,177 for the first three years of operation.

INDUSTRY ANALYSIS

The following information provides estimates of growth for retail sales projected in the *1994 US Industrial Outlook.*

Total retail sales were projected to reach $2.2 trillion in 1994, up seven percent from 1993. Total revenue earned by stores concentrating in nondurable product lines will exceed $1.4 trillion, an increase of more than six percent over 1993, largely reflecting higher prices. These projected increases reflect the general view of business forecasters that consumer spending in 1994 will provide the underlying strength for the three percent growth rate in the GDP forecast for the 1993-94 period. During 1993, consumer spending, reflecting uneasiness about the future, was projected to remain flat as consumers continued to reduce their debt burden.

Year-to-year changes in sales of retail stores concentrating on nondurable merchandise lines, such as food and clothing, tend to mirror changes in general business conditions as indicated by the gross domestic product (GDP), which was forecast to grow about three percent in 1994. In contrast, year-to-year changes in sales of retail stores concentrating in durable goods, such as furniture and major household appliances, tend to exaggerate changes in business conditions by increasing more than the GDP during good years and declining more than the GDP during slowdowns. In addition to overall business conditions, retail sales reflect changes in prices, merchandise mix, and shifts to alternative channels of distribution.

Stores selling mostly nondurables accounted for nearly 64 percent of total retail sales, with 1993 revenues topping $1.3 trillion, up 5.7 percent over 1992. Sales of durable goods totaled $757 billion in current dollars, up more than seven percent from 1992 and accounted for 36 percent of the total.

Retailers of nondurable merchandise face a dual challenge of a slow-growing market and changes in demographics and consumer buying habits that have spawned structural changes within the industry. The retailers that adjust their competitive strategies to these new realities, and take advantage of new marketing techniques such as electronic retailing, catalog marketing, smaller stores, and improved customer service, should succeed in improving their market positions in the changing retailing era of the 1990s.

Retail customers of the 1990s are significantly different from retail customers of a decade ago, and retail strategies need to be reassessed in view of the changing demographics and new buying patterns.

The most significant demographic change is the declining importance of households composed of married couples, dropping from 60.8 percent in 1980 to 55.3 percent in 1991. At the same time, the number of people living alone increased, influencing consumer buying habits and forcing retailers to respond with appropriate packaging and marketing, as evidenced by the increase in "single serving" products.

Some retailers depend on groups other than households for their target markets. For instance, men between the ages of 18 and 34 are the mainstay customers of convenience stores. However, the number of men in this age group is expected to decline during the 1990s, portending a difficult period for convenience stores. Another demographic change is the expected surge in the number of teenagers and young adults in the next five years. This group will be more inclined to embrace electronic shopping channels and interactive television, sometimes referred to as "storeless" shopping.

Changing buying patterns projected for the 1990s reflect new priorities for households composed of married couples and a different lifestyle for single-person households. Many married couples, consisting of maturing baby boomers, have changed their priorities to emphasize more leisure time. Increasingly they have rejected the day-long shopping trips of the past in favor of quick "buy and go" patterns. These changing attitudes toward shopping appear to have had an effect on the retailing scene. Sales at super regional malls—those with at least three anchor stores—dropped 7.3 percent between 1990 and 1992, after increasing 18 percent during the previous years. During the same period, retail sales at smaller community shopping centers increased 15 percent and sales at neighborhood strip centers increased nearly seven percent.

Bridal Industry

Economic factors influencing bridal shops include products and services, competition, demographics, pricing, seasonality, marketing, ownership, and location. The typical bridal shop borrows short-term to finance its sample and accessory inventories. Long-term borrowing would be for permanent furniture and fixtures, leasehold improvements, expansion, equipment, and working capital. Cash flow from operations is the primary source of loan repayment. Recourse to the collateral securing the loans is a secondary source of repayment. Loans to bridal shops should be guaranteed jointly and severally by the owners of the business.

Although the bridal market has been targeted for years by marketers of products and services usually associated with weddings, marketers of everything from credit cards to contraceptives are now fighting for their share of the $32 billion bridal business. For example, Freixenet USA, marketers of Cordon Negro sparkling wine, is targeting the wedding market with an aggressive advertising campaign. Additionally, previously only offered at department stores, bridal registries are showing up everywhere, from the Metropolitan Museum of Art to Ace Hardware to Tower Records.

The wedding industry is a recession-proof industry. It is one of the few segments of the retail economy that saw its profits rise — from 10 percent to 12 percent, during the recessionary year of 1990. This is the reason for the startling growth of industry participants. In 1986, there were fewer than 50 wedding-dress manufacturers in the United States. The figure has since quadrupled. The number of bridal-apparel shops has doubled since 1986 to 7,000.

Virtually all of the 7,000 bridal shops are small, individually owned, and family operated. Opening a store in an urban area will cost a minimum of $100,000, with most of the total going to the wedding gown inventory. Competition is getting stiff and is causing many stores to diversify their inventories to include accessories, shoes, lingerie, and wedding cake cutters. It is important to note, however, that since 1987, ten percent of new bridal-gown businesses have failed annually — this according to National Bride Service. In addition, many department stores are closing their bridal boutiques, citing the special demands and high costs of the business as the reasons.

In 1991 the wedding industry had total revenues of $32 billion. Of that amount, $3.3 billion, or 10.3 percent, went to engagement/wedding rings, while $4.5 billion, or 14.1 percent, went to honeymoon travel and apparel. A total of $7.8 billion, or 24.3 percent, went to home furnishings and household equipment, while $16.4 billion, or 51.3 percent, went to the wedding apparel, invitations, flowers, receptions, photos, and gifts.

One-third of the wedding cost actually goes to the reception. Wedding gowns, on the other hand, represent only $2 billion of the $32 billion total. Standard retail rules don't apply to the wedding-gown business. Only one percent of the population is getting married at any one time. For instance, if 5,000 people live in your area, then only 50 of them are likely to be in the marriage market. Therefore, store sales don't bring an increased demand for dresses.

The amount of money being spent on the honeymoon has greatly increased. In 1987, first-time marriages spent $2.5 billion on honeymoons. By 1991, the figure had jumped to a startling $3.6 billion. Couples are now honeymooning at offshore locations, reversing the trend of a few years ago.

The bridesmaid market, alone, is $200 million.

Positive changes in consumer behavior for the bridal industry are that repeat engagements and remarriages add approximately 25% – 30% to wedding-related revenues each year and that restaged weddings are popular. According to the Census Bureau, one million couples divorce each year, and almost 75% of them will remarry. The National Center for Health Statistics (NCHS) reports that a majority of women who divorce eventually remarry, an average of four years after the previous marriage ended. The average divorced woman who remarries is 35 years old and has been divorced for 3.9 years. The average divorced man who remarries is 39 years old and has waited 3.6 years.

Forty-six percent of weddings in 1988 were remarriages for at least one member of the happy couple — this according to the NCHS. NCHS also reports that in 1988, 1.1 million remarriages took place. Forty percent of those united two divorced persons. For 50 percent, it was the remarriage of one of the happy twosome. For 11 percent, one or both members of the happy couple were widowed. This was a 14 percentage point increase over 1970.

According to the NCHS, in 1990 there were 2,448,000 marriages, compared to 2,404,000 in 1989 — a two percent increase. The 1990 figure, representing the third highest number of marriages in US history, was the highest since 1984. However, in 1993, only 2.3 million couples got married, the lowest figure since 1975. This decline, predicts the National Center for Health Statistics, could last for a decade.

The bridal business is dependent on population trends, and since 1985 the number of weddings has actually decreased. Because of this trend, much of the retail business is going very upscale or very downscale. Stores fighting to maintain the middle position are engaged in a very tough battle. Many in the industry believe that expansion and advertising are among the key strategies for winning over the 1990s bride.

More Americans are putting off their marriages until their late 20s and early 30s when they're earning more money and are firmly established in their careers. In 1988, the first-marriage age was 24.6 years for women and 26.5 years for men. The figure increased from 1985, when it had been 24 years for women and 25.9 years for men.

Most first-time brides (62 percent) consider their weddings to be formal. Only one-fifth of second-time brides have formal weddings. Second-time brides spend 35 percent as much as first-timers on their wedding receptions. Unless she is quite young, a second-time bride is likely to choose a nontraditional gown, a low-key ceremony, and a scaled-down reception.

Typically, 50 to 100 people attend a divorced person's remarriage. On the other hand, 175 to 200 guests attend a first-time wedding, with the guests spending between $70 and $100 on a gift. Although etiquette suggests that it is not necessary to bring a gift to a second marriage, most people disregard this practice in favor of bringing gifts. Americans love weddings. According to a 1989 Gallup poll, more than four in ten adults had attended a wedding within the previous year.

According to *Bride's* Magazine, the average engaged couple in the United States has an income of $48,000, or 30 percent above the U.S. average. Wedding costs range from $8,000 to $25,000. According to *Modern Bride*, weddings average $16,698 each.

The formal wear and rental business may be seasonal, but its growth has been stable, always improving by about five percent per year. Weddings account for approximately 60 percent of tuxedo rental business. Basic black coats remain the preference of most men, and vests have replaced the cummerbund as the accessory of choice in two out of three orders. The vests come in a wide variety of prints. Tuxedo styles are in vogue for four or five years. With a bridal dress or gown, in six months it's ancient history.

For bridal dresses, satin has become very popular in the last four years, and in the last two years, silk has become popular. Lace boots have become very popular with brides.

One of the key ingredients in the successful selling of bridal attire is identifying the price range a bride and her family can afford. It is a big mistake to let a bride fall in love with a dress that won't fit her budget. All prospective brides must be treated with the same courtesies, regardless of the price of their dresses. One very successful bridal shop owner gives each bride a sixpence to put in her shoe.

Independent bridal consulting is one of the hottest segments of the bridal market. Consultants can start business with as little as $2,000 to $3,000. Most consultants sell their services for $25 per hour, or 10% to 15% of the total bridal package.

The traditional wedding season runs from May through August.

PRODUCTS AND SERVICES

Something Old, Something New Bridal Boutique will carry the following brand/product lines: dresses by Alfred Angelo, Bridal Originals, Moonlight Design Inc., Joelle, Dometrios, Victorian Visions, Bridals by Justine, et al; flowers by Castle Pierpont; headpieces by Marionat Inc., Washington Millinery, and Regalia Veils; bridal accessories by Private Cellars, LTD, Golden Ring Publishing, Vermont Stoneworks, Treasured Moments, Beverly Clark Collectibles, D'Giovanna's, Wine Designs, et al; jewelry by Rain Maker, Cathy's Concepts, Carly Designs, et al; lingerie by Shirley of Hollywood; invitations by McPherson's, Stylart, Wedding Ware, Masterpiece Studio, et al; music by Novelle Records and Daywind Music Group; shoes by Benjamin Walk Corp. and Coloriffics; tuxedos by P-Taks, Capital, and After Six; and reception rentals by Mirror Centerpiece.

Something Old, Something New Bridal Boutique will offer only quality products. The reputation the business will create as a premier service provider, when combined with its product offerings, will be largely responsible for the success of this business. Something Old, Something New Bridal Boutique will offer the sale or rental of women's special occasion attire; floral arrangements for weddings; the sale of wedding accessories, favors and decorations, invitations, and miscellaneous items; tuxedo rentals; rental of miscellaneous items for wedding ceremonies and receptions; and bridal consulting services. The store will also offer decorating and clean-up services.

Weather plays a major role in the clothing market. The weather in Pennsylvania's long and wet fall, winter, and spring seasons will be a factor in the choice of inventory offerings. However, as sales are seasonal with approximately 75 percent of sales derived from weddings, most of which occur in the warmer months of the year, it will require a great deal of planning and finesse to stock the appropriate product offerings. Ms. Black believes that her personal event planning experience and innate good taste, and the experience of her family employee, who has had six years of experience in the bridal industry, will provide her with a good basis for inventory decision making, a crucial consideration in the effective, profitable operation of a bridal shop.

Careful buying, inventory control, and using profit margins to the fullest extent is the key to cash flow in the store. Profit realized, for the most part, will be reinvested into the business through enhancement of the inventory. This will allow for the planned expansion of the primary offerings. In three years, with these planned improvements and the expansion well established, the goal is to increase the market share, beyond the initially planned seven percent, and to increase total sales revenue to make Something Old, Something New Bridal Boutique the market leader for bridal and special life-event attire and services in the three county region.

TARGET MARKET AND MARKETING STRATEGY

A majority of the sales revenue will be derived from residents from the counties of Clarion, Venango, and Forest. These areas include Clarion, Fryburg, Shippenville, Strattanville, Foxburg, Sligo, Rimersburg, New Bethlehem, Pleasantville, Oil City, Franklin, Sugarcreek, Kennerdale, Emlenton, Clintonville, Polk, Tionesta, Cooksburg, and Marienville. The target customers for Something Old, Something New Bridal Boutique include the following four different segments: men and women between the ages of 16 and 18 for proms; young women between the ages of 15 and 25 for beauty pageants; men and women between the ages of 18 and 35 for weddings; and men and women between the ages of 25 and 60 for formal party wear.

Market Share

Based upon market research, the following statistics were compiled from information received from courthouses in Ms. Black's three-county primary market area.

Table 1. MARRIAGE LICENSES IN CLARION, FOREST, & VENANGO COUNTIES

County	1990	1991	1992	1993	1994	1/1-6/30/95
Clarion	396	348	326	378	311	170
Forest	41	41	41	41	41	20
Venango	458	453	421	437	441	268

This indicates that the arithmetical average number of weddings is 350 per year for Clarion County, 41 for Forest County, and 442 for Venango County. Ms. Black is assuming that all marriage licenses issued result in weddings, as the difference between number of licenses issued and number of resultant weddings should be minimal. This results in a total annual average, in the primary market area of Something Old, Something New Bridal Boutique, of 833 weddings. Ms. Black calculates that she will secure a slightly less than seven percent market share, or 56 weddings, her first year of business. Ms. Black anticipates that her business will increase in year two in the following manner: ten percent. In year three, Ms. Black expects her business will increase by 15 percent.

Pricing

The pricing strategy at Something Old, Something New Bridal Boutique will be a 100 percent markup on dresses and gowns; a 50 percent markup on invitations, gifts, accessories, flowers, and shoes; and a 20 percent markup on favors. Ms. Black will charge $50 per hour for her consulting services, with the total price bid based on estimated time to perform each task in the selected package. See Appendix M for a complete listing of bridal consulting services offered by Something Old, Something New Bridal Boutique. Tuxedo rentals will include a 20 percent markup. Reception hall rental merchandise will be priced at 30 percent of the cost of the item. In addition, should the customer destroy or lose the rental item, the customer is responsible for replacement cost. See Appendix J for information on rental items. Dress rentals will be priced at 33 percent of their retail price.

Advertising

Ms. Black will certainly endeavor to use whatever low-cost methods will be most effective for her business. She plans to network with area businesses through her consulting services. She will display her cooperative partners' promotional literature in her bridal consulting book, and they will display her promotional materials in their shops. Ms. Black is developing a business card that presents her business as a comprehensive, dignified, and reliable provider of wedding products and services. The cooperative promotional partners, who will display Ms. Black's business card and other promotional pieces, include Coke's Creative Cutters, Designing Minds, Hair Logics by Brenda, Shear Cheveux, The New Wave, Cuts & Curls, Shear Effects, Shear Magic, The Classic Salon, Golden Touch, Shear Expressions, Top Knotch, Carousel Portrait Studio, Carl and Don Studio, Petulla Studio, Richard Lucas Photography, Photograffs, EJ the DJ, Touch of Class, Joel Miller, Sharp DJ Sounds, B & B Limousine, Clearfield Transport, Armstrong Limousine, Inc., Lawrence's Limousine Service, Sara Jane's Deli, Uzi's Pastries, and A Personal Touch. She will work with the following businesses to provide reception hall services: St. Michael's, St. Joseph's, St. Mary's, Kugler Enterprises, and the Holiday Inns of Oil City and Clarion.

Ms. Black will volunteer her services as part of school and community fund raisers by having her business designated as a pick-up or drop-off point. This will involve no actual outlay of funds, but will require a degree of logistic finesse, which Ms. Black is prepared to provide.

Something Old, Something New Bridal Boutique will send a letter of congratulation to those individuals who publish an announcement of their engagements. She has developed a formal letter that will both congratulate and introduce the services that can be provided by the management of Something Old, Something New Bridal Boutique. See Appendix K for a copy of this letter. Ms. Black believes that this will inform those who are definitely in the market for bridal industry services and that it will provide a strong basis for word-of-mouth trade development. The cost for the publication and mailing of the letters will be minimal. Ms. Black will be sending these letters to all engaged couples announcing their impending marriages in the following newspapers: *The Derrick*, *The Clarion News*, *The Forest Press*, and *The News Herald*.

Newspaper advertising will be utilized to promote the Grand Opening of the store and to advertise the monthly special promotions. Such advertising will also serve to keep the name of Something Old, Something New Bridal Boutique in the public's eye, as well as to promote special events, such as fashion shows and new product lines.

The store will run advertisements which should prove to be quite effective. Often the store will feature a block ad in the newspaper, at a price of $10.99 per column inch. Ms. Black plans to advertise by purchasing banner space at a local bowling alley, as bowling participants are often within her primary target customer base. It will cost approximately $150 to have the banner constructed, and Mt. Joy Lanes of R. D. # 3, Knox, PA will charge Something Old, Something New Bridal Boutique $150 per year in rental fees for displaying the banner.

Ms. Black plans to schedule at least two fashion shows each year. A bridal fashion show will be held in December at the Holiday Inn of Clarion. The costs will include $300 for rental of a room and the courtyard. Three advertisements in *The Derrick* will cost a total of $495. Radio advertising will cost $120. Refreshments will not have a cost to Ms. Black as a cooperative catering partner will cosponsor and will provide the food at his/her cost. Ms. Black estimates that 50 brides will attend this function, and she will provide promotional packets to them at a cost of $4 per bride, for a total of $200. This will result in a total cost to Something Old, Something New Bridal Boutique of $1,115 for the bridal show. Ms. Black will use volunteer models and will offer them a 20 percent discount on the attire they wear in the show. She will provide informational packets for all brides-to-be in attendance. Ms. Black will secure the folders, which are emblazoned with the shop name, logo, address, and telephone number, from Banker's Supply House. The folders will include a business card, a calendar and checklist (see Appendix K for a sample of this promotional piece), a checklist of dresses in the bridal show (which simplifies selection as the bride can indicate which dresses she is interested in selecting), sample favors & candies, and brochures from the shop's suppliers.

There will also be at least one fashion show for prom season. It will be held in the month of March and will usually be held at a high school. Ms. Black anticipates the cooperation of the North Clarion School District and the Keystone Area School District. The costs for this fashion show will again be low, aside from the advertising, as Ms. Black will again use volunteer models, who will be offered the dresses they wear in the fashion show at a 20 percent discount. Each show will cost approximately $825, which will include refreshments of $100. Folders for the prom show will be less expensive than those for the bridal show. Ms. Black will include in the prom folders, business cards, a checklist of dresses in the prom show, and tuxedo pamphlets. These folders will cost $1.50 each, and Ms. Black anticipates that 75 students will attend. There will be a door prize awarded at each fashion show, with the approximate cost of each door prize being $15.

The wedding fashion show will be advertised in the following manner: *The Derrick* for three days prior to the week of the bridal show, at $165 per advertisement, or a total of $495 for newspaper advertising. Ms. Black will also advertise the bridal show on C-93, running five, 30-second spots from 2:30 p.m. on. These will also be run during the week prior to the bridal fashion show, alternating with the three days of newspaper advertisements. The cost of the radio will be $60 per day, for a total of $120.

The prom fashion show will be advertised via school newspaper advertisements and/or sports booklets advertisements in the appropriate school district publications. The cost will be approximately $25 per ad and will be run in school newspapers in March. In the future, Something Old, Something New Bridal Boutique hopes to expand its prom fashion shows to include the following school districts: Brookville Area Schools, Clarion-Limestone School District, Clarion Area School District, Allegheny-Clarion Valley School District, Redbank Valley Area School District, East Brady Area School District, Oil City Area School District, Franklin Area School District, and the Cranberry Area School District. Ms. Black will also place a name ad in the various sports booklets, although it is too late to be included in the 1995–96 sports booklets. The cost will be approximately $5 per advertisement.

The cost of Ms. Black's business cards will be $35 per 1,000 cards, and she will secure these from Banker's Supply House of Clarion.

Ms. Black will purchase promotional items which will be used to advertise her business, as well. Items such as bookmarks and matchbooks will be printed at a cost of $74.25 for 200 of each. She will provide the matchbooks as samples in the store, and bookmarks will be for sale in the store. These items will be imprinted with the business name, address, and telephone number.

Something Old, Something New Bridal Boutique will list in the Yellow Pages in Oil City/Franklin-GTE at a cost of $20 per month for a 3¼ inch, six-line, 6-point type advertisement. She will place a similar advertisement in the Knox/Alltell book at a cost of $17 per month. The cost to include such an advertisement in the Clarion/Bell Telephone Company Yellow Pages will be $20 per month.

Ms. Black will create window displays for the two windows of the store. The cost of the window displays will be negligible as she will use products from her inventory and a few supplies from the supplies inventory. Her assistant, Becky Black, has six years of experience in creating bridal store windows. There will also be in-store floor and wall displays, both of which will be changed frequently. This particular advertising method, that is visual merchandising and point-of-sale displays, will be less expensive than most other methods, as the materials will be reusable in future displays and the inventory displayed will be sold as a matter of course.

Flyers will be developed for the store and will be distributed in the following manner: Ms. Black will include the flyers in the folders for the fashion shows and in the shops of her various cooperative partners. Ms. Black will develop the flyers on her personal computer equipment at a cost of $5 per 500 flyers.

Something Old, Something New Bridal Boutique will offer monthly specials, which will be advertised in newspapers. The chart on the following page provides details on what these offers constitute.

Table 2. MONTHLY PROMOTIONAL SPECIALS

Month	Special
January	Ten percent off invitations
February	Free groom tuxedo rental with party of seven or more
March	Ten percent off shoes
April	Ten percent off prom flowers
May	Ten percent off mothers' dresses or suits
June	June brides receive free gift
July	July grooms receive free gift
August	Ten percent off gift items
September	Ten percent off homecoming flowers
October	Ten percent off wedding flowers ordered for December, January, or February weddings
November	Ten percent off special occasion dresses
December	Ten percent off accessories

The final method of advertising the business will be through signage on SR3007. A sign that is two feet high by three feet wide will be placed five feet off the ground on property owned by Kerle Tire Service, R. D. #3, Knox, PA. There will be no leasing fee. Mr. Black will be able to construct and install the sign at a cost of $60. Ms. Black and Miss Melissa Smith will paint the sign.

Primary advertising seasons are November through March, which will stimulate business during the slower selling period. Something Old, Something New Bridal Boutique will participate in whatever cooperative advertising programs become available from suppliers.

Initial Selling Method

Something Old, Something New Bridal Boutique will accept VISA, Mastercard, and DISCOVER. Approximately four percent of sales will be via charge cards, and the average discount for charge card bank service is three percent.

Something Old, Something New Bridal Boutique will also provide a layaway service for its customers. The store will keep the merchandise until the customer has completed all payments. There are specific time limits for paying for the various product lines, and historical industry statistics indicate that almost all customers will pay for the merchandise within the specified period. Something Old, Something New Bridal Boutique will require a 50 percent down payment on all bridal gowns and a ten percent monthly payment thereafter, for a total of five additional payments. Something Old, Something New Bridal Boutique will require a 50 percent down payment on all bridesmaids, flower girl dresses, mother-of-the-bride dresses and suits, and formal attire and a 25 percent monthly payment thereafter, for a total of two additional payments. Tuxedo rentals will require a $25 down payment, with the balance to be paid at the time of pickup.

When the manager observes that a customer has not made a payment in a particular month, she will notify the customer, in a friendly manner, that a payment is due. If the customer fails to complete the payments, the 50 percent deposit paid by the customer is retained by the store, and the customer relinquishes receipt of the product. Something Old, Something New Bridal Boutique will return any payments made in excess of the 50 percent deposit. The bride or groom has the alternative of completing the payments and taking the merchandise.

Ms. Black will recommend that customers order bridal gowns, bridesmaids' dresses, and flower girl dresses at least six months in advance. Industry experience reveals, that as regards wedding attire, 12 percent of customers order one year in advance, 52 percent of customers order nine months in advance, 30 percent of customers order six months in advance, three percent of customers order three months in advance, and one percent of customers order one month in advance.

Selling Method, Near Term

The sales strategy that will be utilized during the first year of operation will be direct contact with customers. Efforts will be made to encourage customers to enter Something Old, Something New Bridal Boutique so that the trained sales staff can introduce themselves and ascertain the customers' preferences and needs. This personal approach will make it easier for these customers to depend on Something Old, Something New Bridal Boutique for their wedding products and services needs and for future occasions requiring formal attire.

The five months experiencing heaviest sales during the year are March through July, for proms and weddings. The marketing emphasis for the slower sales periods will be to hold fashion shows. Other methods will include scheduling speaking engagements at local clubs and purchasing advertisements in the local newspapers and on radio to advertise, among other things, the monthly specials that can be purchased at Something Old, Something New Bridal Boutique. In addition to these methods, see the various strategies detailed in the above paragraphs of this section. Many initial efforts will be low-cost, but labor intensive.

Selling Method, Long-Term

Over a period of time, the advertising methods mentioned above will be ingrained into the everyday operations of Something Old, Something New Bridal Boutique. Eventually, these methods will be expanded into sponsorship of sorority functions at Clarion University of Pennsylvania and civic events and into memberships in professional organizations.

Marketing Plan Specifics

Both radio and newspaper advertising are appropriate. The practice of advertising on radio and newspaper will be continued to keep the name of Something Old, Something New Bridal Boutique in the public's mind. Specialty advertisements will be used with discretion, as this increases advertising expense dramatically. Radio advertisements on Magic 96 cost approximately $300 monthly. Something Old, Something New Bridal Boutique will purchase 30, 30-second spots, plus 12 headliners, all of which will air between noon and midnight. For the Grand Opening, Ms. Black will purchase three days of advertisements, which includes 24, 15-second commercials, one every hour of the day, for a total of 72 commercials. Ms. Black will also advertise on C-93 for 30-second spots during her target audience's listening times. Advertising on C-93 will cost $275 for a series of promotional advertisements, 30 seconds in length, run ten times per day during her target audience's listening period for a total of four days. Ms. Black plans to advertise on Magic 96 during the months of October, December, and February. She plans to advertise on C-93 during the months of November, January, and March.

Newspaper advertisements also carry a high cost per inch of space, but have the advantages of being available for reference and the incorporation of graphics to attract attention. The advertising rate for *The Derrick* per column inch is $10.90 regardless of size. Ms. Black plans to advertise the store's monthly specials in *The Derrick*.

Fashion shows should always cause sales to increase, and they should have the added effect of inviting individuals, who may not have entered the shop, into Something Old, Something New Bridal Boutique. The intent is to have new and regular customers of Something Old, Something New Bridal Boutique become acquainted with the business and/or the new line of product offerings.

COMPETITION

The bridal industry is a competitive market. Some department stores, such as JCPenney, carry lines of bridal and formal attire. In the immediate region, however, it would be necessary to order such clothing from a specialized JCPenney Company catalog, as the regional stores are too small to carry this inventory in stock. Formal attire is also sold through mail order warehouses and numerous general fashion retail outlets. There is also direct competition from other bridal shops. Dry cleaners and some men's fashion retail outlets also engage in the rental of tuxedos. Again, there will be direct competition from other bridal shops that offer tuxedo rentals. Floral shops and some bridal shops will compete for the floral trade. Several businesses will compete for the rental of wedding items and for the sale of miscellaneous wedding items. Of course, gifts can be bought in numerous retail outlets or ordered through a multitude of mail order catalogs.

Local Competition

Something Old, Something New Bridal Boutique will compete most closely geographically with Jeanne's Bridal Shop of Route 322, Van. This competitor will compete in many of the product offerings. Jeanne's Bridal Shop specializes in the sale of formal attire, rental of tuxedos, and the sale of accessories. Something Old, Something New Bridal Boutique will sell gifts and favors, the consulting services, decorating and cleanup of the church and reception hall, floral arrangements, rental of formal dresses, custom-made dresses (primarily for flower girls), sale of lingerie, and rental of reception and church items. Jeanne's Bridal Shop offers none of these products and services.

Other bridal shops which are considered to be in the local market are Northrop's Bridal & Tuxedo Shop of Titusville, Bridal Sweet of Punxsutawney, Forever Yours Bridal Boutique of Titusville, and Helen Freed's Bridal of Sharon. All of these shops are located within approximately a one-hour drive of Something Old, Something New Bridal Boutique.

Non-Local Competition

Because of the nature of bridal shops as being specialty retail stores, customers will travel some distance to access their products and services, particularly for the bridal gown. Therefore, bridal shop retailers will probably always be in a secondarily competitive position with non-local shops or shops in more metropolitan areas that are located within a two to two-and-a-half hour drive. Located within this non-local, regional competitive market area are the following establishments: Bridal Elegance of Erie (which advertises in some of the local telephone Yellow Pages), Sharon Syed's of Union City, Bridal Creations of DuBois, Kaufman's Wedding World of Indiana, That Special Touch of Indiana, The Bridal Train of Homer City, Occasionally Yours Bridal Shop of Clearfield, Susan's Bridal & Fashion Shoppe of Clearfield, Bridal Reflections by Karen Zambotti of Kittanning, Town & Country Floral & Bridal of Kittanning, Catalina's Bridal & Dress Shoppe of Osceola Mills, Diamonds & Lace of Boalsburg, Petrino's Bridal Shoppe of State College, Ann Marie's Brides & Formals of Butler, Precious Moments Boutique of Butler, plus a multitude of shops in the Erie and Pittsburgh areas.

In addition, small local bridal shops will always be in competition for some bridal attire and, certainly, for formal attire, including bridesmaids' dresses, flower girl dresses, and mother-of-the-bride attire, with a multitude of local and regional retail stores and the mail order operations of national retailers such as JCPenney Company (as previously mentioned, JCPenney retails bridal gowns, also), Talbots, Laura Ashley, Ann Taylor, Saks Fifth Avenue, Bloomingdale's, etc. The large buying capacity of JCPenney Company will enable this company to sell products at very reasonable prices. The prestige of the other national retailers will impact sales to upper-end customers, regardless of their rural location.

The following tables indicate the "local" competitors in the various product/service offering categories of Something Old, Something New Bridal Boutique.

Table 3. LOCAL COMPETITORS — BRIDAL SHOPS: A COMPARISON OF PRODUCT & SERVICE OFFERINGS

Bridal Shop	Address, Telephone	Products/ Services
Jeanne's Bridal Shop	R. D. 1, Box 39, Cranberry, PA 16319-9605 (814) 676-1337	1, 2, 3, 4, 5, 6, 8
Northrop's Bridal & Tuxedo Shop	R. D. 3, Box 108, Titusville, PA 16354-8921 (814) 827-1369	1, 2, 3, 4, 5, 6, 8
Bridal Sweet	109 E. Mahoning Street, Punxsutawney, PA 15767-2012 (814) 938-5997	1, 2, 3, 4, 5, 6, 8
Forever Yours Bridal Boutique	Enterprise Road, R. D. 2, Titusville, PA 16354 (814) 589-5270	1, 2, 3, 4
Helen Freed's Bridal	169 East State Street Sharon, PA 16146-1734 (412) 981-0200	1, 2, 3, 4, 5, 8

Table Index: Products/Services

    1 = BRIDAL GOWNS
    2 = BRIDESMAIDS' DRESSES
    3 = FLOWER GIRL DRESSES
    4 = MOTHER-OF-THE-BRIDE DRESSES
    5 = BRIDAL ACCESSORIES SALES
    6 = TUXEDO RENTALS
    7 = FLORAL ARRANGEMENTS & BOUQUETS
    8 = FORMAL ATTIRE
    9 = FORMAL GOWN RENTAL

SAMPLE BUSINESS PLANS
Something Old, Something New Bridal Boutique

Table 4. LOCAL COMPETITORS — BRIDAL SHOPS: ADVANTAGES & DISADVANTAGES

Bridal Shop	Advantages	Disadvantages
Jeanne's Bridal Shop	• Established business • Free alterations on new bridal gowns	• Planning to retire • Nothing behind closet doors is well displayed
Northrop's Bridal & Tuxedo Shop	• Established business 30+ yrs • Very good selection	• Recently changed ownership for first time • Rural location with no access via major roadways
Bridal Sweet	• Good selection • Good range of prices	• Some distance from Clarion area • Rude salesperson
Forever Yours Bridal Boutique	• No response	• Difficult to contact
Helen Freed's Bridal	• Good customer service • Established business: 26 yrs	• Some distance from Clarion area • Do not rent tuxedos

Ms. Black believes that the geographical range for competition for tuxedo rentals is approximately a 45-minute to one-hour drive from her establishment. This would include Oil City, Franklin, Clarion, and Brookville as primary competitor locations. In addition to the bridal shop competitors that offer tuxedo rentals and that are listed on the previous page, her primary competitors also include Town & Country Cleaners, Wear Else, Crooks Clothing, Ray L Way Menswear, and Faller's Flowers of Distinction.

Table 5. LOCAL COMPETITORS — TUXEDO RENTAL

TUXEDO RENTAL	ADDRESS, TELEPHONE
Town & Country Cleaners	542 Liberty Avenue, Clarion, PA 16214-1057 (814) 226-4781
	278 Main Street, Brookville, PA 15825-1251 (814) 849-3371
Wear Else	Clarion Mall, Clarion, PA 16214 (814) 227-2533
Crooks Clothing	539 Main Street, Clarion, PA 16214-1197 (814) 226-8020
Ray L Way Menswear	216 Seneca Street, Oil City, PA 16301-1383 (814) 677-4019
Faller's Flowers of Distinction	1217 Liberty Street, Franklin, PA 16323-1329 (814) 432-5680

Table 6. LOCAL COMPETITORS — TUXEDO RENTALS: ADVANTAGES & DISADVANTAGES

Tuxedo Rental	Advantages	Disadvantages
Town & Country Cleaners	• Multiple locations • Inexpensive rental	• Crowded aisles • No private fitting rooms
Wear Else	• Good lighting • Neat & organized	• Poor selection • Not the best fit in a mall location
Crooks Clothing	• Main Street location • Established business many years	• Not immediately evident in the store that they do tuxedo rentals
Ray L Way Menswear	• Competitive prices • Friendly customer service	• Carry only one line of tuxedos • Don't advertise much to bring in outlying traffic
Faller's Flowers of Distinction	• Main Street location • Only provider in Franklin	• Just started the service, not widely known they offer it • Not necessarily a good fit with a flower shop

Table 7. LOCAL COMPETITORS — FLORAL PROVIDERS

Floral Shops	Address, Telephone
The Flower Center	Clarion Mall, Clarion, PA 16214 (814) 226-5470
Flowers and Bows	625 Wood Street, Clarion, PA 16214-1543 (814) 226-7171
Geyers Silk Flowers	R. D. # 1, Marienville, PA 16239 (814) 927-8646
Faller's Flowers of Distinction	1217 Liberty Street, Franklin, PA 16323-1330 (814) 432-5680
Phillips Flowers	East Main Street, Clarion, PA 16214 (814) 226-8460
Wilshire's Flowers & Gifts	90 Merle Street, Clarion, PA 16214-1897 (814) 226-7070
Blose's Florist and Greenhouse	426 Broad Street, New Bethlehem, PA 16242-1214 (814) 275-1349
The Flower Shoppe	238 Broad Street, New Bethlehem, PA 16242-1210 (814) 275-3535
Anderson's Greenhouse	612 Grant Street, Franklin, PA 16323-2299 (814) 432-2109
Phillip's Flowers & Gifts and Balloon Express	1237 Liberty Street, Franklin, PA 16323-1327 (814) 432-2317
Country Baskets and Gifts by Sue	502 West 1st Street, Oil City, PA 16301-2918 (814) 676-4588
Country Gardens Giftshop	R. D. # 3, Titusville, PA 16354 (814) 827-9142
Double Bloom Flower Shop	233 Seneca Street, Oil City, PA 16301-1339 (814) 677-2973
Sloan's Florists	552 Colbert Avenue, Oil City, PA 16301-2253 (814) 677-3028
Gustafson Greenhouse & Floral Shop	Horsecreek Road, Cranberry, PA 16319 (814) 676-2453
Knot N' Plant Place	19 South Fifth Avenue, Clarion, PA 16214-1552 (814) 226-4974
Clarion Greenhouses	55 North Fifth Avenue, Clarion, PA 16214-1142 (814) 226-7260
Vickers Florist	412 Main Street, Knox, PA 16232 (814) 797-1076
Gehres Gift & Flower Shop	383 East State Street, Knox, PA 16232-0357 (814) 797-1198

Table 8. LOCAL COMPETITORS — FLORAL PROVIDERS: ADVANTAGES & DISADVANTAGES

Floral Shops	Advantages	Disadvantages
The Flower Center	• Original designs • Free consultations	• No privacy or area to sit • Shop is small & cluttered
Flowers and Bows	• Top Yellow Page box advertisement • Multiple product/service offerings	• Only deliver on $100 orders and above
Geyers Silk Flowers	• Multiple product/service offerings • Very friendly & informative service	• Telephone answers as "Carol's"—a restaurant owned by same party • Services don't fit name
Faller's Flowers of Distinction	• No response	• Hard to contact
Phillips Flowers	• Good selection • Nice arrangements	• No weddings on Mother's Day
Wilshire's Flowers & Gifts	• Very friendly • Small to very large weddings	• Do not advertise free delivery for weddings • Back street location
Blose's Florist and Greenhouse	• Decorate balloons • Friendly service	• Competition on same street • Closed Wednesdays
The Flower Shoppe	• Supply extra services (pin on corsages, etc.) • Will order anything you need	• Competition on same street
Anderson's Greenhouse	• Only small deposit required • Will set up flowers	• Just flowers
Phillips Flowers & Gifts and Balloon Express	• Good main street location • Good selection of items	• Only do one wedding per weekend
Country Baskets and Gifts by Sue	• Good selection • Will deliver	• Large deposit required
Country Gardens Giftshop	• Only small deposit required	• Extra charge for delivery • Very rural location
Double Bloom Flower Shop	• Do pinning and instructions on how to carry the flowers • Allow books out overnight	• Need an appointment • Large deposit required
Sloan's Florists	• Established neighborhood business	• Not very helpful • Limited selection & delivery area • Large deposit required
Gustafson Greenhouse & Floral Shop	• Only small deposit required • Good selection	• Limited delivery area

Table 8. LOCAL COMPETITORS — FLORAL PROVIDERS *(continued)*

Floral Shops	Advantages	Disadvantages
Knot N' Plant Place	• Attractive little shop	• Uninformed personnel • Owner is the business & rumor has it that she is ill
Clarion Greenhouses	• Good selection of flowers • Good range of prices	• Wedding flowers not a regular service • Large deposit required
Vickers Florist	• Only small deposit required • Good selection of items & services	• Need an appointment
Gehres Gift & Flower Shop	• Very kind service • Good range of prices	• Large deposit required • Business is in the home

Advantages Over Competition

The advantages Something Old, Something New Bridal Boutique has over the competition are significant.

Something Old, Something New Bridal Boutique has a good location immediately off Exit 7 of I-80, allowing easy access for most of the region. An additional advantage that Ms. Black's business will enjoy is its parking lot, with additional spaces available at adjacent commercial establishments. In addition, some of the special accommodations Something Old, Something New Bridal Boutique offers are the monthly specials it offers to its customers, such as the free rental of the bridegroom's tuxedo with a bridal party of seven groomsmen, when the order is placed in February; rental of reception and ceremony items; sale of party favors, invitations, flowers; rental of formal attire; and comprehensive bridal consulting services.

Something Old, Something New Bridal Boutique is not an established business with a solid reputation for value and professional integrity within the community, such as Northrop's Bridal & Tuxedo, Helen Freed's Bridal, and Jeanne's Bridal Shop. However, even lacking this firm base of income and reputation, Ms. Black believes that she will gain immediate word-of-mouth market acceptance based on her products, services, and integrity of customer relations, as well as via a sophisticated and creative advertising campaign. This acceptance quickly will serve as a foundation for future growth for Something Old, Something New Bridal Boutique. This growth will be accomplished initially through superior management of resources and costs, insightful advertising, and employee training. Growth in the future will be accomplished through expansion of existing services and the addition of new products and services.

Something Old, Something New Bridal Boutique will excel in the provision of bridal consulting services and in product reliability. The knowledge and the range of bridal industry products available at Something Old, Something New Bridal Boutique will be superior in this area of northwest Pennsylvania. Something Old, Something New Bridal Boutique has an advantage over the national retailers in the areas of location and personal service. Something Old, Something New Bridal Boutique will use layaway, credit card sales, and services to encourage the sale of the high-priced inventory common in bridal salons. The store will also compete by offering the rental of formal attire. Ms. Black, alone among her local competitors, will offer comprehensive bridal consulting services to her customers. See Appendix M for a complete listing of bridal consulting services packages. Something Old, Something New Bridal Boutique will constantly monitor its business environments and initiate product and service innovations to respond to a changing market.

The main focus of the business will be bridal industry retail sales. Since future plans are to expand services within this market to respond to changes in customer tastes and needs, this allows the freedom to make periodic changes without requiring a serious investment of time and finances.

Barriers to Entry

A primary barrier to entry in the bridal store industry is the cost of individual inventory items and the level of inventory that must be maintained to be competitive. The extensive competitive environment of local, regional and national retailers also provides a significant barrier to the individual who is contemplating the establishment of a bridal shop.

Strategic Opportunities

Something Old, Something New Bridal Boutique will greatly benefit from the available information on management systems and marketing strategies. With quality systems of management, primarily by tight control of the inventory system, the computerization of the accounting system, and comprehensive sales training for staff, costs will be controlled, and Something Old, Something New Bridal Boutique then will be able to reinvest a greater net income into expanding on the lines of goods and customer services being offered.

Observing the competition and their respective marketing styles will be made part of the regular business operations, and this information will allow Something Old, Something New Bridal Boutique to create and implement an improved marketing plan.

MANAGEMENT

Something Old, Something New Bridal Boutique, to be located on SR 3007, just off of Exit 7 of I-80, will be owned and operated by Rebecca Black of Marble, Pennsylvania. The prospective owner's resume, financial statements, and individual income tax returns can be found in Appendices C, D, and E, respectively.

Key Employees

The owner will serve as manager. She will be responsible for overseeing all the day-to-day operations of the business.

Rebecca Black will be responsible, as manager/owner, for professional customer service; ordering inventory; planning and overseeing all business promotions of Something Old, Something New Bridal Boutique; training employees, directing employees' work performance, and handling employee problems; completing end of day bookkeeping and balancing the money in cash drawer; maintaining the professional image of the business by keeping work stations neat and inventory in order and by monitoring the appearance of the outside of the premises and of outside signage; writing sales tickets for sales and rentals; maintaining customer files, preparation of monthly customer charge statements, and customer contact to inform the customer concerning ordered merchandise; directing customer fittings, alterations, and garment reconstruction; planning and setting up of sales displays; custom dyeing of shoes; and the constant promotion of sales for the business. She also will help to stock shelves.

One full-time employee will be hired at $6.00 per hour for forty hours a week. This individual will be responsible for professional customer service; assisting in all business promotions of Something Old, Something New Bridal Boutique; in the absence of management, completing end-of-day bookkeeping and balancing money in the cash drawer; maintaining the professional image of the business by keeping work stations neat and inventory in order and by monitoring the appearance of the outside of the premises and of outside signage; writing sales tickets for sales and rentals; customer contact to inform the customer concerning ordered merchandise; completing and properly filing customer files; assisting in customer fittings, alterations, and garment reconstruction; assisting in the setting up of sales displays; and the constant promotion of sales for the business. This person will also help to stock shelves.

A second individual will be hired part-time for 20 hours per week at $4.25 per hour. This person will help in all phases of operations as directed by either Ms. Black.

Rebecca Black has been employed since 1990. She received a high school degree in cosmetology, with certificates in a number of business and communications courses. She then received a diploma in the "Barber Operator Course, Manager/Teacher Course" programs and a certificate in the "Computer Operator Course" at J. H. Thompson Academies of Erie.

From 1991 to 1992, Rebecca Black managed the We Care Hair establishment in Clarion. She directed the activities of 11 employees, conducted personnel interviews and training programs, maintained employee payroll records, supervised customer service, performed market tests of products for pricing and customer acceptance, and maintained compliance with all governmental agencies' regulations.

From 1992 to 1995, Rebecca Black was a stylist/nail technician at Coke's Creative Cutters of Clarion. She was responsible for maintaining customer service for her clients; planning, organizing, and implementing promotional activities; and planning and organizing the shop's participation in the annual local prom show.

Since 1994, Rebecca Black has been employed as a pharmacy secretary by the Clarion Hospital. She is responsible for recording and calculating monthly records for both Clarion Hospital and Clarion Psychiatric Center. These records include statistics for both operations, Clarion Hospital departmental charges, emergency medical service pharmacy charges, Stat-Medivac charges, and quality assurance reports.

In addition to her various job tasks, Ms. Black has upgraded both manual and computer filing systems and redesigned procedures for product returns policies, including designing standard form letters which have been adopted by the pharmacy department. Ms. Black is familiar with the following computer software programs: WordPerfect and Lotus 1-2-3.

Rebecca Black will hire Becky Black, her sister-in-law, as the first full-time employee. Becky Black has six years experience in the bridal industry, having worked for La Memory Lane of Clarion, which has since been sold and is now known as Cloud Nine and which is selling its assets to Rebecca Black. Becky Black has experience in all phases of bridal industry operations.

Additional employees will be added to the business as it grows in order to sustain the level of customer service required by Ms. Black. It is anticipated that Ms. Black will employ additional family members in the future, some of whom will work for minimum wage and some of whom will not charge for their services.

Outside Consultants

Something Old, Something New Bridal Boutique will seek counsel from the individuals and organizations detailed in the table on the following page.

Table 9. OUTSIDE CONSULTANTS

Organization/ Individual	Name	Address	Telephone
Attorney	Maria Battista Kerle	721 White Avenue Knox, PA 16232	814-797-2091
Accountant	Rhoads & Rhoads, CPA	Box 525, Clarion, PA 16214-0025	814-226-4039
Insurance Agent	R. James Smathers Agency	400 Main Street Clarion, PA 16214-1021	814-226-5000
Small Business Development Center	Jeanne Haas	Clarion University of Pennsylvania Room 102 Still Building Clarion, PA 16214-1232	814-226-2060
Lenders	Mellon Bank	Main Street, Box 310 Knox, PA 16232-0310	814-797-1136

DEVELOPMENT

Goals of the Company

The long-term goal for Something Old, Something New Bridal Boutique is to expand its local market share by educating the public about the bridal and formal attire industries through a marketing strategy that targets Clarion, Venango, and Forest Counties. Through promotion of the bridal and formal attire industries as a whole and Something Old, Something New Bridal Boutique in specific, the business will become a market leader in the area for these goods and services. Development of new goods and services and the expansion of existing practices will be dictated by the needs and concerns of Something Old, Something New Bridal Boutique's customers: needs and concerns which will be determined from information provided by one-on-one customer contact.

Ms. Black anticipates constructing a building to house the business within a matter of several years. She also anticipates hiring several additional employees as the business grows.

Strategies for Achieving Goals

In the first year, in addition to the initial costs of establishing the business, the priority for expending funds will be to gain tight control over daily costs. Ms. Black will also refurbish the interior and exterior of the store premises prior to opening. Ms. Black will purchase a Packard Bell computer system and a Canon color printer for the business, which will greatly assist in the recordkeeping and inventory control functions of the business.

With the purchase occurring at the end of the year, which is the beginning of the major annual advertising period and with the planned advertising funds available, Ms. Black should be able to quickly create awareness for Something Old, Something New Bridal Boutique. She will also employ readily available resources to expand sales. A positive image will be projected through methods such as training of all staff in appropriate sales techniques. These methods will assist in the promotion of a positive, caring image, as well as permit staff resources to be used in a productive manner during the normally busy months. The use of monthly percentage-off sales will be employed and a policy of high quality products at fair prices will be promoted.

SOMETHING OLD, SOMETHING NEW BRIDAL BOUTIQUE
Sources and Applications of Funds Statement

SOURCES OF FUNDS:

Commercial Loan	$50,000
Owner Investment	13,000
TOTAL SOURCES	**$63,000**

APPLICATION OF FUNDS:

Inventory	$27,300
Furniture & Fixtures	8,443
Leasehold Improvements	16,713
Alarm System	300
Supplies Inventory	1,000
Rental Inventory	1,000
Gifts Inventory	300
Computer System	3,350
Working Capital	4,594
TOTAL USES	**$63,000**

SOMETHING OLD, SOMETHING NEW BRIDAL BOUTIQUE
Balance Sheet
November 1, 1996, 1997, 1998

ASSETS

Current Assets

Cash	$5,000	6.1	$16,360	17.2	$33,697	28.7
Accounts Receivable	21,928	26.8	24,509	25.7	29,240	24.9
Inventory	27,300	33.4	30,167	31.7	33,334	28.4
Supplies Inventory	1,000	1.2	1,105	1.2	1,287	1.1
Gifts Inventory	300	0.4	332	0.3	386	0.3
Total Current Assets	**$55,528**	**67.9**	**$72,471**	**76.1**	**$97,944**	**83.5**

Fixed Assets

Furniture & Fixtures	$8,443	10.3	$8,443	8.9	$8,443	7.2
Leasehold Improvements	16,713	20.4	16,713	17.6	16,713	14.2
Alarm System	300	0.4	300	0.3	300	0.3
Rental Inventory	1,000	1.2	1,105	1.2	1,287	1.1
Computer System	3,350	4.1	3,350	3.5	3,350	2.9
Less: Accumulated Depreciation	(3,579)	(4.4)	(7,158)	(7.5)	(10,737)	(9.2)
Total Fixed Assets	**$26,227**	**32.1**	**$22,753**	**23.9**	**$19,356**	**16.5**

TOTAL ASSETS	**$81,755**	**100.0**	**$95,224**	**100.0**	**$117,301**	**100.0**

LIABILITIES AND OWNER'S EQUITY

Current Liabilities

Accounts Payable	$11,670	14.3	$13,094	13.8	16,174	13.8
Line of Credit	921	1.1	0	0.0	0	0.0
Current Portion of Debt	9,043	11.1	9,916	10.4	10,873	9.3
Total Current Liabilities	**$21,634**	**26.5**	**$23,009**	**24.2**	**$27,046**	**23.1**

Long–Term Liabilities

Long–Term Portion of Debt	$32,710	40.0	$22,795	23.9	$11,922	10.2
Total Long–Term Liabilities	**$32,710**	**40.0**	**$22,795**	**23.9**	**$11,922**	**10.2**

TOTAL LIABILITIES	**$54,344**	**66.5**	**$45,804**	**48.1**	**$38,969**	**33.2**

OWNER'S EQUITY

Beginning Capital	$13,000	15.9	$27,411	28.8	$49,420	42.1
Net Income	20,411	25.0	29,209	30.7	41,511	35.4
Owner Withdrawals	(6,000)	(7.3)	(7,200)	(7.6)	(12,600)	(10.7)
TOTAL OWNER'S EQUITY	**$27,411**	**33.5**	**$49,420**	**51.9**	**$78,332**	**66.8**

TOTAL LIABILITIES & OWNER'S EQUITY	**$81,755**	**100.0**	**$95,224**	**100.0**	**$117,301**	**100.0**

See Summary of Forecast Assumptions

SOMETHING OLD, SOMETHING NEW BRIDAL BOUTIQUE

Projected Income Statement
For the Three Years Ending October 31, 1996, 1997, & 1998

	YEAR 1	%	YEAR 2	%	YEAR 3	%
SALES						
Wedding Gowns	$39,200	27.3	$45,570	27.4	$54,794	27.4
Other Dresses	61,200	42.7	71,064	42.8	85,532	42.8
Accessories	4,200	2.9	4,851	2.9	5,858	2.9
Services	5,602	3.9	6,470	3.9	7,813	3.9
Rentals	2,750	1.9	3,596	2.2	4,432	2.2
Invitations	2,160	1.5	2,495	1.5	3,012	1.5
Gifts/Favors	1,600	1.1	1,848	1.1	2,231	1.1
Tuxedos	26,700	18.6	31,059	18.7	37,375	18.7
Less: Sales Returns & Allowances	32	(0.0)	911	(0.5)	1,096	(0.5)
NET SALES	**$143,380**	**100.0**	**$166,042**	**100.0**	**$199,952**	**100.0**
COST OF GOODS SOLD						
Wedding Gowns	$19,600	13.7	$22,785	13.7	$27,397	13.7
Other Dresses	30,600	21.3	35,532	21.4	42,766	21.4
Accessories	2,801	2.0	3,235	1.9	3,906	2.0
Rentals	0	0.0	270	0.2	330	0.2
Invitations	1,440	1.0	1,664	1.0	2,009	1.0
Gifts/Favors	1,292	0.9	1,492	0.9	1,802	0.9
Tuxedos	22,400	15.6	26,040	15.7	31,311	15.7
TOTAL COST OF SALES	**$78,133**	**54.5**	**$91,017**	**54.8**	**$109,520**	**54.8**
GROSS MARGIN	**$65,247**	**45.5**	**$75,025**	**45.2**	**$90,432**	**45.2**
OPERATING EXPENSES						
Wages	$16,900	11.8	$18,369	11.1	$20,206	10.1
Payroll Taxes	2,028	1.4	2,204	1.3	2,425	1.2
Insurance	1,666	1.2	1,709	1.0	1,805	0.9
Telephone	960	0.7	1,109	0.7	1,339	0.7
Rent	2,400	1.7	2,400	1.4	2,400	1.2
Utilities	960	0.7	1,008	0.6	1,058	0.5
Outside Services	2,880	2.0	2,880	1.7	2,880	1.4
Supplies	560	0.4	647	0.4	781	0.4
Accounting/Legal	150	0.1	110	0.1	121	0.1
Advertising/Promotion	6,325	4.4	6,150	3.7	7,427	3.7
Car/Delivery/Travel	480	0.3	954	0.6	1,089	0.5
Donations	180	0.1	189	0.1	198	0.1
Security System Maintenance	240	0.2	264	0.2	290	0.1
Bank Charges	322	0.2	500	0.3	541	0.3
Miscellaneous	120	0.1	139	0.1	167	0.1
Interest	5,086	3.5	3,604	2.2	2,612	1.3
Depreciation	3,579	2.5	3,579	2.2	3,579	1.8
TOTAL OPERATING EXPENSES	**$44,836**	**31.3**	**$45,815**	**27.6**	**$48,920**	**24.5**
NET INCOME	**$20,411**	**14.2**	**$29,209**	**17.6**	**$41,511**	**20.8**

See Summary of Forecast Assumptions

SOMETHING OLD, SOMETHING NEW BRIDAL BOUTIQUE
Projected Cash Flow Statement
For the Three Years Ending October 31, 1996, 1997, & 1998

	YEAR 1	YEAR 2	YEAR 3
CASH INFLOWS			
Wedding Gowns	$33,110	$44,678	$52,747
Other Dresses	56,115	70,479	84,207
Accessories	3,835	4,794	5,770
Services	5,152	6,401	7,705
Rentals	2,300	3,458	4,296
Invitations	1,901	2,455	2,950
Gifts/Favors	1,431	1,754	2,259
Tuxedos	17,640	29,480	35,332
Less: Sales Returns & Allowances	32	37	45
TOTAL INFLOWS	**$121,452**	**$163,461**	**$195,221**
CASH OUTFLOWS			
Purchases: Gowns & Dresses	$45,130	$58,064	$69,015
Purchases: Tuxedos	15,800	24,870	29,379
Purchases: Other	5,533	6,660	8,046
Wages	16,900	18,369	20,206
Payroll Taxes	2,028	2,204	2,425
Insurance	1,666	1,709	1,805
Telephone	960	1,109	1,339
Rent	2,400	2,400	2,400
Utilities	960	1,008	1,058
Outside Services	2,880	2,880	2,880
Supplies	560	647	781
Accounting/Legal	150	110	121
Advertising/Promotion	6,325	6,150	7,427
Car/Delivery/Travel	480	954	1,089
Donations	180	189	198
Security System Maintenance	240	264	290
Bank Charges	322	500	541
Miscellaneous	120	139	167
Loan Payment	13,333	12,647	12,528
TOTAL CASH OUTFLOWS	**$115,967**	**$140,873**	**$161,697**
NET CASH FLOW	**$5,485**	**$22,588**	**$33,524**
BEGINNING CASH BALANCE	**$0**	**4,079**	**16,360**
OPERATING ACTIVITIES			
Net Cash Flow	$5,485	$22,588	$33,524
FINANCING ACTIVITIES			
Loan Proceeds	$50,000	$0	$0
Owner Investment	13,000	0	0
Owner Withdrawals	(6,000)	(7,200)	(12,600)
INVESTING ACTIVITIES			
Furniture & Fixtures	($8,443)	$0	$0
Inventory	(27,300)	(2,867)	(3,167)
Leasehold Improvements	(16,713)	0	0
Alarm System	(300)	0	0
Supplies Inventory	(1,000)	(105)	(182)
Rental Inventory	(1,000)	(105)	(182)
Gifts Inventory	(300)	(32)	(55)
Computer System	(3,350)	0	0
ENDING CASH BALANCE	**$4,079**	**$16,360**	**$33,697**
LINE OF CREDIT			
Borrowed on Line of Credit	$17,161	$6,774	$0
Paid on Line of Credit	16,240	7,694	0
ENDING CASH BALANCE	**$5,000**	**$16,360**	**$33,697**

See Summary of Forecast Assumptions

Summary of Forecast Assumptions/Projected Balance Sheet

These financial forecasts present, to the best of management's knowledge and belief, the company's expected financial position, results of operations, and cash-flow position for the forecast periods. Accordingly, the forecasts reflect management's judgment of the expected conditions and its expected course of action. The assumptions disclosed herein are those that management believes to be significant to the forecasts. There usually will be differences between the forecasted and the actual results because events and circumstances frequently do not occur as expected, and those differences may be material.

The projected statements assume that Something Old, Something New Bridal Boutique will begin operations on November 1, 1995. The fiscal year, for purposes of the projected financial statements, will extend from November 1 to October 31.

ASSETS

Current Assets

Cash

Cash amounts are derived from the ending cash balances of the projected cash-flow statements. It is assumed, but not reflected within these statements, that accumulated cash will be invested in interest-bearing accounts or will be reinvested in the business.

Accounts Receivable

Accounts receivable reflects the differences between revenue and cash inflow. Management predicts the following cash lag for the revenue categories of Something Old, Something New Bridal Boutique:

Wedding Gowns: One-half of the total price is required as a deposit at ordering. Subsequent payments will be ten percent of the total price each month for the following five months.

Other Dresses: One-half of the total price is required as a deposit at ordering. Subsequent payments will be 25 percent of the total price each month for the following two months.

Accessories: Shoes, veils, jewelry, and flowers: One-half of the total price is required as a deposit at ordering. Subsequent payments will be 25 percent of the total price each month for the following two months.

Services: Alterations require full cash at time of delivery. Decorating requires one-half of the total price as a deposit at time of contract issuance. Subsequent payments will be ten percent of the total price each month for the following five months. Bridal Consulting requires 25 percent of total price as a deposit at time of contract issuance. Subsequent payments will be 15 percent of the total price each month for the following five months.

Rentals: Wedding and Reception Equipment requires one-half of the total price as a deposit at time of contract issuance. Subsequent payments will be ten percent of the total price each month for the following five months. Gown Rental, which begins in year two, is on a cash-only basis.

Invitations: One-half of the total price is required as a deposit at ordering. Subsequent payments will be ten percent of the total price each month for the following five months.

Gifts/Favors: One-half of the total price is required as a deposit at ordering. Subsequent payments will be 25 percent of the total price each month for the following two months.

Inventory

Based on the owner's initial purchase of $27,300 in inventory from Cloud Nine of Clarion, broken down into the following inventory lines and amounts: Wedding Gowns ($11,041); Bridesmaids' Dresses ($3,767); Prom/Party Attire ($2,898); Flower Girl Dresses ($537); Mother-of-the-Bride Dresses/Suits

($2,154); Veils ($1,984); Shoes ($1,388); Jewelry ($1,821); Underwear ($954); Purses ($191); Gloves ($417); and Miscellaneous ($148).

Supplies Inventory
Includes owner's initial purchase of $808 in supplies from Cloud Nine of Clarion. This category also includes favors inventory ($100) and invitation ordering books ($75), plus a minor extra amount.

Gifts Inventory
Initial purchases of gifts inventory is $300. Additional purchases to support sales increases of ten percent in year two and 15 percent in year are also recognized. There is a five percent inflationary factor for each of years two and three.

Fixed Assets
Fixed assets are stated at cost and include Furniture & Fixtures — $7,443 in equipment purchased from Cloud Nine of Clarion and $1,000 for new furniture; Leasehold Improvements — $16,713; Alarm System — $300; Rental Inventory — $140 from Cloud Nine of Clarion, plus an additional $860 for other items; and a Computer System — $3,350. Depreciation includes the annual Furniture & Fixtures depreciation that is calculated on a straight-line basis with a useful life of ten years, resulting in an annual depreciation of $844. The Leasehold Improvements of $16,713 will be depreciated over a period of ten years at $1,671 per year. The Alarm System will be depreciated over a period of five years at an annual depreciation of $60. The Computer System depreciation, that is calculated on a straight-line basis with a useful life of five years, results in an annual depreciation of $670. The Rental Inventory of $1,000, that will be depreciated over a period of three years, results in an annual depreciation of $333. Total annual depreciation expense will be $3,579.

LIABILITIES AND OWNER'S EQUITY

Current Liabilities

Accounts Payable
Accounts Payable reflects the differences between Cost of Goods and moneys that actually are an outflow in payment. The following terms will be utilized for each of the Cost of Goods expense categories:

Purchases: Gowns & Dresses: Starting in month seven of year one, Something Old, Something New Bridal Boutique will be extended terms of 30 days by its wedding gown vendors. There is no payment reflected for month seven. Cost of goods is 50 percent of selling price.

Purchases: Tuxedos: $25 is due at time of ordering. Six months later at pick-up, the other $25 will be due.

Purchases: Others: All other cost of goods categories are paid for at time of expensing. Hence, there is no Accounts Payable for any of the other categories of revenue.

Line of Credit
Something Old, Something New Bridal Boutique will also negotiate a line of credit to assist in the payment of inventory bills. There is a current balance at year-end reflected in the balance sheet in year one only. The amount is $921. The line of credit is calculated at 10 percent per annum. Borrowings and payments against the line of credit in 1996, 1997, and 1998 will be $17,161; $6,774; and $0, respectively, for borrowings and $16,240; $7,694; and $0, respectively, for the payments. A line of credit will only be used if circumstances require.

Current Portion of Long-Term Debt
The current portion of long-term debt includes all principal payments due within the next fiscal year. The loan will be a principal of $50,000 for five years, with an interest rate of 9.3 percent. Monthly loan payments will be $1,044.

Long-Term Liabilities

The long-term portion of the loans payable consists of principal payments due in subsequent years. The terms of the new loan are assumed, for the purposes of these projected financial statements, to be as follows: A commercial loan of $50,000 with an assumed interest rate of 9.3 percent for a term of five years and monthly loan payments of $1,044, including interest and principal.

OWNER'S EQUITY

Beginning Capital

Beginning capital at November 1, 1995 of $13,000 will be contributed by Rebecca Black.

Net Income

Net income for the year. See the Three-Year Projected Income Statement on page 29.

Owner Withdrawals

Amounts Ms. Black removes from the business for personal use. She will withdraw $6,000; $7,200; and $12,600 in 1996, 1997, and 1998, respectively.

Summary of Forecast Assumptions
Projected Income Statements
for the Three Years Ending October 31, 1998

All income statement projections were based on calculations made by Rebecca Black. These projections were based on historical sales for another bridal business, with consideration being given to policies and procedures that will be instituted by Ms. Black. For the purposes of these financial statements the fiscal year will begin on November 1 and end on October 31.

SALES

Total Sales

Sales figures in the first three years of operations are based on historical figures of the currently existing business, Cloud Nine of Clarion. Ms. Black will be purchasing the assets of Cloud Nine. In the first three years of operations, November 1, 1995 through October 31, 1998, total sales are based on the following assumptions: Discrete individual sales figures were developed for each revenue category and for each component within each revenue category for year one. There was a flat ten percent increase in sales revenue for year two and a flat 15 percent increase in sales revenue for year three. A five percent inflationary factor is included for each of years two and three.

The following are the individual revenue categories and their respective components.

Wedding gowns: Only the wedding gowns. Average sales revenue per wedding gown is $700.

Other dresses: Bridesmaids' dresses, mother-of-the-bride dresses and suits, flower girl dresses, and prom/party attire. Average sales revenue for dresses in this category is $180.

Accessories: Shoes, flowers, veils, and jewelry. Average sales revenue for items in this category are: Shoes ($30), flowers ($300), veils ($80), and jewelry ($20).

Services: Decorating services, clothes altering services, and bridal consulting services. Decorating services will average sales revenue of $250 per event. Approximately three items per wedding will be altered at a charge of $14 per item. Bridal consulting services will average sales revenue of $1,000 per wedding.

Rentals: Year one — wedding and reception decorations and equipment. Year two and forward — wedding and reception decorations and equipment, and prom/party attire. Wedding and reception decorations and equipment rentals will average $250 per event. Average rental per prom/party dress will be $60 per event. In addition, four out of five prom/party dress rentals will include a $30 cleaning fee, which is the entire cost to Something Old, Something New Bridal Boutique to have the rental item dry cleaned. Hence, there is no margin made on the dry cleaning of the rental dresses.

Invitations: Invitations will sell at $1.08 per person, with an average wedding list of 200 guests. This makes total sales revenue per wedding for invitations an average of $216.

Gifts /Favors: Gifts for various members of the wedding party and favors for the reception. Gifts will average $25 per item. Favors are calculated at 90 cents per favor, with 150 guests per wedding. This makes total sales revenue per wedding for favors an average of $135.

Tuxedos: Only the tuxedos. Average rental is $60 per tuxedo. The three major revenue categories are: wedding gowns at 27.4 percent of total sales revenues; other dresses at 42.8 percent of total sales revenues; and tuxedos at 18.6 percent of total sales revenues. These three categories combine for a total of 88.8 percent of total revenues.

Sales Returns & Allowances

Sales returns & allowances is based on management assumptions provided by Ms. Black. An average percentage of two percent per year has been employed for purposes of these financial projections. This represents merchandise returned to the store following purchase and relates only to sales in the gifts/favors revenue category. All other sales are contractual arrangements, not subject to return of deposits, etc. Industry history demonstrates that non-fulfillment of contracts is negligible and, therefore, no consideration of this is given in the projections.

Net Sales

Net sales equals the difference between total sales and sales returns & allowances.

Cost of Goods Sold

Represents the cost basis of inventory sold to realize net sales. Cost of goods sold for the various revenue categories is as follows:

Wedding gowns: Average cost of goods per wedding gown is $350.

Other dresses: Average cost of goods for dresses in this category is $90.

Accessories: Average cost of goods for items in this category are: Shoes ($20), flowers ($200), veils ($53), and jewelry ($13).

Rentals: The average cost of goods per prom/party attire will be $30 per event. Management believes that each rental dress will be worn a total of three times. That would allow its original average cost of $90 to be recovered in three wearings, at $30 per wearing. There is no prom/party dress rental until year two. Four out of five dresses rented will purchase dry cleaning services from Something Old, Something New Bridal Boutique. The cost to the store is $30 and that is what is charged to the customer. No margin is made on the dry cleaning of the rental dresses. There is no cost of goods sold expense for wedding & reception equipment, as this category is depreciated over three years.

Invitations: Invitations will cost $0.72 per guest, for an average total cost of $144 per wedding.

Gifts /Favors: Gifts will have a 50 percent markup and will cost an average of $16.67 each. Favors will cost $0.75 cents per favor for a total cost of $112.50 for an average wedding of 150 guests.

Tuxedos: Average rental cost to Something Old, Something New Bridal Boutique is $50 per tuxedo.

GROSS MARGIN

Gross margin represents that portion of net sales that remains after cost of goods sold has been deducted. Gross margin is used to pay operating expenses.

OPERATING EXPENSES

Operating expenses are based on management experience and expectations and are provided by Rebecca Black.

Wages

	Hrs/Week	Rate/Hr	1995
CLERK (FULL-TIME)	40	HOURLY	$6.00 PER HOUR
CLERK (PART-TIME)	20	HOURLY	$4.25 PER HOUR

Due to the seasonal nature of the business, overtime will be used as needed. A 10 percent wage increase will be given in each of years two and three to the full-time clerk, and a five percent wage increase will be given in year two and a 10 percent increase will be given in year three to the part-time clerk.

Payroll Taxes

Assumed to be 12 percent of wages. Includes employer's share of social security and Medicare contributions and state and federal unemployment tax.

Insurance

Based on a rate quote provided by R. James Smathers Agency, 400 Main Street, Clarion, Pennsylvania. The premium of $1,666 per year is based on a quote for all insurable aspects of the business and includes Worker's Compensation. Worker's Compensation is based on a payroll of $16,900, and the insurance rate is $2.92 per $100 insurance, for a total of $493 for year one. The annual premium was divided evenly among the 12 months for purposes of the projected income statement. For purposes of the cash-flow statement, the insurance premiums are paid on a quarterly basis. As the first years premium is guaranteed for three years, there is no increase in insurance rates for years two and three, aside from a small increase in Worker's Compensation for the increasing payrolls in years two and three.

Telephone

This projection is based on management experience and expectation. A 10 percent activity increase factor for year two and a 15 percent activity increase factor for year three have been built into the projections. A five percent inflationary factor has been recognized in both years two and three.

Rent

Rent is calculated at a total of $400 per month. However, because of the extensive renovations being done to the property by Ms. Black, a special arrangement has been concluded with the owners. Something Old, Something New Bridal Boutique will pay only $200 per month until the entire leasehold improvement cost of $16,713 has been recovered. This will constitute a seven year period of time. This rental fee will be paid to Robert L. and Vivian L. Russell of Okeechobee, Florida. Rent will remain flat at $200 per month throughout the projection period.

Utilities

This projection is based on management experience and expectation. The expense includes $80 per month for electric and gas. Water and sewage are provided by the lessor. A five percent inflationary factor has been recognized in both years two and three.

Outside Services

This expense is based on payment to a family member to keep the premises neat and clean. A flat rate of $240 per month will be paid throughout the three year projection period.

Supplies

This expense category includes payments for office supplies, marking labels, shopping bags, boxes, shoe dyes, in-store signs, cleaning equipment, and many miscellaneous items. It also includes the expense of wrapping paper and miscellaneous visual merchandising expense for window displays. This projection is based on management experience and expectation. A 10 percent activity increase factor is included for year two and a 15 percent activity increase factor is included for year three. A five percent inflationary factor has been recognized in both years two and three.

Accounting/Legal
This projection is based upon a quote provided by Rhoads & Rhoads, Box 525, Clarion, PA, for annual business income tax returns. The charge is $100 for this service. In year one only, there will be a $50 charge for review of Ms. Black's leasing contracts. Legal services will be provided by Maria Battista-Kerle, 721 White Street, Knox, PA. A ten percent inflationary factor has been recognized in both years two and three for the accounting service.

Advertising/Promotion
This projection is based on management experience and expectation. It includes advertising moneys to be spent on radio, newspapers, and special events such as fashion shows and the Grand Opening. A ten percent activity increase factor has been included for year two and a 15 percent activity increase factor has been included for year three. A five percent inflationary factor has been recognized in both years two and three.

Car/Delivery/Travel
This expense category includes the financing of one buying trip per year. A ten percent activity increase factor has been included for year two and a 15 percent activity increase factor has been included for year three. A five percent inflationary factor has been recognized in both years two and three. In addition, in year two a $400 amount has been included for a trip to the bridal industry trade show in Chicago. It is held in September each year. The amount was increased to $420 for year three.

Donations
This projection is based on management expectation. It includes donations to local civic organizations for public relations purposes. A five percent inflationary factor has been recognized in both years two and three.

Security System Maintenance
This projection is based on a contractual arrangement with Security Systems of Pennsylvania, 601 Grant Street, Franklin, Pennsylvania. A 10 percent inflationary factor has been recognized in both years two and three.

Bank Charges
This represents a $25 per month checking account charge beginning in month seven and discounts of three percent on the four percent of sales revenue that is realized through utilization of credit cards.

Miscellaneous
This expense category includes a small monthly amount to purchase miscellaneous items not recognized elsewhere in the projections. A 10 percent activity increase factor has been included for year two and a 15 percent activity increase factor has been included for year three. A five percent inflationary factor has been recognized in both years two and three.

Interest
See details on interest expense under "Long-Term Liabilities" in the Summary for Forecast Assumptions for the Projected Balance Sheet on page 28. Interest also includes payments against a line of credit for each of the three projected years. At ten percent per annum, the amounts borrowed in 1996, 1997, and 1998 will be $17,161; $6,774; and $0, respectively. Interest payments on the line of credit in 1996, 1997, and 1998 will be $805; $119; and $0, respectively.

Depreciation
See details on depreciation expense under "Fixed Assets" in the Summary for Forecast Assumptions for the Projected Balance Sheet on page 30.

Summary of Forecast Assumptions
Projected Cash-Flow Statements
for the Three Years Ending October 31, 1998

Cash Inflows

The projected Cash Flow Statements are divided into two sections. In the top portion, the net cash inflows (outflows) for the period are computed. The bottom portion of the Projected Cash Flow Statements shows the calculation of the period-end cash balance.

Cash Outflows

Figures in this part of the statement are taken directly from the corresponding Projected Net Income Statements except as follows:

Depreciation

Depreciation does not appear on the cash-flow statements, since depreciation does not involve the disbursement of cash.

Loan Payment

While the income statements show only interest expense, the cash-flow statements show interest and principal for the outstanding loan and loan proceeds.

Owner Withdrawals

Amounts withdrawn from the business for the personal use of the owner do not constitute an expense and will not appear on the income statements. Ms. Black will withdraw $500 per month in the first year, $600 per month in the second year, and $1,000 per month in the third year of the business. The withdrawal will increase in year three in the tenth month, to $1,200.

SOMETHING OLD, SOMETHING NEW BRIDAL BOUTIQUE

Projected Quarterly Income Statement
For the Year Ending October 31, 1997

	1ST QTR	2ND QTR	3RD QTR	4TH QTR	TOTAL
SALES					
Wedding Gowns	$9,555	$8,820	$16,170	$11,025	$45,570
Other Dresses	14,553	16,821	21,357	18,333	71,064
Accessories	1,005	693	1,871	1,282	4,851
Services	1,160	1,111	3,520	679	6,470
Rentals	289	818	1,444	1,046	3,596
Invitations	249	748	998	499	2,495
Gifts/Favors	185	185	924	554	1,848
Tuxedos	6,552	5,859	11,088	7,560	31,059
Less: Sales Returns & Allowances	4	4	18	11	911
NET SALES	$33,544	$35,051	$57,354	$40,968	$166,042
COST OF GOODS SOLD					
Wedding Gowns	$4,778	$4,410	$8,085	$5,513	$22,785
Other Dresses	7,277	8,411	10,679	9,167	35,532
Accessories	670	462	1,248	855	3,235
Rentals	0	150	0	120	270
Invitations	166	499	665	333	1,664
Gifts/Favors	149	149	746	448	1,492
Tuxedos	5,460	5,040	9,240	6,300	26,040
TOTAL COST OF SALES	$18,500	$19,121	$30,663	$22,734	$91,017
GROSS MARGIN	$15,044	$15,930	$26,691	$18,233	$75,025
OPERATING EXPENSES					
Wages	$4,592	$4,592	$4,592	$4,592	$18,369
Payroll Taxes	551	551	551	551	2,204
Insurance	427	427	427	427	1,709
Telephone	277	277	277	277	1,109
Rent	600	600	600	600	2,400
Utilities	252	252	252	252	1,008
Outside Services	720	720	720	720	2,880
Supplies	162	162	162	162	647
Accounting/Legal	28	28	28	28	110
Advertising/Promotion	1,538	1,538	1,538	1,538	6,150
Car/Delivery/Travel	239	239	239	239	954
Donations	47	47	47	47	189
Security System Maintenance	66	66	66	66	264
Bank Charges	115	117	144	124	500
Miscellaneous	35	35	35	35	139
Interest	978	962	871	793	3,604
Depreciation	895	895	895	895	3,579
TOTAL OPERATING EXPENSES	$11,521	$11,507	$11,443	$11,345	$45,815
NET INCOME	$3,523	$4,423	$15,248	$6,889	$29,209

See Summary of Forecast Assumptions

SOMETHING OLD, SOMETHING NEW BRIDAL BOUTIQUE

Projected Cash Flow Statement
For the Year Ending October 31, 1997

	1ST QTR	2ND QTR	3RD QTR	4TH QTR	TOTAL
CASH INFLOWS					
Wedding Gowns	$10,490	$9,198	$12,716	$12,275	$44,678
Other Dresses	16,047	14,742	19,656	20,034	70,479
Accessories	1,058	684	1,429	1,623	4,794
Services	1,379	1,024	2,106	1,892	6,401
Rentals	571	565	1,177	1,144	3,458
Invitations	412	546	798	699	2,455
Gifts/Favors	247	146	690	671	1,754
Tuxedos	6,712	7,599	8,329	6,840	29,480
Less: Sales Returns & Allowances	4	4	18	11	37
TOTAL INFLOWS	**$36,912**	**$34,501**	**$46,882**	**$45,166**	**$163,461**
CASH OUTFLOWS					
Purchases: Gowns & Dresses	$13,764	$9,629	$16,076	$18,596	$58,064
Purchases: Tuxedos	6,530	5,320	7,350	5,670	24,870
Purchases: Other	986	1,260	2,659	1,755	6,660
Wages	4,592	4,592	4,592	4,592	18,369
Payroll Taxes	551	551	551	551	2,204
Insurance	427	427	427	427	1,709
Telephone	277	277	277	277	1,109
Rent	600	600	600	600	2,400
Utilities	252	252	252	252	1,008
Outside Services	720	720	720	720	2,880
Supplies	162	162	162	162	647
Accounting/Legal	0	110	0	0	110
Advertising/Promotion	2,252	924	1,675	1,299	6,150
Car/Delivery/Travel	139	139	139	539	954
Donations	47	47	47	47	189
Security System Maintenance	264	0	0	0	264
Bank Charges	115	117	144	124	500
Miscellaneous	35	35	35	35	139
Loan Payment	3,161	3,196	3,157	3,132	12,647
TOTAL CASH OUTFLOWS	**$34,874**	**$28,358**	**$38,863**	**$38,778**	**$140,873**
NET CASH FLOW	**$2,038**	**$6,143**	**$8,020**	**$6,388**	**$22,588**
BEGINNING CASH BALANCE	$5,000	$5,000	$5,552	$11,772	
OPERATING ACTIVITIES					
Net Cash Flow	$2,038	$6,143	$8,020	$6,388	
FINANCING ACTIVITIES					
Owner Withdrawals	($1,800)	($1,800)	($1,800)	($1,800)	
INVESTING ACTIVITIES					
Inventory	($2,867)	$0	$0	$0	
Supplies Inventory	(105)	0	0	0	
Rental Inventory	(105)	0	0	0	
Gifts Inventory	(32)	0	0	0	
ENDING CASH BALANCE	**$2,115**	**$9,343**	**$11,772**	**$16,360**	
LINE OF CREDIT					
Borrowed on Line of Credit	$3,611	$106	$3,057	$0	
Paid on Line of Credit	741	3,897	3,057	0	
ENDING CASH BALANCE	**$5,000**	**$5,552**	**$11,772**	**$16,360**	

See Summary of Forecast Assumption

Something Old, Something New Bridal Boutique

SOMETHING OLD, SOMETHING NEW BRIDAL BOUTIQUE
Projected Monthly Income Statement
For the Year Ending October 31, 1996

	NOV	DEC	JAN	FEB	MAR	APR	MAY	JUN	JUL	AUG	SEP	OCT	TOTAL
SALES													
Wedding Gowns	$2,100	$3,500	$2,800	$2,100	$2,100	$3,500	$1,400	$4,900	$7,000	$1,400	$4,200	$4,200	$39,200
Other Dresses	3,600	5,400	3,600	2,700	4,860	7,200	2,160	6,480	9,000	1,800	8,460	5,940	61,200
Accessories	30	600	240	30	30	540	30	540	1,050	110	540	460	4,200
Services	376	210	418	126	376	460	334	1,294	1,420	84	252	252	5,602
Rentals	0	250	0	250	0	250	250	500	500	250	250	250	2,750
Invitations	216	0	0	216	216	216	216	216	432	216	216	0	2,160
Gifts/Favors	0	160	0	0	0	160	0	320	480	0	160	320	1,600
Tuxedos	1,440	2,400	1,920	1,260	1,440	2,400	960	3,360	4,800	960	2,880	2,880	26,700
Less: Sales Returns & Allowances	0	3	0	0	0	3	0	6	10	0	3	6	32
NET SALES	$7,762	$12,517	$8,978	$6,682	$9,022	$14,723	$5,350	$17,604	$24,672	$4,820	$16,955	$14,296	$143,380
COST OF GOODS SOLD													
Wedding Gowns	$1,050	$1,750	$1,400	$1,050	$1,050	$1,750	$700	$2,450	$3,500	$700	$2,100	$2,100	$19,600
Other Dresses	1,800	2,700	1,800	1,350	2,430	3,600	1,080	3,240	4,500	900	4,230	2,970	30,600
Accessories	20	400	160	20	20	360	20	360	700	73	360	307	2,801
Invitations	144	0	0	144	144	144	144	144	288	144	144	0	1,440
Gifts/Favors	0	129	0	0	0	129	0	258	388	0	129	258	1,292
Tuxedos	1,200	2,000	1,600	1,200	1,200	2,000	800	2,800	4,000	800	2,400	2,400	22,400
TOTAL COST OF SALES	$4,214	$6,979	$4,960	$3,764	$4,844	$7,983	$2,744	$9,252	$13,376	$2,617	$9,363	$8,035	$78,133
GROSS MARGIN	$3,548	$5,538	$4,018	$2,918	$4,178	$6,740	$2,606	$8,351	$11,297	$2,203	$7,592	$6,261	$65,247

SOMETHING OLD, SOMETHING NEW BRIDAL BOUTIQUE
Projected Monthly Income Statement, Continued
For the Year Ending October 31, 1996

	NOV	DEC	JAN	FEB	MAR	APR	MAY	JUN	JUL	AUG	SEP	OCT	TOTAL
OPERATING EXPENSES													
Wages	$1,408	$1,408	$1,408	$1,408	$1,408	$1,408	$1,408	$1,408	$1,408	$1,408	$1,408	$1,408	$16,900
Payroll Taxes	169	169	169	169	169	169	169	169	169	169	169	169	2,028
Insurance	139	139	139	139	139	139	139	139	139	139	139	139	1,666
Telephone	80	80	80	80	80	80	80	80	80	80	80	80	960
Rent	200	200	200	200	200	200	200	200	200	200	200	200	2,400
Utilities	80	80	80	80	80	80	80	80	80	80	80	80	960
Outside Services	240	240	240	240	240	240	240	240	240	240	240	240	2,880
Supplies	20	20	100	20	20	100	20	20	100	20	20	100	560
Accounting/Legal	13	13	13	13	13	13	13	13	13	13	13	13	150
Advertising/Promotion	527	527	527	527	527	527	527	527	527	527	527	527	6,325
Car/Delivery/Travel	40	40	40	40	40	40	40	40	40	40	40	40	480
Donations	15	15	15	15	15	15	15	15	15	15	15	15	180
Security System Maintenance	20	20	20	20	20	20	20	20	20	20	20	20	240
Bank Charges	9	15	11	8	11	18	31	46	55	31	45	42	322
Miscellaneous	10	10	10	10	10	10	10	10	10	10	10	10	120
Interest	385	433	456	460	463	468	468	445	404	372	396	336	5,086
Depreciation	298	298	298	298	298	298	298	298	298	298	298	298	3,579
TOTAL OPERATING EXPENSES	$3,654	$3,707	$3,806	$3,727	$3,733	$3,825	$3,759	$3,750	$3,798	$3,662	$3,700	$3,717	$44,838
NET INCOME	($106)	$1,830	$212	($809)	$445	$2,915	($1,153)	$4,601	$7,499	($1,459)	$3,892	$2,544	$20,411

See Summary of Forecast Assumptions

SOMETHING OLD, SOMETHING NEW BRIDAL BOUTIQUE
Projected Cash Flow Statement
For the Year Ending October 31, 1996

	NOV	DEC	JAN	FEB	MAR	APR	MAY	JUN	JUL	AUG	SEP	OCT	TOTAL
CASH INFLOWS													
Wedding Gowns	$1,050	$1,960	$1,960	$1,890	$2,100	$3,010	$2,100	$3,640	$4,900	$2,590	$3,920	$3,990	$33,110
Other Dresses	1,800	3,600	4,050	3,600	4,005	5,490	4,095	5,580	6,660	4,770	6,930	5,535	56,115
Accessories	15	308	278	225	83	285	158	413	668	453	560	393	3,835
Services	251	235	318	176	301	410	284	644	895	459	602	577	5,152
Rentals	0	125	25	150	50	175	200	325	375	275	300	300	2,300
Invitations	108	22	22	130	151	173	173	194	324	238	238	130	1,901
Gifts/Favors	0	93	34	34	0	93	34	219	345	169	194	219	1,431
Tuxedos	600	1,000	800	600	600	1,000	1,240	2,800	3,120	1,240	2,040	2,600	17,640
Less: Sales Returns & Allowances	0	3	0	0	0	3	0	6	10	0	3	6	32
TOTAL INFLOWS	**$3,824**	**$7,338**	**$7,486**	**$6,804**	**$7,290**	**$10,632**	**$8,283**	**$13,808**	**$17,277**	**$10,193**	**$14,780**	**$13,736**	**$121,452**
CASH OUTFLOWS													
Purchases: Gowns & Dresses	$2,850	$4,450	$3,200	$2,400	$3,480	$5,350	$0	$1,780	$5,690	$8,000	$1,600	$6,330	$45,130
Purchases: Tuxedos	600	1,000	800	600	600	1,000	1,000	2,400	2,800	1,000	1,800	2,200	15,800
Purchases: Other	164	529	160	164	164	633	164	762	1,376	217	633	565	5,533
Wages	1,408	1,408	1,408	1,408	1,408	1,408	1,408	1,408	1,408	1,408	1,408	1,408	16,900
Payroll Taxes	169	169	169	169	169	169	169	169	169	169	169	169	2,028
Insurance	417	0	0	417	0	0	417	0	0	417	0	0	1,666
Telephone	80	80	80	80	80	80	80	80	80	80	80	80	960
Rent	200	200	200	200	200	200	200	200	200	200	200	200	2,400
Utilities	80	80	80	80	80	80	80	80	80	80	80	80	960
Outside Services	240	240	240	240	240	240	240	240	240	240	240	240	2,880
Supplies	20	20	100	20	20	100	20	20	100	20	20	100	560
Accounting/Legal	50	0	0	0	0	100	0	0	0	0	0	0	150
Advertising/Promotion	1,625	825	500	300	300	200	625	625	200	200	300	625	6,325
Car/Delivery/Travel	40	40	40	40	40	40	40	40	40	40	40	40	480
Donations	15	15	15	15	15	15	15	15	15	15	15	15	180
Security System Maintenance	240	0	0	0	0	0	0	0	0	0	0	0	240
Bank Charges	9	15	11	8	11	18	31	46	55	31	45	42	322
Miscellaneous	10	10	10	10	10	10	10	10	10	10	10	10	120
Loan Payment	1,044	1,097	1,125	1,134	1,142	1,152	1,158	1,140	1,104	1,078	1,107	1,052	13,333
TOTAL CASH OUTFLOWS	**$9,261**	**$10,178**	**$8,138**	**$7,285**	**$7,960**	**$10,795**	**$5,657**	**$9,016**	**$13,567**	**$13,204**	**$7,748**	**$13,157**	**$115,967**
NET CASH FLOW	**($5,437)**	**($2,840)**	**($652)**	**($481)**	**($670)**	**($163)**	**$2,626**	**$4,792**	**$3,710**	**($3,012)**	**$7,032**	**$580**	**$5,485**

SOMETHING OLD, SOMETHING NEW BRIDAL BOUTIQUE
Projected Cash Flow Statement, Continued
For the Year Ending October 31, 1996

BEGINNING CASH BALANCE	$0	$5,000	$5,000	$5,000	$5,000	$5,000	$5,000	$5,000	$5,000	$5,000	$5,000	$5,000
OPERATING ACTIVITIES												
Net Cash Flow	($5,437)	($2,840)	($652)	($481)	($670)	($163)	$2,626	$4,792	$3,710	($3,012)	$7,032	$580
FINANCING ACTIVITIES												
Loan Proceeds	$50,000	$0	$0	$0	$0	$0	$0	$0	$0	$0	$0	$0
Owner Investment	13,000	0	0	0	0	0	0	0	0	0	0	0
Owner Withdrawals	(500)	(500)	(500)	(500)	(500)	(500)	(500)	(500)	(500)	(500)	(500)	(500)
INVESTING ACTIVITIES												
Furniture & Fixtures	($8,443)	$0	$0	$0	$0	$0	$0	$0	$0	$0	$0	$0
Inventory	(27,300)	0	0	0	0	0	0	0	0	0	0	0
Leasehold Improvements	(16,713)	0	0	0	0	0	0	0	0	0	0	0
Alarm System	(300)	0	0	0	0	0	0	0	0	0	0	0
Supplies Inventory	(1,000)	0	0	0	0	0	0	0	0	0	0	0
Rental Inventory	(1,000)	0	0	0	0	0	0	0	0	0	0	0
Gifts Inventory	(300)	0	0	0	0	0	0	0	0	0	0	0
Computer System	(3,350)	0	0	0	0	0	0	0	0	0	0	0
ENDING CASH BALANCE	**($1,343)**	**$1,660**	**$3,848**	**$4,019**	**$3,830**	**$4,337**	**$7,126**	**$9,292**	**$8,210**	**$1,488**	**$11,532**	**$5,080**
LINE OF CREDIT												
Borrowed on Line of Credit	$6,343	$3,340	$1,152	$981	$1,170	$663	$0	$0	$0	$3,512	$0	$0
Paid on Line of Credit	0	0	0	0	0	0	2,126	4,292	3,210	0	6,532	80
ENDING CASH BALANCE	**$5,000**	**$5,000**	**$5,000**	**$5,000**	**$5,000**	**$5,000**	**$5,000**	**$5,000**	**$5,000**	**$5,000**	**$5,000**	**$5,000**

See Summary of Forecast Assumptions

SOMETHING OLD, SOMETHING NEW BRIDAL BOUTIQUE
Break−Even Analysis*
For the Three Years Ending October 31, 1996, 1997, & 1998

VARIABLE COSTS

Cost of Goods Sold	$78,133	$91,017	$109,520

PERCENT VARIABLE COST	54.49%	54.82%	54.77%

FIXED COSTS

Wages	$16,900	$18,369	$20,206
Payroll Taxes	2,028	2,204	2,425
Insurance	1,666	1,709	1,805
Telephone	960	1,109	1,339
Rent	2,400	2,400	2,400
Utilities	960	1,008	1,058
Outside Services	2,880	2,880	2,880
Supplies	560	647	781
Accounting/Legal	150	110	121
Advertising/Promotion	6,325	6,150	7,427
Car/Delivery/Travel	480	954	1,089
Donations	180	189	198
Security System Maintenance	240	264	290
Bank Charges	322	500	541
Miscellaneous	120	139	167
Loan Payment	13,333	12,647	12,528

TOTAL FIXED COSTS	$49,504	$51,279	$55,257

BREAK−EVEN SALES	$108,785	$113,489	$122,177

Break−even sales = Total Fixed Costs/(1 − Variable Cost Percentage)

Break−even sales were prepared on a cash flow basis. Therefore, there was no allowance
for depreciation. Loan Payments were added into the analysis.

Learning Express

Company:	Learning Express
Entrepreneurs:	Deirdre & Michael Robinson
Location:	Nashua, N.H.
Business Description:	Educational Toy Store
Projected Opening Date:	Start-Up
Starting Capital:	$240,000
Owners' Equity:	$80,000
Employees:	4 to 6 (including owners) at start-up
Education:	Deirdre—B.A., Economics, Boston University, 1991 J.D., Boston College, 1994
	Michael—B.S., Finance, University of Wisconsin, 1989 Candidate for M.B.A. at Boston College

As a successful lawyer and a businessman, Deirdre and Michael Robinson felt that too much of their time was spent on the job instead of in family activities. In addition, they wanted to continue working with the public, but they wanted to be more imaginative and creative in their work. Combining their individual talents, family needs, and professional careers, the Robinsons decided to look into running a business of their own.

They bought a franchise directory and started looking through it to see what caught their eye. They noticed a juvenile furniture business, as well as other family-oriented opportunities. Deirdre's parents recommended they look at Learning Express because they knew other Learning Express franchise owners personally. Some research into the franchise revealed that it was just what the Robinsons were looking for. They felt very comfortable with the franchisor because the company was clearly willing to work very closely with its franchisees.

Both franchisor and the Robinsons had been eyeing the Nashua, N.H. area as a possible store location. The Robinsons had selected Nashua after researching the types of businesses that existed in the area and what kind of customers were available. They also did a competitive analysis by walking around (CABWA). In addition, the Robinsons talked to people they knew who lived in the area, to develop a feel for the territory. It was quite evident that this was where they wanted to be. It took only two and a half months from first look to signing with Learning Express for the exclusive rights for Nashua.

While they haven't opened their store yet (they are still scouting for the perfect location in Nashua), both franchisor and franchisee are very comfortable with the current timetable. Because the franchisor maintains both a personal and professional relationship with all of its franchisees, the Robinsons and Learning Express are looking forward to a long and prosperous association. According to the Robinsons, *"You have to be comfortable with the franchisor, because you are putting your life on the line. You may quit your job, maybe mortgage your house. You are putting a lot of faith in the franchisor. Watch out for the franchisor that is doing a hard sell. Working with a franchisor has to be a team effort. We chose Learning Express, not just because of the product, but because of the company behind it."*

SECTION

Executive Summary: This section is direct and to the point. It could stand to be augmented, however, by more information about why Learning Express is unique to the area and why the franchise is successful.

Description of Business: This section could be used to explain further what makes the company unique. The plan and the owners stress high customer service. This section should detail the attributes that will set this store apart from other, similar shops.

Market: This section identifies the target markets clearly. The addition of a few demographic figures (such as dollars spent per household on toys) would help give this section a broader view.

Competition: This section is well presented, and the "competitive advantage" comparisons are particularly good. The concept of a learning toy store is not unique, but Learning Express's presentation is. Some reviewers may like to see information about other general toy competitors as well (e.g., Kay-Bee Toy and Hobby, Wal-Mart, etc.).

Market Share: The addition of demographics in the Market section would give this section on market share a needed boost. This is a competitive market, and good demographics are necessary to show how you plan to attain your piece of the pie.

Location: Logic of a mall vs. non-mall location is clear. Mall-traffic statistics (which should be easily attainable) could enhance this section.

Pricing: This section adequately covers the pricing policy and philosophy that will be used. To link this section with the local market, the owners may want to include information about pricing strategies used by competitors.

Promotion: This plan details an extensive marketing and advertising campaign used by the franchisor. Franchisee application of this program is well presented, and shows thorough research. By adding results of the campaign from other stores, this section can provide great confidence in the business.

Form of Ownership: It is clear this is a franchise business, and the key elements of the organization have been covered.

Management and Personnel: While the franchisees do not have considerable experience in retail, the plan documents the backgrounds of key personnel and other outside resources involved in the operation of the business. If the franchisor is going to play a large role in the actual running of the business, it might be wise to include a list of things the franchisor has actually agreed to do.

Financial Information: This section is clear, well laid out, and contains good information on SBA start-up requirements. Showing balance sheet expenditures below the cash-flow line is excellent and gives the reader a clear picture of the start-up costs.

Insurance: This issue was not covered until the very end. With the high percentage of children in the store and the hands-on style of the product displays, liability insurance should be explored with some detail.

Overall Comments: This plan is well written and includes much of the basic information required for financing. The format is well thought out and easy to read. Firming up a few sections should garner this business the investments it needs.

FINANCING PROPOSAL

FUTURE ENDEAVORS, INCORPORATED

d/b/a
LEARNING EXPRESS
NASHUA, NEW HAMPSHIRE

Submitted to:

Small Business Administration

Prepared by:

Deirdre Robinson

Michael Robinson

November 23, 1996

TABLE OF CONTENTS

PLAN OBJECTIVE

PART ONE—THE BUSINESS

1. BUSINESS PROFILE
2. MARKET PROFILE
3. COMPETITION PROFILE
4. LOCATION AND FACILITIES
5. MANAGEMENT PROFILE
6. PERSONNEL PROFILE

PART TWO—FINANCIAL DATA

1. LOAN APPLICATION SUMMARY
2. START UP EXPENSES
3. CAPITAL EQUIPMENT LIST*
4. PROFIT-AND-LOSS PROJECTION 1ST YEAR BY MONTH
   NOTES AND EXPLANATIONS TO P&L PROJECTION
5. CASH-FLOW PROJECTION 1ST YEAR BY MONTH
   NOTES AND EXPLANATIONS TO CASH FLOW
6. BALANCE SHEET—AT START OF BUSINESS AND
   PROJECTED BALANCE SHEET AFTER 1 YEAR
7. PROFIT-AND-LOSS PROJECTIONS YEARS 2 & 3 BY QUARTER
8. BREAK-EVEN ANALYSIS

PART THREE—SUPPORTING DOCUMENTS*

1. PERSONAL RESUMES
2. PERSONAL FINANCIAL STATEMENT
3. SELECTED SUPPORTING DOCUMENTS

SAMPLE BUSINESS PLANS — Learning Express

> *All sales projections, operating expenses, and income projections have been made without the input of Learning Express Inc. These figures, along with the estimated start-up costs, are subject to change based on a number of factors including location, size of start store, time of opening, etc. Learning Express Inc. makes no actual or projected claims of sales, profits, or earnings of Learning Express local store franchises.*

*Note: omitted because of space limitations.

PLAN OBJECTIVE

This plan will serve as a financing proposal for a retail store, Learning Express, that will be owned and operated by Future Endeavors, Incorporated.

Learning Express is a national franchise with an exciting approach to the traditional toy store. It is committed to providing an assortment of innovative products that stimulate a curious mind and provide the tools that help "the kid in all of us" develop to our full potential.[1]

Shopping and browsing at the Learning Express is an interactive experience. Its creative approach to product presentation, its hands-on philosophy of "trying before buying" and its unique store design set Learning Express apart from other stores.[2]

The Learning Express approach to the toy business goes beyond what it sells — to how it sells it. Learning Express has thrown out old ideas about how a toy store should look and has developed its unique concept by designing fixtures and displays that create the impact to best show off its merchandise. You know at once that you're in a different kind of store, one that involves you and entertains you.[3]

Future Endeavors, Incorporated is requesting a term loan in the amount of $160,000. It plans to use $120,000 of the money for start-up with the remaining $40,000 to be used for working capital as needed by the business. We propose to repay the loan over seven years, at the current small business lending rate with no prepayment penalty.

In addition to the money that Future Endeavors, Inc. is seeking to borrow, the principals, Deirdre Robinson and Michael Robinson, will be making an equity investment of $80,000. This money will be used to purchase inventory, equipment, fixtures and supplies as well as make leasehold improvements, pay for start-up expenses and have sufficient money in reserve for working capital during the first year of operation.

The proposed Learning Express will be opened in an outdoor shopping complex in Nashua, N.H. This location will attract both drive-by and walk-by traffic. In addition, the extensive marketing and advertising campaign that Learning Express has developed will also make this store a destination shop.

BUSINESS PROFILE

Learning Express is a national retail franchise chain that specializes in selling educational toys and products to children from infancy through the young teenager. It has been franchising since 1987 and currently has forty-four (44) stores in seventeen (17) states. It plans on opening another thirty (30) stores during 1997. During this time it has developed name recognition, successful business plans and a strong marketing strategy that has allowed its franchise to grow. Much of its success can be attributed to its philosophy of strong customer service, its ability to create a store that encourages experimentation and its extensive marketing and outreach programs. These have allowed Learning Express to grow both in numbers and popularity.

The store that we propose to open would be located on the Daniel Webster Highway in Nashua, N.H., right over the Massachusetts border. This is the primary shopping area for Nashua residents as well as both New Hampshire and Massachusetts residents in surrounding towns. There is a large regional mall as well as 15 shopping centers within a half-mile stretch of road. The proposed location for our store would be in one of the highly visible shopping centers, just outside the mall.

In addition to purchasing the right to use the Learning Express name, business concept and marketing plans, we also purchase an exclusive territory in which to open the proposed Learning Express. This means that we will have the exclusive right to open all stores within this territory. The territory we propose to purchase includes the entire city of Nashua. (See map attached) While our immediate plans are to open a Learning Express along the Daniel Webster Highway in Southern Nashua, our longer term plans will be to open a second store in Northern Nashua.

Our goal is to create a store in which people enjoy shopping. Where families begin shopping when their children are young and continue to come back as their children grow. We believe the best way to accomplish this goal is by developing relationships with our customers, giving them excellent customer service and creating a comfortable shopping environment.

In order to develop relationships with our customers, we feel that it is very important that the store be owner occupied. This not only allows the owners to meet and greet their customers but, more importantly, it allows the customers to meet and talk with the owner. The hope is that when they leave they will be able to associate a person with the store and this will help draw them back. In today's market, there are fewer and fewer stores where customers have the opportunity to meet and talk with the owner. We believe that this personal relationship will help to keep customers coming back.

As for service, we expect that all customers will be greeted as they enter the store and asked if they need assistance. If they do, the sales associate will talk to the customers about their needs and make suggestions about various products. If they do not need assistance, the sales associate will be on the floor and easily accessible for questions. Employees will be easily identified by the colorful aprons and name tags they will be wearing.

While we recognize the importance of service, we acknowledge that good service alone does not ensure a store's success. It is equally important to create a comfortable shopping environment for both children and adults. We believe the combination of ongoing games and activities for the children will make the shopping experience more enjoyable for the adults. It will allow them to shop at leisure while their children are busy coloring, watching a video, playing on the computer or building with Legos.® We also plan on offering free gift wrapping of all purchases to save customers time and money.

MARKET PROFILE

Industry Analysis

A niche market exists in the children's retail educational toy business servicing middle and upper income families. As more families become concerned about how their children are spending their free time, they are searching for ways to keep their children busy while, at the same time, stimulating their senses and learning. To date, it has been difficult for these families to find a wide range of high quality educational toy products. While traditional toy stores carry a few of these items, their selection is very limited, with their primary focus on computer software.

The educational toy industry is growing at a rapid rate. Last year, the market for these products amounted to 20%, or $4 billion, of the $20 billion U.S. toy industry, with some analysts predicting it to grow as high as $9 billion annually. Industry sources agree that the major trend is for the expansion to continue. As parents become increasingly concerned with the public school system and how their children are spending their time, industry analysts predict that parents will seek out educational alternatives to the typical toys. Furthermore, industry analysts believe that the real potential for retail growth lies in smaller specialty stores, which can successfully market to a niche audience, provide high quality or "leading edge" products and offer customer service. This is what Learning Express offers.

Target Audience

Nashua is a city of approximately 85,000 people with an average income of $54,000. Census statistics indicate that the average family in Nashua has two children and that the number of families is growing. In addition, national census data indicate that the number of children in school will continue to increase over the next decade as the baby boomers' children begin having their own children. In addition to the 85,000 Nashua residents, the proposed location for the store is the primary shopping area for families living in the suburbs surrounding Nashua, both in New Hampshire and Massachusetts.

Census data also indicate that there is an increasing number of people who are becoming grandparents, and retail analysts predict that they will become one of the largest toy-buying segments of the population. This is especially important for Learning Express, since studies indicate that grandparents much prefer to shop in smaller stores where they receive more personalized attention. We believe Learning Express can offer them the product selection as well as the personalized shopping environment they desire.

Inventory and Pricing

When the store first opens, the initial inventory order will be written with the assistance of Learning Express founder and owner Sharon DiMinico. After this initial order, we will have autonomy over all future inventory orders. This freedom will allow us to best meet the needs of our customers. The Franchisor recognizes that while some products may work well in one store, that does not automatically mean that they will work well in every store. That is why the ability to customize our inventory is so important.

One of the strengths of being a member of a franchise is the power to negotiate lower prices with manufacturers and vendors. Inventory is ordered directly from the manufacturers or distributors, it is not purchased from the Franchisor. With Learning Express, the Franchisor negotiates discounts and prices with individual vendors and then each store has the option of purchasing that product. This allow us to take advantage of even greater savings. The fact that there are now forty-four (44) stores nationwide gives the Franchisor greater leverage when negotiating pricing terms and discounts. We expect to benefit from larger discounts and pricing terms in the future, as the number of Learning Express stores increases.

Once the inventory is received, it is up to each individual store owner to set the price for the product. Retail price is not dictated by the Franchisor, although it suggests using the manufacturer's suggested retail price. While Learning Express is not a discount store, we realize that situations will arise where other stores may sell the same product for less. In these situations we propose to adopt a "meet it or beat it" pricing policy, where if a customer sees the same product at another store for less, we will meet the lower price.

Marketing and Advertising

One of the strengths of Learning Express is its dynamic and broad reaching approach to marketing on both a local and regional level. Its marketing strategy is based on its belief and commitment to building ongoing relationships with its customers. The Franchisor requires that 2% of gross sales be spent on advertising but does not specify the type of advertising. It is up to each store to determine which type of local advertising would be most effective. The Franchisor also reserves the right to collect an additional 1% of sales to be used for a national advertising campaign. While this is not yet in place, as the number of stores nationwide continues to grow, this would be the next logical step.

Regional Advertising

The proposed Learning Express is part of an existing franchise network, with 19 sites in Eastern Massachusetts, Rhode Island and New Hampshire, that will allow us to take advantage of the regional advertising. Since Nashua is only forty (40) miles north of Boston, the television programming is the same as that in Boston and most of Massachusetts. In addition, most residents receive the *Boston Globe* or Boston *Herald,* and many Nashua residents commute to Boston or its suburbs on a daily basis for work.

In the past, Learning Express has placed print ads in the *Boston Globe* and the *Boston Parents Paper* and television ads on WGBH-Boston. In addition, this year, Learning Express has teamed up with WRKO, a local Boston radio station, for its annual "Toys for Tots" benefit. This means that when WRKO promotes this benefit, it will mention Learning Express. All this advertising helps promote name recognition.

Local Advertising

On a more local level, the Learning Express franchisor has created several marketing programs that have proven successful and are used by all Learning Express Franchisees.

Monthly Newsletter: The Learning Express Franchisor publishes a bimonthly newsletter that includes information about upcoming promotions, product information, workshops, and safety tips. These newsletters are individualized for each store to promote workshops and specials specific to that location. These newsletters are then sent to everyone on the store's mailing list. This helps to keep customers informed of any special promotions, as well as upcoming events and workshops that they may want to attend.

Catalog: The catalog is produced once a year, approximately three months before Christmas. Each store owner decides how many catalogs to purchase and how to distribute them. The Franchisor recommends distribution in local community newspapers, mailing them to customers who receive the newsletter, as well as making them available in store for shoppers who may not be on the list or look in the newspaper. The catalog is customized for each location, containing each store's address and phone number.

Local School Fund-Raising Services: This program involves an outreach to local preschools, elementary and middle schools by offering them the opportunity to participate in a fund-raising program. Each school is given one night during November and December when parents, family members and faculty can shop at the store and receive a 20% discount. After the evening of shopping is complete, 20% of the total sales from that evening are given back to the local school.

Corporate Toy Services: This program gives the corporate community an opportunity to purchase toys at a substantial savings for their family outings, holiday parties, or charitable gift giving. The Franchisee Owner meets with the corporate representative at Learning Express to discuss possible age appropriate toy suggestions to suit the company's particular requirements. Then, if the company decides to purchase the toys, it receives a discount that varies depending upon the size of the order. Over $500 = 15% discount; over $1,000 = 20% discount; and over $5,000 = 25% discount. In addition, employees of the company will receive coupons giving them a 15% discount on any in-stock merchandise.

Birthday Registry: This program allows children to come into the store and make wish lists of all the toys and games that they would like for their birthdays. Then parents, relatives and friends can come to the store and pick a present from the list. This can be done in person or over the phone. The item is then gift-wrapped, at no extra charge, and can be taken when the customer leaves the store or picked up on the way to the party. This is a convenience that many busy parents have found convenient. As an incentive for joining the birthday registry, many store owners offer additional discounts or free balloon bouquets.

Frequent Shopper Program: Each time a shopper comes into the store and makes a purchase for $10.00 or more it is recorded on a "Frequent Shopper Card." After ten purchases the total of the purchases are averaged, and the buyer will receive a store credit in that amount.

Workshops: Each store is encouraged to hold weekly workshops for children ages 3 to 6. These workshops are free and generally consist of arts-and-crafts-type projects such as making a hot plate, puzzles, claydough or decorating a tee shirt. In addition to arts-and-crafts workshops, each store is encouraged to bring in entertainment such as magicians, authors for readings of favorite books as well as appearances by favorite characters. Here are some examples of what other Learning Express stores have done:

- Brought in a person dressed as Madeline the doll.
- Local author to read from her recently published children's book.
- Representative from a local animal shelter to talk to families about choosing their first pet.
- Spelling Bee/Geography Bee with prizes for the winners.
- Face painting.
- Lego building contest.
- Halloween costume contest.

In addition to the programs created by the Franchisor and used by all franchise owners, Learning Express encourages each store owner to cater workshops, special events and promotions that would best suit the individual store and the customers. Several programs that we intend to develop at the proposed Learning Express would be:

Birthday Month: We propose to post a "birthday board" where we would put up pictures of customers' children celebrating a birthday in that month. Then, sometime during the month, the child could come into the store and receive 20% off any product not already on sale.

New Families: We propose to contact the local hospital maternity wards and have them distribute a Learning Express Newsletter and coupon to new families.

The Store as a Destination Shop and as a Walk-In

The nature of Learning Express's products, as well as its strategic location in Nashua, will support both destination shopping and a walk-in trade. People in the market for educational toy products are likely to make a single-purpose trip to such a specialty store. At the same time, the product lends itself to impulse buying by shoppers just passing by.

Once customers are aware of Learning Express's presence, they will recall it and seek us out when looking for a product for their own children or a gift for someone else's. The awareness will develop over several months due to the strong advertising campaign, word of mouth and simply by being observed by shoppers in the center and driving by.

COMPETITION PROFILE

Currently the educational toy market in the Northeast is shared by two other participants. These are LearningSmith and Noodle Kidoodle. Within a 15-mile radius of Nashua's downtown shopping area there are no other shopping areas of comparable size. The closest shopping center of comparable size to the south is Burlington, Mass., to the east is Salem, N.H., and to the north is Manchester, N.H. Learning Express's primary competition would come from a LearningSmith that is located in the Pheasant Lane Mall.

LearningSmith: LearningSmith has approximately 12 stores, primarily in the Northeast. They are located in regional malls, and while they carry educational products for children through adults, its stores' real appeal is to teenagers and adults. This is partly due to the fact that its stores have the feel of a bookstore, whereas Learning Express has the feel of a toy store. Its stores are run by managers, rather than owners, and it does not have the outreach programs or weekly workshops of a Learning Express. Currently, there is a LearningSmith in the Pheasant Lane Mall. While LearningSmith carries some similar products, the store itself, including its layout and majority of products, appeals to adults. Pricing of like products is similar.

Noodle Kidoodle: Noodle Kidoodle is based in New York and has approximately 20 stores. Its stores range in size from 12,000 square feet to 16,000 square feet and are designed to attract children between the ages of infant through fourteen. While it offers more inventory than the typical Learning Express, due to its sheer size, it does not have the customer service or as extensive a marketing plan as Learning Express. There is no Noodle Kidoodle in Nashua, nor does the company currently have plans to open in that region. The closest Noodle Kidoodle is almost 20 miles away, in Burlington, and we do not expect buyers to travel to Burlington to shop at this store.

There are several distinguishing features of Learning Express that set it apart from its competition.

1. The first is that the proposed store will be owner occupied. This factor will afford a high level of personal service that customers cannot find in any of the competitors.

2. Second is the unique marketing plan, described above, that targets families at their homes, schools and work.

3. Third are the weekly workshops the store will offer, for free. These workshops will not only bring families into the store, they will help promote customer loyalty. No other store in the Nashua area offers this type of program.

4. Fourth is free gift wrapping. While many stores offer free gift wrapping during the holiday season, Learning Express offers it year-round.

In addition to the close proximity of LearningSmith, we feel that it is important to note that Toys "R" Us is also present in the downtown shopping area but we do not feel that they can be considered direct competition.

Toys "R" Us: Toys "R" Us is a large, national chain store whose primary product is toys. It carries very few educational products, and most of these are computer-related software. Currently,

Toys "R" Us is in the process of developing a new concept called "Concept 2000." This is its attempt to create a section of its store devoted to educational products. At this point in time, this concept is being tried in several stores but there are not plans to implement this program throughout the chain. Unlike Learning Express, there is little or no customer assistance. Our analysis, as well as other Learning Express stores' experience, indicates that Toys "R" Us will not provide substantial competition for what Learning Express is intending to do. The only products that are the same between the two stores are Lego and K'nex.

LOCATION AND FACILITIES

The proposed Learning Express will be located in an outdoor shopping center with high visibility, outside the Pheasant Lane Mall. The Pheasant Lane Mall, with over 70 stores and anchors such as Macy's, Filene's, Sears and Lechmere, attracts a high volume of traffic into the area on a daily basis.

Outside of the Mall there are several large shopping centers with high visibility. All these shopping centers have strong anchor stores, such as Filene's Basement, Pier One Imports, Marshalls, Blockbuster Video, Home Depot and major grocery stores. The proposed store will go into one of these shopping centers. We believe the best location for the proposed Learning Express would be in a shopping center with an anchor store that attracts families, especially women. This would include large clothing stores, discount stores such as Filene's Basement or Marshalls or major supermarkets.

The rent in the proposed shopping centers ranges from $18–$22/square foot. Since we do not know the exact shopping center at this time, we cannot give an exact monthly rent, but we have estimated based on $22 a square foot. All shopping centers have ample parking facilities and large glass window storefronts. This is important to attract both walk-by and drive-by customers.

We need approximately 3,000 square feet of space. This size will allow sufficient space for inventory displays as well as ample space for workshops and children to play and experiment with the toys. These activities not only market a variety of products found in the store, they help to occupy children so parents can take their time browsing through the store. We plan to have a built-in television with VCR that will be showing children's videos that can be purchased at the store. We also plan on having a computer on which customers can try the latest software, before buying.

The store is divided into 8 sections, Little Tots, Arts & Crafts, Puzzles & Games, Science & Nature, Pretend/Imagine, Construction & Transit, Books, and Music & Videos. Each section of the store is clearly labeled to assist customers in finding the section and product they need.

MANAGEMENT PROFILE

The owners of the proposed Learning Express will be Deirdre and Michael Robinson. Deirdre is an attorney with several years of experience in the areas of real estate and business law. Michael Robinson has an undergraduate degree in finance and has almost completed his Master's in Business Administration. He has spent the past six years working for State Street Bank & Trust in a variety of positions including management accounting and financial analyst.

Management Team—Franchisee

Deirdre Robinson, President: Deirdre Robinson's formal training is as a lawyer. She graduated from Boston University in 1991 with a degree in Economics and from Boston College Law School in 1994. She worked in retail sales during college and law school. Currently she works for a small real estate law firm specializing in commercial and residential real estate, business law and civil litigation.

Michael Robinson, Vice President: Michael graduated from the University of Wisconsin—Madison in 1989 with a degree in Finance/Banking. After graduation he took a job with State Street Bank & Trust and worked in the Comptrollers Division before transferring to the bank's investment division, State Street Global Advisors. Michael is currently working towards his M.B.A. in entrepreneurial studies at Boston College and expects to graduate in Spring 1998.

In addition to the owners, the outside management support will consist of:

- Alan Suvalle of Friedman, Suvalle and Salomon, an accountant specializing in start-up retail businesses and franchises.

- Evan Tobasky of Rodman Insurance Agency, an insurance representative.

Management Team—Franchisor[4]

The directors, principal officers and other executives who have management responsibility in connection with the operation of Learning Express and who act as a team of advisors for all franchisees are as follows:

Sharon DiMinico, President, Treasurer and Director: Ms. DiMinico has been actively involved in the conceptualization and development of the Learning Express system since 1987. She has served as president, treasurer and a director since the Franchisor's inception in 1987. From 1987 to 1993, Ms. DiMinico opened and operated two (2) retail Learning Express stores along with two (2) partners. She opened Learning Express of Needham with her partners in 1987 and sold it as a franchise in July 1993. She purchased Toy Chest Inc. with her partners, a business in which she retains an ownership interest. From 1974 to 1983, Ms. DiMinico was President of UPSTAIRS DOWNSTAIRS of Acton, Mass., a retail ceramic tile and installation company.

Louis DiMinico, Clerk and Director of Leasing: Mr. DiMinico has been the clerk and a director of Learning Express since its inception. From 1971 through the present, Mr. DiMinico has been president of the Groton Corporation, a real estate development company.

Sandra Luzzi, Vice President and Director: Since the Franchisor's inception, Ms. Luzzi has been vice president and a director of Learning Express. She has been a co-owner and the toy department manager of Toy Chest Inc., West Hartford, Conn., since 1989.

Steven P. Manfredi, Vice President: Mr. Manfredi became the vice president and chief operating officer of Learning Express in April 1996. From 1991 to 1994, Mr. Manfredi owned the Learning Express local store franchise in Salem, N.H. He had previously served as regional manager of Siemens/Rolm Corporation from 1982 to 1991. From 1978 until 1991, Mr. Manfredi served as a senior fiscal advisor for the House of Representatives for the State of Rhode Island. Mr. Manfredi received his B.S. from Bentley College, Waltham, Mass.

Kathy Troknya, Director of Franchise Operations: Ms. Troknya joined the Learning Express system in 1989, when she became the manager of a local Learning Express store. In 1990, she became the director of franchise operations for the Franchisor. Ms. Troknya assists local store franchisees in opening stores, and provides training and ongoing support.

Teresa E. Cartier, Director of Communications: Ms. Cartier joined Learning Express in June 1996 as director of communications. From March 1995 through May 1996, Ms. Cartier was an editor for Community Newspaper Company. She was the editor of the *Gardner News* from September 1988 through March 1995 and a reporter and assistant editor for the *Athol Daily News* from February 1986 until September 1988.

Chip Will: Mr. Will is the regional owner for New Hampshire, Vermont and Maine. He will be our local contact. In addition to being a regional owner he owns two stores himself, one in the Rockingham Mall in Salem, N.H., and the second in Andover, Mass. He has extensive experience in the opening and daily operation of a Learning Express.

PERSONNEL PROFILE

The employment needs of the typical Learning Express depend upon its size and the store hours. We expect the hours of operation of the Learning Express we propose to open will be from 10:00 a.m.–9:00 p.m. Monday through Saturday and 12:00 p.m.–6:00 p.m. on Sunday. Given these hours of operation, the proposed business needs to employ the following:

Manager (full-time)	$ 10.00–12.00/hour
3–4 Part-Time Employees	$ 6.00–8.00/hour
Part-Time Bookkeeper	$ 8.00–10.00/hour

Monday–Friday: During the week we expect to need three (3) people in the store during the busiest hours. This will include the owner, manager and one part-time sales associate. We expect the busiest hours to be between 10:00 a.m. and 6:00 p.m. After 6:00 in the evening, when the store is slower, we expect to need two (2) salespeople.

Saturday–Sunday: We expect the weekend to be significantly busier than during the week, and therefore we would require more sales help, a manager and two part-time sales associates. During this period we expect to have four (4) salespeople, including the owner, on the floor.

We expect to contract with a payroll company to handle the payroll, and we do not expect to pay health benefits for any employee.

[1]   Learning Express Informational Brochure, 1996

[2]   Learning Express Informational Brochure, 1996

[3]   Learning Express Informational Brochure, 1996

[4]   This information is from the Learning Express Uniform Franchise Offering Circular, 1997

LOAN APPLICATION SUMMARY

DMR Corporation, a Learning Express Franchisee
Nashua, New Hampshire

Amount Requested:	$160,000. We expect to need $120,000 to open the store and would then use the remaining $40,000 for working capital if needed.
Terms:	Term loan for 7 years
Purpose:	The above amount, along with the principals' equity investment of $80,000, will allow the applicants to purchase inventory, furniture, fixtures and to do leasehold improvements and to have enough working capital to operate a profitable business.

SOURCE OF FUNDS

USE OF FUNDS	EQUITY	LOAN	TOTAL
Inventory	$22,000	$58,000	$80,000
Fixtures/Equipment	20,000	20,000	40,000
Franchise Fee	5,000	25,000	30,000
Renovations	12,000		12,000
Supplies & Misc.	7,000		7,000
Computers/Software		17,000	17,000
Working Capital	500	40,000	40,500
Grand Opening	3,000		3,000
Lease Deposit	5,500		5,500
Sign	4,000		4,000
Utility Deposit	1,000		1,000
TOTAL	**$80,000**	**$160,000**	**$240,000**

COLLATERAL AND CONDITIONS:

The following collateral and conditions are offered on the loan:

1. First Lien on all equipment, furniture, fixtures and inventory are offered as security.
2. The company will assign life insurance on the principals to the lender.
3. The company will maintain hazard insurance in the amount and type required by the lender with loss payable endorsements.
4. All principals will give personal guarantees against the loan.

SAMPLE BUSINESS PLANS Learning Express

START-UP EXPENSES

Inventory $80,000.00
Fixtures & Equipment 40,000.00
Franchise Fee 30,000.00
Computer Equipment 17,000.00
Leasehold Improvements 12,000.00
Rent Deposit 5,500.00
Sign 4,000.00
Grand Opening 3,000.00
Supplies 7,000.00
Utility Deposits 1,000.00

TOTAL START-UP COSTS $199,500.00

SAMPLE BUSINESS PLANS Learning Express

*** BALANCE SHEET ***
Start of Business

Assets
Current Assets

Cash	$40,500	
Inventory	$80,000	
Supplies	$7,000	
Rent Deposit	$5,500	
Sign	$4,000	
Utilities Deposit	$1,000	
Total Current Assets		$138,000

Fixed Assets

Computers	$17,000	
Fixtures/Equipment	$40,000	
		$57,000
Franchise Fee	$30,000	
Grand Opening	$3,000	
Leasehold Improvement	$12,000	
Total Fixed Assets		$45,000
Total Assets		$240,000

Liabilities
Current Liabilities

Notes Payable	$160,000	
Accrued Taxes Payable	$0	
Total Liabilities		$160,000

Owners Equity

Owners Capital	$80,000	
Retained Earnings	$0	
Total Capital		$80,000
Total Liabilities & Equity		$240,000

*** BALANCE SHEET ***
End of Year

Assets
Current Assets

Cash	$96,837	
Inventory	$80,000	
Supplies	$7,000	
Rent Deposit	$5,500	
Sign	$4,000	
Utilities Deposit	$1,000	
Total Current Assets		$194,337

Fixed Assets

Computers	$17,000	
Computer Depreciation	($2,004)	
Fixtures/Equipment	$40,000	
F&E Depreciation	($5,712)	
Total Fixed Assets		$49,284
Franchise Fee	$30,000	
Amortization Franchise Fee	($3,000)	
Grand Opening	$3,000	
Depreciation Grand Open	($3,000)	
Leasehold Improvement	$12,000	
Depreciation of Leasehold	($1,740)	
		$37,260
Total Assets		$280,881

Liabilities
Current Liabilities

Notes Payable	$18,254	
Accrued Taxes Payable	$12,150	
Total Current Liabilities		$30,404

Longterm Liabilities

Notes Payable	$125,260	
Total Longterm Liabilities		$125,260

Owners Equity

Owners Capital	$80,000	
Retained Earnings	45,217	
Total Capital		$125,217

NOTES AND EXPLANATIONS TO THE PROFIT-AND-LOSS PROJECTION

Gross Sales:	Retail sales of children's toys are cyclical in nature. They tend to be higher in the spring, decrease in the summer, then steadily increase from September through Christmas.
Expected Returns:	Calculated at 2% of Gross Sales.
Net Sales:	This is equal to Gross Sales minus Expected Returns.
Cost of Goods:	53% including freight and discounted products due to sales and specials.
Rent:	Will be set as agreed in lease.
Owner's Salary:	$10/hr. for 40-hour week ($20,800)
Manager's Salary:	$10/hr. for 40-hour week ($20,800)
Part-time Salary:	40 hours Monday–Friday at $7.00/hr split between 2–3 people 2 people each for 8 hours on Saturday at $7.00/hr. 2 people each for 6 hours on Sunday at $10.50/hr.
Payroll Taxes:	Company obligation to FICA and Social Security calculated at 11% of salaries.
Interest Payment:	The portion of payment to bank that is interest only.
Insurance:	Fire, liability, workers compensation and business interruption calculated at $3,100/yr.
Telephone:	Estimated at $2,400/yr. amortized monthly.
Utilities:	Estimated at $6,000/yr. amortized monthly.
Postage & Deliveries:	Estimated at $600/yr. amortized monthly.
Office Supplies:	Estimated at $5,040/yr. amortized monthly.
Merchant Credit Fees:	Calculated at 3% of credit card sales with credit card sales accounting for 80% of all sales.
Misc:	Estimated at $6,000/yr. amortized monthly.
In-Store Activity:	Estimated at $600/yr. amortized monthly.
Computer Lease:	Lease of computer equipment at $400/month.
Depreciation:	7 years straight-line method.
Amortization:	Franchise Fee amortized over 10 years.
Royalty:	Calculated at 5% of gross receipts.*
Advertising:	Calculated at 2% of gross receipts.*

*Gross receipts are defined, according to the franchise agreement, as gross sales minus returns.

SAMPLE BUSINESS PLANS — Learning Express

*** CASH FLOWS (STATEMENT of CHANGES in FINANCIAL POSITION: Year 1 by month) ***

	START UP	Mar-97	Apr-97	May-97	Jun-97	Jul-97	Aug-97	Sep-97	Oct-97	Nov-97	Dec-97	Jan-98	Feb-98	Year 1
BEGINNING BALANCE		$40,500	$41,475	$41,688	$40,756	$39,061	$36,222	$34,528	$35,503	$39,529	$59,575	$100,597	$97,758	$607,192
Loan Receipts	$160,000	$0	$0	$0	$0	$0	$0	$0	$0	$0	$0	$0	$0	$0
Equity Invested	$80,000	$0	$0	$0	$0	$0	$0	$0	$0	$0	$0	$0	$0	$0
Cash Receipts	$0	$44,100	$42,140	$39,200	$37,240	$34,300	$37,240	$44,100	$51,940	$93,100	$147,000	$34,300	$39,200	$643,860
Accounts Receivable		$0	$0	$0	$0	$0	$0	$0	$0	$0	$0	$0	$0	$0
TOTAL CASH AVAILABLE	$240,000	$84,600	$83,615	$80,888	$77,996	$73,361	$73,462	$78,628	$87,443	$132,629	$206,575	$134,897	$136,958	$1,251,052
DISBURSEMENTS:														
Cost of Goods		$23,850	$22,790	$21,200	$20,140	$18,550	$20,140	$23,850	$28,090	$50,350	$79,500	$18,550	$21,200	$348,210
Rent		$5,500	$5,500	$5,500	$5,500	$5,500	$5,500	$5,500	$5,500	$5,500	$5,500	$5,500	$5,500	$66,000
Wages Owner		$1,733	$1,733	$1,733	$1,733	$1,733	$1,733	$1,733	$1,733	$1,733	$1,733	$1,733	$1,733	$20,796
Wages Employees		$3,700	$3,700	$3,700	$3,700	$3,700	$3,700	$3,700	$3,700	$3,700	$3,700	$3,700	$3,700	$44,400
Interest Payment		$1,367	$1,355	$1,344	$1,333	$1,321	$1,310	$1,298	$1,286	$1,274	$1,262	$1,250	$1,238	$15,638
Principal Payment		$1,310	$1,321	$1,333	$1,344	$1,356	$1,367	$1,379	$1,391	$1,402	$1,415	$1,427	$1,439	$16,484
Payroll Taxes		$598	$598	$598	$598	$598	$598	$598	$598	$598	$598	$598	$598	$7,176
Insurance		$260	$260	$260	$260	$260	$260	$260	$260	$260	$260	$260	$260	$3,120
Telephone		$200	$200	$200	$200	$200	$200	$200	$200	$200	$200	$200	$200	$2,400
Utilities		$500	$500	$500	$500	$500	$500	$500	$500	$500	$500	$500	$500	$6,000
Postage & Deliveries		$50	$50	$50	$50	$50	$50	$50	$50	$50	$50	$50	$50	$600
Office Supplies & Expenses		$420	$420	$420	$420	$420	$420	$420	$420	$420	$420	$420	$420	$5,040
Misc.		$500	$500	$500	$500	$500	$500	$500	$500	$500	$500	$500	$500	$6,000
In Store Activities		$50	$50	$50	$50	$50	$50	$50	$50	$50	$50	$50	$50	$600
Royalty		$2,205	$2,107	$1,960	$1,862	$1,715	$1,862	$2,205	$2,597	$4,655	$7,350	$1,715	$1,960	$32,193
Advertising		$882	$843	$784	$745	$686	$745	$882	$1,039	$1,862	$2,940	$686	$784	$12,877
TOTAL DISBURSED		$43,125	$41,927	$40,132	$38,935	$37,139	$38,935	$43,125	$47,914	$73,054	$105,978	$37,139	$40,132	$587,534
Change in Cash Balance														
Beginning Cash Balance		$84,600	$83,615	$80,888	$77,996	$73,361	$73,462	$78,628	$87,443	$132,629	$206,575	$134,897	$136,958	$1,251,052
Increase/(Decrease) in Cash		$43,125	$41,927	$40,132	$38,935	$37,139	$38,935	$43,125	$47,914	$73,054	$105,978	$37,139	$40,132	$587,534
Ending Cash Balance		$41,475	$41,688	$40,756	$39,061	$36,222	$34,528	$35,503	$39,529	$59,575	$100,597	$97,758	$96,826	$663,517
START UP EXPENSES														
Inventory	$80,000													
Fixtures & Equipment	$40,000													
Computer	$17,000													
Franchise Fee	$30,000													
Leasehold Improvements	$12,000													
Rent Deposit	$5,500													
Sign	$4,000													
Grand Opening	$3,000													
Supplies	$7,000													
Utility Deposits	$1,000													
TOTAL	$199,500													
CASH FLOW	$40,500	$41,475	$41,688	$40,756	$39,061	$36,222	$34,528	$35,503	$39,529	$59,575	$100,597	$97,758	$96,826	$663,517

(Left margin:) SAMPLE BUSINESS PLANS — Learning Express

NOTES AND EXPLANATIONS TO THE CASH-FLOW PROJECTION

Beginning Balance:	Cash balance at the beginning of the month.
Loan Receipts:	Cash received from loans.
Equity:	Equity invested by the owners.
Sales Receipts:	Sales, received from cash/credit card/check sales.
Total Available:	Cash available to pay expenses monthly.
Cost of Goods:	Initial inventory and replacement of goods sold.
Rent:	Monthly lease paid in advance each month.
Salary Owner:	Salaries are paid in month cost incurred.
Salary Employees:	Salaries are paid in month cost incurred.
Interest Payment:	Interest paid monthly.
Principal Payment:	Principal paid monthly.
Payroll Taxes:	Company's share of FICA/Social Security.
Insurance:	Fire, Hazard, Liability and Workers Comp at $3,100/yr.
Telephone:	Monthly expense paid monthly.
Utilities:	Monthly expense paid monthly.
Postage & Delivery:	Cost paid in month incurred.
Office Supplies:	Cost paid in month incurred.
Misc.:	Cost paid in month incurred.
In-Store Activity:	Estimated at $50/month, paid in month incurred.
Royalty:	5% paid in each month incurred.
Advertising:	2% paid in each month advertising costs incurred.
Total Disbursed:	Total cash paid out monthly.
Ending Cash Balance/ Cash Flow:	End of the month cash balance becomes the beginning balance of the next month.
Start-Up Expense:	Expenses incurred to start the business.

<table>
<tr><td colspan="3">

*** BALANCE SHEET ***
Start of Business

Assets
  Current Assets
Cash	$40,500	
Inventory	$80,000	
Supplies	$7,000	
Rent Deposit	$5,500	
Sign	$4,000	
Utilities Deposit	$1,000	
Total Current Assets		$138,000

  Fixed Assets
Computers	$17,000	
Fixtures/Equipment	$40,000	
		$57,000
Franchise Fee	$30,000	
Grand Opening	$3,000	
Leasehold Improvement	$12,000	
Total Fixed Assets		$45,000
Total Assets		$240,000

Liabilities
  Current Liabilities
Notes Payable	$160,000	
Accrued Taxes Payable	$0	
Total Liabilities		$160,000

Owners Equity
Owners Capital	$80,000	
Retained Earnings	$0	
Total Capital		$80,000
Total Liabilities & Equity		$240,000

</td><td colspan="3">

*** BALANCE SHEET ***
End of Year

Assets
  Current Assets
Cash	$96,837	
Inventory	$80,000	
Supplies	$7,000	
Rent Deposit	$5,500	
Sign	$4,000	
Utilities Deposit	$1,000	
Total Current Assets		$194,337

  Fixed Assets
Computers	$17,000	
Computer Depreciation	($2,004)	
Fixtures/Equipment	$40,000	
F&E Depreciation	($5,712)	
Total Fixed Assets		$49,284
Franchise Fee	$30,000	
Amortization Franchise Fee	($3,000)	
Grand Opening	$3,000	
Depreciation Grand Open	($3,000)	
Leasehold Improvement	$12,000	
Depreciation of Leasehold	($1,740)	
		$37,260
Total Assets		$280,881

Liabilities
  Current Liabilities
Notes Payable	$18,254	
Accrued Taxes Payable	$12,150	
Total Current Liabilities		$30,404

  Longterm Liabilities
Notes Payable	$125,260	
Total Longterm Liabilities		$125,260

Owners Equity
Owners Capital	$80,000	
Retained Earnings	45,217	
Total Capital		$125,217
Total Liabilities & Equity		$280,881

</td></tr>
</table>

SAMPLE BUSINESS PLANS
Learning Express

*** INCOME STATEMENT (Year 2 by quarter) ***

Quarters	1st	2nd	3rd	4th	Total	% of Total Sales
Total Sales	$113,000	$116,000	$200,000	$248,000	$697,000	100.00%
Cost of Goods Sold						
Material & Freight	$59,890	$61,480	$106,000	$131,440	$369,410	53.00%
% of Total Sales	53.00%	53.00%	53.00%	53.00%	53.00%	
Total Cost of Goods Sold	$59,890	$61,480	$106,000	$131,440	$369,410	53.00%
Gross Profit	$53,110	$54,520	$94,000	$116,560	$327,590	47.00%
% of Total Sales	47.00%	47.00%	47.00%	47.00%	47.00%	
Operating Expenses						
Rent	$16,500	$16,500	$16,500	$16,500	$66,000	9.47%
Owners Payroll	$5,200	$5,200	$5,200	$5,200	$20,800	2.98%
Employees Payroll	$11,100	$11,100	$11,100	$11,100	$44,400	6.37%
Interest Payment	$3,548	$3,436	$3,322	$3,205	$13,511	1.94%
Payroll Tax	$1,793	$1,793	$1,793	$1,793	$7,172	1.03%
Insurance	$780	$780	$780	$780	$3,120	0.45%
Telephone	$600	$600	$600	$600	$2,400	0.34%
Utilities	$1,500	$1,500	$1,500	$1,500	$6,000	0.86%
Postage & Deliveries	$150	$150	$150	$150	$600	0.09%
Office Supplies & Expense	$1,260	$1,260	$1,260	$1,260	$5,040	0.72%
Merchant Credit Cards	$3,192	$2,784	$4,800	$5,952	$16,728	2.40%
Misc.	$1,500	$1,500	$1,500	$1,500	$6,000	0.86%
In Store Activities	$150	$150	$150	$150	$600	0.09%
Computer Depreciation	$501	$501	$501	$501	$2,004	0.29%
F&E Depreciation	$1,428	$1,428	$1,428	$1,428	$5,712	0.82%
Lease Improv. Depreciation	$435	$435	$435	$435	$1,740	0.25%
Amortization of Franchise Fee	$750	$750	$750	$750	$3,000	0.43%
Royalty	$5,650	$5,800	$10,000	$12,400	$34,850	5.00%
Advertising	$2,260	$2,320	$4,000	$4,960	$13,940	2.00%
Total Operating Expenses	$58,297	$57,987	$65,769	$70,164	$253,617	36.39%
Income From Operations	($5,187)	($3,467)	$28,231	$46,396	$73,973	10.61%
Income before Taxes	($5,187)	($3,467)	$28,231	$46,396	$73,973	10.61%
Taxes on Income	($1,556)	($1,040)	$8,469	$13,919	$22,192	3.18%
Net Income After Taxes	($3,631)	($2,427)	$19,762	$32,477	$51,781	7.43%
% of Total Sales	-3.21%	-2.09%	9.88%	13.10%	7.43%	

*** INCOME STATEMENT (Year 3 by quarter) ***

Quarters	1st	2nd	3rd	4th	Total	% of Total Sales
Total Sales	$144,000	$123,000	$218,000	$285,000	$770,000	100.00%
Cost of Goods Sold						
Material & Freight	$76,320	$65,190	$115,540	$151,050	$408,100	53.00%
% of Total Sales	53.00%	53.00%	53.00%	53.00%	53.00%	
Total Cost of Goods Sold	$76,320	$65,190	$115,540	$151,050	$408,100	53.00%
Gross Profit	$67,680	$57,810	$102,460	$133,950	$361,900	47.00%
% of Total Sales	47.00%	47.00%	47.00%	47.00%	47.00%	
Operating Expenses						
Rent	$16,500	$16,500	$16,500	$16,500	$66,000	8.57%
Owners Payroll	$5,200	$5,200	$5,200	$5,200	$20,800	2.70%
Employees Payroll	$11,100	$11,100	$11,100	$11,100	$44,400	5.77%
Interest Payment	$3,085	$2,962	$2,836	$2,706	$11,589	1.51%
Payroll Tax	$1,793	$1,793	$1,793	$1,793	$7,172	0.93%
Insurance	$780	$780	$780	$780	$3,120	0.41%
Telephone	$600	$600	$600	$600	$2,400	0.31%
Utilities	$1,500	$1,500	$1,500	$1,500	$6,000	0.78%
Postage & Deliveries	$150	$150	$150	$150	$600	0.08%
Office Supplies & Expense	$1,260	$1,260	$1,260	$1,260	$5,040	0.65%
Merchant Credit Cards	$3,456	$2,952	$5,232	$6,840	$18,480	2.40%
Misc.	$1,500	$1,500	$1,500	$1,500	$6,000	0.78%
In Store Activities	$150	$150	$150	$150	$600	0.08%
Computer Lease	$501	$501	$501	$501	$2,004	0.26%
F&E Depreciation	$1,428	$1,428	$1,428	$1,428	$5,712	0.74%
Lease Improv. Depreciation	$435	$435	$435	$435	$1,740	0.23%
Amortization of Franchise Fee	$750	$750	$750	$750	$3,000	0.39%
Royalty	$7,200	$6,150	$10,900	$14,250	$38,500	5.00%
Advertising	$2,880	$2,460	$4,360	$5,700	$15,400	2.00%
Total Operating Expenses	$60,268	$58,171	$66,975	$73,143	$258,557	33.58%
Income From Operations	$7,412	($361)	$35,485	$60,807	$103,343	13.42%
Income before Taxes	$7,412	($361)	$35,485	$60,807	$103,343	13.42%
Taxes on Income	$2,224	($108)	$10,646	$18,242	$72,987	9.48%
Net Income After Taxes	$5,188	($253)	$24,840	$42,565	$72,340	9.39%
% of Total Sales	3.60%	-0.21%	11.39%	14.94%	9.39%	

BREAK-EVEN ANALYSIS

FIXED COSTS

Rent	$66,000.00
Utilities	6,000.00
Insurance	3,100.00
Bank	31,874.00
Salaries, Manager	20,800.00
Payroll Taxes	2,288.00
Telephone	2,400.00
TOTAL	$132,461.00

$$\$132,461 \div 47\% = \$281,832/\text{year}$$

Feasibility Analysis: $\$281,832 \div 362 \text{ days} = \$778.54/\text{day}$

$$\$778.54 \div \$20/\text{sale} = 38.92 \text{ sales per day.}$$

1-800-BATTERIES

Company:	1-800-BATTERIES
Entrepreneur:	Ken Hawk
Location:	San Jose, Calif.
Business Description:	Mail-Order Electronics Batteries
Opening Date:	June 1993
Starting Capital:	$10,000
1996 Sales:	$4.7 million
Owners' Equity:	$10,000. Investor added $50,000 in December 1993.
Employees:	2 at start-up; 31 in June 1997
Education:	B.S., Electrical Engineering, University of Michigan, 1986 M.B.A., Stanford University, 1993

While a student in the M.B.A. program at Stanford University, Ken Hawk was approached by his friend, John Mackall. John needed a replacement battery for his portable computer and could not find one locally at a reasonable price. Ken instantly recognized a niche market that was worth exploring. Ken had been working for Microsoft, so he was familiar with the electronics industry as well as the distribution channels for replacement parts and accessories. Ken also knew that the computer portables market was growing at a rate of 30% per year, driving an increasing need for replacement batteries.

By combining focus groups and mall interviews in nearby Silicon Valley with his industry knowledge and research, Ken determined there was indeed a niche that a new retail business could fill. *"Rechargeable batteries are like the trash business: something everybody needs but nobody wants to handle,"* says Ken. The overwhelming response from potential customers was that they wanted a replacement battery at a fair price, with quick service. Currently, they had to go to six or seven stores, place an order, wait several weeks for delivery, and pay outrageous prices.

Ken decided to start 1-800-BATTERIES. His mission was to sell batteries at a fair price, with fast delivery, to win a lifetime customer.

To obtain financing, he needed to develop a quality business plan. With the assistance of Irv Grousebeck, a professor at Stanford University, Ken began to put his plan together. His first step was to put a timeline on his plan: 10 sections in 10 weeks. Ken found a potential investor and faxed him one section of his business plan per week. *"There is nothing like a schedule to force progress,"* according to Ken.

Ken had read several business plans that included tremendous amounts of superfluous information. *"Don't overanalyze to the point of analysis paralysis! A business plan's number one priority is to figure out your business: Who are you going to sell to? What are you going to sell? What is the potential market? Who do you have on your team? Next, a business plan helps you talk with potential investors. Be brutally honest in your plan. It is easy to get tunnel vision and ignore the potential downfalls of your business. Show the bad with the good. Not only will it help your business develop a realistic viewpoint, but your investors will be impressed with your maturity."*

SECTION

Executive Summary: Although this is a venture plan, the Executive Summary should include intended location, legal form of ownership, and the market's potential.

Description of Business: The identification of the current state of technology is very good, and the unique delivery approach—from distributor to customer—is clearly defined.

Market: Excellent analysis of opportunities in the marketplace. Data on the battery market and expected growth are a plus. The plan should discuss the specific target audience as well.

Competition: Good, useful information on the overall competitive landscape. Because of the business's venture status, identification of potential alliances makes this a strong section.

Market Share: The plan should include information on market share of all possible competitors.

Location: This is not covered in the plan. However, because of the nature of the business, it could operate from almost anywhere.

Pricing: No mention is made of pricing policy or pricing strategy compared to the competition. There is also no pricing analysis in light of customer needs and buying behavior.

Promotion: The 800 phone number concept is very good. The plan also outlines some exceptional ideas on promotional campaigns.

Form of Ownership: Because of the small size of the company, the simple structure described is appropriate. This company is not capital intensive, so the form of ownership is not significant. If certain segments take off (such as cellular and camcorder battery sales), then corporate status might be indicated.

Management and Personnel: Other than the principal, little information is provided about key personnel and others in the management structure. When the entrepreneur is still in school and has little experience in the market, experienced advisers will be vital to a plan's success.

Financial Information: Good analysis of factors related to operations and breakdown of unit sales. For a venture plan, you only need to include a cursory overview of your projected revenues.

Insurance: Not covered.

Overall Comments: This plan clearly identifies the need for a business such as this. It is a great concept, but potentially has a considerable number of competitors. As a venture plan, it has all the required elements. Additions to all sections would be required to turn it into a working plan capable of obtaining financing.

Business Plan
3/13/93

Prepared by Ken Hawk

TABLE OF CONTENTS

EXECUTIVE SUMMARY

Business Objectives

1-800-Batteries was formed in March 1993 to distribute rechargeable batteries for portable electronics products to people who have a hard time finding them.

Initially, we plan to focus on selling rechargeable batteries through the mail to professionals and small businesses that use portable computers, portable cellular phones, and camcorders. These customers value battery life and have trouble finding rechargeable batteries for their products. By using mail order, we believe we can deliver a broad range of rechargeable batteries to these customers more effectively than resellers. Because of the large variety of battery models and the difficulty resellers have in stocking batteries, we believe we can offer customers a strong value proposition. For example, the retail price of the Compaq LTE/286 battery is $130, but it can be purchased from distributors for roughly $45. An opportunity exists for a quality mail order provider to sell these batteries to end users for about $80.

We expect to earn higher gross margins than a typical mail order company because our customers are buying convenience, service, and selection, not price.

Product Line/Technology Sourcing

We will initially offer all NiCad replacements for camcorders, portable computers, and portable cellular phones.

However, our value to the customer will go beyond being a more convenient source for rechargeable batteries. We will actively seek out better products and more advanced technologies. For example, we will have a line of Nickel Metal Hydride batteries which will be slightly more expensive than the NiCad batteries but can provide up to 50% increases in time between charges. Also, we will offer battery rechargers, that can recharge batteries faster than conventional rechargers or eliminate the memory effect, thereby lengthening the life of NiCad and NiMH batteries. Finally, we will offer power management software, which also has potential to increase battery life in portable computers.

By focusing on one core value benefit to the customer, longer battery life, we believe we can offer an array of products that the customer cannot easily find anywhere else.

Market

The total market for rechargeable batteries for the three target products is estimated to be approximately $150MM in retail sales. However, the market will expand rapidly. First, sales of portable computers and portable cellular phones will likely grow at 30%–40% per year for the next few years. Second, as new battery technologies evolve over the next two years, the installed base will have a strong incentive to replace their current 2–3 hour batteries with 3–4 hour batteries based on more advanced technology. Finally, sales of other technologies, such as fast chargers or power management software, will augment sales of batteries.

The demographics of our target audience suit mail order distribution. They are wealthy professionals who value their time. As a result, battery life is very important to them. For example, an extra hour of battery life for an executive on an airplane may be worth much more than the cost of the battery. Furthermore, they are receptive to buying through the mail because it saves them time and hassle.

Our preliminary market survey asked owners of our target electronics products a very simple question: "Would you consider buying a second rechargeable battery via mail order if it were 20% less expensive than retail and could be shipped overnight free of charge?" 87% of respondents said they would "Definitely" or "Probably" purchase the battery.

SAMPLE BUSINESS PLANS — 1-800-Batteries

Management Team

The board of advisers currently consists of three candidates for the MBA degree at the Stanford Graduate School of Business. Combined, they have several years of experience in high tech sales and marketing of both hardware and software. Two of the three have had exposure to the mail order business. They are very comfortable working as a small close-knit team. Ken Hawk, with extensive sales and marketing experience at Microsoft, Venture Manufacturing Singapore and Silicon Systems, will found the company.

Operations and Financing Requirements

One of the most appealing aspects of this business is that it can be started with extremely low overhead.

We will establish contracts with existing regional battery distributors and assemblers to ship direct from their warehouses to our customers for a nominal fulfillment fee. Therefore, we will have limited inventory investment. Also, we will contract out any overflow customer service requirements. This allows us to grow our telemarketing operation slowly, thus limiting fixed costs. Finally, we will reduce our customer acquisition costs by making deals with OEMs and other partners to supply batteries to their customers. We are currently discussing this possibility with OEM portable computer manufacturers and leading battery management software firms.

RISK FACTORS

Technological Change

Microsoft and other software firms are actively developing power management software. This software will extend battery life and thus reduce the need for extra batteries or higher performance replacement batteries. However, Microsoft's push in this area also will increase the awareness of the need for longer battery life. This is also an opportunity since battery management software firms will provide us with an easy and effective way to reach power sensitive portable owners.

Semiconductor firms including Intel are developing 3 Volt microprocessors that use less power and actively manage battery usage, thus reducing the need for extra batteries or higher performance replacement batteries.

Duracell is pushing a set of three standard size NiMH batteries that will be sampled to OEMs in April 1993. If the OEMs adopt standard size batteries, the retailers will jump into the market. It is our view that the continuous pressure to pack more into a smaller portable product will thwart Duracell's efforts to standardize rechargeables.

Compaq has developed a battery with a ROM encoded chip, effectively preventing third party batteries from working in Compaq notebooks. The other manufacturers are not following Compaq's move. In addition, we can still make a profit selling Compaq brand batteries through our channel.

Battery technology is improving. The average monochrome notebook battery now lasts just under three hours. Battery improvements will slowly erode the need for extra batteries. However, this improvement in battery life is being mitigated by the increasing use of power hungry active matrix color displays, fax modems, and larger hard drives.

Battery recharging has made great strides in the last few years. Rapid chargers coupled with quick-charge batteries can now recharge a battery in less than an hour where it used to take overnight. However, these rapid chargers are not in widespread use, and 1-800-Batteries plans to sell these chargers and therefore benefit from this trend.

We feel these risk factors are manageable as described above.

Competition

This is an attractive opportunity that will draw competitors. Our goal is to increase the barriers to entry and reduce our customer acquisition costs by forging key relationships with OEMs, joint marketing partners, and resellers. Moreover, we will offer better service and higher quality products than the existing small competitors.

Management

Ken Hawk has a well rounded technical sales and marketing background; however, he has little mail order experience. We recognize the need for additional mail order business experience and will add an experienced mail order person to our board of advisers.

PRODUCTS

1-800-Batteries's primary products will be replacement and extra rechargeable batteries used in portable electronic items. The initial product focus will be rechargeable batteries for portable computers, portable cellular phones, and camcorders.

Portable Computers

The portable computer market over the last several years has been characterized by rapid product innovation and consequent short life cycles (often only six months). As portable computers have shrunk from laptops to notebooks to subnotebooks, battery specifications have continued to evolve as designers looked for ways to make them smaller, lighter, and more powerful.

Virtually no standardization has taken place for battery specifications in this market. Even within the same manufacturer, different models often require different batteries. The battery cells for computers are either enclosed within a hard plastic case or shrink-wrapped together. While many of these battery packs are easily removable (e.g., the Apple Powerbook battery which pops right out), some battery packs are more difficult to remove and replace. The average retail price range is $80–$120.

The dominant battery technology today is nickel-cadmium ("NiCads") which still accounts for over 90% of rechargeable battery sales. Battery life on one charge ranges from one to four hours, depending on the specific batteries and computer involved. The new Nickel Metal Hydride technology ("NiMH"), which offers up to twice the performance of NiCads as well as lighter weight and less environmental impact, is gaining rapid acceptance.

Portable Cellular Phones

Portable cellular phones have been evolving almost as fast as portable computers. For instance, the 7.5-ounce state-of-the-art Motorola Micro Tac Lite is several times lighter than the industry leader only two years ago. Battery specifications have changed along with the improved product designs.

Again, little product standardization exists. Different models require different batteries, even if they are made by the same manufacturer. Most batteries are enclosed within a hard plastic case. All are easy to remove and replace. The average retail price is approximately $80.

NiCad batteries currently dominate the market, but NiMH batteries are rapidly gaining popularity.

Camcorders

Product innovation in the camcorder market has also been constant, e.g., the introduction of tiny palmcorders and the increased use of fuzzy logic. However, battery specifications have shown more standardization in this market than in the above two. For instance, a number of models manufactured by Panasonic, Mitsubishi, NEC, and Akai all share the exact same battery. Nevertheless, a wide variety of battery specifi-

SAMPLE BUSINESS PLANS 1-800-Batteries

cations still exists in this market. At least 25 different batteries are required by models sold in the market today.

Battery packs for camcorders are generally enclosed within a hard plastic case. All are easy to remove and replace. The average retail price is approximately $60.

NiCad batteries currently dominate the market, but NiMHs are rapidly gaining popularity.

Product Technology

The dominant technological trend in rechargeable batteries is the move from NiCads to NiMHs. As discussed, NiMH batteries can provide up to twice the performance of NiCads as well as being lighter weight and quicker to recharge. A disputed advantage of NiMHs is that they are supposedly free of the "memory effect" that troubles NiCads. This effect occurs when a NiCad is repeatedly recharged before being fully discharged. The outcome is that the NiCad loses its capacity to fully recharge, so that a normal three-hour battery can end up lasting only one hour. NiMHs are touted as being free from this memory-effect problem.

Moreover, NiMH batteries are free from the highly toxic cadmium which is used in NiCads. Many governments are taking action to ban NiCads because of the difficulty in safely disposing of them. NiCad batteries are the largest source of cadmium pollution in the U.S. In fact, by the end of 1993, up to ten states in the U.S. and several European countries may declare NiCads to be illegal. Minnesota has led the way with its recently implemented legislation, which forces manufacturers, and manufacturers of products that use NiCads, to make the batteries easily removable so that they can safely be disposed of separately from the products.

Compaq recently launched a battery pack recycling program to help address this environmental issue. Rechargeable batteries as a whole are beneficial to the environment in the sense that they dramatically reduce the number of disposable batteries that find their ways to dump sites. An estimated 88% of all mercury found in landfills comes from alkaline batteries.

Given these favorable dynamics for NiMH batteries, analysts expect unit sales could grow by 20% a year. Current manufacturers of NiMHs include Sanyo, Matsushita, and Toshiba. New entrants into this market include Hitachi Maxell, Furukawa Battery, and Duracell as part of a joint venture with Varta and Toshiba.

Beyond NiMHs, the technology of the future looks to be rechargeable lithium-ion batteries. While a number of manufacturers make disposable lithium cells, usually as little "button" cells for computer memory back-up, manufacturers have struggled to design rechargeable lithium batteries. Recently, however, Sony Energytec seems to have found the answer. They currently are producing over 100,000 lithium batteries a month for cellular phones and intend to increase production sharply to service the portable computer market. They already include lithium-ion batteries in their newest camcorders.

The performance of lithium rechargeables allows them to offer three times the power of the best NiCads at half the weight. Given this performance edge, most of the major battery manufacturers are focusing on this technology as well. The consensus in the industry is that it will likely be two or three years before all the technical impediments are removed and the costs come down so that lithiums can truly challenge NiCads and NiMHs for the bulk of the market.

The most cutting edge battery technology today is lithium-polymer. Developed by Valence Technology, these batteries are composed of a thin plastic-type material which can be shaped into any convenient form. According to Valence, lithium-polymer batteries will be able to offer four times the power of comparable-sized NiCads at a tenth of the price. However, most analysts believe that this technology won't be economically viable for at least several years.

Despite near-term uncertainty over the rate of introduction of these new battery technologies, it is apparent that together they represent the potential for enormous market expansion, especially if they can be utilized in the existing installed base.

MARKET

Market Size and Growth

The market will be driven by three factors:

- Need for extra batteries
- Need for longer life batteries
- Need for replacement batteries[1]

The target market initially will be consumers and small businesses with either a portable computer, cellular phone, or camcorder.

The laptop/notebook computer installed base is approximately 3 million units. Unit sales are expected to double next year, and rapid growth is expected for the next 3–5 years.

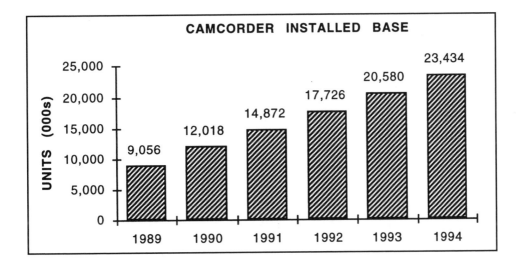

------
[1] *NiCD and NiMH batteries can only sustain 500–700 charge/discharge cycles.*

The portable cellular phone installed base is almost 2 million units. Unit sales are expected to increase by 20% next year, and rapid growth is expected for the foreseeable future.

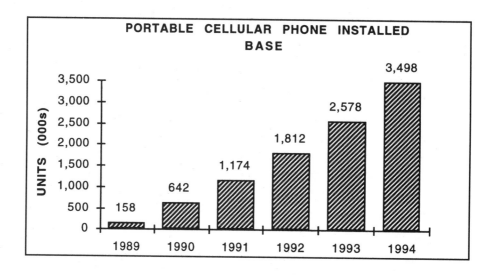

The camcorder installed base is the largest of the three, with about 18 million units in U.S. households. Year-to-year sales growth is slow, but installed base growth is steady.

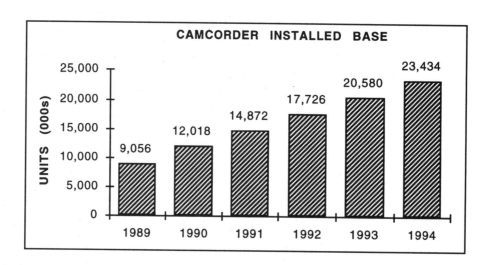

While the total U.S. retail battery market is estimated to be over $3 billion, the retail rechargeable battery market is approximately $650 million, with about $360 million in sales of nonstandardized[2] rechargeable batteries. Within this segment, the relative sizes of our target markets are as follows:

Camcorder batteries	$80 million
Portable computer batteries	$35 million
Portable cellular phone batteries	$35 million
Total initial target market	$150 million

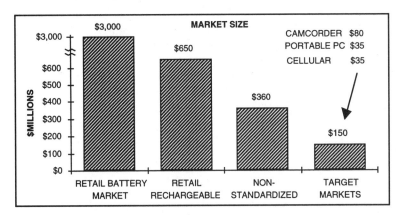

Analysts expect the retail rechargeable battery market to increase to approximately $1 billion by 1995, an expected annual growth rate of 20%–25%. Growth in the portable computer and portable cellular phone segments will likely be more rapid.

One interesting point is that many of those surveyed were not willing to pay current market prices for rechargeable batteries or were not aware of current market prices. For example, only 9% of portable PC owners said they would be willing to pay over $75 for a second rechargeable battery, yet most such batteries cost in excess of $80 at retail. Interestingly, 25% of owners said they would be willing to pay over $75 if the second battery lasted 50% longer than their existing battery. Technology that is coming to market shortly is expected to achieve this performance increase.

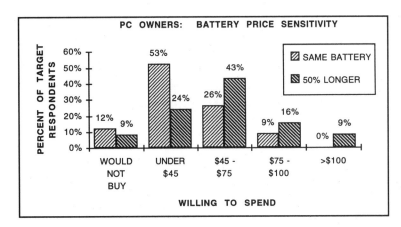

In conclusion, the market appears ripe for a rechargeable battery distribution specialist, particularly one that specializes in notebook computer batteries. Portable electronics users value battery life, are frustrated by the cost and availability of batteries through conventional channels, and are very receptive to mail order as a distribution method.

---

[2] Non-standardized rechargeable batteries include all rechargeables that do not fall into the conventional round cell categories (A, B, D, C, etc.). Most are custom made for a particular product or products on the market.

COMPETITION

1-800-Batteries's competition in selling replacement rechargeable batteries falls into three general categories: resellers, computer manufacturers selling direct, and mail order companies.

Most replacement rechargeable batteries are sold through resellers. Customers often return to the stores where they purchased their units to buy replacement batteries. While some retail stores carry the batteries in stock, others choose to serve their customers by special ordering the batteries from their distributors.

The time delay for these orders ranges anywhere from one to ten business days. Generally, portable computer batteries are the least likely to be kept in inventory, given that they are the most expensive and come in the widest variety of specifications.

Through discussions with various resellers, 1-800-Batteries has learned that many of them view the sale of replacement rechargeable batteries as a nuisance. Besides the inventory costs and hassles consistent with a multitude of ever-changing SKUs, resellers are concerned about the theft of these products, given their small size and relative high value. As one reseller put it, "Batteries are like cash." For this reason, they often must keep them locked up or off the floor. Finally, resellers view dealing with these issues as an undesirable drain on their sale forces' time.

This generalization is not true for all resellers. For instance, Fry's Electronics, a superstore, views its mission as being all things to all people. When interviewed, a Fry's manager responded that stocking many different battery types is consistent with their overall strategy. They don't question the value of this approach.

To help partially compensate for the expense involved, resellers generally mark up rechargeable batteries from 100% to 200%. For instance, the Toshiba 2200SX notebook battery retails for $159.95, yet costs under $57 at the wholesale level (180% markup over cost).

Besides the resellers, the computer manufacturers themselves represent another source of competition for 1-800-Batteries. Especially based on the success of the Dell model, computer manufacturers are increasingly choosing to reach their customers directly over the phone and through the mail. Manufacturers such as Altima and Dell have toll-free 800 numbers, which customers can call to have replacement batteries shipped out the next day. ACER is grudgingly organizing a mail order program to supply batteries for their notebook customers as a response to the customers' frustrations with the existing distribution channels.

The prices quoted by most manufacturers still represent at least a healthy 100% over wholesale.

Besides selling batteries themselves, some manufactures such as Toshiba and Texas Instruments choose to refer customers to dealers in their area, with varying degrees of efficiency. For instance, the most convenient dealer that Toshiba could recommend to 1-800-Batteries was one in Fremont, CA.

The mail order competition falls into two categories: broad mail order computer resellers and battery manufacturers selling through mail order. The computer mail order companies advertise in the trade magazines and offer batteries as one line item among a wide array of products. Consequently, they do a poor job of serving a broad laptop customer base, due to limited selection of batteries and other power management products.

Not surprisingly, 1-800-Batteries is not the first company to focus on selling rechargeable batteries via mail order. Several different battery assemblers such as Battery Biz, Alexander Batteries, and Yakar Systems can be found by scanning the advertisements in magazines such as *PC Laptop*. Generally, these competitors appear to be fairly new and unsophisticated at this time. Marketing efforts are limited to magazine ads. Their primary selling propositions are prices 20%–40% cheaper than retail. Please see Exhibit 1 for sample competitive advertisements.

Some of these entrants into the market appear to be distributors that have just decided to add some retail sales to their sales mix. Others are consumer-oriented mail order houses that offer batteries along with a full line of other computer products and accessories.

1-800-Batteries is confident that it can successfully compete with these other mail order battery companies through the use of more sophisticated marketing and service plans as well as through some relationships with major players in the industry. This strategy is discussed in depth in our Marketing Program.

MARKETING PROGRAM

Objectives

The first objective of our marketing program is to quickly generate profitable sales. The second objective is to secure key relationships that will build barriers to entry against our current and potential competitors.

Marketing Strategy

The thrust of our marketing strategy is focus and leverage. We will focus on the programs with the highest success ratio and lowest costs, rather than taking a shotgun approach. We plan to leverage the customer base and marketing resources of strategic partners. This strategy will be executed in three phases.

PHASE ONE (FY1)

The objectives of phase one are to quickly reach customers without heavy marketing expenses and to lock up key relationships, thus building competitive barriers to entry.

Joint Marketing

Joint marketing is focused on three software companies that sell battery management software. Our basic concept is to include our $5 off coupon in each of these retail software packages. In exchange for their help, we will give the software companies user registration information and will act as a sales channel for their software. After developing a strong relationship, we envision these firms' software flashing our 800# when the battery has degraded to 80% of the original charge capacity.

Company	Software Product	Reseller	Retail
Traveling Software	BatteryWatch Pro 4.0	$29	$49.95
Lucid Group	Battery Boost	$45	$79.95
Diagsoft	PowerMeter 1.08	$55	$99.95

Lucid is currently selling approximately 10,000 units per month of Battery Boost.

Reseller

The reseller program will consist of a small point of sale display offering next day delivery of rechargeable batteries. We will pay the resellers $5.00 for each order their customers place. Additionally, we will provide the reseller with the relevant customer information surrounding each purchase so that they would not lose track of this valuable information. This will give us increased distribution for the low cost of producing the POS material. The resellers will be able to offer their customers batteries without having to carry any stock, set up special locked display cases, train their salesforce, waste valuable shelf space with slow moving batteries, or refer business to their competitors. We will initially target small computer dealers, Office Depot, and Bizmart.

The resellers we interviewed responded favorably to a proposal by 1-800-Batteries to handle their replacement rechargeable battery business. According to Ernest Bruch, owner of Computer HQ, "We do this [refer customers elsewhere] with other things we don't want to stock . . It's an excellent idea." Ricardo Carlos, store manager of USM Computer said, "Sure, I would be interested. I want to make money. Now I just tell them [customers] where they can get one [and receive nothing in return]."

OEM

We will partner with OEMs through a battery sticker program in which our 800# is placed directly on the rechargeable batteries in their products. OEMs, including ACER, have told us they do not want to be in the battery replacement business, yet they are unhappy with the way resellers are serving customers' battery needs. We will offer to handle all of the OEMs' customers' battery replacement needs, and in exchange OEMs will place a sticker with our 800# on every battery that goes into their new notebooks. As their customers order batteries from us, we will collect product registration information and forward it to the OEMs. Thus OEMs gets two benefits: no more hassle with battery fulfillment and increased product registration rates. According to ACER, each registered user is worth $10–$15.

PHASE TWO (FY2)

Launch Direct Mail and Advertising

Our direct mail and advertising programs will be focused on the narrow segment of notebook power users. We will test and measure each program, expanding the programs with a positive return on marketing investment, and improving or eliminating the nonperforming programs. Our first test advertising will be placed with in-flight magazines.

PHASE THREE (FY3)

Launch Catalog

The catalog will be launched after the second year of operations once we have sourced a stable of quality products including fast rechargers and higher performance NiMH batteries. In addition, by this time we will have a substantial qualified customer list.

Phase	Channel	FY1	FY2	FY3	FY4	FY5
One	Joint Marketing	$331,200	$624,000	$1,116,000	$1,450,800	$1,886,040
	Reseller POS	$66,240	$187,200	$535,680	$696,384	$905,299
	OEM Stickers	$276,000	$520,000	$1,116,000	$1,450,800	$1,886,040
Two	Direct Mail	$0	$156,000	$148,800	$193,440	$251,472
	Advertising	$0	$156,000	$148,800	$193,440	$251,472
Three	Catalog	$0	$0	$124,000	$161,200	$209,560
	Total Sales	$673,440	$1,643,200	$3,189,280	$4,146,064	$5,389,883
	Profit Before Tax	$79,986	$137,504	$305,573	$345,505	$449,157
	Taxes	$31,994	$55,002	$122,229	$138,202	$179,663
	Profit After Tax	$47,991	$82,502	$183,344	$207,303	$269,494
	ROS	7.1%	5.0%	5.7%	5.0%	5.0%

Customers

We will focus on the end user consumer who is frustrated with the current method of buying batteries in a retail environment. These customers are affluent consumers who own at least one and usually more than one portable electronic device. They are somewhat price conscious; however, they are willing to pay for good service and convenience. We will also target small business portable users, who normally shop at computer dealers and superstores.

Staffing

Our goal is to slightly understaff relative to our projected order entry needs and handle overflow when necessary via a telemarketing service. Our rationale for keeping order entry in-house is to receive accurate market feedback and deliver excellent customer service. With our three-phase marketing strategy and assumed sales level, we need the following people over time:

PHASE ONE (FY1)

Administrator/Order Entry

This person will handle an average of 40 customer orders and 40 informational calls per day. This person will have basic computer skills and will:

- Enter all customer order data

- Send the battery order to the appropriate vendor

- Send the registration information and spiff to the source of the sale

President/Founder

This person will develop the key relationships with OEMs, battery software firms, resellers, and battery suppliers. In addition he will hire the administrator, select the office location, and contract the programming of the order entry system.

Phase Two (FY2)

Sales/Marketing

This person will implement the targeted advertising and direct mail campaigns. This person will also assist the President in securing additional OEM and reseller relationships.

Order Entry

Additional people would be hired based on the projected sales/call volume. These people would be trained by the original administrator.

Phase Three (FY3)

Sales/Marketing

This person will implement the catalog program and would source appropriate additional products.

Order Entry

Additional people would be hired based on the projected sales/call volume. These people would be trained by the original administrator.

MANAGEMENT

Ken W. Hawk

Experience	**MICROSOFT, Redmond, Washington**	**Summer, 1992**

Product Manager, Multimedia Systems Group

- Developed a detailed channel marketing strategy including channel launch plan for Microsoft Video for Windows.
- Executed first phase of launch strategy by securing major commitments from Egghead, CompUSA, and Computer City.
- Organized a group of nine multimedia product managers into the "CD/Multimedia Family" for joint channel marketing projects.

VENTURE MANUFACTURING SINGAPORE, Palo Alto, California   **1989–1991**

U.S. Sales and Marketing Manager

Venture Manufacturing Singapore is an electronics contract manufacturing company with factories in Singapore, Malaysia, and Indonesia.

- Ran U.S. office, managed $160,000 operating budget, and reported to the managing Director in Singapore.
- Built strong relationships and sold contract manufacturing services to executives at top electronic companies in the U.S.
- Developed and executed annual U.S. sales and marketing plan.

SILICON SYSTEMS, Tustin, California   **1986–1989**

Field Sales Engineer

- Sold custom semiconductors to Original Equipment Manufacturers in Silicon Valley, exceeded quota of $3.5 Million by $2.1 Million.
- Pioneered field sales engineer program after convincing our president of its merits.
- Successfully completed one year rotational engineer training program including intense assignments in product engineering, tactical and strategic marketing.

Education   **STANFORD GRADUATE SCHOOL OF BUSINESS, Palo Alto, California** **1991–1993**

- Candidate for M.B.A. degree, June 1993
- Co-President Entrepreneur Club, Rugby Club

UNIVERSITY OF MICHIGAN, Ann Arbor, Michigan   **1981–1986**

- Bachelor of Science, Electrical Engineering
- Elected Captain of the Rugby Team, Social Chairman SAE Fraternity

Personal
- Completed Mountain Man Triathlon 1991
- Volunteer sixth grade teacher through Junior Achievement

Board of Advisers

Eric Bunting worked for two years as a consultant at Monitor Company, a management consulting firm in Cambridge, MA. One of his clients was a major mail order company that was looking at ways to optimize additional warehouse space by potentially entering the third-party fulfillment business. After working at Monitor Company, Eric was a cofounder and director of Bunting Resources, Inc., a $1,000,000 oil and gas company.

Sanjeev Kriplani worked on distribution strategy for small third-party developers for Apple Computer during the summer of 1992. Prior to business school, Sanjeev worked as the marketing manager of a division of a towel wholesaler in Chicago. Sanjeev had P&L responsibility for the division and managed a $400K expense budget. As part of his responsibilities, he ran a small direct mail and telemarketing operation. Prior to this, Sanjeev worked as an Associate in the San Francisco office of Booz, Allen & Hamilton, a general management consulting firm.

FINANCIAL ASSUMPTIONS

1. Major expenses, other than founder's salary, do not begin until a deal is signed with a software partner or OEM.

2. Gross margins are 35%–40% versus 20%–25% for a typical mail order company. This is due to four main reasons. First, we are offering convenience and performance at a fair price. Our customers will be less price conscious since they currently have a hard time buying batteries. Second, our target customers are less price conscious since they own premium portable products. The battery represents a small fraction of their total system cost, and the benefits of battery life outweigh the cost so they will pay a fair price. Third, the majority of our customers learn about us without ever seeing a catalog. These are not typical mail order customers. Fourth, by leveraging the distributors we do not carry inventory.

3. Only 10% of the orders will be handled by the overflow telemarketing service at $4.00 per order.

4. Marketing expenses are partially variable, due to aggressive commission plan for salesforce.

5. Property, plant, and equipment will be limited to office lease ($2000/month) and Macintosh IISI, Laser Printer, Database Software: $3,000.

6. Employee benefits are estimated at 18% and payroll taxes at 10%.

7. Reduction in ASP and gross margin is due to the following sales mix assumptions:

	Computer	Cellular	Camcorder
FY1	100%	0%	0%
FY2	90%	5%	5%
FY3	80%	10%	10%

FINANCIAL PROJECTIONS

	FY1 Per Month *Phase One*	FY2 Per Month *Phase Two*	FY3 Per Month *Phase Three*
Fixed Costs			
Admin. Costs	$2,500	$5,000	$7,500
Office/Computer Rental	$2,300	$2,530	$2,783
Telephone Expense	$750	$1,500	$2,250
R&D Investment	$0	$0	$0
Advertising Costs/Direct Mail	$100	$10,000	$20,000
Selling Costs (Salary)	0	$2,500	$5,000
Founder Salary Cost	$4,167	$4,167	$4,167
Payroll Taxes and Employee Benefits (28%)	$1,867	$2,567	$3,267
Total Fixed Costs	$11,683	$28,263	$44,966
Variable Costs			
Total Cost of Goods Sold	$34,794	$89,007	$178,068
Overflow Fulfillment (10% Orders, $4/Order)	$325	$843	$1,715
Reseller Commission	$407	$1,200	$3,600
Salesforce Commission	$0	$685	$1,329
Return Restocking Fees (1% Sales)	$561	$1,369	$2,658
Visa/MC Fees (3% Sales)	$1,684	$4,108	$7,973
Total Variable Costs	$37,771	$97,211	$195,343
Pricing & Unit Sales Variables			
Sales	$56,120	$136,933	$265,773
Average Selling Price	$69.00	$65.00	$62.00
Number of Units	813	2107	4287
Sales/Day (20 Days/Mo.)	41	105	214
Gross Margin	38%	35%	33%
Cost of Goods Sold/Unit	$42.78	$42.25	$41.54
Total Variable Cost/Unit	$46.44	$46.14	$45.57
Break-even Unit Volume	518	1,499	2,737
Break-even Sales/Day (20 Days/Mo.)	25.9	74.9	136.8
Gross Profit/Month	$6,665	$11,459	$25,464
Annual Profit	$79,986	$137,504	$305,573
Annual Sales	$673,440	$1,643,200	$3,189,280
Total Units Shipped Per Year	9,760	25,280	51,440
Installed Base Portable Computers	5,500,000	8,500,000	10,500,000
Installed Base Penetration	0.18%	0.30%	0.49%

Sources of Sales	Annual Shipments	Annual Penetration	Annual Sales	Monthly Sales	% Sales	Assumptions
Phase One						
Software Joint Mktg Deal 1	12,0000	4%	4800	400	49%	
Reseller POS (Ten Deals)			960	80	10%	2 units/store/week
OEM Deal #1	200,000	2%	4000	333	41%	
Total				813	100%	
Phase Two						
Software Joint Mktg Deal 2	240,000	4%	9600	800	38%	
Reseller POS (Thirty Deals)			2880	240	11%	3 units/store/week
OEM Deal #2	400,000	2%	8000	667	32%	
Direct Mail	120,000	2%	2400	200	9%	
Advertising			2400	200	9%	
Total				2107	100%	
Phase Three						
Software Joint Mktg Deal 3	360,000	5%	18000	1500	35%	
Reseller POS (Sixty Deals)			8640	720	17%	3 units/store/week
OEM Deal #3	600,000	3%	18000	1500	35%	
Direct Mail	120,000	2%	2400	200	5%	
Advertising			2400	200	5%	
Catalog			2000	167	4%	
Total				4287	100%	

SAMPLE BUSINESS PLANS

1-800-Batteries

Battery Express, Inc.
DBA 1-800-Batteries
Financial Statements
for the two years ended
December 31, 1994

Battery Express, Inc.
Balance Sheets

	December 31, 1993	December 31, 1993
Current Assets:		
Cash and cash equivalents	$6,394	$28,961
Accounts receivable, net	8,142	93,535
Inventory	3,680	29,928
Prepaid expenses	–	1,200
Deferred catalog costs	–	–
Total current assets	18,216	153,624
Plant and Equipment, net	18,399	17,800
Other Assets	130,000	130,000
Total assets	$166,615	$301,424
Current Liabilities:		
Line of credit	$ –	$ –
Accounts payable	15,250	84,306
Other accrued expenses	–	42,349
Total Current Liabilities	15,250	126,655
Notes Payable to ACS	50,000	75,000
Stockholders' Equity:		
Common stock	180,000	180,000
Preferred stock	–	–
Retained earnings	(78,635)	(80,231)
Total stockholders' equity	101,365	99,769
Total liabilities and stockholders' equity	$166,615	$301,424

SAMPLE BUSINESS PLANS

1-800-Batteries

Battery Express, Inc.
Statement of Operations

	Period from inception June 30, 1993, to December 31, 1993	Year ended December 31, 1994
Net product and freight revenue	$61,955	$666,312
Cost of goods sold and freight expense	45,403	433,094
Gross margin	16,552	233,218
Selling, general and administrative expense	95,187	234,814
Operating income	(78,635)	(1,596)
Other expenses, net	–	–
Net income before taxes	(78,635)	(1,596)
Income taxes	–	–
Net income	$(78,635)	($1,596)

Battery Express, Inc.
Statement of Cash Flows

	Period from inception June 30, 1993, to December 31, 1993	Year ended December 31, 1994
Operations:		
Net income	$(78,635)	$1,596)
Reconciliation of non-cash expenses - depreciation	1,857	5,428
Increase in accounts receivable	(8,142)	(85,393)
Increase in inventory	(3,680)	(26,248)
Increase in prepaid	–	(1,200)
Increase in deferred catalog	–	–
Increase in other assets	–	–
Increase in accounts payable	15,250	69,056
Increase (decrease) in accrued expenses	–	42,349
Net cash used by operations	(73,350)	2,396
Investment:		
Purchase of equipment	(20,256)	(4,829)
Financing:		
Proceeds from issuance of common stock	50,000	–
Proceeds from issuance of note payable	50,000	25,000
Proceeds from issuance of preferred stock	–	–
Net increase in cash and equivalents	6,394	22,567
Cash at the beginning of the period	–	6,394
Cash and equivalents at the end of the period	$6,394	$28,961

Section IV

Inc.Sheets

Inc.Sheets are hands-on worksheets you can use to build your business. They were developed to facilitate the gathering and analysis of data that should be included in your business plan. *Inc.Sheets* are a combination of checklists, templates, and forms that closely parallel each section of the planning guide. Make copies as tools for drafting your plan. Use them as you complete the corresponding sections of your business plan, and then file them by topic as suggested in Section I.

Notes

Executive Summary Checklist/Worksheet

As a statement of your vision for your business, the Executive Summary should be well thought out and drafted prior to developing your plan. It can be revised or corrected once your plan has been completed. It must give concise answers to the following questions:

What merchandise and services will be offered?
❑ Now—

❑ Future—

What is the projected demand for your merchandise?
❑ Now—

❑ Future—

Who constitutes the primary market?
❑ Now—

❑ Future—

How large is the primary market?
❑ Now—

❑ Future—

. . . continued

Inc.
SHEETS
Worksheets
To Build
Your Business

When will the business begin operations?

Where will the business be located?

Who will make up your management team?

What organizational structure will your business have?

What are your business's major short-term and long-term goals?

What are your financing needs and potential sources?

INC.SHEETS
Executive Summary

Mission Statement

Your mission statement will serve as the centerpiece around which your business plan will be built. A mission statement in its simplest form is a statement of your company's purpose, vision, values, and goals.

What are your company's:

❑ Purpose—

❑ Vision—

❑ Values—

❑ Goals—

What business is your company in?

What products and services do you provide?

What are your strengths and competitive advantages?

Who are your target markets/customers?

What are the basic beliefs and values your company holds?

Business Description Checklist

A Description of Business section may be necessary to elaborate on certain aspects of your business that cannot be adequately covered in your Executive Summary. Following are four situations in which a Description of Business section may help clarify to the reader exactly what your business is trying to accomplish and how you plan to do it.

Buying an Existing Business

- ❏ The company's history
- ❏ Organizational structure
- ❏ Performance history
- ❏ Reason the owner(s) are selling
- ❏ Existing customer base
- ❏ Ownership transition strategies you will use
- ❏ Business valuation

A New Type of Business (New Product/Merchandise)

- ❏ Why is your business really different?
- ❏ What existing product(s) represent your closest competition?
- ❏ What new technology and/or methods are you using?
- ❏ Why do you feel there is a demand for this product?

Complex Product Offerings/Target Markets

- ❏ What is the rationale for your product offerings?
- ❏ Explain each product (or group of products) you will carry and how they interrelate.
- ❏ Identify all your potential target markets.

Franchise

- ❏ Where is the franchisor located, and how long has it been in business?
- ❏ Outline the provisions of the franchise contract. Be sure to include the complete contract in an appendix.
- ❏ What is unique about the product line?

Information Needs Assessment

Identifying information needs before actually looking for data will help maximize your research efforts. Refer to the Resource Directory for possible sources, or ask your library's reference librarian for additional help. Use one *Inc.Sheet* for each level.

❏ National Level   ❏ Regional Level   ❏ Local Level

Data/Information Needed	Potential Sources

INC.SHEETS | Information Needs

Trend Information

This worksheet helps you examine the trends in your market to assist you in your planning effort. To get you started, a few generic questions are provided. You will also need to develop additional topics that are specific to your business's market environment. Refer to the Resource Directory for possible sources of trend information. Use one worksheet for each question.

❏ How are other businesses similar to yours doing? Are they experiencing growth, at a plateau, or in decline? If the industry is in decline, how will your company avoid the trend?

❏ If the industry is growing, how will you compete with companies already in existence?

❏ Is the field becoming overcrowded with competitors?

❏ Are trends in your local marketplace different from those on the national and regional levels? If so, how can they be used to your advantage?

Question:

❏ National   ❏ Regional   ❏ Local

Specific Data/Information:

Segmentation Strategy: The Consumer Market

There are several ways to define a *target market(s)* (i.e., those consumers toward whom you are *specifically* aiming your products and services). This worksheet helps identify the characteristics of those markets that are most important, serving as a guide to developing your target-market profile(s). Fill out one worksheet for each of your proposed target-market segments.

Inc. SHEETS
Worksheets
To Build
Your Business

Age:	Sex:	Marital/family status:	Family size:

Education level:

Occupation:

Income:

Geographic location:

Housing (rent/own):

Interests:

Projected purchase frequency:

Other:

INC.SHEETS
Segmentation Strategy

Segmentation Strategy: The Business Market

If you plan on targeting business/institutional clients (for example, an office-supply store servicing area businesses as well as the home-office market), you will need to complete a similar profile for this target market. The worksheet, like the one for the consumer market, helps identify the characteristics of those business markets that are most important, serving as a guide to developing your target-market profile(s). General categories have been provided; however, characteristics will vary with the types of businesses being targeted. Fill out one worksheet for each of your proposed target market segments.

Business type:

Size of business:

Geographic location:

Possible uses of your products or services:

Frequency of need for your products or services:

Other:

Analyzing Product Cycle, Diversification, and Seasonality

In the course of developing information for your business plan, have you identified any factors that may affect your product cycle? Is your merchandise diverse enough to offset any trends, and if so, how? Are you likely to experience seasonal fluctuations? If you are already in business, where do your products fit into the Boston Consulting Group Matrix? What are your "staple" items?

Product diversity:

Seasonal fluctuations or changes:

Boston Consulting Group Matrix:

RELATIVE MARKET SHARE

	High	Low
High	Stars:	Question Marks:
Low	Cash Cows:	Dogs:

INDUSTRY GROWTH RATE

Inc. SHEETS
Worksheets
To Build
Your Business

Competitive Data

Fill out this sheet for each competitor identified. Some of the data may be impossible to obtain; therefore, estimates will be necessary. The information collected will be used in developing your competitive grid.

Company: _____

Street address: _____

City: _____ State: _____ Zip: _____

Years in business: _____

Telephone: (_____) _____ – _____ Fax: (_____) _____ – _____

E-mail address: _____

Merchandise offered:

Business attributes (hours, pricing, customer service, etc.):

Location factors (surroundings):

Estimated size:

❏ Annual sales

❏ Market share

❏ Number of employees

Advertising methods used (give names of newspapers, radio stations, outdoor locations, Web sites, etc.):

Worksheets
To Build
Your Business

....

Greatest perceived strength:

....

Greatest perceived weakness:

INC.SHEETS Competitive Data

....

How will you compete with this company
(i.e., what are your competitive advantages)?

Inc. SHEETS
Worksheets
To Build
Your Business

Competitive Grid

After completing a Competitive Data sheet on each competitor in your market area, collect the most significant information on this table for inclusion in your business plan. Your actual worksheet will probably contain more detail than the completed grid.

Company	Market Share & Sales (estimated)	Merchandise Offered	Business Attributes
Name: _____ Address: _____ City: _____ State: _____ Zip: _____ Years in business: _____ Telephone: (_____) ____–_____ E-mail address: _____	Market Share: Annual Sales: No. of Employees:		
Name: _____ Address: _____ City: _____ State: _____ Zip: _____ Years in business: _____ Telephone: (_____) ____–_____ E-mail address: _____	Market Share: Annual Sales: No. of Employees:		
Name: _____ Address: _____ City: _____ State: _____ Zip: _____ Years in business: _____ Telephone: (_____) ____–_____ E-mail address: _____	Market Share: Annual Sales: No. of Employees:		

INC.SHEETS Competitive Grid

Strengths	Weaknesses	My Competitive Advantages

INC.SHEETS — Competitive Grid

Worksheets To Build Your Business

Estimated Competitor Sales and Customer Base

The following calculations will provide you with an estimate of the **average sales** *(in dollars)* and the **average number of people served** per existing competitor.

Average Competitor Sales

Sales: What are the total sales for competitors' merchandise statewide?
[Note: This can also be calculated at the city, regional, or national levels.]

(Source: State Bureau of Taxation or Census of Retail Trade)

Number of Establishments: How many competitors are in your state?

(Source: County Business Patterns or Census of Retail Trade)

$$\text{Average Sales per Establishment} = \frac{\text{Total Sales}}{\text{Number of Establishments}}$$

$ _____ \quad = \quad _____

Average Customer Base

Population: What is the total number of people in your state?

(Source: Statistical Abstract)

$$\text{Average Number of People per Business} = \frac{\text{Population}}{\text{Number of Establishments}}$$

_____ \quad = \quad _____

Projections Using National Data

If it has been difficult to access demand data for your market area, you can gather it for regional or national markets, then apply that information to your local market to obtain demand estimates. Use the Reference Guide to identify appropriate sources.

**Worksheets
To Build
Your Business**

Example:

You plan to open a lawn-and-garden store featuring power equipment (lawn tractors, mowers, and tillers) in the greater San Antonio area. Your customer profile includes homeowners with an income of $40,000 or more per year who already own some kind of power lawn equipment. According to historical data, these people are most likely to purchase additional (or replacement) equipment. This also eliminates city residents of downtown neighborhoods, where there is a high probability that homeowners do not have a lawn. Since there is no local survey information on how many people own power lawn equipment in the San Antonio area, you will have to use national data to help determine market size.

From *national* demographic data, you find out that:

❏ 55.4% of all adults in the United States who own any lawn and garden equipment (indicating they have a lawn of some kind) own their own home.

(Source: Simmons Study of Media and Markets*)*

❏ 55% of all power-equipment owners have an annual household income of $40,000 or more.   *(Source:* Simmons Study of Media and Markets*)*

Combine the data: $.554 \times .55 = .3047$

Result: Of the given population, 30.47% fit your customer profile (people who own their home, own power equipment, and have an annual income of $40,000 or more).

Local Market Conditions: There are 935,327 people in San Antonio. *(Source: U.S. Bureau of the Census)*

By applying the 30.47% to the local market population, you get:

$935,327 \times .3047 = 284,994$

Conclusion: Approximately 284,994 people fit your customer profile in San Antonio.

Note: When combining data from different sources, bear in mind that the data sets may include different categories (e.g., income class or time periods). It may be necessary to interpolate the data to fit your needs. Remember that you are looking for approximations. The results of your calculations are just estimates that, combined with other data (such as break-even), can be used to reduce uncertainty about market size and sales projections.

. . . continued

Projection Worksheet

Target Profile:

Develop a target customer profile by using factors such as:

- ❏ Income
- ❏ Family size
- ❏ Cable subscribers
- ❏ Marital status
- ❏ Geographic region
- ❏ Pet owners
- ❏ Occupation
- ❏ Home ownership
- ❏ Frequent travelers

Be sure to note the source, category description, and time frame of each piece of data you collect.

My target customer's characteristics are:	____% of national/regional population	Source
A		
B		

Calculate the national/regional percentage:

$$\frac{\_\_\_\_\%}{(A)} \quad \times \quad \frac{\_\_\_\_\%}{(B)} \quad =$$

Result: _____ %

Local Market Conditions:

(Population in your trading area) _____

Estimated size of my target market:

$$\frac{_____}{\text{(National/regional percent)}} \quad \times \quad \frac{_____}{\text{(Trading area population)}} \quad = \quad \frac{_____}{\text{(No. of potential customers)}}$$

> **Note:** There may be situations in which you use more than two characteristics to define your target population.

INC.SHEETS — Demand Projections

Calculating Market Saturation

Using the most current census data, adjusted for local conditions, and expenditure data from the U.S. Census of Retail Trade, you can determine approximately how much each consumer in your trading area spends on your type of merchandise. Use the following formula to compare several areas in terms of saturation level.

$$\text{Index}^1 = \frac{C^1 \times RE^1}{RF^1}$$

Where:

Index^1 = Index of Retail Saturation for area 1

C^1 = Number of customers in area 1
(Source: U.S. Census, CACI)

RE^1 = Retail expenditures per consumer in area 1
(Source: U.S. Census of Retail Trade)

RF^1 = Square footage of retail facilities in area 1
(Source: Observation, Yellow Pages, and County Business Patterns)

Index for Location 1 _____ = _____X_____

Index for Location 2 _____ = _____X_____

Index for Location 3 _____ = _____X_____

Index for Location 4 _____ = _____X_____

INC.SHEETS
Market Saturation

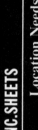

Location Needs Assessment

The first step in choosing your new location is determining the operating environment your business needs. Once you have identified your business location requirements, you can use this information to identify locations that best fulfill those needs. (Some of the categories given here may not be applicable to your business.)

Budget range: improvements/deposits/utilities/rent/or debt service (if you plan on purchasing your business's premises) $_____ to $ _____

Location Factors	Your Requirements
Site Requirements Square footage, improvements, utilities, zoning/future expansion, office sharing, other *Note: If you are considering a home office, include any improvements you will have to make to the space.*	
Proximity to Customers Considering type of products sold (convenience, shopping, or specialty), how important is proximity?	
Proximity to Competition Optimum distance to competitors	
Traffic Patterns Customer volume required Foot traffic Vehicular traffic	
Parking Customer, employee	
Permits & Licenses Federal, state, and local	
Other Considerations	

Site Evaluation

Use this form to gather information on each potential business location. Cross-check with the information on the "Location Needs Assessment" to evaluate the site's advantages and disadvantages to determine an overall "grade" for the site.

Location Address:_____

Structure (configuration, square footage, age, materials, condition, architecture, heating/air):

Rent/Lease (duration, cost, terms, etc.):

Other Costs:

Proximity to Customers:

Proximity to Competition:

Traffic Patterns (foot and vehicular):

. . . continued

Inc. SHEETS
Worksheets
To Build
Your Business

Parking:

....

Zoning:

....

Permits/Licenses Required:

....

Key Advantages:

....

Key Disadvantages:

....

Other:

....

Site Grade:	❏ A	❏ B	❏ C	❏ D	❏ F
(check one)	(Ideal)	(Desirable)	(Suitable)	(Last resort)	(Unsuitable)

INC.SHEETS Site Evaluation

Estimating Your Trading Area

Prior to selecting a specific location for your business, you need to evaluate your trading area. Draw a circle around your potential location, with a 15-mile radius for an urban area and up to a 50-mile radius for rural markets. Then divide this trading area into primary, secondary, and fringe zones. Once you have broken down your trading area, you can find the demographic characteristics of those living there, which will be critical as you begin the process of projecting sales.

Example:

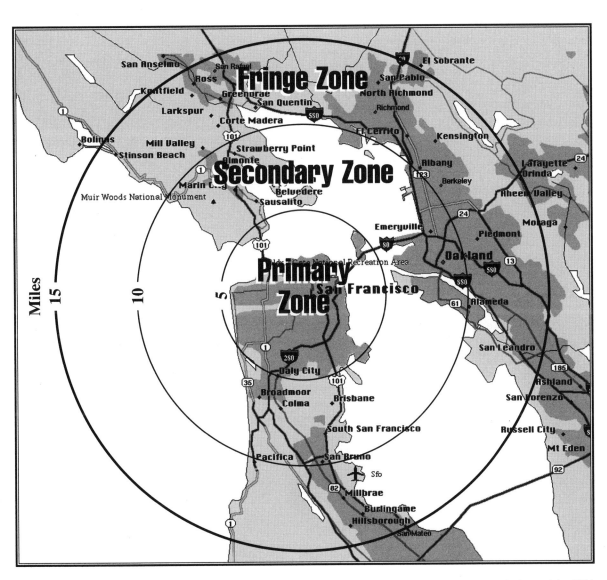

Source: DeLorme's Street Atlas USA

Store Layout and Design

Draw the layout of your store on the grid below. Indicate windows, doors, cash register station(s), fixtures, stock room, and office space. Make four or five copies of this worksheet. Use the copies to create maps that show design themes, parking, and proximity to other businesses, but don't get carried away. One or two drawings should be sufficient. If this is a mall location, add a layout of the mall, and show your intended location.

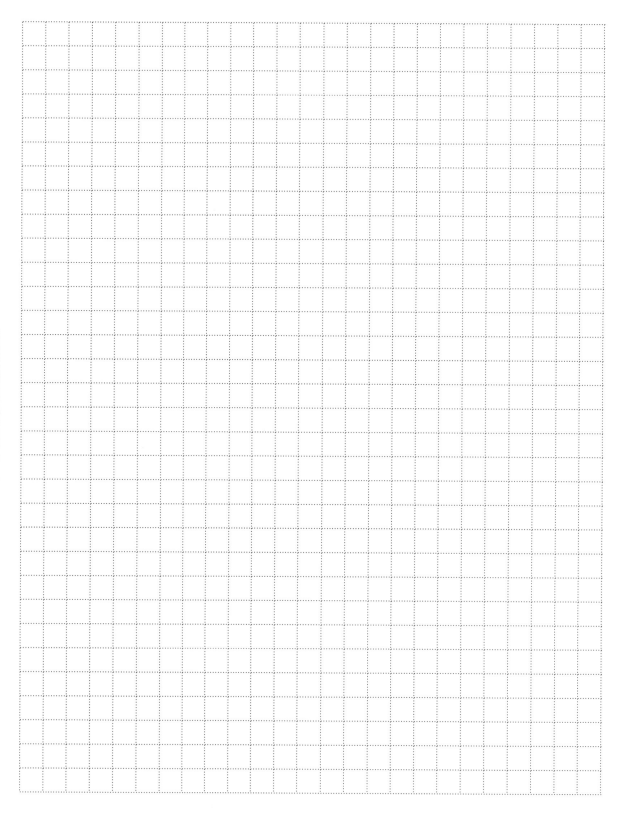

Pricing Strategy

In most mature markets, you will find merchandise offered at different price levels (high, moderate, low) reflecting varying degrees of consumer demand, ability and willingness of customers to pay, and the retailers' ability to differentiate their offerings. What pricing strategy do you intend to use, and why?

Penetration Pricing

❑ Can you achieve your financial goals at these lower price levels? How?

❑ How do you expect your competitors to react to such a pricing policy?

Premium Pricing

❑ Will your market support higher prices due to higher perceived value? Explain.

❑ On what basis other than price can you differentiate your products?

Differential Pricing

❑ How will you implement this plan?

Inc.
SHEETS
Worksheets
To Build
Your Business

Break-Even Quantity (Sales)

Calculate the break-even quantity (sales) for your business.

$$\text{BEQ (sales)} = \frac{FC}{P - VC}$$

BEQ (sales)	=	Dollar amount of sales necessary to break even
FC	=	Fixed costs for one year
P	=	Price you plan to charge for a single product or group of products (i.e., estimated sale per customer, which may include several items)
VC	=	Direct or variable costs related to each product

BEQ = _____

−

Break-Even Quantity (Sales)

Contribution Margin method:

Contribution Margin	=	Sales	−	VC

Contribution Margin = _____ − _____

$$\text{Break-Even Sales} = \frac{\text{Total Fixed Costs}}{\text{Contribution Margin (as a \% of Sales)}}$$

BEQ = _____

Break-Even (Customers)

Calculate how many customers you need to break even.

$$\text{Number of Customers needed to break even} = \frac{\text{Break-Even Sales}}{\text{Estimated Average Purchase/Customer}}$$

BEC = _____

INC.SHEETS Break-Even Formulas

Objectives

From the following list, prioritize your objectives to help form your promotional strategy. In the early stage of your business, you may have only one or two goals on which to focus.

✍ **Establish and/or expand customer base**

✍ **Differentiate merchandise and/or customer service**

✍ **Influence people to become customers**

✍ **Build goodwill**

Objectives	Methods to Achieve Objectives

Using Promotion

Promotion is a key element for any business plan. There are a variety of ways to promote your merchandise and your business to your customers. How will you set your company apart from the others? Consider each of the following topics, and respond to them in your plan.

Differentiation

How does the promotional activity make your store and merchandise look unique, different from those offered by your competitors?

Publicity

What attributes of your business might garner free publicity? Who are your contacts at the local media outlets?

Customer Service

Is a strong commitment to customer service evident in your plan? Does it justify repeat sales projections? What special services (such as personal notes to customers when special inventory arrives, individual in-store attention, accurate billing, good return policies) do you plan to provide?

Packaging

How does your packaging add to your overall promotional strategy? Does it correctly represent the image you want for your business?

Advertising Options

Use this worksheet to evaluate potential media options for your business message. List the name and type of each media support (e.g., radio: KSEA, WBWK; TV: Channel 6, ABC; print: *Washington Journal, Rye Examiner*), its reach, its cost, and the message you plan to promote via that medium. This information, coupled with a calculation of CPM (cost per thousand potential customers reached) for each vehicle, will further assist you in determining which media mix will be most cost-effective.

Promotional Medium: _____

Reach: _____ Cost: _____ CPM: _____

Market Targeted: _____

Message:

Promotional Medium: _____

Reach: _____ Cost: _____ CPM: _____

Market Targeted: _____

Message:

Promotional Medium: _____

Reach: _____ Cost: _____ CPM: _____

Market Targeted: _____

Message:

Preferred Form of Ownership

Identify the most advantageous form of ownership for your business and your reasons for choosing it.

Sole Proprietorship

Reasons:

Partnership

Reasons:

C Corporation

Reasons:

S Corporation

Reasons:

Limited Liability Corporation (Partnership)

Reasons:

Information Needs Checklist

You will need to gather information on each of the following items for the Management section of your business plan. As you complete each section, use this checklist to track your progress.

**Worksheets
To Build
Your Business**

Biographical Sketch and Qualifications

- ❏ Yourself
- ❏ Partners
- ❏ Other management
- ❏ Key personnel (nonmanagement)
- ❏ Franchise principals (for franchised business)

Professional Advisers

- ❏ Attorney
- ❏ Accountant
- ❏ Insurance agent
- ❏ Consultants (qualifications and descriptions of services)
- ❏ Other

Staff and Organization

- ❏ Description of jobs
- ❏ Salary and benefits
- ❏ Special requirements/qualifications

Other

- ❏ Board of directors/advisers (qualifications)
- ❏ Organizational chart
- ❏ Staffing plan

INC.SHEETS Information Needs

INC.SHEETS
Capital Asset List

Capital Asset List

List all the capital equipment you need to buy for your business. Be sure to note any major items and list the vendors' names, addresses, and phone numbers. This form will help you to project how much fixed-asset financing you may need.

Capital Equipment List

Item	Description	Quantity	Unit Cost	Total Cost
			$	$
TOTAL COST				$

Notes

Start-Up Cost Estimate Statement

This statement helps you calculate the amount of funds required to open and maintain your business until your sales revenues can support operations. This first section identifies Pre-Start-Up expenses, including items such as equipment, legal and professional fees, and Grand Openings. The second section identifies other start-up costs and allows for estimating a "financial cushion" to get you through the first few months of business. Some common business expense items have been included. Be sure to expand your worksheet to include all of your specific business needs.

Inc. SHEETS
Worksheets
To Build
Your Business

Start-Up Cost Estimate

Pre-Start-Up Items			Estimated Cost
			$
		Subtotal	$

Other Start-Up Items	Est. Cost per Month	# Months Coverage	
Salary of Owner	$		$
Other Salaries/Wages/Fees			
Taxes, Social Security			
Rent/Mortgage			
Advertising			
Delivery			
Supplies			
Telephone/Fax/Postage			
Utilities			
Insurance			
Debt Service			
Maintenance			
Legal/Professional Assistance			
Other			
TOTAL START-UP COSTS	$		$

Sources and Uses of Cash

On this worksheet, you must list all individual sources of funds used to start your business and the specific uses for this money. Sources must *always* equal uses.

Sources and Uses of Cash

Sources	Amount
	$
TOTAL SOURCES:	$

Uses	Amount
	$
TOTAL USES:	$

Balance Sheet

A balance sheet is calculated on an annual basis reflecting your business condition as of a particular date. Fill out this balance sheet projected for the day you open your business (pro forma). Your specific business may require additional categories, and some of those listed below may not apply to you. Adjust your balance sheet accordingly.

Inc. SHEETS
Worksheets
To Build
Your Business

BALANCE SHEET
Date: _____

ASSETS		LIABILITIES	
CURRENT ASSETS		**CURRENT LIABILITIES**	
Cash (on hand and in banks)	$_____	Accounts Payable	$_____
Accounts Receivable	_____	Current Portion of Long-Term Debt	_____
Notes Receivable	_____	Notes Payable	_____
Inventory	_____	Taxes Payable	_____
Other Current Assets	_____	Accrued Payroll	_____
TOTAL CURRENT ASSETS	$_____	Other Liabilities	_____
		TOTAL CURRENT LIABILITIES	$_____
FIXED ASSETS			
Leasehold Improvements	$_____	**LONG-TERM LIABILITIES**	
Equipment	_____	Notes Payable (bank)	$_____
Furniture/Fixtures	_____	(less current portion)	(_____)
(less accumulated depreciation)	(_____)	**TOTAL LONG-TERM LIABILITIES**	$_____
TOTAL FIXED ASSETS	$_____	**STOCKHOLDERS' EQUITY**	
TOTAL ASSETS	$_____	Capital Stock	$_____
		Current Earnings	_____
		TOTAL EQUITY	$_____
		TOTAL LIABILITIES & EQUITY	$_____

INC.SHEETS | Balance Sheet

SHEETS
Worksheets
To Build
Your Business

Income Statement

The income statement is a record of your business's financial activities over a period of time, and is generally calculated on a quarterly basis. Fill out this income statement on a pro forma basis before you open. You may also complete this statement at various times throughout the year to obtain an idea of your current finances. Your particular business may require additional categories, and some of those listed below may not apply to you. Adjust your income statement accordingly.

INCOME STATEMENT

For Quarter Ending: _____

GROSS SALES	$ _____
Less: Returns & Allowances	$ _____
NET SALES	$ _____
COST OF GOODS SOLD	$ _____
GROSS PROFIT	$ _____

OPERATING EXPENSES

Salaries & Wages	$ _____
Accounting/Legal	$ _____
Rent	$ _____
Maintenance	$ _____
Utilities	$ _____
Telephone	$ _____
Office Supplies	$ _____
Marketing & Advertising	$ _____
Interest Expense	$ _____
Depreciation	$ _____
Insurance	$ _____
Travel	$ _____
Miscellaneous	$ _____

TOTAL OPERATING EXPENSES	$ _____
OTHER REVENUE (EXPENSES)	$ _____
NET INCOME	$ _____

Monthly Cash-Flow Projection Statement

On the following pages you will find an expanded version of the statement to the right. Make five copies of each page and tape them together to form a 12-month cash-flow statement. Add "Pre-Start-Up" to the first column, and fill in Months 1–12. Use the column after Month 12 for "Totals." You can insert a final column that records the difference, or variance, between estimates and actuals for the year.

The cash-flow statement documents all cash transactions (income and expenses) on a monthly basis. Begin with figures from your Sources and Uses of Cash statements. As you receive funds and accrue expenses, be sure to fill in the "Actual" column for each month (including Pre-Start-Up).

This statement can be modified to suit your specific needs. It can be more easily created and updated using spreadsheet software.

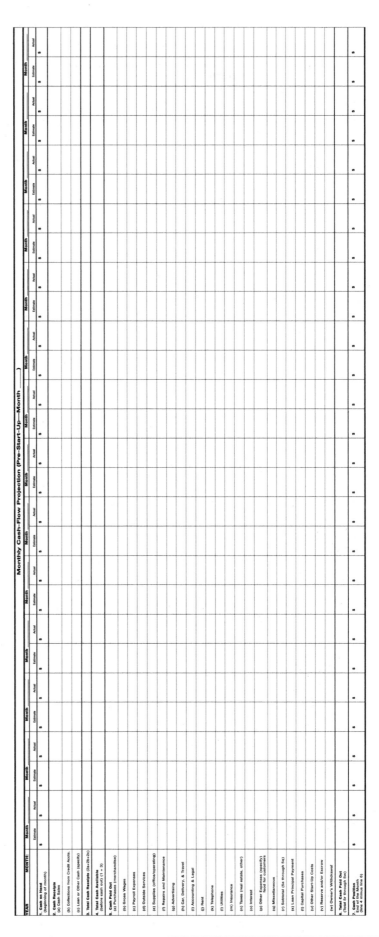

Inc. SHEETS

Worksheets To Build Your Business

Monthly Cash-Flow Projection (Pre-Start-Up/Month _____ – Month_____)

YEAR MONTH:	Month _____		Month _____		Month _____	
	Estimate	Actual	Estimate	Actual	Estimate	Actual
1. Cash on Hand (beginning of month)	$	$	$	$	$	$
2. Cash Receipts (a) Cash Sales						
(b) Collections from Credit Accts.						
(c) Loan or Other Cash (specify)						
3. Total Cash Receipts (2a+2b+2c)						
4. Total Cash Available (before cash out) (1 + 3)						
5. Cash Paid Out (a) Purchases (merchandise)						
(b) Gross Wages						
(c) Payroll Expenses						
(d) Outside Services						
(e) Supplies (office/operating)						
(f) Repairs and Maintenance						
(g) Advertising						
(h) Car, Delivery, & Travel						
(i) Accounting & Legal						
(j) Rent						

Attach to top of next page.

Inc.
SHEETS
Worksheets
To Build
Your Business

Cash Paid Out (*cont.*)	$	$	$	$	$	$
(k) Telephone						
(l) Utilities						
(m) Insurance						
(n) Taxes (real estate, other)						
(o) Interest						
(p) Other Expenses (specify) food for customers						
(q) Miscellaneous						
(r) Subtotal (5a through 5q)						
(s) Loan Principal Payment						
(t) Capital Purchases						
(u) Other Start-Up Costs						
(v) Reserve and/or Escrow						
(w) Owner's Withdrawal						
Total Cash Paid Out (Total 5r through 5w)						
Cash Position End of the Month (line 4 minus line 6)	$	$	$	$	$	$

INC.SHEETS Monthly Cash Flow

Insurance Needs Checklist

There are various types of insurance your business will need. Before contacting an insurance agent, list each type you anticipate needing, including information such as coverage levels required, deductible limits, and maximum premium costs. You can usually find this information through trade associations, in industry publications, and by asking local counterparts. Examples include: fire, theft, health, workers' compensation, fidelity bonding, title, and other risks specific to your business.

Type of insurance: _____

Coverage required: _____

Deductible limit: _____

Maximum premium: _____

Questions for agent: _____

_____

Type of insurance: _____

Coverage required: _____

Deductible limit: _____

Maximum premium: _____

Questions for agent: _____

_____

Type of insurance: _____

Coverage required: _____

Deductible limit: _____

Maximum premium: _____

Questions for agent: _____

_____

INC.SHEETS Insurance Needs

Insurance Quotes

Use this worksheet to identify vendors that can provide services to meet your insurance needs. Create grids for each potential insurance category required by your business, and use them to evaluate and select policies that best meet your needs.

Note: As you speak to insurance brokers, they may inform you of coverage/plans that you had not previously considered.

Broker	Premium/ Deductible	Coverage Provided
Name: _____ Address: _____ City: _____ State: _____ Zip: _____ Telephone: (_____) _____–_____ Fax: (_____) _____–_____ E-mail address: _____ Policy Carrier: _____		
Name: _____ Address: _____ City: _____ State: _____ Zip: _____ Telephone: (_____) _____–_____ Fax: (_____) _____–_____ E-mail address: _____ Policy Carrier: _____		
Name: _____ Address: _____ City: _____ State: _____ Zip: _____ Telephone: (_____) _____–_____ Fax: (_____) _____–_____ E-mail address: _____ Policy Carrier: _____		

Inc. SHEETS
Worksheets To Build Your Business

INC.SHEETS Insurance Quotes

Franchise Questions

When considering a franchise business, part of your research should include interviews with other franchisees and with the franchisor. Ask questions about their experiences, the territory, and the contract. Use the following questions, along with others you develop, as an interview guide for gathering information.

Questions to Ask Franchisees

1. What was the total investment required by the franchisor?

2. Were there hidden or unexpected costs?

3. How long did it take you to hit the break-even point?

4. How long before the franchise was able to support you?

5. Where were you trained, and was the training adequate?

6. Have you required any follow-up management or training support?

7. Have you ever had a serious disagreement with the franchisor? What about? How was it settled?

8. What type of reports do you have to provide to the franchisor?

9. Are you satisfied with the marketing, promotional, and advertising assistance that you receive from the company?

10. Would you advise someone else to start a franchise with this particular franchisor?

Questions to Ask the Franchisor

1. How long has the franchisor been in business? How long has it been offering franchises?

2. What is the business experience of the franchise company's directors and officers?

3. Have any of the franchisor's partners or company members ever gone bankrupt?

4. When would I get to see the contract and disclosure statement?

5. Does the franchisor provide a profit projection? What bases are used for these projections? How long have the outlets used for the projection been in operation?

6. Does the franchisor provide the initial training program? Who pays for this?

7. Does the franchisor have a system for inspection of the franchises?

8. Will the franchisor help hire and train my staff?

9. Does the franchisor design store layouts and displays?

10. Does the franchisor provide inventory control? Does it provide volume-purchasing discounts?

11. Does the franchisor provide pre-opening advertising?

12. What is the advertising program? What do I pay toward local advertising? What do I pay toward national advertising?

Questions About the Territory

1. Is the proposed territory exclusive? What assurances do I have that it is exclusive?

2. How near to me is the franchisor's next franchisee or company-owned unit going to be?

3. Is the territory well defined? Is it large enough? What are my expansion possibilities?

4. What is the present population? What is the expected population in five years? Ten years?

5. Are there any new highways planned? What about industrial growth?

    What is the traffic count near this location (both auto and pedestrian)?

6. What are the current zoning laws? Are zoning licenses required?

7. What is the average income level in the area?

8. What is the competition in the area? How are other businesses similar to mine doing?

9. Does the franchisor decide where my location will be? Do I buy or lease the location?

10. Has the franchisor conducted feasibility studies of the market potential in my proposed territory?

General Questions About the Contract

1. Does the contract protect both parties?

2. Are all costs, payments, and royalties clearly stated? Are they reasonable?

3. Does the franchisee have to pay a royalty when business is poor?

    How are "poor" business levels defined?

4. Is there a minimum sales quota?

5. How long is the duration of the agreement?

6. What are the conditions for renewal of the contract?

7. Does my lease correspond to the contract in duration?

    Are there parallel renewal options for the contract and the lease?

8. Does the contract cover in detail all the franchisor's verbal promises?

9. Do I have the right to the franchisor's latest innovations?

10. Do I have the right to assign the franchise?

11. How can I terminate the franchise? When and how can the franchisor terminate my franchise?

    How will I be compensated for the "goodwill" I have built up?

12. Is there an arbitration clause for dispute resolution?

13. Do I have to promise not to enter into any other business while

    I am a franchisee ("full time and attention" clause)?

14. Do I have to promise not to enter into any business similar to the franchisor's for a

    period of time after I have separated from the franchisor ("covenant not to compete")?

Notes

Section V

Retail Resource Directory

T he following section contains a variety of resources that you will find helpful in researching and writing your business plan. Although the listings in this section do not include all those available in the marketplace, for most plans they will be more than sufficient, and for others, a good start. Resources are grouped into three categories.

"On-the-shelf" reference materials are listed first. Most are readily available at your local public, college, or university library. Some are also available online, so you may be able to access them from your home computer. These resources are marked with the letter R and include their Internet or World Wide Web addresses. References are organized to correspond to the sections of your business plan. Each one gives a specific example of how the particular reference will help you find the information you need.

General resources, or advisers, available to help you find information and/or develop your business plan, make up the second category. The first part contains listings for some of the major trade associations doing business in the retail industry. The second part covers government-sponsored human resource assistance programs. It is always a good idea to see what type of assistance is available as you start developing your plan. A few phone calls can often identify significant help that is available at low or no cost.

Finally, there is a collection of **financial resources and programs** that are targeted toward small business. Once you have started your plan and have an understanding of what your financing requirements will be, you should review this section. Start by contacting local bankers to apprise them of your situation and to seek their counsel. This will enable them to let you know what they need to see in your plan in order to consider you a good candidate for financing. It often helps to bring the banker in early on, to make him or her a part of your team.

REFERENCES

Here are some of the most useful materials available to assist you in developing your plan. The names and addresses of the publishers are included so that you may contact them if you are unable to find the resource locally. As indicated, some of these resources are available online, and where applicable, their Internet addresses are listed.

You will find references to sources in the Resource Directory throughout Section I to guide you to the appropriate material. As you consult these resources, you are likely to find additional uses for them beyond creating a business plan.

Index Guide to Resources

Type of Information	Almanac of Business & Industrial Ratios p. 228	American Wholesalers & Distributors Directory p. 229	Business Periodicals Index p. 230	Business-to-Business Directory p. 231	Census of Retail Trade p. 232	County Business Patterns p. 233	Demographics USA p. 234	Directory of Business Information Resources p. 235	Encyclopedia of Business Information Sources p. 236	Encyclopedia of Associations p. 260
MARKET										
Customers			X	X			X	X		
Suppliers		X	X			X		X		
Marketing			X				X	X	X	
FINANCIAL										
Industry Norms									X	
Ratios	X									
Salaries/Payroll					X	X				
INDUSTRY										
Employment			X				X		X	
Forecasts			X				X		X	X
Trade Associations			X					X	X	X
Trade Shows			X					X		X
COUNSELING									X	
FINANCING										

Index Guide to Resources

Type of Information	Equifax National Decision Systems	Financial Studies of the Small Business	1997 Franchise Annual	Internet	Lifestyle Market Analyst	New York Times Index	Reader's Guide to Periodical Literature	RMA Annual Statement Studies	Simmons Study of Media and Markets	SBA	SBDCs	SBDC Research Network
	p. 238	p. 240	p. 242	p. 243	p. 244	p. 245	p. 246	p. 247	p. 248	p. 273	p. 264	p. 267
MARKET											X	X
Customers	X			X	X	X	X		X	X	X	X
Suppliers				X							X	X
Marketing	X		X	X			X		X	X		
FINANCIAL											X	X
Industry Norms				X				X		X	X	X
Ratios		X						X			X	X
Salaries/Payroll												
INDUSTRY											X	X
Employment	X				X	X	X			X	X	X
Forecasts	X				X	X	X				X	X
Trade Associations			X	X	X		X				X	X
Trade Shows				X			X				X	X
COUNSELING											X	X
FINANCING				X						X		

Type of Information	Small Business Profiles	Small Business Sourcebook	The Sourcebook of Zip Code Demographics	State Economic Development Agencies	1996 Survey of Buying Power	Thomas Register	Trade Associations	The 1997 TradeShows & Exhibits Schedule	Ulrich's International Periodicals Directory	Wall Street Journal
	p. 250	p. 251	p. 252	p. 268	p. 254	p. 255	p. 260	p. 256	p. 257	p. 258
MARKET										
Customers			X	X		X	X			X
Suppliers		X		X	X	X		X		X
Marketing	X			X			X	X		X
FINANCIAL										
Industry Norms										
Ratios										
Salaries/Payroll										
INDUSTRY										
Employment				X						X
Forecasts	X						X			X
Trade Associations		X		X				X	X	X
Trade Shows				X				X	X	X
COUNSELING										
FINANCING				X						

Almanac of Business and Industrial Financial Ratios

Publisher: Prentice Hall Inc.
200 Old Tappan Rd., Old Tappan, NJ 07675
800-922-0579
Internet: http://www.prenhall.com

Type of information available:

Selected Operating and Income Statement figures and financial ratios for various industries.

How to use it:

Find comparable income statement figures and financial ratios for your industry.

For example:

After two and a half years in business, Hannah's Dress Shoppe has not achieved the amount of sales its owner, Hannah Crown, had been hoping for. Looking at her Balance Sheet, Hannah is concerned that she may have too much of her operating funds tied up in inventory. On the other hand, she wants to be sure to have enough inventory to provide a large selection of styles and colors. Hannah uses the *Almanac* to see what other businesses similar to hers are averaging for inventory levels. In her asset class (under $100,000) most businesses maintain $33,000 in inventory. Since Hannah has $52,500 in inventory, she can carefully cut back, then reallocate some money into promotional efforts to increase sales.

Availability: Bookstores, major libraries; $89.95

Table II — RETAIL TRADE 5600
Corporations with Net Income

APPAREL AND ACCESSORY STORES

Money Amounts and Size of Assets in Thousands of Dollars

Item Description for Accounting Period 7/93 Through 6/94	Total	Zero Assets	Under 100	100 to 250	251 to 500	501 to 1,000	1,001 to 5,000	5,001 to 10,000	10,001 to 25,000	25,001 to 50,000	50,001 to 100,000	100,001 to 250,000	250,001 and over
Number of Enterprises 1	22039	236	8423	7721	2703	1828	843	121	84	22	23	20	15
Revenues ($ in Thousands)													
Net Sales 2	73638606	337494	1998695	3883660	2185609	3005764	3829036	1822026	3626234	1851079	3331894	6137447	41629668
Portfolio Income 3	800280	12071	1449	4511	12898	13010	7361	1591	17719	5839	11050	60033	652747
Other Revenues 4	1673786	4286	22090	110828	14825	28943	24025	6900	36988	51278	42445	120682	1210497
Total Revenues 5	76112672	353851	2022234	3998999	2213332	3047717	3860422	1830517	3680940	1908196	3385389	6318162	43492912
Average Total Revenues 6	3454	1499	240	518	819	1667	4579	15128	43821	86736	147191	315908	2899527
Operating Costs/Operating Income (%)													
Cost of Operations 7	60.4	60.0	58.0	62.8	60.8	60.2	60.1	64.2	60.3	62.4	61.3	58.7	60.2
Rent 8	6.4	3.6	9.8	9.0	6.2	4.2	6.6	5.4	7.0	5.0	5.6	5.1	6.5
Taxes Paid 9	2.2	2.3	2.0	2.2	3.1	2.5	2.6	2.3	2.0	1.9	2.0	2.7	2.1
Interest Paid 10	1.0	0.6	0.5	0.4	0.8	0.7	0.6	1.1	0.7	0.6	1.1	0.7	1.2
Depreciation, Depletion, Amortization 11	2.1	2.3	0.4	0.7	0.6	0.8	1.0	1.0	1.4	1.4	1.7	.1.7	2.7
Pensions and Other Benefits 12	1.1	1.0	0.4	0.2	0.3	0.8	0.8	0.5	0.8	1.1	1.1	1.1	1.3
Other 13	24.0	26.9	18.6	17.3	20.4	23.9	21.3	18.9	24.5	24.8	23.5	26.8	25.1
Officers Compensation 14	1.5	1.1	7.0	4.1	4.2	5.3	4.8	2.0	2.2	1.3	0.8	0.7	0.3
Operating Margin 15	1.5	2.2	3.5	3.3	3.5	1.7	2.2	4.8	1.3	1.7	2.9	2.4	0.6
Oper. Margin Before Officers Compensation 16	2.9	3.2	10.5	7.5	7.8	7.0	7.1	6.8	3.5	3.0	3.7	3.2	0.9
Selected Average Balance Sheet ($ in Thousands)													
Net Receivables 17	222	•	5	15	36	86	113	966	1170	2448	6358	19016	238803
Inventories 18	549	•	33	92	176	333	1016	3557	7491	13405	26783	49769	413563
Net Property, Plant and Equipment 19	399	•	2	14	37	68	305	1027	3908	8011	18313	42804	418259
Total Assets 20	1698	•	53	160	348	683	1974	6902	15418	34742	65917	153027	1627841

Almanac of Business & Industrial Financial Ratios by Leo Troy.
Copyright © 1997, Prentice Hall. Reprinted by permission.

RESOURCE DIRECTORY — On-the-Shelf Resources

American Wholesalers and Distributors Directory

Publisher: Gale Research Inc.
835 Penobscot Bldg., 645 Griswold St.
Detroit, MI 48226-4094
800-877-GALE (877-4253)
800-762-4058 fax

Type of information available:

Identifies more than 28,000 wholesalers and distributors in the United States and Puerto Rico in 61 broad categories. Listing includes company name, address, product lines, SIC code, year established, annual estimated sales, number of employees, and the company principals.

How to use it:

Find sources of supply. Information in this reference is classified by product line, then indexed by SIC code, geography, and alphabetical order.

For example:

Evan owns a building-material supply business in Wichita, Kans., that sells a variety of roofing materials to local contractors. Evan needs to find a source of supply for high-quality adhesives, caulking compounds, and sealants for the many roofing contractors he serves. The category "Adhesives" tells Evan about several national adhesive wholesalers, and the geographic index points Evan to other sources of supply in the Wichita area.

Availability: Most major libraries and universities; $190

(1) Adhesives

Entries in this section are arranged alphabetically by company name. When the company name is a personal name, the company name is alphabetized by the surname unless the first name or initial(s) are part of a trade name. See the User's Guide at the front of this directory for additional information.

■ 1 ■ **Bender Wholesale Distributors**
52705 Moose Trail
Elkhart, IN 46514
Phone: (219)264-4409
Fax: (219)262-8799
Product Line: Adhesives and sealants; Chemical preparations. **SIC:** 5169 (Chemicals & Allied Products Nec). **Founded:** 1948.

■ 2 ■ **William Bernstein Company Inc.**
155 W. 72nd St.
New York, NY 10023
Phone: (212)799-3200
Fax: (212)799-3209
Product Line: Albinium gum. **SIC:** 5149 (Groceries & Related Products Nec). **Founded:** 1939. **Sales:** $3,000,000. **Employees:** 6. **Principals:** President, William Bernstein.

■ 3 ■ **Everitt & Ray Inc.**
1325 Johnson Dr.
City of Industry, CA 91745
Phone: (818)961-3611
Fax: (818)333-7567
Product Line: Abrasives and adhesives, including sanding belts. **SIC:** 5085 (Industrial Supplies). **Sales:** $3,000,000. **Employees:** 15. **Principals:** David Everitt.

■ 4 ■ **Hytec Fastening Systems Div.**
6875 Broadway Ave.
Cleveland, OH 44105
Phone: (216)883-5100
Fax: (216)883-5103
Product Line: Adhesives; Staples; Nails. **SIC:** 5169 (Chemicals & Allied Products Nec). **Founded:** 1981. **Sales:** $1,800,000. **Employees:** 12. **Principals:** President, Edward Kozelka.

■ 5 ■ **International Tape Products Co.**
5 Lawrence St.
Bloomfield, NJ 07003
Phone: (201)748-7870
Fax: (201)748-0408
Product Line: Adhesives and sealants. **SIC:** 5169 (Chemicals & Allied Products Nec). **Founded:** 1965. **Sales:** $6,000,000. **Employees:** 17. **Principals:** President, Pierre Guariglia; Vice President, Gary Guariglia; Manager, Terry Gamba.

■ 7 ■ **J.E. Lenover & Son Inc.**
34119 Autry
Livonia, MI 48150
Phone: (313)427-0000
Toll-free: 800-LEN-OVER
Fax: (313)427-0986
Product Line: Caulking compounds a Adhesives and sealants; Wallboard. (Construction Materials Nec); 5031 (Lumbe Millwork). **Employees:** 5.

■ 8 ■ **Polyken Technologies**
15 Hampshire St.
Mansfield, MA 02048
Phone: (508)261-6256
Toll-free: 800-248-7659
Fax: (508)261-6272
Product Line: Pressure sensitive produ tape. **SIC:** 5113 (Industrial & Personal S

■ 9 ■ **Red Devil Inc.**
2400 Vauxhall Rd.
Union, NJ 07083
Phone: (908)688-6900
Fax: (908)688-8872
Product Line: Hand tools; Caulking con sealants. **SICs:** 5169 (Chemicals & Allied P 5072 (Hardware).

■ 10 ■ **Romar Sales Corp.**
866 Iwilei Rd.
Honolulu, HI 96817
Phone: (808)536-8298
Product Line: Sealants. **SIC:** 5082 (Cc Mining Machinery).

■ 11 ■ **John G. Shelley Company Inc**
16 Mica Ln.
Wellesley Hills, MA 02181
Phone: (617)237-0900
Fax: (617)237-8978
Product Line: Adhesives. **SIC:** 5085 (Industrial Supplies). **Founded:** 1927. **Sales:** $4,000,000. **Employees:** 30. **Principals:** President, H. Chandler Shelley Jr.; CFO, John W. Fachner Jr.

Wichita, KS

Wichita

A-B Sales Inc. (Alcoholic Beverages) [1494]
Action Auto Radio Inc. (Electrical and Electronic Equipment and Supplies) [8621]
Advanced Imaging Technologies Inc. (Medical, Dental, and Optical Equipment) [19294]
Airtechnics Inc. (Electrical and Electronic Equipment and Supplies) [8631]
Alipro Corp. (Wichita, Kansas) (Paints and Varnishes) [21770]
Associated Systems Inc. (Computers and Software) [6362]
Bagatelle (Food) [11009]
Berry Companies Inc. (Construction Materials and Machinery) [7362]
Berry Tractor and Equipment Co. (Construction Materials and Machinery) [7363]
Bevan-Rabell Inc. (Electrical and Electronic Equipment and Supplies) [8789]
Case Supply, Inc. (Wichita, Kansas) (Floorcovering Equipment and Supplies) [10206]
Comfort Supply Inc. (Heating and Cooling Equipment and Supplies) [15072]
Cramer Co. Inc. (Household Appliances) [15770]
Decorator & Craft Corp. (Toys and Hobby Goods) [27046]
F and E Wholesale Food Service Inc. (Food) [11598]
Finn Distributing Co. Inc. (Household Items) [16088]
Foley Tractor Company Inc. (Agricultural Equipment

Geographic Index

American Wholesalers and Distributors Directory

RESOURCE DIRECTORY
On-the-Shelf Resources

Business Periodicals Index

Publisher: H.W. Wilson Co.
950 University Ave., Bronx, NY 10452
718-588-8400

Type of information available:

Index of articles appearing in general business and trade periodicals, organized alphabetically by subject.

How to use it:

Obtain information including general industry trends, news, competitive information, and advances in technology.

For example:

Brad and Joan, two former members of the band "Rhyme Maniacs," retired from the group to open their own record store. They already know a lot about the recording industry, but not very much about record stores. For example, "What are the big record stores doing for advertising campaigns?" "How do we get the hits before they are yesterday's news?" and "Should we carry books on tape?" Brad and Joan will look up a variety of titles on these and other subjects, and then read the articles in the related periodicals.

Availability: most libraries; $225 to $2,990

---

810   BUSINESS PERIODICALS INDEX

Record industry *See* Recording industry
Record stores
    See also the following corporate names
    Bananas Music (St. Petersburg, Fla.)
    Camelot Music Inc.
    Compact Disc World Inc.
    Cut Corner Records & Video (Lexington, Ky.)
    Grand Ole Opry Records
    K. W. C. Management Corporation
    Lucy's Record Shop (Nashville. Tenn.)
    Music Network (Firm)
    Musicland Stores Corp.
    National Record Mart Inc.
    Peppermint Records & Tapes (Firm)
    Poplar Tunes Record Shop Inc.
    Spec's Music, Inc.
    Streetside Records (Firm)
    Tower Records (Firm)
    Virgin Megastores (Firm)
      Acquisitions and mergers
Peppermint's K.W.C. facing sale to Music Network. *Billboard* v109 p62 Ja 18 '97

      Closing
Blockbuster plots shift in int'l retail course: music closures planned. D. Jeffrey. *Billboard* v108 p10+ O 19 '96
Media Play: Musicland tries to fix a good idea gone awry. E. Christman. *Billboard* v108 p46 D 21 '96

Record stores—*cont.*
      Competition
Cross-channel aid for indies: scheme helps small stores compete [EMI Channel concept] J. Ferguson. *Billboard* v108 p36 D 14 '96
Mall-based music stores struggle to survive against tough competition. il *Stores* v78 p58+ O '96
Music retailers try gamely to excite computer-besotted consumers. M. Folb. il *Marketing* v101 p7 D 23-30 '96
Peanut butter and Pearl Jam [Fresh Picks] P. Newcomb. por *Forbes* v159 p152 F 10 '97
      Design and construction
Tower's second splashdown in Lincoln Center: chain expects revamped store to be top U.S. outlet. E. Christman. il *Billboard* v108 p61-2 N 16 '96
Virgin goes to Disney World, eyes U.S. movie theater biz [to open Megastore in Disney World, Fla.] E. Christman. *Billboard* v108 p82 O 19 '96
      Failure
Retailers tread cautiously in '96. E. Christman. *Billboard* v108 p53+ D 28 '96
      Finance
Corporate soap opera contributed to a grim year for indies. C. Morris. *Billboard* v108 p58-9 D 28 '96
Holiday sales results mixed for entertainment biz: music chains report good, bad news. D. Jeffrey and others. *Billboard* v109 p1+ Ja 18 '97

Music retailers try gamely to excite computer-besotted consumers. M. Folb. il *Marketing* v101 p7 D 23-30 '96
Virgin goes to Disney World, eyes U.S. movie theater biz [to open Megastore in Disney World, Fla.] E. Christman. *Billboard* v108 p82 O 19 '96
Vital Dutch scene crosses musical borders: music retailers thrive via niche marketing. B. Bambarger. il *Billboard* v108 p1+ N 2 '96
      Merchandising
Indie chain Streetside Records drums up business according to its own rhythm. P. Bates. por *Billboard* v108 p80-1+ O 19 '96
      Reorganization
A reborn Wherehouse looks to future. E. Christman. *Billboard* v109 p3+ Ja 11 '97
      Sales promotion
Do premiums add value to music retail? E. Christman. *Billboard* v108 p3+ D 7 '96
In-store tours offer alternative: appearances benefit both artists and merchants. F. DiCostanzo. *Billboard* v108 p71-2 N 23 '96
Labels took steps to ease retailers' woes. D. Jeffrey. *Billboard* v108 p53+ D 28 '96
      Securities
Music bland: the recorded music industry is starting to hit some sour notes on Wall Street. E. Dravo. *Financ World* v166 p86 Ja 21 '97
      Security measures
Source-tagging tested in U.K. J. Ferguson. *Billboard* v108 p55 N 16 '96
      Stock
    See Record stores—Inventories
      Web sites
National Record Mart brings Web to retail. D. Jeffrey. *Billboard* v108 p5 N 16 '96
      Asia
Merchants & marketing. il *Billboard* v108 p APQ4+ O 26 '96
Parallel import consensus within reach: weak distribution an obstacle for Asian retailers. K. Cahoon. *Billboard* v109 p6 Ja 11 '97

Tower targets South America: store expansion also planned for Asia. J. Ferguson. *Billboard* v109 p43+ Ja 18 '97
      Australia
Australia launching EPOS-based charts. C. Eliezer. *Billboard* v108 p10+ N 23 '96
      Canada
Music retailers try gamely to excite computer-besotted consumers. M. Folb. il *Marketing* v101 p7 D 23-30 '96
      Cayman Islands
    See also
    Caribbean Rhythm (Firm)
      Great Britain
    See also
    HMV Music Ltd.
    WH Smith Retail (Firm)
Source-tagging tested in U.K. J. Ferguson. *Billboard* v108 p55 N 16 '96

Business Periodicals Index © 1997, H.W. Wilson Co. April 1997, Volume 39, No. 8, Record Stores.

RESOURCE DIRECTORY On-the-Shelf Resources

The Guide to Retail Business Planning

230

Business-to-Business Directory

Type of information available:
A listing of businesses in your local area that sell goods and services principally to other businesses.

How to use it:
Find potential suppliers or competitors.

For example:
Jack and Sally are planning to open a trophy shop in the New York metropolitan area that will specialize in plaques and awards for corporate employee-incentive programs. They want to know what services (such as engraving, one-day turnaround, and delivery) other trophy shops in greater New York are offering. They will then incorporate these services into their offerings to become a full-service supplier.

Availability: Public, university and business libraries or through local phone company; no charge

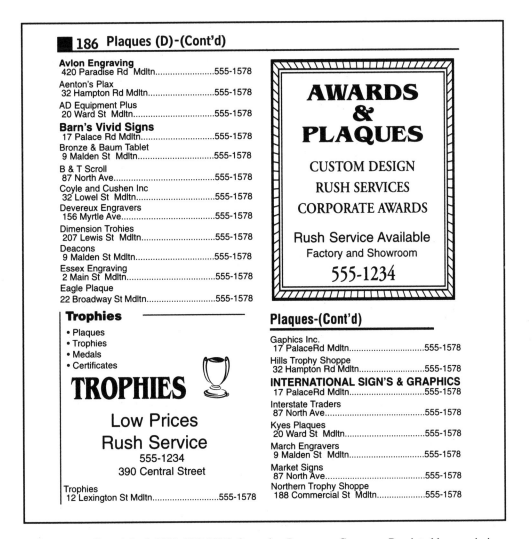

■ 186 Plaques (D)-(Cont'd)

Avlon Engraving
420 Paradise Rd Mdltn........................555-1578

Aenton's Plax
32 Hampton Rd Mdltn............................555-1578

AD Equipment Plus
20 Ward St Mdltn.................................555-1578

Barn's Vivid Signs
17 Palace Rd Mdltn...............................555-1578

Bronze & Baum Tablet
9 Malden St Mdltn...............................555-1578

B & T Scroll
87 North Ave......................................555-1578

Coyle and Cushen Inc
32 Lowel St Mdltn...............................555-1578

Devereux Engravers
156 Myrtle Ave....................................555-1578

Dimension Trohies
207 Lewis St Mdltn.............................555-1578

Deacons
9 Malden St Mdltn................................555-1578

Essex Engraving
2 Main St Mdltn..................................555-1578

Eagle Plaque
22 Broadway St Mdltn...........................555-1578

Trophies

- Plaques
- Trophies
- Medals
- Certificates

TROPHIES

Low Prices
Rush Service
555-1234
390 Central Street

Trophies
12 Lexington St Mdltn...........................555-1578

AWARDS & PLAQUES

CUSTOM DESIGN
RUSH SERVICES
CORPORATE AWARDS

Rush Service Available
Factory and Showroom
555-1234

Plaques-(Cont'd)

Gaphics Inc.
17 PalaceRd Mdltn...............................555-1578

Hills Trophy Shoppe
32 Hampton Rd Mdltn...........................555-1578

INTERNATIONAL SIGN'S & GRAPHICS
17 PalaceRd Mdltn...............................555-1578

Interstate Traders
87 North Ave......................................555-1578

Kyes Plaques
20 Ward St Mdltn...............................555-1578

March Engravers
9 Malden St Mdltn...............................555-1578

Market Signs
87 North Ave......................................555-1578

Northern Trophy Shoppe
188 Commercial St Mdltn....................555-1578

Census of Retail Trade
(Retail Annual Survey)

Publisher: Bureau of the Census
Washington, DC 20233
301-457-4100
Internet: http://www.census.gov

Type of information available:

Numbers of establishments and payroll figures in various industries, organized by town. This source also provides information on how many businesses are individual proprietorships or partnerships rather than corporations.

How to use it:

Determine how many businesses (potential competitors) in a particular industry are located in your market area.

For example:

Anne and Lilly want to open a flower shop in Baton Rouge, La. To determine whether the area is currently underserved by florists, they consult the Census of Retail Trade to see how many florists are in business in Baton Rouge. According to Anne's calculations, Baton Rouge can support 32 florists and still provide adequate sales levels. Lilly finds that there are 19 flower shops with total sales of $17,740,000 (or more than $930,000 each). Anne and Lilly will now target the least served area of Baton Rouge for their location.

Availability: World Wide Web, many libraries; $6

Table 5. **Summary Statistics for Places With 350 Establishments or More: 1992** —Con.

[Includes only establishments with payroll. For meaning of abbreviations and symbols, see introductory text. For explanation of terms and comparability of 1987 and 1992 censuses, see appendix A. For information on geographic areas followed by ▲, see appendix F]

SIC code	Geographic area and kind of business	Estab-lishments (number)	Sales ($1,000)	Annual payroll ($1,000)	First-quarter payroll ($1,000)	Paid employees for pay period including March 12 (number)
	BATON ROUGE					
	Retail trade	1 705	2 659 517	305 209	71 822	26 947
52	Building materials and garden supplies stores	75	124 921	13 163	2 903	781
521, 3	Building materials and supply stores	42	102 523	9 605	2 105	517
525	Hardware stores	23	13 337	2 418	563	167
526	Retail nurseries, lawn and garden supply stores	7	4 578	893	187	89
527	Manufactured (mobile) home dealers	3	4 483	247	48	8
53	**General merchandise stores**	36	450 743	44 909	10 705	3 634
531	Department stores (incl. leased depts.) [1][2]	15	350 915	(NA)		421
531	Department stores (excl. leased depts.) [1]	15			1 639	259
533	Variety stores			6 975	831	57
539	Miscellaneous general merchandise stores	37	48 072	3 510	219	412
54		35	27 790	873	1 534	
		10	7 066	6 572		9 651
		48	57 432		16 751	
5712	Furniture stores			71 668		9 180
5713, 4, 9	Homefurnishings stores	482	268 340		16 066	3 557
572	Household appliance stores			68 534	6 688	EE
573	Radio, television, computer, and music stores	417	251 631	29 247	(D)	4 707
		167	100 813	(D)	7 164	EE
58	**Eating and drinking places**	11	(D)	29 748	(D)	
		213	119 925	(D)		471
	Eating places	26	(D)		685	
5812	Restaurants			3 134		719
5812 pt.	Cafeterias	65	16 709		2 189	
5812 pt.	Refreshment places			9 365		1 946
5812 pt.	Other eating places	46	82 373		5 834	
5812 pt.	Drinking places	318	156 431	24 720		31
5813					64	150
591	**Drug and proprietary stores**	6	2 788	263	441	
		27	9 630	1 990		988
59 ex. 591	**Miscellaneous retail stores**				2 675	CC
		146	85 544	11 232	(D)	CC
592	Liquor stores	26	(D)	(D)	(D)	272
593	Used merchandise stores	20	(D)	(D)	1 066	392
		42	26 781	4 280	781	
594	Miscellaneous shopping goods stores	58	27 203	3 616		210
5941	Sporting goods stores and bicycle shops				838	AA
5942	Book stores			3 602	(D)	
5944	Jewelry stores	30	17 740	(D)		166
5943, 5, 6, 7, 8, 9	Other miscellaneous shopping goods stores	1	(D)		468	AA
				1 879	(D)	AA
596	Nonstore retailers	19	7 795	(D)	(D)	AA
598	Fuel dealers	2	(D)	(D)	(D)	CC
		3	(D)	(D)	887	274
		26	(D)	3 777		
5992	Florists	58	21 707		219	57
5993	Tobacco stores and stands			6 572	1 534	412
5994	News dealers and newsstands					
5995	Optical goods stores					
5999	Miscellaneous retail stores, n.e.c.					

Retail Annual Survey, U.S. Department of Commerce, Bureau of the Census, 1994
Louisiana, LA-21, Baton Rouge, Miscellaneous Retail Stores, Florists.

County Business Patterns

Publisher: U.S. Department of Commerce
Bureau of the Census, Data User Services Div.
Washington, DC 20233
301-457-4100
Internet: http://www.lib.virginia.edu/sosci/cbp/cbp.html

Type of information available:

State and county employment, payroll figures, and numbers of establishments of various industries according to size.

How to use it:

Find out how many businesses in a particular industry are located in a county.

(Updated annually, this resource is similar in content to the *Census of Retail Trade*; however, *County Business Patterns* breaks down the total number of establishments by number of employees, but does not contain information on type of organization.)

For example:

Bob and Corinne recently inherited money from Corinne's parents. They have always wanted to open a grocery store somewhere in northern Maine. Bob and Corinne are wondering how many grocery stores there are in Aroostook County and how large they are. They will use this information, in addition to a recent traffic-patterns study and density calculations, to determine which areas in Aroostook County appear to be underserved.

Availability: CD-ROM, libraries, government bookstores; U.S. book, $650; state by state, $2.50 to $12; CD-ROM (1992–1993), $150

COUNTY BUSINESS PATTERNS   **MAINE 23**

Table 2. **Counties—Employees, Payroll, and Establishments, by Industry: 1994**—Con.

[Excludes most government employees, railroad employees, and self-employed persons. Size class 1 to 4 includes establishments having payroll but no employees during mid-March pay period. (D) denotes figures withheld to avoid disclosing data for individual companies; the data are included in broader industry totals. For explanation of terms, statement on reliability, and comparability with other data, see introductory text]

SIC code	Industry	Number of employees for week including March 12	Payroll ($1,000) First quarter	Payroll ($1,000) Annual	Total number of establishments	1 to 4	5 to 9	10 to 19	20 to 49	50 to 99	100 to 249	250 to 499	500 to 999	1,000 or more
	ANDROSCOGGIN—Con.													
	Services—Con.													
87	Engineering and management services	425	2 920	11 892	82	56	18	5	2	1	—	—	—	—
871	Engineering and architectural services	127	1 153	4 369	16	9	4	2	—	1	—	—	—	—
872	Accounting, auditing, and bookkeeping	227	1 439	6 184	39	25	10	2	2	—	—	—	—	—
—	Administrative and auxiliary	120	1 223	5 425	4	1	1	—	—	2	—	—	—	—
	Unclassified establishments	(A)	(D)	(D)	14	14	—	—	—	—	—	—	—	—
	AROOSTOOK													
	Total	22 641	97 158	413 827	2 383	1 422	472	272	150	37	22	5	3	—
	Agricultural services, forestry, and fishing	156	602	3 193	33	26	2	2	3	—	—	—	—	—
07	Agricultural services	107	335	1 932	22	17	2	1	2	—	—	—	—	—
	Mining	(A)	(D)	(D)	1	1	—	—	—	—	—	—	—	—
15	Construction	678	3 035	19 153	223	177	28	15	3	—	—	—	—	—

Industry	1 411	3 180	13 307	111
Food stores	1 411	3 180	13 307	111
Grocery stores	1 375	3 137	13 008	101
Automotive dealers and service stations	973	3 488	14 803	121
New and used car dealers	257	1 275	5 651	14
Gasoline service stations	534	1 472	6 028	69
Apparel and accessory stores	312	632	2 653	56
Women's clothing stores	118	194	802	22
Family clothing stores	120	268	1 096	11
Furniture and homefurnishings stores	197	547	2 478	29
Furniture and homefurnishings stores	127	365	1 654	15
Furniture stores	109	325	1 442	11

County Business Patterns, U.S. Department of Commerce, Bureau of the Census, 1994, Maine, CBP-94-21.

Demographics USA

Publisher: Market Statistics
355 Park Avenue South, New York, NY 10010
800-685-7828
212-592-6259 fax
http://www.marketstats.com

Type of information available:

Basic demographics including population data and households by Effective Buying Income (EBI). Also includes actual retail sales for major store types and major merchandise lines. Three books are available, sorted by county, city, or zip code.

How to use it:

Find demographic information about potential customers, markets, and product lines. Compare data from region to region to develop market potential.

For example:

A chain of automotive dealers wants to reach men 55 to 64 years of age in Florida and is considering placing advertising in newspapers in one of four metro markets (MSAs): Panama City, Pensacola, Sarasota-Bradenton, or Tallahassee. The chain uses *Demographics USA* to determine that Sarasota-Bradenton not only has a high population of 55-to-64-year-old males, but that automotive dealer sales are highest in this area as well. The chain will therefore focus its advertising efforts in the Sarasota-Bradenton area.

Availability: Most business libraries, university libraries, major public libraries; pricing starts at $435; CD-ROM starts at $999 (includes book)

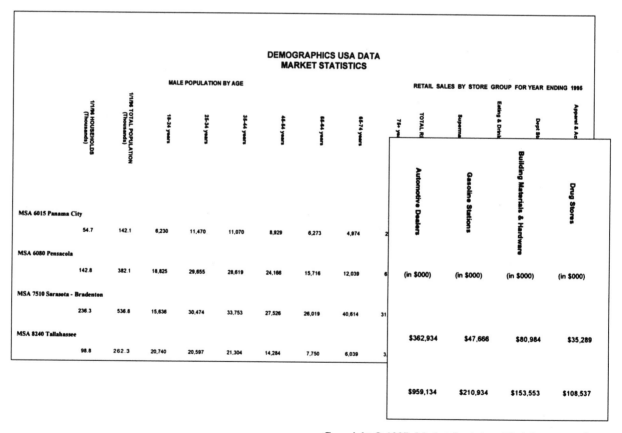

DEMOGRAPHICS USA DATA
MARKET STATISTICS

MALE POPULATION BY AGE

RETAIL SALES BY STORE GROUP FOR YEAR ENDING 1995

	1/1/96 HOUSEHOLDS (Thousands)	1/1/96 TOTAL POPULATION (Thousands)	18-24 years	25-34 years	35-44 years	45-54 years	55-64 years	65-74 years	75+ ye		Automotive Dealers (in $000)	Gasoline Stations (in $000)	Building Materials & Hardware (in $000)	Drug Stores (in $000)
MSA 6015 Panama City	54.7	142.1	6,230	11,470	11,070	8,929	6,273	4,974	2					
MSA 6080 Pensacola	142.8	382.1	18,825	29,655	28,619	24,166	15,716	12,039	6					
MSA 7510 Sarasota - Bradenton	236.3	536.8	15,636	30,474	33,753	27,526	26,019	40,614	31		$362,934	$47,666	$80,984	$35,289
MSA 8240 Tallahassee	98.8	262.3	20,740	20,597	21,304	14,284	7,750	6,039	3		$959,134	$210,934	$153,553	$108,537

Directory of Business Information Resources 1997

Publisher: Grey House Publishing Inc.
Pocket Knife Square, Lakeville, CT 06039
860-435-0868
860-435-0867 fax

Type of information available:

A listing of print media, electronic media, and trade shows for 93 industry groups.

How to use it:

Locate vertical trade associations, organizations, newsletters, directories, databases, and trade shows for your industry.

For example:

Paul is planning on opening his own sporting goods store. In the early stages of his research, he is looking for a variety of trade associations, newsletters, and human resources from which he can draw market information and technical expertise. Looking under "Sports and Recreation," Paul finds several associations listed that may provide industry statistics and demographics. Moving on to the Newsletter and Magazine sections, he identifies media that he would want to subscribe to. Through the media and the associations, he will find critical planning and financial information for establishing a new store.

Availability: Most business and university libraries; $150

12658 National Golf Foundation

1150 South US Highway One
Jupiter, FL 33477
561-744-6006
800-733-6006
FAX 561-744-6107
E-Mail: ngf@ngf.org
Home Page: www.ngf.org

Dr. Joseph Beditz, President & CEO
William Burbaum, Editor/Publisher
Provides market research on the U.S. Golf Industry and serves as an information clearinghouse for the industry and the media. Conducts seminars for golf teachers, coaches and professionals. Conducts golf course development feasibility studies for developers. Publications include instructional guides for playing and teaching; books on all phases of building and operating golf facilities; annual research reports on all aspects of the game; and a bi-monthly newsletter.

6M Members Founded: 1936
Printed in 2 colors on matte stock

12659 National Health Club Association

12596 Bayaud Avenue, 1st Floor
Denver, CO 80228
303-753-6422

Thomas Plummer, Executive Director
Provides services and resources to the fitness center/health club industry nationwide. Emphasizes club and employee quality, sponsors training seminars and educational programs.

3M Members Founded: 1988

12660 National Ski Retailers Association

1699 Wall Street
Mt. Prospect, IL 60056
708-439-4293
FAX 708-439-0111

Thomas B. Doyle, Managing Director
Provides retail support services, legislative representation, marketing support for members.

Members are professionals involved in all aspects of the strength training of athletes.
13.8M Members

12664 National Youth Sports Coaches Association

2050 Vista Parkway
West Palm Beach, FL 33411
407-684-1141

Represents coaches involved in youth athletics.
117M Members

12665 Pop Warner Football

586 Middletown Blvd., Ste. C-100
Langhorne, PA 19047
215-752-2691
FAX 215-752-2879

Jon Butler, Executive Director
A national youth football and cheerleading organization that provides assistance to its various chapters.
285M+ Members Founded: 1929

12666 Professional Bowlers Association

1720 Meriman Road
Akron, OH 44334
216-836-5568
FAX 216-836-2107

Acts on behalf of professional bowlers.
3.7M Members

12667 Professional Golf Club Repairmen's Association

2295 Ben Hogan Drive
Dunedin, FL 34698
813-787-6890
FAX 813-787-4361

Thelma Schloss, Executive Director
Jacqueline L. Bowers, Secretary
Advances repair and clubmaking skills. Conducts specialized education and research programs, eight schools a week running five days.
1M Members Founded: 1977

RESOURCE DIRECTORY
On-the-Shelf Resources

Encyclopedia of Business Information Sources

Publisher: Gale Research Inc.
835 Penobscot Bldg., 645 Griswold St.
Detroit, MI 48226-4094
800-877-GALE (877-4253)
800-762-4058 fax

Type of information available:
A listing of written and human resources arranged alphabetically by topic.

How to use it:
Locate directories, periodicals, newsletters, books, manuals, trade associations, online databases, and statistical sources relating to your industry or area of interest.

For example:
Jim and Ellen are skilled potters. They are considering selling their wares exclusively through direct marketing, since their local market cannot support another retail pottery outlet. They know very little about direct marketing and would like to consult some resources on the subject. Under "Direct Marketing" they find several books that they believe will be helpful. They also find the addresses of various trade associations, and will write for additional information.

Availability: Business and university libraries or through publisher; $299

RESOURCE DIRECTORY
On-the-Shelf Resources

Mail Advertising Service Association International. 1421 Prince St., Suite 200, Alexandria, VA 22314. Phone: (800) 333-6272 or (703) 836-9200. Fax: (703) 548-8204.

Nonprofit Mailers Federation. 815 15th N.W., Suite 822, Washington, DC 20005-2201. Phone: (202) 628-4380. Fax: (202) 628-4383.

DIRECT MARKETING

GENERAL WORKS

Creative Strategy in Direct Marketing. Susan K. Jones. NTC Publishing Group. 1991. $39.95.

Direct Marketing, Direct Selling, and the Mature Consumer: A Research Study. James R. Lumpkin and others. Quorum Books. 1989. $55.00. A study of older consumers and their use of mail order, telephone shopping, party-plans, etc.

Do-It-Yourself Direct Marketing: Secrets for Small Business. Mark S. Bacon. John Wiley & Sons, Inc. 1991. $24.95.

ABSTRACTING AND INDEXING SERVICES

Business Periodicals Index. H. W. Wilson Co. Monthly, except August, with quarterly and annual cumulations. Price on application.

DIRECTORIES

Catalog Age/Direct Sourcebook. Cowles Business Media, Inc. Annual. $25.00. Lists of approximately 300 suppliers of products and services for direct marketing, especially catalog marketing.

Direct Marketing List Source. SRDS. Bimonthly. $354.00 per year. Provides detailed information and rates for business, farm, and consumer mailing lists (U. S., Canadian, and international). Includes current postal information and directories of list brokers, compilers, and managers. Formerly *Direct Mail List Rates and Data.*

Direct Marketing Handbook. Edward L. Nash. McGraw-Hill, Inc. 1991. $69.95. Second edition.

Direct Marketing Success: What Works and Why. F.F. Gosden. John Wiley and Sons, Inc. 1985 $16.95.

Financial Services Direct Marketing: Essential Strategies. James R. Rosenfield. Sourcebooks, Inc. 1990. $55.00. Includes copy and design guidelines.

The New Direct Marketing: How to Implement a Profit-Driven Database Marketing Strategy. David Shepard. Irwin Professional Publishing. 1994. $60.00. Second edition. Discusses the construction, analysis, practical use, and evaluation of direct marketing databases containing primary and/or secondary data.

Sales Manager's Handbook. John P. Steinbrink. Dartnell Corp. 1989. $49.95. 14th edition.

ONLINE DATABASES

ABI/INFORM. UMI/Data Courier. Provides online indexing to business-related material occurring in over 800 periodicals from 1971 to the present. Inquire as to online cost and availability.

WILSONLINE: Wilson Business Abstracts. H. W. Wilson Co. Indexes and abstracts 350 major business periodicals, plus the *Wall Street Journal* and the business section of the *New York Times.* Indexing is from 1982, abstracting from 1990, with the two newspapers included from 1993. Updated daily. Inquire as to online cost and availability. (*Business Periodicals Index* without abstracts is also available online.‡)

PERIODICALS AND NEWSLETTERS

Catalog Age. Cowles Business Media, Inc. Monthly. Free to qualified personnel; others, $65.00 per year. Edited for catalog marketing and management personnel.

Direct Marketing: Using Direct Response Advertising to Enhance Marketing Database. Hoke Communications, Inc. Monthly. $56.00 per year.

Direct Selling Association International Bulletin. World Federation of Direct Selling Associations. Three times a year. Membership.

Direct: The Magazine for Direct Marketing Management. Cowles Business Media, Inc. Monthly. Free to qualified personnel; others, $64.00 per year.

DM News: The Newspaper of Direct Marketing. DM News. 47 times a year. Free to qualified personnel; others, $75.00 per year. Includes special feature issues on catalog marketing, telephone marketing, database marketing, and fundraising. Available on the world wide web at http://www.dmnews.com

Journal of Direct Marketing. John Wiley & Sons, Inc., Journals Div. Quarterly. $320.00 per year. Exchange of ideas in the field of direct marketing.

Who's Mailing What: The Monthly Newsletter Analysis and Record of the Direct Marketing Archive. North American Publishing Co. Monthly. $295.00 per year. Newsletter and listing of promotional mailings. Photocopies of mailings are available to subscribers.

TRADE ASSOCIATIONS AND PROFESSIONAL SOCIETIES

Direct Selling Association. 1666 K St., N.W., Suite 1010, Washington, DC 20006-2808. Phone: (202) 293-5760. Fax: (202) 463-4569.

DIRECTORIES
See: CATALOGS AND DIRECTORIES

DIRECTORS
See: CORPORATE DIRECTORS AND OFFICERS

DISABILITY INSURANCE
See also: EMPLOYEE BENEFIT PLANS

Equifax National Decision Systems

Data Provider: Equifax National Decision Systems
5375 Mira Sorrento Place, Suite 400, San Diego, CA 92121
800-866-6510
619-550-5800
Internet: http://www.ends.com

Type of information available:

Marketing information including detailed databases of demographics, projections, and geographic data; customer segmentation and targeting data; mapping; data-analysis services; and consulting services.

How to use it:

Find information related to location factors for your business, such as traffic flow demographics, data by potential trading area, and street maps.

For example:

Anne and Don want to open a sandwich shop and pub in the Faneuil Hall area of Boston. They are looking for the location with the highest level of foot traffic that consists of white-collar workers with disposable income who eat out for lunch. They would also like a listing of all restaurants within a two-mile radius of their potential site. They call Equifax and speak with a consultant. For a fee (starting at $70 for a single location report), the consultant identifies locations that match Anne and Don's criteria. Armed with detailed maps and traffic-flow patterns, Anne and Don will look for restaurant space near upscale, high-traffic locations

Availability: Reports, maps, customized for your location up to five-mile radius (not in bookstores or libraries); price varies

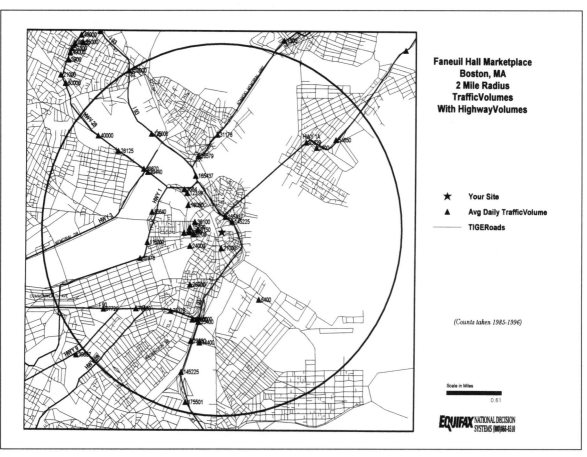

Faneuil Hall Marketplace
Boston, MA
2 Mile Radius
TrafficVolumes
With HighwayVolumes

★ Your Site
▲ Avg Daily TrafficVolume
— TIGERoads

(Counts taken 1985-1996)

Scale in Miles
0.61

RESOURCE DIRECTORY
On-the-Shelf Resources

RESTAURANT: LOCATION DIRECTORY

BY EQUIFAX NATIONAL DECISION SYSTEMS 800-866-6510

COORD: 42:21.81   71:03.58

RESTAURANT NAME CATEGORY	ADDRESS CITY	SIC EMP SIZE	DIST/DIR CHAIN	
BERTUCCI'S BRICK OVEN PIZZERIA QSR PIZZA	799 MAIN ST CAMBRIDGE, MA	581243 50	2.0 NO	W
SAFFRON GRILL NC RESTAURANT	795 MAIN ST CAMBRIDGE, MA	581200 17	1.9 NO	W
ANAGA BISTRO NC RESTAURANT	798 MAIN ST CAMBRIDGE, MA	581200 17	2.0 NO	W
ROYAL EAST NC RESTAURANT	782 MAIN ST CAMBRIDGE, MA	581200 15	1.9 NO	W
HYMIE'S DELICATESSEN QSR OTHER SANDWICH	1060 CAMBRIDGE ST CAMBRIDGE, MA	581244 1	1.9 NO	W
EL RANCHO QSR RETAIL	1126 CAMBRIDGE ST CAMBRIDGE, MA	581251 1	2.0 YES	W
MIDWEST GRILL NC RESTAURANT	1122 CAMBRIDGE ST CAMBRIDGE, MA	581200 17	2.0 NO	W
CAFE CASAL QSR VARIED MENU	1075 CAMBRIDGE ST CAMBRIDGE, MA	581267 2	2.0 NO	W
CORNER DELIGHT RESTAURANT NC RESTAURANT	1093 CAMBRIDGE ST CAMBRIDGE, MA	581200 2	2.0 NO	W
LA GROCERIA ITALIANA RSTAURANT NC RESTAURANT	853 MAIN ST CAMBRIDGE, MA	581200 30	2.0 NO	W
BIGGS RESTAURANT NC RESTAURANT	111 HARVARD ST CAMBRIDGE, MA	581200 17	1.7 NO	W
TAJ INDIA RESTAURANT NC RESTAURANT	781 MAIN ST CAMBRIDGE, MA	581200 3	1.9 NO	W
STEFANI HOUSE OF PIZZA QSR PIZZA	783 MAIN ST CAMBRIDGE, MA	581243 2	1.9 NO	W
IZZY'S RESTAURANT & SUB SHOP QSR OTHER SANDWICH	169 HARVARD ST CAMBRIDGE, MA	581244 5	1.9 NO	W

* IN DIRECTION COLUMN MEANS MATCHED TO ZIP CODE CENTROID

RESOURCE DIRECTORY
On-the-Shelf Resources

Financial Studies of the Small Business

Publisher: Financial Research Associates
P.O. Box 7708, 510 Ave. J SE
Winter Haven, FL 33880
941-299-3969
941-299-2131 fax

Type of information available:
Sales data and ratios for businesses from $10,000 to over $1 million in annual sales. This reference is particularly good for businesses that are anticipating modest sales levels.

How to use it:
Determine whether your business-plan financials and projections are in line with industry norms.

For example:
Leanne is preparing her business plan for an office-supply store. She projects her receivables at 15 to 20 days, but isn't sure if that matches the industry norms. Checking under "Retail Office Supplies," Leanne learns that the industry average (median) is 32 days. Since this is a longer collection period than Leanne expected, she will need more cash to support operations. She changes her plan accordingly, and avoids a cash-flow problem.

Availability: Many libraries and accountants (not available in bookstores); $97 hardbound; $128 diskette; $45 financial statement comparative analysis

```
                                              Page  1
                    FINANCIAL DATA ANALYSIS
Client #   123           PREPARED FOR          Prepared 03/25/97

          ******************************
          *  ANY OFFICE SUPPLY CO.      *
          *  ANYTOWN        US  90001   *
          ******************************
                    12/31/96

              Compared against all businesses
      In the Retail Office Supplies industry for the year 1995-1996
---------------------------------------------------------------------

                             INCOME DATA

                             YOUR FIRM    STANDARD
                             %/NET SALES  %/NET SALES  VARIANCE UNITS
Net Sales (Gross Income)       100.0       100.0        0.0 Pct.
Cost of Sales                   63.9        64.6       -0.7 Pct.
Gross Profit                    36.1        35.4        0.7 Pct.
General / Administrative Expenses 26.1      33.5       -7.4 Pct.
Operating Profit                10.0         1.9        8.1 Pct.
Interest Expense                 0.9         0.4        0.5 Pct.
Depreciation                     0.7         0.8       -0.1 Pct.
Profit Before Taxes              8.5         0.7        7.8 Pct.
```

RESOURCE DIRECTORY On-the-Shelf Resources

```
                          PROOF SHEET                    Page  1
                Client Name  - ANY OFFICE SUPPLY CO.
                Information as of 12/31/96
        Industry Code   11    Client #  123     4 Employees


                             ASSETS
Cash                                         22,560
Accounts Receivable                          35,210
Inventories                                 112,790
TOTAL CURRENT ASSETS                                    170,560
Land,Bldgs., Lse-hold Imp. (Net)             38,400
Equipment (Net)                              12,787
All Other Fixed Assets                        7,800
TOTAL FIXED ASSETS                                       58,987
All Other Assets                             25,000
TOTAL ASSETS                                            254,547

                           LIABILITIES
Accounts Payable, Trade                      52,450
Short Term Bank Loans                         2,500
All Other Current Liabilities                 8,757
TOTAL CURRENT LIABILITIES                                63,707
Notes Payable, Long Term                     10,000
Mortgages Payable                            23,000
Stockholder Loans (Due Owners)               30,000
All Other Long Term Liabilities               2,100
TOTAL LONG TERM LIABILITIES                              65,100
    TOTAL LIABILITIES                                   128,807
    NET WORTH                                           125,740
    TOTAL LIAB & NET WORTH                              254,547
```

INCOME DATA

	YOUR FIRM %/NET SALES	STANDARD %/NET SALES	VARIANCE	UNITS
Net Sales (Gross Income)	100.0	100.0	0.0	Pct.
Cost of Sales	63.9	64.6	-0.7	Pct.
Gross Profit	36.1	35.4	0.7	Pct.
General / Administrative Expenses	26.1	33.5	-7.4	Pct.
Operating Profit	10.0	1.9	8.1	Pct.
Interest Expense	0.9	0.4	0.5	Pct.
Depreciation	0.7	0.8	-0.1	Pct.
Profit Before Taxes	8.5	0.7	7.8	Pct.

ADDITIONAL OPERATING ITEMS

	YOUR FIRM %/NET SALES	STANDARD %/NET SALES	VARIANCE	UNITS
Labor	7.3	11.8	-4.5	Pct.
Rent	0.0	2.6	-2.6	Pct.
Advertising	1.3	1.0	0.3	Pct.
Insurance	1.2	1.2	0.0	Pct.
Travel	0.3	0.4	-0.1	Pct.
Officer / Executive Salaries	8.1	5.6	2.5	Pct.

Copyright © 1996, Financial Research Associates.

Publisher: Info Press Inc.
P.O. Box 550, Lewiston, NY 14092
716-754-4669
E-mail: infopress@infonews.com
Internet: http://infonews.com/franchise

Type of information available:

Alphabetical listing of available franchise opportunities containing addresses, phone numbers, product lines, years in business, years franchising, franchise fees, royalty fees, financing assistance (if any).

How to use it:

Obtain contact and investment information on thousands of franchises in hundreds of industries.

For example:

Ken and Caroline have lived in Cincinnati for 10 years. Ken has worked for McDonald's as a general manager, and Caroline has been working for a local stationer. On the basis of some recent research, Ken and Caroline find that the area they live in is currently underserved by party paper-supply houses. Unfortunately, Ken and Caroline do not have enough money to open their own store, but they might be able to afford to enter into a franchise opportunity. Looking under "Retail" in the 1997 Franchise Annual, they spot six franchises requiring total investment and fees ranging from $85,000 to $500,000.

Availability: Many universities, libraries, and SBDCs; $39.95

RESOURCE DIRECTORY
On-the-Shelf Resources

PAPER BY DESIGN
11401 Pine Blvd., Pembroke Pines, FL, 33026. Contact: Dave Earnest, Bus. Dev. Mgr. - Tel: (402) 484-7100, (800) 301-9504, Fax: (402) 484-7811. Retail concept specializing in the custom printing of cards, invitations and gifts, etc. Established: 1993 - Franchising Since: 1994 - No. of Units: Company Owned: 2 - Franchise Fee: $20,000 - Royalty: 5% - Total Inv: $56,600 - Financing: No.

PAPER FIRST/PAPERTOWN
Paper First Franchising, Inc.
3623 Latrobe #203 Fairway Office Condo., Charlotte, NC, 28211. Contact: Melvin W. Frank, Owner - Tel: (704) 364-1785, Fax: (704) 364-2466. Paper products, party supplies and janitorial supplies. Established: 1980 - Franchising Since: 1988 - No. of Units: Company Owned: 1 - Franchised: 68 - Franchise Fee: $15,000 - Royalty: downscale from 2.5% to .5% - Total Inv: $85,000 - $120,000 incl. fran. fee - Financing: Assistance.

PAPER WAREHOUSE
7630 Excelsior Blvd., Minneapolis, MN, 55426. Contact: Jan Pithey, Dir. of Fran. Sales - Tel: (800) 229-1792. Retail party stores. Three store profiles: 4,000 and 6,500 and 8,500 square feet. Established: 1983 - Franchising Since: 1987 - No. of Units: Company Owned: 50 - Franchised: 45 - Franchise Fee: $19,000 - $25,000 - Royalty: 4% - Total Inv: $149,100 - $464,500 - Financing: No.

PARTY CITY
Party City Corp.
400 Commons Way, Rockaway, NJ, 07866. Contact: Valeria Szymaniak, V.P. Real Estate & Franchise - Tel: (800) 883-2100, Fax: (201) 983-1333. Deep discount party supply superstore. 6,000 - 10,000 sq. ft.

Established: 1986 - Franchising Since: 1987 - No. of Units: Company Owned: 12 - Franchised: 115 - Franchise Fee: $30,000 - Royalty: 4% - Total Inv: $290,000 min. investment - Financing: Assistance in securing financing.

PARTY FAIR FRANCHISING CO., INC.
Pond Road Shopping Center, Freehold, NJ, 07728. Contact: David Silverstein - Tel: (908) 780-1110. One-stop party supply store. Attractive, well designed retail locations offering the consumer selection, quality and value. Established: 1983 - Franchising Since: 1987 - No. of Units: Company Owned: 4 - Franchised: 16 - Franchise Fee: $24,000 - Royalty: 5% - Total Inv: $80,000 - $120,000 - Financing: Yes.

PARTY LAND
5215 Militia Hill Rd., Plymouth Meeting, PA, 19462. Contact: John Barry, V.P., Sales - Tel: (610) 941-6200. World's largest international retail party supply franchise, specializing in service, selection & savings. Established: 1986 - Franchising Since: 1988 - No. of Units: Company Owned: 11 - Franchised: 90 - Franchise Fee: $25,000 - Royalty: 5%, 4% adv. - Total Inv: $149,000 to $229,000 - Financing: No.

The Internet

The Internet is a system that integrates literally millions of computers, from major university mainframes to small PCs. Virtually any information that can be found in a library can be accessed online through File Transfer Protocol (FTP) sites. In addition, the government maintains information—from census-bureau files, labor statistics, and law documents to the hours the White House is available for tours—in huge libraries located on the Net. Universities maintain research documents, academic and industrial studies, course descriptions, and library card catalogs. The importance the Internet plays in the research process cannot be overstated. For example, a large portion of the research for this book was done on the Net, and practically all of the text traveled on the information superhighway from author to editor and back again.

Marketing on the Internet has grown exponentially over the past year. Large corporations like AT&T, Hewlett-Packard, and General Motors have sites on the Net that not only advertise their products and services but also offer financial data about their companies and may have links to other resources for information relating to their industries. Even "mom & pop" stores are joining the Information Age by hosting a Web site to advertise their business. Individuals have FTP sites that contain data for special-interest groups on many different topics, such as environmentalism or military reenactments. Many trade associations, industrial organizations, and retail groups maintain Web sites of their own, with gateways to statistical data, membership information, listings of services provided, and current political initiatives.

The Internet can be accessed through most colleges and universities around the globe (some restrictions for usage may apply if you are not directly affiliated with the institution). In addition, you can log on to the Internet via "Internet Gateways," which are virtual "on-ramps" to the information highway. Most online services such as America Online, CompuServe, and Prodigy have gateways, as do most large corporate E-mail systems. You'll also need Web browser software such as Netscape or Microsoft Internet Explorer. Through such connections you can use the Internet at home with your own PC.

For more on the Internet, search engines, and keyword searches, see Human Resources (Trade Associations): How to find a vertical trade association.

For example:

Nathaniel's boss, Blake, is retiring after 40 years of service to the College of Business Administration. In honor of his retirement, Nathaniel would like to get a humidor for Blake, who happens to be a connoisseur of fine cigars. Using his computer to do a keyword search with the "Excite" search engine, Nathaniel finds thousands of listings, including humidor manufacturers, retailers, and articles on humidors and cigar accessories. Among them, he finds "The Humidor Store" (Internet: http://www.humidorstore.com) in Tampa, Fla., which offers a large variety of humidors at prices ranging from $169 to $995. The Web site has complete product descriptions, order information, frequently asked questions (FAQ), and color pictures of several different humidors.

Another example:

Sarah is thinking about opening her own candy kiosk at one of four malls in her area. She would like to evaluate each location in terms of traffic flow and customer demographics, but is not sure about the mechanics of location analysis. She does a keyword search using "location analysis NEAR kiosk," and receives links to 200,000 Web pages containing the words "location," "analysis," and "kiosk," listed in order of the probability that they meet what Sarah is looking for. The first few articles are helpful, and she completes her analysis with confidence.

The Lifestyle Market Analyst

Publisher: SRDS
1700 Higgins Rd., Des Plaines, IL 60018
800-851-SRDS (851-7737), 847-375-5000
847-375-5001 fax
Internet: http://www.srds.com

Type of information available:

Demographic information on popular activities, broken down by geographic market.

How to use it:

Cross-reference specific data to calculate potential market for your business. In addition, you could put together several kinds of information and calculate the total market for a particular product or line.

For example:

Mark has lived in coastal Charleston, S.C., all his life and loves to sail. With his business degree, he would like to open a marine supply store on the waterfront. He is trying to develop a customer profile so he can determine the potential market for marine products. In *The Lifestyle Market Analyst,* Mark finds that national demographics of boating enthusiasts show that 75.8% are between the ages of 25 and 54, 60.3% are married, 70.4% own their homes, the median household income is $48,300, and overwhelmingly 81.1% have some form of bank credit card. Mark can use the data from the national market to determine his local market potential.

Availability: Only through university and public libraries; $310

Boating/Sailing

Demographics
Base Index US = 100

Total Households 10,136,515

Age of Head of Household	Households	%	Index
18-24 years old	537,235	5.3	102
25-34 years old	2,270,579	22.4	117
35-44 years old	2,736,859	27.0	119
45-54 years old	2,138,805	21.1	117
55-64 years old	1,256,000		
65-74 years old			

Income Earners			
Married, One Income	2,544,265	25.1	90
Married, Two Incomes	3,568,053	35.2	127
Single	4,024,196	39.7	89
Dual Income Households			

Boating/Sailing

Alphabetical Listing of DMAs Ranked by Index

▓ : Denotes DMAs ranked 1 - 10

Designated Market Areas	Lifestyle Rank	Households	%	Index
Abilene-Sweetwater, TX	177	8,268	7.5	72
Albany, GA	193	9,409	7.0	67
Albany-Schenectady-Troy, NY	51	59,163	11.5	111
Albuquerque-Santa Fe, NM	167	41,912	7.7	74
Alexandria, LA	178	6,014	7.5	72
Alpena, MI	18	2,358	14.3	138
Amarillo, TX	197	12,655	6.8	65
Anchorage, AK	21	18,087	14.1	136
Anniston, AL	189	3,232	7.2	69
Atlanta, GA	94	153,745	9.7	93
Augusta, GA	111	20,570	9.2	88
Austin, TX	53	47,953	11.4	110
Bakersfield, CA	174	12,219	7.5	72

Designated Market Areas	Lifestyle Rank	Households	%	Index
Cedar Rapids-Waterloo & Dubuque,IA	157	25,001	8.1	78
Champaign & Springfield-Decatur,IL	163	27,074	7.9	76
Charleston, SC	3	39,840	17.2	165
Charleston-Huntington, WV	190	34,523	7.1	68
Charlotte, NC	85	80,171	10.0	96
Charlottesville, VA	187	3,373	7.3	70
Chattanooga, TN	135	27,917	8.7	84
Cheyenne-Scottsblf-Strlng,WY-NE	137	4,341	8.7	84
Chicago, IL	116	286,810	9.1	88
Chico-Redding, CA	31	23,021	13.3	128
Cincinnati, OH	144	67,219	8.4	81
Clarksburg-Weston, WV	203	6,993	6.6	63
Cleveland, OH	92	143,935	9.8	94

The Lifestyle Market Analyst. Copyright © 1997, SRDS with data supplied by the Polk Company.

RESOURCE DIRECTORY
On-the-Shelf Resources

New York Times Index

Publisher: The New York Times Co.
229 W. 43rd St. (9th Fl.), New York, NY 10036-3913
212-556-1989; 212-556-1629 fax
212-221-5065 (for Index)

Type of information available:

Brief digests of articles related to your business that have appeared in *The New York Times* and its subsidiary publications.

How to use it:

Find articles addressing topics relating to your business or industry.

For example:

Mike owns three used-appliance stores in the Groton, Conn., area. As a part of his business, he routinely buys refrigerator compressors and installs them in older units to resell. Recently, a salesman from a compressor plant in Northern Ireland visited Mike's store and offered him a bulk deal on low-cost compressors, but requested an exclusive contract to supply all of Mike's compressors. If Mike severs all his local compressor-supply relations, it would be unlikely that he could reestablish them at current rates should the new supplier be unable to produce. Mike was also concerned that political unrest in Northern Ireland might make distribution a problem. He decided to read what *The New York Times* and its subsidiaries have written recently about Northern Ireland, and make his decision on whether to sign an exclusive contract after some additional research.

Availability: University and major public libraries; $735 to $1,120 (monthly, quarterly, annually)

NORTH SEA. See also
Gas (Fuel), Ja 24
NORTH VIETNAM. Use Vietnam
NORTHEASTERN STATES (US). See also
Air Pollution, Ja 19
NORTHERN IRELAND
  Novelist Edna O'Brien Op-Ed article on increasing terror in Northern Ireland; deplores vitriolic tone of debate; scores British Prime Min John Major's praise of unionist leader David Trimble; drawing (M), Ja 25, I,23:2
  Thomas J Flynn letter contends that he finds it hard to believe that Charles F Feeney, New Jersey businessman who has anonymously contributed millions of dollars to various charities and causes, can be so taken by myth of Irish nationalism that he thinks his donations to Sinn Fein supported only nonviolent activities, Ja 28,A,20:4
  New book, Eyewitness: Bloody Sunday by Don Mullan, has inflamed Irish feelings about killing of 14 Catholics by British paratroopers in Northern Ireland 25 years ago; photo (M), Ja 30,A,6:3
  British Government says it will appoint commission in Northern Ireland to try to control religious-patriotic parades that have led to violence (S), Ja 31,A,13:1
NORTHLINE MALL (HOUSTON, TEX). See also
Retail Stores and Trade, Ja 31
NORTHROP GRUMMAN CORP. See also
Airlines and Airplanes, Ja 16,17,20
  Northrop Grumman Corp sells largest building on its Bethpage, LI, property to Steel-Los (S), Ja 30,B,5:6
NORTON, EDWARD. See also
Motion Pictures, Ja 19
NOSSITER, JONATHAN. See also

NOSSITER, JONATHAN. See also
Motion Pictures, Ja 27
NOYES MUSEUM (OCEANVILLE, NJ). See also
Fish and Other Marine Life, Ja 19
NTSHANGASE, JABULANI. See also
Alcoholic Beverages, Ja 31
NUCLEAR WASTES. See also
Atomic Weapons, Ja 27
Water Pollution, Ja 26
NUCLEAR WEAPONS. Use Atomic Weapons
NULAND, SHERWIN B. See also
Death and Dying, Ja 17
NUMBERS. See also
Mathematics
NUNS. See also
Art, Ja 26
Colleges and Universities, Ja 26
Sectarian Schools
NUNZIATO, LINDA A. See also
Police, Ja 29
NURSING AND NURSES. See also
Medicine and Health, Ja 25,26,29,31
NUTRITION. Use Diet and Nutrition
NUTRITION 21 (CO). See also
Weight, Ja 29
NYACK (NY)
  Profile of the Nyacks in Rockland County, NY, as a place to live; map; photos (L), Ja 26,IX,3:2
NYNEX CORP. See also
Telephones and Telecommunications, Ja 19,22
Television, Ja 16
  Reports fourth-quarter 1996 net of $379.7 million, up from $235.6 million in 1995 Period (M), Ja 22,D,4:3
NYU. Use New York University

Reader's Guide to Periodical Literature

Publisher: H.W. Wilson Co.
950 University Ave., Bronx, NY 10452
718-588-8400

Type of information available:

Listings of recent articles appearing in more than 200 popular periodicals, indexed by subject and author in one alphabetical list. Also available in an abridged format covering more than 50 publications.

How to use it:

Find an index of recent articles about your industry or service.

For example:

Morgan owns a small computer store and carries a small line of multimedia accessories. She would like to add digital cameras to her line and market them to her photography customers. Morgan does not know much about photography, so she consults the *Reader's Guide to Periodical Literature* for articles about digital cameras. She finds several articles on digital cameras, some appearing in *Popular Photography* and *Rolling Stone*.

Availability: Most libraries (not available in bookstores); $200

DIGITAL CAMERAS
  Digital cameras give an instant view. J. Pournelle. il *Byte* v21 p32 D '96
  Instant images. il *Fortune* Special Issue p184-7 Wint '97
              Testing
  20 top digital cameras. M. J. McNamara. il *Popular Photography* v60 p22-3+ D '96
  Buying a camera? The good news is that you have lots of choices. That's the bad news, too. R. Day. il *Rolling Stone* p81 F 20 '97
  Color QuickCam. D. McClelland. il *Macworld* v13 p79 S '96
  Digital cameras give your documents snap. M. J. Himowitz. il *Fortune* v135 p144+ F 17 '97
  Digital cameras grow up. J. Shapiro. il *Popular Mechanics* v173 p63-6 D '96
  Fujix DS-220. D. McClelland. il *Macworld* v13 p85 S '96
  Get the digital picture. C. O'Malley. il *Popular Science* v250 p64-8 Mr '97
  What's new in digital imaging. il *Fortune* Special Issue p188-9 Wint '97
DIGITAL CELLULAR RADIO
  Talk is cheaper. il *Fortune* Special Issue p128-9+ Wint '97
  Vaulting the walls with wireless: AT&T may use cellular to invade the Bells' local-phone turf. A. Barrett and others. il map *Business Week* p85+ Ja 20 '97
              Standards
  Uncle Sam, please pick a cell-phone standard. C. Arnst. il *Business Week* p44 F 24 '97
DIGITAL CLOCKS *See* Clocks, Electronic
DIGITAL COMPACT DISC PLAYERS *See* Compact disc players

RMA Annual Statement Studies

Publisher: Robert Morris Associates (RMA)
The Association of Lending and Credit Risk Professionals
One Liberty Place, Suite 2300, Philadelphia, PA 19103-7398
800-677-7621
215-446-4101 fax

Type of information available:

Balance Sheet, Income Statement, and representative financial ratio information for more than 400 industries. This resource is also available on computer disk.

How to use it:

Determine whether the projections and assumptions on your trial Balance Sheet are representative of the industry, or check to see whether a company's ratios are within industry norms.

(RMA cautions that the Studies should be regarded as a general guideline and not an absolute industry norm. This is because of limited samples within categories, the categorization of companies by their primary Standard Industrial Classification (SIC) number only, and different methods of operation by companies within the same industry.)

For example:

Peter and Susan have been building financial projections for their musical-instruments store and want to know whether their assumptions are close to the actual industry averages. In the RMA Annual Statement Studies, they will find historical comparative data that average Balance Sheet and Income Statement figures, sorted by size of business. They can compare the assumptions they have made on their projections to the ratios in the guide, to see whether they line up with the norms for the musical-instrument retailers.

Availability: University and business libraries, some bookstores; $125

---

628 RETAILERS—MUSICAL INSTRUMENTS & SUPPLIES. SIC# 5736

						# Postretirement Benefits		
						Type of Statement		
1	7	1	1	1		Unqualified	11	9
		3	8	2	1	Reviewed	23	14
2	6	15	3			Compiled	55	57
17	26	8				Tax Returns	6	7
5	6					Other	24	19
5	6	8					4/1/91-3/31/92	4/1/92-3/31/93
	63 (4/1-9/30/95)		58 (10/1/95-3/31/96)				ALL	ALL
0-500M	500M-2MM	2-10MM	10-50MM	50-100MM	100-250MM	**NUMBER OF STATEMENTS**	119	106
29	44	34	11	2	1			
%	%	%	%	%	%	**ASSETS**	%	%
9.7	5.7	5.0	.9			Cash & Equivalents	4.8	5.2
7.1	13.9	11.9	25.5			Trade Receivables - (net)	17.1	15.8
63.9	61.6	52.0	48.2			Inventory	59.0	57.5
.6	1.6	3.3	3.8			All Other Current	1.7	1.1
81.3	82.9	72.1	78.5			Total Current	82.6	79.6
14.0	11.0	20.1	14.9			Fixed Assets (net)	12.0	13.5
2.4	.4	.9	.6			Intangibles (net)	.5	.4
2.3	5.7	6.9	6.0			All Other Non-Current	4.9	6.5
100.0	100.0	100.0	100.0			Total	100.0	100.0
						LIABILITIES		
26.8	13.0	17.5	21.9			Notes Payable-Short Term	18.7	18.1
5.0	3.3	4.6	4.9			Cur. Mat.-L/T/D	3.0	3.3
19.5	20.0	19.5	25.1			Trade Payables	19.5	18.0
1.0	.2	.6	.3			Income Taxes Payable	.5	.3
6.4	7.6	8.2	8.6			All Other Current	6.0	7.1
58.7	44.1	50.3	60.7			Total Current	47.6	46.8
14.3	11.8	9.7	13.8			Long Term Debt	10.4	10.8
.0	.0	.2	.6			Deferred Taxes	.1	.2
5.6	6.7	3.1	2.6			All Other Non-Current	4.2	3.6
21.4	37.5	36.7	22.3			Net Worth	37.8	38.6
100.0	100.0	100.0	100.0			Total Liabilities & Net Worth	100.0	100.0
						INCOME DATA		
100.0	100.0	100.0	100.0			Net Sales	100.0	100.0
40.7	40.1	40.6	40.6			Gross Profit	42.3	42.4
38.0	36.4	35.9	36.9			Operating Expenses	39.5	39.0
2.7	3.7	4.7	3.7			Operating Profit	2.8	3.3
1.9	.8	1.3	.0			All Other Expenses (net)	.2	.3
.8	2.8	3.4	3.8			Profit Before Taxes	2.6	3.0
						RATIOS		
2.0	2.7	1.9	1.5				2.5	2.5
1.4	1.9	1.5	1.2			Current	1.7	1.7
1.0	1.4	1.3	1.0				1.3	1.3
.5	.8	.7	.6				.8	.9
.3 (28)	.3	.3	.4			Quick	.4	.4
.1	.2	.2	.1				.2	.1
0 UND	9 41.9	9 42.0	24 15.0				9 42.9 8 46.2	
5 68.7	15 24.7	20 18.0	47 7.8			Sales/Receivables	25 14.5 18 20.6	
24 15.4	30 12.2	33 10.9	76 4.8				46 7.9 37 10.0	
104 3.5	140 2.6	111 3.3	104 3.5				140 2.6 126 2.9	
166 2.2	192 1.9	174 2.1	174 2.1			Cost of Sales/Inventory	183 2.0 192 1.9	
243 1.5	261 1.4	243 1.5	332 1.1				281 1.3 281 1.3	

RESOURCE DIRECTORY
On-the-Shelf Resources

Simmons Study of Media and Markets

Publisher: Simmons Market Research Bureau Inc.
309 W. 49th St., 14th Fl., New York, NY 10019-7316
800-999-SMRB (7672)
212-373-8900, 212-373-8918 fax

Type of information available:

Extensive information about the consumers of about 800 products. For example, for a given product, one can determine the age, income, educational level, race, and television-viewing habits of its typical consumer.

How to use it:

Develop a demographic profile of your customers, determine market share and size, and position your advertising according to your findings.

For example:

Eleanor owns "Kid's Klothes," a children's apparel store in Savannah, Ga. She is thinking about adding a shoe department. According to the information in the *Simmons Study of Media and Markets*, the customer profile (purchaser) for children's apparel is a 35-year-old married mother of two, with a household income of $30,000 to $40,000, who reads the weekend paper more than the daily paper. Eleanor will spend more of the store's advertising dollars in the weekend edition, since it is read by most of her potential customers, and offer "2 for 1" deals on shoes.

Availability: By subscription, also in university and business libraries; price varies

	TOTAL U.S. '000	SHOES-ATHLETIC BOUGHT IN LAST 12 MONTHS				SHOES-CANVAS BOUGHT IN LAST 12 MONTHS				SHOES-OTHER BOUGHT IN LAST 12 MONTHS				RAIN OR SNOW BOOTS BOUGHT IN LAST 12 MONTHS			
		A '000	B DOWN	C % ACROSS	D INDX	A '000	B DOWN	C % ACROSS	D INDX	A '000	B DOWN	C % ACROSS	D INDX	A '000	B DOWN	C % ACROSS	D INDX
TOTAL PRINCIPAL SHOPPERS	112018	10484	100.0	9.4	100	7614	100.0	6.8	100	7727	100.0	6.9	100	5355	100.0	4.8	100
18-24	9907	1341	12.8	13.5	145	953	12.5	9.6	142	1046	13.5	10.6	153	689	12.9	7.0	146
25-34	26761	4781	45.6	17.9	191	3667	48.2	13.7	202	3590	46.5	13.4	194	2374	44.3	8.9	186
35-44	24489	2516	24.0	10.3	110	1674	22.0	6.8	101	1807	23.4	7.4	107	1164	21.7	4.8	99
45-54	17156	1099	10.5	6.4	68	733	9.6	4.3	63	*570	7.4	3.3	48	*649	12.1	3.8	79
55-64	13145	*437	4.2	3.3	36	*238	3.1	1.8	27	*330	4.3	2.5	36	*281	5.3	2.1	45
65 OR OLDER	20561	311	3.0	1.5	16	350	4.6	1.7	25	385	5.0	1.9	27	*198	3.7	1.0	20
18-34	36668	6122	58.4	16.7	178	4620	60.7	12.6	185	4636	60.0	12.6	183	3063	57.2	8.4	175
18-49	70908	9231	88.0	13.0	139	6684	87.8	9.4	139	6783	87.5	9.5	138	4590	85.7	6.5	135
25-54	68406	8396	80.1	12.3	131	6074	79.8	8.9	131	5967	77.2	8.7	126	4187	78.2	6.1	128
35-49	34240	3109	29.7	9.1	97	2064	27.1	6.0	89	2128	27.5	6.2	90	1527	28.5	4.5	93
50 OR OLDER	41110	1253	12.0	3.0	33	931	12.2	2.3	33	964	12.5	2.3	34	765	14.3	1.9	39
GRADUATED COLLEGE	21089	2173	20.7	10.3	110	1454	19.1	6.9	101	1625	21.0	7.7	112	1049	19.6	5.0	104
ATTENDED COLLEGE	26996	3044	29.0	11.3	120	2252	29.6	8.3	123	1971	25.5	7.3	106	1626	30.4	6.0	126
GRADUATED HIGH SCHOOL	40781	3803	36.3	9.3	100	2646	34.8	6.5	95	2722	35.2	6.7	97	1914	35.7	4.7	98
DID NOT GRADUATE HIGH SCHOOL	23153	1465	14.0	6.3	68	1262	16.6	5.5	80	1409	18.2	6.1	88	767	14.3	3.3	69
EMPLOYED FULL-TIME	60901	6233	59.5	10.2	109	4330	56.9	7.1	105	4245	54.9	7.0	101	2983	55.7	4.9	102
EMPLOYED PART-TIME	8081	1192	11.4	14.8	158	819	10.8	10.1	149	677	8.8	8.4	121	791	14.8	9.8	205
NOT EMPLOYED	43036	3059	29.2	7.1	76	2465	32.4	5.7	84	2805	36.3	6.5	94	1581	29.5	3.7	77
PROFESSIONAL/MANAGER	17631	1826	17.4	10.4	111	1219	16.0	6.9	102	1193	15.4	6.8	98	824	15.4	4.7	98
TECHNICAL/CLERICAL/SALES	25183	3109	29.6	12.3	132	2156	28.3	8.6	126	1983	25.7	7.9	114	1598	29.8	6.3	133
PRECISION/CRAFT	5284	*412	3.9	7.8	83	*255	3.4	4.8	71	*267	3.5	5.1	73	**158	2.9	3.0	62
OTHER EMPLOYED	20884	2079	19.8	10.0	106	1519	19.9	7.3	107	1480	19.1	7.1	103	1195	22.3	5.7	120
SINGLE	21858	1596	15.2	7.3	78	1058	13.9	4.8	71	1159	15.0	5.3	77	950	17.7	4.3	91
MARRIED	60339	7396	70.5	12.3	131	5344	70.2	8.9	130	5363	69.4	8.9	129	3597	67.2	6.0	125
DIVORCED/SEPARATED/WIDOWED	29821	1492	14.2	5.0	53	1213	15.9	4.1	60	1205	15.6	4.0	59	807	15.1	2.7	57
PARENTS	38281	8036	76.6	21.0	224	5918	77.7	15.5	227	5974	77.3	15.6	226	3871	72.3	10.1	212
WHITE	95676	8698	83.0	9.1	97	6384	83.8	6.7	98	6606	85.5	6.9	100	4456	83.2	4.7	97
BLACK	13160	1445	13.8	11.0	117	1128	14.8	8.6	126	892	11.5	6.8	98	764	14.3	5.8	122
OTHER	3181	*341	3.2	10.7	114	**103	1.4	3.2	48	*229	3.0	7.2	104	**135	2.5	4.2	89
NORTHEAST-CENSUS	23405	1859	17.7	7.9	85	1299	17.1	5.6	82	1316	17.0	5.6	82	1279	23.9	5.5	114
MIDWEST	27743	2738	26.1	9.9	105	2104	27.6	7.6	112	1766	22.8	6.4	92	1556	29.1	5.6	117
SOUTH	38561	3765	35.9	9.8	104	2613	34.3	6.8	100	3034	39.3	7.9	114	1469	27.4	3.8	80
WEST	22308	2122	20.2	9.5	102	1599	21.0	7.2	105	1611	20.8	7.2	105	1052	19.6	4.7	99
COUNTY SIZE A	46371	4341	41.4	9.4	100	2912	38.2	6.3	92	2922	37.8	6.3	91	2276	42.5	4.9	103
COUNTY SIZE B	34346	3026	28.9	8.8	94	2417	31.7	7.0	104	2616	33.8	7.6	110	1508	28.2	4.4	92
COUNTY SIZE C	17023	1859	17.7	10.9	117	1354	17.8	8.0	117	1334	17.3	7.8	114	1028	19.2	6.0	126
COUNTY SIZE D	14278	1259	12.0	8.8	94	932	12.2	6.5	96	856	11.1	6.0	87	*544	10.2	3.8	80
METRO CENTRAL CITY	36068	3027	28.9	8.4	90	2149	28.2	6.0	88	2256	29.2	6.3	91	1483	27.7	4.1	86
METRO SUBURBAN	53010	5072	48.4	9.6	102	3617	47.5	6.8	100	3818	49.4	7.2	104	2716	50.7	5.1	107
NON METRO	22941	2385	22.7	10.4	111	1848	24.3	8.1	119	1653	21.4	7.2	104	1156	21.6	5.0	105
TOP 5 ADI'S	24784	2038	19.4	8.2	88	1505	19.8	6.1	89	1554	20.1	6.3	91	1235	23.1	5.0	104
TOP 10 ADI'S	35718	2993	28.5	8.4	90	2201	28.9	6.2	91	2178	28.2	6.1	88	1634	30.5	4.6	96
TOP 20 ADI'S	49710	4397	41.9	8.8	94	2982	39.2	6.0	88	3041	39.4	6.1	89	2321	43.3	4.7	98
HSHLD. INC. $75,000 OR MORE	11767	1084	10.3	9.2	98	792	10.4	6.7	99	634	8.2	5.4	78	*528	9.9	4.5	94
$60,000 OR MORE	21066	2240	21.4	10.6	114	1454	19.1	6.9	102	1382	17.9	6.6	95	1049	19.6	5.0	104
$50,000 OR MORE	30037	3227	30.8	10.7	115	2012	26.4	6.7	99	1900	24.6	6.3	92	1490	27.8	5.0	104
$40,000 OR MORE	42698	4490	42.8	10.5	112	2990	39.3	7.0	103	2802	36.3	6.6	95	2080	38.8	4.9	102
$30,000 OR MORE	58197	6129	58.5	10.5	113	4242	55.7	7.3	107	4072	52.7	7.0	101	3022	56.4	5.2	109
$30,000 - $39,000	15499	1638	15.6	10.6	113	1252	16.4	8.1	119	1270	16.4	8.2	119	942	17.6	6.1	127
$20,000 - $29,000	19616	1751	16.7	8.9	95	1271	16.7	6.5	95	1461	18.9	7.4	108	927	17.3	4.7	99
$10,000 - $19,999	20256	1611	15.4	8.0	85	1250	16.4	6.2	91	1305	16.9	6.4	93	789	14.7	3.9	82
UNDER $10,000	13949	993	9.5	7.1	76	850	11.2	6.1	90	889	11.5	6.4	92	617	11.5	4.4	92
HOUSEHOLD OF 1 PERSON	23484	544	5.2	2.3	25	488	6.4	2.1	31	479	6.2	2.0	30	431	8.1	1.8	38
2 PEOPLE	36820	1311	12.5	3.6	38	1034	13.6	2.8	41	981	12.7	2.7	39	716	13.4	1.9	41
3 OR 4 PEOPLE	38721	5738	54.7	14.8	158	4127	54.2	10.7	157	4301	55.7	11.1	161	3016	56.3	7.8	163
5 OR MORE PEOPLE	12994	2892	27.6	22.3	238	1966	25.8	15.1	223	1966	25.4	15.1	219	1191	22.2	9.2	192
NO CHILD IN HOUSEHOLD	69729	1813	17.3	2.6	28	1369	18.0	2.0	29	1327	17.2	1.9	28	1127	21.1	1.6	34
CHILD(REN) UNDER 2 YEARS	8732	2866	27.3	32.8	351	2229	29.3	25.5	376	2148	27.8	24.6	357	1269	23.7	14.5	304
2 - 5 YEARS	15547	6518	62.2	41.9	448	4754	62.4	30.6	450	4715	61.0	30.3	440	3131	58.5	20.1	421
6 - 11 YEARS	19131	3479	33.2	18.2	194	2431	31.9	12.7	187	2587	33.5	13.5	196	1797	33.6	9.4	196
12 - 17 YEARS	18671	1616	15.4	8.7	92	1188	15.6	6.4	94	1180	15.3	6.3	92	*652	12.2	3.5	73
RESIDENCE OWNED	73147	6679	63.7	9.1	98	4837	63.5	6.6	97	4830	62.5	6.6	96	3247	60.6	4.4	93
VALUE: $70,000 OR MORE	42927	4102	39.1	9.6	102	2751	36.1	6.4	94	2624	34.0	6.1	89	1943	36.3	4.5	95
VALUE: UNDER $70,000	30220	2577	24.6	8.5	91	2086	27.4	6.9	102	2207	28.6	7.3	106	1303	24.3	4.3	90
RESIDENCE RENTED	37137	3642	34.7	9.8	105	2582	33.9	7.0	102	2642	34.2	7.1	103	1998	37.3	5.4	113
DAILY NEWSPAPERS																	
NET ONE DAY REACH	68512	5862	55.9	8.6	91	4252	55.8	6.2	91	4231	54.8	6.2	90	2911	54.4	4.2	89
READ ONLY ONE	56809	4981	47.5	8.8	94	3648	47.9	6.4	94	3494	45.2	6.2	89	2440	45.6	4.3	90
READ TWO OR MORE	11703	882	8.4	7.5	80	604	7.9	5.2	76	737	9.5	6.3	91	471	8.8	4.0	84
WEEKEND/SUNDAY NEWSPAPERS																	
NET ONE DAY REACH	77332	7662	73.1	9.9	106	5600	73.5	7.2	107	5508	71.3	7.1	103	3820	71.3	4.9	103
READ ONLY ONE	69793	6997	66.7	10.0	107	5094	66.9	7.3	107	4984	64.5	7.1	104	3441	64.3	4.9	103
READ TWO OR MORE	7539	665	6.3	8.8	94	505	6.6	6.7	99	524	6.8	6.9	101	379	7.1	5.0	105

RESOURCE DIRECTORY
On-the-Shelf Resources

Small Business Profiles

Publisher: Gale Research Inc.
835 Penobscot Bldg., Detroit, MI 48226-4094
313-961-2242
800-877-4253

Type of information available:

This source contains information for 60 different business types on various aspects of starting a business. Information given includes estimates of start-up costs and profit potential, choosing a location, franchise opportunities, and obtaining licenses and insurance.

How to use it:

Gain targeted, industry-specific information relating to starting your small business.

For example:

Stephen has been the golf pro at Keystone Country Club for seven years. Now he would like to open his own golf shop to serve the three country clubs in the area. Because of a confusing road system, Stephen is not exactly sure where he should locate his business. He wants to know what other golf shops have done and where to get detailed location analysis specifically designed for businesses such as his. Looking under "Golf Shop," Stephen finds a section on location that includes the name of a company that will do a location analysis, assist with market estimates, and evaluate competition.

Availability: Major business libraries; $95 per volume

GOLF SHOP

Small Business Profiles • Volume 1

REFERENCES AND TRADE PUBLICATIONS

References:

Golf Equipment & Supplies—Retail Directory: American Business Directones, Inc., 5711 S. 86th Circle, Omaha, NE 68127; phone: (402) 593-4600.

Golf Tips: Werner and Werner Corp., 16000 Ventura Blvd., Suite 201, Encino, CA 91436, phone: (310) 820-1500.

Sporting Goods Retailers Directory: American Business Directones, Inc.; 5711 S. 86th Circle; Omaha, NE 68127; phone: (402) 593-4600.

Sports Market Place: Sportsguide. Inc., P.O. Box 1417, Princeton, NJ 08540; phone: (609) 921-8599.

Publications:

Golf Shop Operations: Golf Digest/Tennis, Inc., P.O. Box 0395, Trumbull, CT 06611-0395; phone: (203) 373-7231.

Golf Industry: Sterling Southeast, Inc., 1450 NE 123rd St., North Miami, FL 33161-6051; phone: (305) 893-8771.

Golf Market Today: National Golf Foundation (NGF), 1150 S. U.S. Highway 1, Jupiter, FL 33477; phone: (407) 744-6006.

Sporting Goods Business: Gralla Publications. 1515 Broadway, New York, NY 10036; phone: (212) 869-1300.

Sports Trend: Shore Communications, Inc.; 180 Allen Rd., NE, Bldg. N., Ste. 300, Atlanta, GA 30328; phone: (404) 252-8831.

LOCATION AND MANAGEMENT

For the independently owned or franchised golf shop, it is not enough to locate your store on or near a high traffic area. You should be accessible to foot traffic as well, and to public transportation. Ideally, you should be situated close to a public golf course and, if possible, in or near an affluent neighborhood. If that is not feasible, being situated in a shopping mall or near one can be a plus, although this can mean high rent expenses.

For a $2,000 fee, Integrity Golf in Edmond, Oklahoma will do a detailed survey of potential locations for your business, or will examine the location you have selected and help you with gauging your market and assessing your competition.

A country club golf pro shop will take its clientele from the club membership. In most clubs, members must go to the pro shop to make reservations and pay greens fees. Set up your counter in the rear of the store so that customers and members must pass by your merchandise each time they play golf. What the golf pro shop may lack in variety of merchandise or personal services is made up for in clothing and other merchandise that bears the particular country club's logo. Club members will naturally be interested in these personalized items, and, because they are usually affluent, they may be willing to pay higher prices for the latest fashions and merchandise.

Small Business Profiles. Edited by Suzanne Bourgoin.
Copyright © 1994, Gale Research. All rights reserved. Reproduced by permission.

Small Business Sourcebook

Publisher: Gale Research Inc.
835 Penobscot Bldg., Detroit, MI 48226-4094
313-961-2242
800-877-4253

Type of information available:

This resource gives an overview of information resources, arranged by business type, for start-ups or established businesses. Material includes: start-up information, primary trade associations, educational programs, reference works, sources of supply, statistical sources, and trade periodicals. Volume II of the set contains information on topics of general interest such as venture capital, funding, and compensation. Volume II also contains listings of governmental, academic, and commercial organizations helpful to small business.

How to use it:

Look up a wide range of sources of start-up information—background, figures, financing, training, networking, and more—for more than 100 types of businesses.

For example:

Laura and Karen are planning to open a pet store in a local strip mall. They are planning to carry a full variety of dogs, cats, fish, and iguanas. They would also like to carry pet food and pet accessories. Laura and Karen have been having difficulty finding statistics on the pet food industry to include in their plan. Under "Pet Shop," Laura and Karen find three different statistical sources on the pet food and accessories market. They also note several trade periodicals for pet dealers, to which they will subscribe.

Availability: Business libraries;
$305 (two volumes)

18917 ● *Pet Supplies and Food—Retail Directory*
American Business Directories, Inc.
5711 S. 86th Circle
Omaha, NE 68127
(402)593-4600 ● Toll-Free: 800-555-6124
    ● Fax: (402)331-5481

Annual. **Price:** Please inquire. **Number of Listings:** 12,775 (U.S. edition); 1,584 (Canadian edition). **Entries Include:** Name, address, phone (including area code), size of advertisement, year first in "Yellow Pages," name of owner or manager, number of employees. Compiled from telephone company "Yellow Pages," nationwide. **Arrangement:** Geographical.

18918 ● *Pet Supplies Marketing Directory*
Fancy Publications
PO Box 6050
Mission Viejo, CA 92690
(213)385-2222

Jack Sweet, Editor. Three times per year. **Price:** $75. **Publication Includes:** More than 2,000 trade associations, manufacturers and distributors of pet supplies and equipment, manufacturers' representatives, wholesalers of pets, and industry publishers. **Entries Include:** Company name, address, phone, line of business, name and

Statistical Sources

18921 ● *The Pet Food Market*
Rector Press, Ltd.
130 Rattlesnake
Leverett, MA 01054-9726
(413)548-9708 ● Toll-Free: 800-247-3473
    ● Fax: (413)367-2853

1995. **Price:** $2,195.00; $1,495.00 (trade paper).

18922 ● *The Pet Supplies and Accessories Market*
Packaged Facts
581 Avenue of the Americas
New York, NY 10011
(212)645-4500 ● Toll-Free: 800-346-3787
    ● Fax: (212)645-7681

1992. **Price:** $1650.00 ($1567.50 for Find/SVP cardholders). Published by Packaged Facts. Analyzes the dynamics of the pet supplies and accessories market. Covers a wide range of pets, but concentrates on dogs, cats, birds, and fish. Pinpoints the major factors impacting market growth. Includes sales projections to 1996; leading marketers; the competitive situation; new-product development; distribution channels, including distributors and rack jobbers; the retail level,

Small Business Sourcebook. Edited by Amy Lynn Park.
Copyright © 1997, Gale Research. All rights reserved. Reproduced by permission.

RESOURCE DIRECTORY On-the-Shelf Resources

The Sourcebook of Zip Code Demographics

Publisher: CACI Marketing Systems
1100 N. Glebe Rd., Arlington, VA 22201
800-282-CACI (2224)
703-841-2916, 703-522-6376 fax

Type of information available:
Provides demographic information such as population, income, race, age, and purchase potential, from the national to the local level, arranged by zip code.

How to use it:
Determine the demographic characteristics of inhabitants of a certain geographic area.

For example:
Brad and Lillian want to open a religious bookstore in Salt Lake City. They want to be sure there are enough people in their trading area who fit the demographic profile they have established for their target customer. They will find income data on the particular area of Salt Lake City they are considering for their retail location. They can also determine the disposable income of residents of the areas near their business, as well as the number of customers who have graduated from college.

Availability: Most major libraries;
$395 (county), $495 (zip);
$995 (CD-ROM)

UTAH — POPULATION CHANGE

A 84117-84712

ZIP CODE # / POST OFFICE NAME	COUNTY FIPS CODE	POPULATION 1980	1990	1996	2001	1990-96 ANNUAL CHANGE % Rate	State Centile	HOUSEHOLDS 1990	1996	2001	% Annual Rate 1990-96	1996 Average HH Size	FAMILIES 1990	1996	% Annual Rate 1990-96
84117 SALT LAKE CITY	035	21553	23063	24752	26314	1.1	18	9039	9661	10258	1.1	2.54	6214	6645	1.1
84118 SALT LAKE CITY	035	40921	55972	64038	70406	2.2	54	14853	16836	18441	2.0	3.80	13219	15016	2.1
84119 SALT LAKE CITY	035	33663	38892	42844	46173	1.6	30	13422	14781	15937	1.6	2.89	9732	10687	1.5
84120 SALT LAKE CITY	035	39939	52881	60522	66500	2.2	55	14370	16348	17920	2.1	3.69	12646	14396	2.1
84121 SALT LAKE CITY	035	38042	40235	44567	48114	1.6	35	12719	14024	15117	1.6	3.16	10247	11305	1.6
84123 SALT LAKE CITY	035	20331	27597	30506	32903	1.6	34	9686	10671	11499	1.6	2.85	6615	7273	1.5
84124 SALT LAKE CITY	035	21534	20402	22178	23733	1.3	23	7067	7659	8189	1.3	2.89	5543	6001	1.3
84302 BRIGHAM CITY	003	16830	17119	18390	19510	1.2	19	5351	5722	6062	1.1	3.19	4300	4598	1.1
84305 CLARKSTON	005	567	665	724	776	1.4	25	190	206	220	1.3	3.51	159	172	1.3
84306 COLLINSTON	003	810	959	1074	1162	1.8	45	257	286	309	1.7	3.76	217	241	1.7

POPULATION COMPOSITION — UTAH 84117-84712 B

ZIP CODE # / POST OFFICE NAME	White 1990	White 1996	Black 1990	Black 1996	Asian/Pacific 1990	Asian/Pacific 1996	%Hisp 1990	%Hisp 1996	0-4	5-9	10-14	15-19	20-24	25-44	45-64	65-84	85+	18+	MED AGE 1990	MED AGE 1996	M/F (×100)
84117 SALT LAKE CITY	97.1	96.6	0.3	0.3	1.7	2.1	2.3	2.7	5.6	7.5	7.4	7.5	6.4	29.0	21.0	13.8	1.9	74.9	34.1	35.0	89.6
84118 SALT LAKE CITY	94.0	93.0	0.5	0.6	2.7	3.2	6.7	7.8	9.1	10.5	12.7	11.5	7.9	31.8	12.8	4.3	0.2	59.7	23.1	24.4	98.6
84119 SALT LAKE CITY	88.9	86.9	1.2	1.4	4.5	5.3	7.7	7.7	8.9	9.8	11.4	11.6	8.6	30.7	15.3	6.0	0.7	68.8	26.2	28.1	98.2
84120 SALT LAKE CITY	92.3	91.1	0.6	0.6	3.4	4.1	2.1	2.5	8.4	8.2	8.8	10.2	9.1	30.7	15.3	6.0	0.4	62.1	23.2	24.8	99.1
84121 SALT LAKE CITY	97.7	97.2	0.2	0.2	1.4	1.7	5.6	6.6	5.8	7.9	8.9	9.1	7.0	28.5	23.4	8.8	0.7	71.7	30.4	32.4	96.3
84123 SALT LAKE CITY	93.8	92.7	0.8	0.9	2.6	3.0	2.3	2.8	7.5	9.0	8.1	7.6	6.3	27.1	19.9	9.8	1.3	69.8	27.5	29.2	96.0
84124 SALT LAKE CITY	97.2	96.7	0.2	0.2	1.7	2.0	4.8	5.2	5.9	8.0	8.1	7.6	7.0	24.8	17.0	7.3	1.5	73.4	34.2	35.4	95.5
84302 BRIGHAM CITY	95.0	95.1	0.1	0.1	0.9	1.1	2.4	3.2	8.3	9.5	11.2	12.7	6.8	23.2	14.8	7.3	0.8	63.4	28.3	28.0	97.4
84305 CLARKSTON	97.7	97.1	0.0	0.0	0.3	0.4	2.9	3.1	10.0	10.2	13.4	11.6	7.2	24.9	14.9	7.1		58.1	23.4	22.7	100.3
84306 COLLINSTON	96.4	96.2	0.0	0.0	1.5	1.7	4.4	4.8	9.8	10.5	13.2	11.6		24.1	23.4			59.7	24.1	23.4	104.2

UTAH — INCOME C 84117-84712

ZIP CODE # / POST OFFICE NAME	1996 Per Capita Income	1996 HH Income Base	Less than $15,000	$15,000-$24,999	$25,000-$49,999	$50,000-$99,999	$100,000-$149,999	$150,000 or More	Median HH Income 1996	2001	1996 Natl Centile	1996 State Centile	All Ages	<35	35-44	45-54	55-64	65+
84117 SALT LAKE CITY	21511	9660	9.3	15.1	37.1	27.0	8.0	3.5	40510	41315	83	77	40048	31774	45515	54272	47526	29803
84118 SALT LAKE CITY	11904	16836	6.5	13.7	46.6	30.1	2.8	0.3	40222	41725	82	74	34101	31269	36996	40151	33994	22531
84119 SALT LAKE CITY	12743	14782	17.3	18.6	41.4	20.6	1.7	0.4	31472	32222	61	47	28557	29967	36343	41567	33228	22093
84120 SALT LAKE CITY	11906	16349	7.5	12.8	46.2	31.2	2.2	0.2	40179	41391	82	73	33859	25087	33202	37364	29744	19103
84121 SALT LAKE CITY	20592	14024	6.9	9.0	30.8	37.9	11.4	4.1	52514	53464	94	96	45633	35716	52181	57431	57121	32945
84123 SALT LAKE CITY	15770	10671	12.9	16.6	41.2	25.1	3.5	0.6	35062	35758	70	57	32017	28476	38058	41923	31712	19696
84124 SALT LAKE CITY	22102	7659	8.4	11.4	32.4	31.9	10.9	5.0	41667	48347	91	93	46330	32017	28476	38058	41923	32093
84302 BRIGHAM CITY	15587	5721	9.8	8.7	42.8	32.5	5.3	0.9	41739	45907	85	82	45633	35938	51745	62851	53325	33689
84305 CLARKSTON	10875	205	14.6	15.1	43.9	24.9	1.0	0.5	35109	38564	70	58	37301	32749	43325	53325	33689	
84306 COLLINSTON	12330	287	10.5	10.8	42.2	32.1	3.5	1.0	40517	44243	83	78	29915	28056				

SPENDING POTENTIAL INDEXES — UTAH 84117-84712 D

ZIP CODE # / POST OFFICE NAME	Auto Loan	Home Loan	Investments	Retirement Plans	Home Repair	Lawn & Garden	Remodeling	Appliances	Electronics	Furniture	Restaurants	Sporting Goods	Theater & Concerts	Toys & Hobbies	Travel	Video Rental	Apparel	Auto Aftermarket	Health Insurance	Pets & Supplies
84117 SALT LAKE CITY	102	106	117	114	112	102	111	102	101	105	109	99	109	101	112	101	105	107	103	99
84118 SALT LAKE CITY	100	101	83	99	98	88	99	98	95	96	97	97	92	99	91	94	103	105	96	95
84119 SALT LAKE CITY	95	93	82	88	95	91	97	102	100	101	120	105	112	106	115	100	98	101	95	104
84120 SALT LAKE CITY	99	100	78	96	110	106	119	105	111	115	111	93	109	101	112	98	96	107	99	96
84121 SALT LAKE CITY	108	113	105	126	98	90	99	98	98	105	98	99	96	97	95	98	86	91	102	99
84123 SALT LAKE CITY	97	85	94		112	103	112	102	112	110	89	93	87	92	83	96	94	98		99
84124 SALT LAKE CITY	103	104	118	117	101	93	101	100	96	100	96	95	92	96	89	99				
84302 BRIGHAM CITY	97	91	93	92	94	100	93	97	93	95										
84305 CLARKSTON	98	87	81	88	95	96	96	100	96											
84306 COLLINSTON																				

Copyright © 1996, CACI Marketing Systems.

1996 Survey of Buying Power

Publisher: *Sales & Marketing Management* magazine
Bill Communications Inc., 355 Park Ave. South
New York, NY 10010-1789
212-592-6300
800-443-2155

Type of information available:

Annual issue published by *Sales & Marketing Management* magazine. Contains information on population and income for every state by cities and counties, including per capita and per household incomes.

How to use it:

Determine the buying power of a particular city or county, or find cities or counties with certain buying-power characteristics.

For example:

Jim and Patty decided to add a second furniture store to their location in Mesa, Ariz. Their established customer profile leads them to the Phoenix–Scottsdale area because of the age and population-density demographics. They want to know the effective buying income (EBI) of these two cities to determine which location is preferable. The population of Phoenix is considerably larger than Scottsdale's, and the EBI of Phoenix is more than four times that of Scottsdale. On the basis of this and competition information (such as the number of furniture stores already serving Phoenix, their average sales, and location), Jim and Patty will open their new store in Phoenix.

Availability: most major libraries; $95 (free with subscription to *Sales & Marketing Management* magazine, $48 per year)

METRO & COUNTY TOTALS

METRO AREA / COUNTY / City	Total Population (000s)	18-24	25-34	35-49	50+	House-holds (000s)	Total Retail Sales	Food	Eating & Drinking Places	General Mdse.	Furniture/ Furnish. Appliance	Auto-motive	Total EBI ($000)	Median Hsld. EBI	A $20,000-$34,999	B $35,000-$49,999	C $50,000 & Over	Buying Power Index
Arizona																		
FLAGSTAFF	119.0	14.2	15.2	22.2	16.2	37.1	1,226,770	237,362	247,444	175,042	36,646	156,105	1,317,292	27,595	25.5	16.9	21.4	.0414
COCONINO	112.9	14.7	15.4	22.3	15.7	35.0	1,183,743	228,222	239,669	171,379	36,246	154,738	1,259,237	27,936	25.4	17.0	21.9	.0395
• Flagstaff	52.9	22.7	16.1	21.7	13.1	16.6	825,839	150,035	155,463	132,864	32,998	137,651	639,957	29,986	25.3	17.8	24.2	.0226
KANE, UTAH	6.1	5.8	9.9	21.1	26.5	2.1	43,027	9,140	7,775	3,663	400	1,367	58,055	22,668	29.2	15.3	11.5	.0019
PHOENIX-MESA	2,612.0	9.2	16.4	22.6	25.1	986.0	25,349,890	4,912,388	3,453,806	3,005,005	1,599,026	6,036,293	37,004,777	30,039	26.4	18.9	23.2	.9870
MARICOPA	2,470.6	9.2	16.6	22.7	24.9	941.0	24,575,533	4,687,783	3,350,235	2,930,190	1,581,387	5,930,248	35,819,085	30,609	26.4	19.1	23.9	.9515
Chandler	135.3	8.1	22.5	23.9	13.1	47.3	941,513	242,448	135,262	127,804	86,870	137,557	1,937,087	37,577	25.1	25.4	29.3	.0466
Glendale	178.1	10.0	16.1	25.2	19.3	64.8	1,787,845	304,931	165,983	231,483	84,469	726,924	2,357,415	31,624	25.0	20.2	24.6	.0660
• Mesa	332.2	9.5	16.7	20.9	24.2	124.3	3,629,192	591,017	416,316	590,727	275,161	796,873	4,402,463	30,056	28.8	20.1	21.3	.1268
Peoria	80.7	5.1	17.1	21.0	28.6	29.3	630,927	164,964	62,786	91,128	20,539	119,686	1,114,948	33,958	27.6	24.2	24.0	.0282
• Phoenix	1,088.2	9.3	17.5	23.8	21.7	409.9	10,818,838	2,216,888	1,641,651	1,184,901	752,601	2,207,735	14,903,951	29,106	26.8	18.3	22.1	.4080
• Scottsdale	163.7	7.6	15.3	25.3	33.4	72.7	3,180,344	393,329	424,512	405,338	159,498	1,159,540	3,814,928	38,373	22.5	18.7	35.9	.0985
• Tempe	145.8	18.4	19.0	23.4	16.8	57.3	1,923,723	331,922	294,589	121,906	119,983	494,129	2,196,216	31,813	24.2	19.3	26.0	.0632
PINAL	141.4	8.4	14.5	21.4	27.6	45.0	774,357	224,605	103,571	74,815	17,639	106,045	1,185,692	20,595	27.8	14.1	9.5	.0355
TUCSON	768.8	10.1	15.3	22.3	26.9	301.7	6,826,194	1,253,111	892,669	1,055,419	374,109	1,314,247	9,968,305	25,542	26.8	16.0	18.1	.2707
PIMA	768.8	10.1	15.3	22.3	26.9	301.7	6,826,194	1,253,111	892,669	1,055,419	374,109	1,314,247	9,968,305	25,542	26.8	16.0	18.1	.2707
• Tucson	451.5	13.0	17.2	20.5	24.4	181.4	5,523,176	945,076	697,632	815,651	335,837	1,176,608	5,057,921	22,227	27.6	14.6	12.5	.1682
YUMA	131.1	9.7	14.2	18.8	26.8	43.7	971,681	199,060	116,220	188,482	35,758	199,630	1,283,015	22,544	27.8	14.7	13.3	.0385
YUMA	131.1	9.7	14.2	18.8	26.8	43.7	971,681	199,060	116,220	188,482	35,758	199,630	1,283,015	22,544	27.8	14.7	13.3	.0385
• Yuma	71.3	8.8	16.3	19.6	23.6	24.8	789,237	155,987	98,004	167,854	30,587	156,353	765,280	25,392	29.6	17.9	14.7	.0251
OTHER COUNTIES																		
APACHE	66.7	8.9	13.4	18.2	16.9	17.2	222,418	76,074	17,567	12,233	1,183	3,974	366,610	14,886	19.9	11.7	9.0	.0125
COCHISE	115.3	8.8	14.2	21.8	27.0	40.0	667,477	189,036	101,520	90,769	18,348	113,794	1,244,673	23,900	25.9	16.2	15.5	.0329
GILA	46.6	5.8	10.2	20.7	36.4	18.1	345,011	102,500	66,545	44,890	4,489	48,459	504,877	22,504	27.8	14.7	12.9	.0142
GRAHAM	31.2	10.0	14.2	20.2	24.2	8.7	204,296	52,316	20,998	34,052	7,787	44,468	291,331	21,240	25.3	13.9	13.7	.0087
GREENLEE	9.3	5.1	12.6	22.6	25.3	3.2	21,427	10,462	3,487	165	20		105,188	31,093	26.6	26.2	16.1	.0022
LA PAZ	16.7	6.6	11.5	19.5	35.6	6.4	108,859	18,767	19,848	2,628	1,346	5,709	170,816	19,070	23.7	12.2	11.8	.0048
∞ MOHAVE	125.7	5.8	11.7	20.6	39.0	49.4	1,247,662	261,229	136,987	148,030	36,151	307,364	1,488,215	24,113	30.0	15.0	14.3	.0440
NAVAJO	90.9	8.2	13.7	19.6	19.9	25.2	560,182	147,030	70,703	78,012	15,888	93,357	671,087	19,978	22.4	15.3	12.3	.0225
SANTA CRUZ	36.1	8.0	13.0	20.6	23.4	10.5	414,408	108,777	49,136	63,831	10,093	37,585	298,432	21,228	24.8	15.3	12.1	.0118
YAVAPAI	135.9	6.0	10.1	21.3	40.9	57.0	1,199,175	302,205	152,482	128,360	50,012	212,620	1,741,960	22,975	29.0	14.6	13.1	.0474
TOTAL METRO COUNTIES	3,750.5	9.5	15.9	22.3	25.7	1,415.8	35,579,170	6,854,010	4,839,351	4,568,315	2,081,290	8,012,272	51,003,549	28,536	26.7	18.0	21.4	1.3797
TOTAL STATE	4,299.2	9.2	15.5	22.1	26.1	1,602.1	39,322,423	7,862,176	5,341,637	5,023,255	2,190,456	8,572,238	56,398,523	27,733	26.6	17.6	20.5	1.5367

Survey of Buying Power. Copyright © 1996, Sales and Marketing Management. Reprinted by permission.

Thomas Register of American Manufacturers

Publisher: Thomas Publishing Co.
Five Penn Plaza, New York, NY 10001
212-695-0500, 212-290-7206 fax
Internet: http://www.thomasregister.com

Type of information available:

Lists companies and the products that they produce. Published annually in February, information is organized by product and services and company name.

How to use it:

Identify potential customers, competitors, or suppliers.

For example:

Jenette and Susan are planning to open a garden supply store in Leominster, Mass. They need fix-

tures on which to display a wide variety of products of varying weights. They plan to carry everything from 75-lb. terra-cotta plant pots to one-oz. packages of seeds. Consulting the *Thomas Register,* they look under "Fixtures." Sources of supply are listed alphabetically by state and city. They can then contact any one of several local suppliers or several hundred national suppliers from which to purchase their store fixtures.

Availability: Most libraries,
CD-ROM and Internet;
$240 (plus $16 shipping)

THOMAS REGISTER 1997

FIXTURES: STORE (Contd)

FIXTURES: STORE (Contd)
FL: CLEARWATER (Contd)
(See Our Full Page Ads At "Displays: Electronic" & "Signs: Advertising"; See Our Lit-By-Fax Information In The Catalog File)

▲ SEE OUR CATALOG   IN CATALOG FILE SECTION

FL: FORT LAUDERDALE
Wells Construction Service 1081 N.E. 43rd Court..........NR
FL: FORT MYERS
Tampa Plastics Corp. 2177-T Andrea Lane (Wooden & Acrylic).....................................NR
FL: FORT WALTON BEACH
Tri-Plex, Inc. 155-T Lovejoy Rd. N.W.......................NR
FL: HALLANDALE
Fiero Enterprises, Inc. 203 N.W. 5th Ave...................NR
FL: HIALEAH
Alva Fixtures, Inc. 1629-T W. 33rd Place...................NR
Continental Wood Products, Inc. 7990 W. 25th Ave....NR
G & X Woodworks, Inc. 795-T W. 18th St..................NR
FL: HOLLY HILL
Moss Matrix, Inc. 1705-T State Ave. (Stock, Custom Point-Of-Purchase Displays, Signage, Fixtures, Enclosures, Exhibits)..................1M−
FL: JACKSONVILLE
Doro, George, Fixture Co. Dept. TR, P.O. Box 1836.....1M+
Load King Mfg. Co., Inc. P.O. Box 40606-T (Wood Fixtures, Aluminum/Stainless Backroom Equipment)....................................10M+
Nu-Lite Cabinets, Inc. 11246-T Distribution Ave. E.18...NR
Southside Fixtures 3470-T St. Augustine Rd..............NR
FL: MIAMI
Amertec-Granada, Inc. 7007-T N. Waterway Dr..........1M−
ART-PHYL CREATIONS 16250-T N.W. 48th Ave. (ZIP 33014) (Peghooks, Garment Hooks, Utility Hooks For Perfboard & Slatwall, Plastic, Wire, Stock P.O.P. Displays, Merchandising Aids) (FAX: 305-621-4093) (800-327-8318)............................5M+
Happy Face Enterprises 2456 N.W. 77th (Wood)........NR
Modern Manufacturing Inc. 351 N.E. 185 St..............1M+
S & L Store Fixture Co., Inc. 2685-T N.W. 105th Ave....NR
T & R Stone Fixtures, Inc. 2700-T N. Miami Ave.........NR
FL: OCALA
SEMCO SOUTHEASTERN MFG. CO., INC., A LEGGETT & PLATT COMPANY P.O. Box 1899 D-6 (ZIP 34478-1899) (Display Hooks & Hangers, Wire Display Racks, Baskets, Wire Forms, Fourslide Stampings, Custom & Standard Mfg. & Powder Coating) (800-835-7321)......................1M+
FL: PINELLAS PARK
JAD Construction Co. Inc. P.O. Box 1366.................1M−
FL: ST. AUGUSTINE
Harwil Fixtures, Inc. 3705-T Old Lewis Speedway.......NR
FL: SANFORD
TCM Imagineering, Inc. 3850-T E. Hwy. 46...............NR
FL: SEFFNER
Amcraft Fixtures, Inc. 928-T W. Sligh Ave................NR
FL: SPRING HILL
Creative Design Mfg. Co., Inc. 252-T Shady Hill Rd., P.O. Box 11001.......................................NR
FL: TAMPA
Custom Craft Laminates, Inc. Dept. T, P.O. Box 15795..NR
Faulkner Plastics, Inc. 2808-T Beach Dr.................5M+
Woodcraft Products Inc. 2417-T N. 70th Sts.............1M−
FL: WEST MELBOURNE
Cleve Craft Cabinets 7715-T Ellis Rd....................NR
FL: WEST PALM BEACH

Partitions, Racks, Stove Fixtures & Workstations; Service Capabilities: Electrostatic Powder Coating, Water Based Painting & Laser Cutting) (800-638-7334)....................................50M+
Regal Plastics, Inc. 2335-T N. Cicero Ave. (Acrylic)......1M−
Saco Metals, Inc. 457-T N. Leavitt St....................NR
SEE ALL INDUSTRIES, INC. 3623-T S. Laflin Place (ZIP 60609-1304) (Convex, Magnifying & Flat Glass, Impact Resistant Plexiglass, Steel, Tempered Flat & Convex, For Safety & Surveillance) (800-873-1313)....................................NR

▲ SEE OUR CATALOG   IN CATALOG FILE SECTION

Tesko Welding & Mfg. Co. 4425-T W. Kinze St..........1M−
IL: DEERFIELD
Hirsh Display Fixtures P.O. Box 43.......................1M−
IL: ELK GROVE VILLAGE
TOTAL PLASTICS, INC. 1872 Brummel Dr. (ZIP 60007) (Mfr. Of Plastic Components & Complete Assemblies In Numerous Industries With The Ability To Form, Cut, Machine, Decorate & Assemble. Fabrication Of Plastic Sheet, Rod, Film, Tubing, Shapes & Other Fabricated Parts. Other Applications In Pressure Sensitive Tapes & Adhesives) (800-456-0400).......................5M+
(See Our 2 Page Insert At Plastic Materials)
IL: ELMHURST
Crown Metal Mfg. Co. 765-T S. State Rte. 83...........5M+
IL: FRANKLIN PARK
Fixture Craft, Inc. 10235-T Pacific Ave...................NR
IL: GURNEE
KHM Plastics 4165-T Grove Ave. (Design/ Fabrication-Screen Printing; Fabricated Displays, Store Fixtures)....................................NR
IL: KANKAKEE
Intrinsic Molding Mfg. Co. P.O. Box 1247................1M−
IL: LAKE BLUFF
MERCHANDISING INVENTIVES, INC. 917 North Shore Dr. (ZIP 60044) (Merchandising Sign & Display Accessories) (847-295-9700).......................NR
(See Our Full-Page Ad At Displays)
IL: LAKE FOREST
Richter Industries Inc. 220 Keith Ln....................NR
IL: LIBERTYVILLE
Capitol Interiors 14052-T W. Petronella Dr.............1M+
IL: LINCOLN
Mll Inc. 2100-T W. 5th St. Rd. (Wood & Metal).........10M+
IL: LINCOLNWOOD
Midwest Tropical, Inc. 3700 W. Morse Ave., Dept. R....NR
IL: LOMBARD
Rardin, L.W., Custom Furniture 846-T N Ridge Ave......NR
IL: MELROSE PARK
Garcy Corp. 1400-T 25th Ave............................25M+
H/J Products, Inc. 2121-T N. 15th Ave..................1M+
RHC/Spacemaster Corp. 1400-T 25th Ave..............100M+
IL: MOKENA
Sharn Enterprise, Inc. 10838-T Walnut..................NR
IL: OREGON
Dye Store Fixture & Display Co. 201-T N. Third St.......1M−
IL: PALATINE
Accent Store Fixtures 306-T E. Helen Rd., P.O. Box 1787....................................NR
IL: ROCKFORD
Pierce Laminated Products, Inc. 2430-T N. Court St.....1M+
SOUTHERN IMPERIAL, INC. P.O. Box 2308 (ZIP 61131) (Display Fixtures, Perforated Board Hardware, Display Hooks, End Cap Merchandisers) (815-877-7041).......................NR

Display Craft Mfg. Co. 3939-T Washington Blvd.........5M+
Dittmar, John, & Sons, Inc. 8924-T Yellow Brick Rd. (Laminate)....................................1M+
MD: KINGSVILLE
Cherryworks Ltd 12609 Hartford Rd......................NR
MD: ODENTON
Russell-William Ltd. 1710-T Midway Rd.................5M+
MD: OWINGS MILLS
Saga Design 11422 Cronhill Dr...........................1M+
MD: ROCKVILLE
Merchandising Concepts 11910-T Parklawn Dr..........1M−
MA: ARLINGTON
Brass Works 1167-T Massachusetts Ave...................NR
MA: BROCKTON
AQUATECH SYSTEMS, INC. 93 Centre St. (ZIP 02401) (Specialty Fabricator Of Decorative & Architectural Aquariums & Terrarium Exhibits & Systems) (800-537-3002)....................................NR
MA: EAST BOSTON
Ginsberg, I., & Sons, Inc. 98-T Condor St...............1M+
MA: EASTON
Architects Studio, Inc. 68-T Main St.....................1M−
MA: FALL RIVER
Spectrum Display Inc. 915-T Dwelly St. (Retail).........NR
MA: GRAFTON
Larrivee, W.J., Mfg. Co., Inc. 12-T Collette St...........NR
MA: HINGHAM
Fifield, C. W., Co., Inc. 72 Sharp St., Unit C-4 (Simulated Velvets, Suedes, Leather & Flannel Materials, Custom Developed Fabrics, Flocked Fabrics, Non-Woven).......NR
MA: LOWELL
GENERAL WOODWORKING, INC. 105-T Pevey St. (ZIP 01851) (Workstations For Use In Assembly, Warehouse, Electronics, Computer & Material Handling. Height Adjustable, Ergonomic & ESD. Stands, Racks & Carts (All Powder Coat). Dist. Of Chairs & Weber Knapp) (508-458-6625)...............NR
MA: MALDEN
Sabco Industries, Inc. 56-T Waite St., Ext................NR
MA: MARLBOROUGH
Automatic Specialties, Inc. 422 Northboro Rd............NR
MA: MEDWAY
General Display, Inc. 6-T Industrial Park Rd.............NR
MA: NEEDHAM
Cheviot Corp. 55-T Fourth St.............................NR
MA: WEST HANOVER
Crawford Products Inc. 301-T Winter St., P.O. Box 1215 (Display)....................................5M+
MA: WILMINGTON
Paramount Mfg. Co. P.O. Box 559.......................1M+
MI: ALPENA
PANEL PROCESSING, INC. 120 N. Industrial Hwy. (ZIP 49707-0457) (Pegboard, Hardboard, Fiberboard, Particleboard: Painted, CNC Machined, Edge Finishing, Vinyl & Melamine Laminating; Woodgrain Printing, Screen Printing, Custom Perforating, Chalkboard, Total Panel Fabrication Services) (800-433-7142)....................................10M+
(See Our Full Page Ad At Hardboard)
(See Our Company Profile In Volume 24)
MI: AUBURN HILLS
Pontiac Plastics 4260 Giddings Ave.....................1M+
MI: BATTLE CREEK
Battle Creek Wire Products, Inc. 77 Leonard Wood Dr....................................1M−
MI: BENTON HARBOR
MODAR, INC. 1394 E. Empire Ave. (ZIP 49022-1407) (Laminated, Edgebanded, & Fully CNC Machined

---

RESOURCE DIRECTORY
On-the-Shelf Resources

Copyright © 1997, Thomas Publishing Co.

The Guide to Retail Business Planning | **255**

The 1997 TradeShows & Exhibits Schedule

Publisher: Bill Communications
P.O. Box 888, Vineland, NJ 08360
800-266-4712, 609-691-5800
609-691-3371 fax

Type of information available:

Information about trade shows and exhibitions throughout the country. Listings are indexed by industrial/professional classification as well as geographically, chronologically, and alphabetically by event name. They include such information as contact person, phone and fax numbers, number and type of exhibits, dates, and number and type of attendees.

How to use it:

Locate trade shows or exhibitions with participants from your market area or specialty, enabling you to meet potential suppliers, customers, and others in similar businesses.

For example:

Brett and Jeannie are planning to open a wine (and beer) cellar, and need to stock it with a large variety of wines from around the world. Since they cannot afford to visit hundreds of wineries, they plan to attend several wine trade shows where they can sample dozens of vintages in one location. They will make purchases to fill their cellar with labels that will appeal to their customers. In the 1997 TradeShows and Exhibits Schedule, they find four domestic trade shows, and several more international shows.

Availability: Many libraries; $185 prepaid;
$195 invoiced;
prices include midyear update

TRADESHOWS & EXHIBITS SCHEDULE - Industrial/Professional Section

FOOD/BEVERAGE (continued)

SWISS VINICULTURE & AGRICULTURE FAIR (AGROVINA)
EXHIBIT MANAGER
FOIRE DU VALAIS
RUE DU LEVANT 91, CP 224
MARTIGNY, SWITZERLAND CH-1920
PHONE: 026-22-1495 FAX: 026-22-9891
SCOPE: FOREIGN FREQ: BIENNIAL
EXHIBITS: 91 BOOTHS
EXHIBIT NOTES: EXHIBITS OF MACHINERY AND PRODUCTS FOR VINICULTURE AND WINE CELLARS.
SHOW DATES, LOCATIONS & ATTENDANCE:
98 FEB 4 - 7 MARTIGNY CENTRE D'EXPOSITIONS 15,300

TAIPEI INTL FOOD INDUSTRY SHOW
EXHIBIT MANAGER
CHINA EXTRNL TRDE DEV CNCL
5 HSINYI RD, SEC 5
TAIPEI, TAIWAN
PHONE: 886-2-725-1111 FAX: 886-2-7251314
SCOPE: FOREIGN FREQ: ANNUAL
EXHIBITS: 11,925 SQ METERS
EXHIBIT NOTES: EXHIBITS OF VEGETABLES & FRUITS, CEREALS, MEAT PRODUCTS, CANDIES, DAIRY PRODUCTS, HEALTH PRODUCTS, BEVERAGES, WINES & LIQUORS, CONDIMENTS, REFRIGERATION EQUIPMENT, FROZEN FOODS, HOTEL CATERING & FOOD PREPARATION EQUIPMENT, FOOD PACKAGING & PROCESSING MACHINERY, VENDING MACHINES, ETC.
SHOW DATES, LOCATIONS & ATTENDANCE:
97 JUN 12 - 16 TAIPEI WORLD TRADE CENTER 87,250

TEXAS FOOD INDUSTRY ASSN
PAUL HARDIN
7333 HIGHWAY 290 EAST
AUSTIN, TX 78723
PHONE: (512) 926-9285 FAX: (512) 926-0917
SCOPE: STATE FREQ: ANNUAL
EXHIBITS: 1,700 BOOTHS PRE/POST MTG: YES
EXHIBIT NOTES: LARGEST SUPERMARKET & CONVENIENCE STORE EXPO IN THE SOUTHWEST, FEATURES EQUIPMENT, SERVICES AND FOOD SOLD IN SUPERMARKETS AND CONVENIENCE STORES.
ATTENDEES: OWNERS, PRESIDENTS, OPERATORS & MANAGERS OF CONVENIENCE STORES & SUPERMARKETS - BOTH INDEPENDENT & CHAIN.
SHOW DATES, LOCATIONS & ATTENDANCE:
97 JUN 29 - JUL 1 DALLAS TX CONV CENTER 3,000

TOBACCO & CANDY DISTRS ASSN OH
JACK ADVENT, EXEC DIR

B

TRI-STATE DAIRY-DELI ASSN EXPO
CARLA JEREMIAS, CONV/TRDE SHOW MGR
PO BOX 870
CAMP HILL, PA 17001-0870
PHONE: (800) 345-0108 FAX: (814) 658-3645
SCOPE: REGIONAL FREQ: ANNUAL
EXHIBITS: 70,000 SQ FT GROSS
SHOW DATES, LOCATIONS & ATTENDANCE:
97 JUN 8 - 12 ATLANTIC CITY NJ TAJ MAHAL 5,000

US MEAT EXPORT FED
JEFF OATES, VP COM & IND RLTNS
1050 17TH ST STE 2200
DENVER, CO 80265
PHONE: (303) 623-6328 FAX: (303) 623-0297
SCOPE: NATIONAL FREQ: SEMI-ANNUAL
EXHIBITS: 30 BOOTHS PRE/POST MTG: NO
EXHIBIT NOTES: EXHIBITS OF BEEF, PORK, VEAL, LAMB PRODUCTS, CUTTING/COOKING DEMONSTRATIONS.
ATTENDEES: MEAT PACKERS, GRAIN, CATTLE & HOG PRODUCERS, TRADE OFFICIALS, AGRIBUSINESS, AND FOREIGN BUYERS.
SHOW DATES, LOCATIONS & ATTENDANCE:
97 MAY 27 - 31 ATLANTA GA 200

VIENNA INTL WINE FAIR (VINOVA)
EXHIBIT MANAGER
WIENER MESSEN & CONGRS GES,MBH
PO BOX 277
LAGERHAUSSTRABE 7
VIENNA, AUSTRIA A-1021
PHONE: 43-1-72-720-260 FAX: 43-1-727-20-440
SCOPE: FOREIGN FREQ: BIENNIAL
EXHIBITS: 29,128 SQ METERS
EXHIBIT NOTES: EXHIBITION OF AUSTRIAN & FOREIGN WINES, VITICULTURAL & CELLERAGE TECHNOLOGY, EQUIPMENT & ACCESSORIES.
SHOW DATES, LOCATIONS & ATTENDANCE:
98 MAY 8 - 12 VIENNA MESSEGELANDE 16,480

VINEGAR INST
LARRY DAVENPORT, EXEC DIR
5775 PEACHTREE DUNWOODY
STE 500G
ATLANTA, GA 30342-1558
PHONE: (404) 252-3663 FAX: (404) 252-0774
SCOPE: NATIONAL FREQ: ANNUAL

C

WINE EDUCATORS SOC
JAMES HOLSING, EXEC DIR
132 SHAKER RD, STE 14
E LONGMEADOW, MA 01028
PHONE: (413) 567-8272
SCOPE: INTERNATIONAL FREQ: ANNUAL
EXHIBITS: 20 BOOTHS PRE/POST MTG: YES
ATTENDEES: RESTAURANTEURS, WHOLESALERS RETAILERS.
SHOW DATES, LOCATIONS & ATTENDANCE:
97 AUG 1 - 3 ORLANDO FL
  HYATT REGENCY ORLANDO INTL APT 500
98 AUG SAN FRANCISCO CA 500

WINE FESTIVAL MONTEREY ANNUAL MTG
TOM CORCORAN, FEST MGR
CORCORAN EXPOSITIONS INC
33 NO DEARBORN, STE 505
CHICAGO, IL 60602
PHONE: (312) 541-0567 FAX: (312) 541-0573
SCOPE: DISTRICT FREQ: ANNUAL
EXHIBITS: 200 BOOTHS PRE/POST MTG: NO
EXHIBIT NOTES: EXHIBITS CONSIST OF CALIFORNIA WHITE, RED AND SPARKLING WINES, ALONG WITH NEW RELEASES.
ATTENDEES: RESTAURANTEURS, DISTRIBUTORS, HOTELIERS, CLUB MANAGERS, SOMMELIERS AND WINE BUFFS.
SHOW DATES, LOCATIONS & ATTENDANCE:
97 APR 10 - 13 MONTEREY CA CONF CENTER 5,000

WINE SPIRITS WHOLESALERS AMER
JOSEPH C. GEGG, SR VVP
1023 15TH ST,NW
WASHINGTON, DC 20005
PHONE: (202) 371-9792 FAX: (202) 789-2405
SCOPE: INTERNATIONAL FREQ: ANNUAL
EXHIBITS: 150 BOOTHS PRE/POST MTG: NO
EXHIBIT NOTES: PROVIDES AN OPPORTUNITY FOR SUPPLIERS OF ALCOHOL BEVERAGES FROM AROUND THE WORLD TO SHOW THEIR BRANDS & DISCUSS SALES & PROMOTIONS OF PRODUCTS. NO RETAILERS OR CONSUMERS ARE ADMITTED TO THE SHOW.
ATTENDEES: US WHOLESALERS OF WINES AND SPIRITS AND NEARLY EVERY SPIRIT BRAND. MOST WINE LABELS ARE REPRESENTED.
SHOW DATES, LOCATIONS & ATTENDANCE:
97 MAY 17 - 21 ORLANDO FL
  MARRIOTT HOTEL WORLD CENTER 2,200
98 APR 25 - 29 SAN FRANCISCO CA
  MARRIOTT HOTEL 2,500

Successful Meetings magazine. Copyright © 1997, Bill Communications Inc.

Ulrich's International Periodicals Directory

Publisher: R.R. Bowker
121 Chanlon Rd., New Providence, NJ 07974
888-BOWKER2, 908-771-7725 fax
Internet: http://www.bowker.com

Type of information available:

Magazines, journals, and all other serials that are published worldwide are listed alphabetically within subject category. The data include items such as subscription rates, publisher address and contact information, description of the periodical, and ISSN (International Standard Serial Number). This directory is updated annually in November.

How to use it:

Find periodicals (domestic and international) that cover the area of your business.

For example:

Jerry and Corinne would like to open a collectible shop featuring baseball cards, stamps, bottles, tins, and other antiques. They are aware that the collectible market is very volatile, and they want to keep up to date with all the trends affecting their inventory. They use *Ulrich's International Periodicals Directory* to find magazines that carry articles on collecting trends, both in the United States and abroad.

Availability: Many libraries; $425;
CD-ROM, $525

HOBBIES   3505

790.13   US   ISSN 0733-2130
AM201
COLLECTOR EDITIONS. 1973. bi-m. $19.97. Collector Communications Corp., 170 Fifth Ave., New York, NY 10010. TEL 212-989-8700.
FAX 212-645-8976. (Subscr. to: Box 1941, Marion, OH 43305) Ed. Joan M. Pursley; Pub. Robert C. Rowe. adv. contact: Diane G. Kane. bk.rev.; charts; illus. circ. 100,000. (also avail. in microform from UMI) **Document type:** consumer publication. —UMI.
   Former titles (until 1981): Collector Editions Quarterly (ISSN 0199-929X); (until 1977): Acquire.

795.4 808.836   US
COLLECTORS CHRONICLE. 1991. m. $12.50. Sporting World, Box 10151, Oakland Lake Sta., Oakland, CA 94610. TEL 510-428-2000. Ed. George Epstein. adv. contact: J. Miller. bk.rev. circ. 49,000. (tabloid format; back issues avail.) **Document type:** newspaper.
   Formerly: Card Collectors Chronicle.
   Description: Covers news and trends in collecting baseball cards and comic books.

790.13   AT   ISSN 1036-6997
COLLECTORS DIRECTORY; for everyone interested in collecting. 1990. q. Aus.$10 (foreign $20). Stephen & Joni Coleman. Ed. & Pub., P.O. Box 1357, Penrith, N.S.W. 2751, Australia. TEL 047-392652. adv. contact: Joni Coleman. bk.rev.; illus. circ. 500. (back issues avail.) **Document type:** newspaper.)
   Description: Contains contacts by phone or address. Provides a service to buy, sell, swap, or chat with others interested in anything old, interesting, antique or collectible

790.12   UK   ISSN 1350-1119
COLLECTORS MART. 1980. q. £10.30 (Ireland and rest of Europe £11.70; elsewhere £12.20). Collectors Mart Ltd., Parkgate House, 27 High St., Hampton Hill, Mddx. TW12 1NB, England.
TEL 44-181-941-4512. FAX 44-181-941-8630. E-mail: cmart@easynet.co.uk. Ed. John Pitman. R&P contact: John Pitman. adv.: B&W page £250; adv. contact: Anne Morrell. bk.rev.; illus. circ. 3,000.
Document type: consumer publication.
   Formerly (until 1984): New Collecting Lines; Incorporates: Finders Keepers (Wellingborough) (ISSN 0260-5236)
   Description: Covers trade ephemera and

808.836   US   ISSN 0745-4570
COMICS BUYERS GUIDE. 1971. w. $36.95 (effective 1996). Krause Publications, Inc., 700 E. State St., Iola, WI 54990. TEL 715-445-2214.
FAX 715-445-4087. TELEX 556461 KRAUSE PUB UD. Ed. Maggie Thompson; Pub. Greg Loescher. adv. contact: Jim Felhofer. circ. 19,379. (tabloid format; also avail. in microform from UMI)
   Description: Directed to comics fans, collectors and the comics industry. Contains articles and news about comics from the past and the present and the people who write, draw and publish them.

790.1 355   US   ISSN 1054-5174
COMMAND POST. 1993. q. $24. Game Designers Workshop, Box 1646, Bloomington, IL 61702-1646.

790.13   US
COMPETITION (HARRISBURG). 1989. a. $16.95. Stackpole, Inc., 5067 Ritter Rd., Mechanicsburg, PA 17055-6921. TEL 717-234-5091.
FAX 717-234-1359. Ed. Cathy Hart. adv. circ. 7,000.

745.592   US   ISSN 1052-486X
NK4894.U6
CONTEMPORARY DOLL MAGAZINE. 1990. bi-m. $19.90 (foreign $37.90). Scott Advertising & Publishing Co., 30595 Eight Mile Rd., Livonia, MI 48152-1798. TEL 810-477-6650.
FAX 810-477-6795. Ed. Barbara Campbell. circ. 43,000. **Document type:** consumer publication.
   Description: Covers contemporary dolls of all types, including artists' dolls, one-of-a-kind dolls and limited editions; also includes advice for collectors and profiles of artists and manufacturers here and abroad.

790.13   US   ISSN 0195-9735
CONTEST HOTLINE.* 1977. m. $12. Nationwide Shopper, Box 3197, Burbank, CA 91508-3197. Ed. Jerry Haws. (tabloid format)

790.13   US   ISSN 1071-8672
CONTEST NEWS-LETTER. 1975. m. $15.97. Contest Partners, Box 1266, Bethany Beach, DE 19930-1226. (Subscr. to: Box 58637, Boulder, CO 80322-8637) Eds. Deni Rich Henderson, Ann Faith.

739   GW   ISSN 0341-8936
D W J - DEUTSCHES WAFFEN-JOURNAL. 1965. m. DM.102 (foreign DM.125.30). Journal Verlag Schwend GmbH, Schmollerstr. 31, 74523 Schwaebisch Hall, Germany. TEL 49-791-404500. FAX 49-791-404505. Eds. Gerhard Wirnsberger, Klaus Schinmeyer. adv.: B&W page DM.4664, color page DM.6238.10; trim 197 x 265; adv. contact: Norbert Rieger. bk.rev.; illus.; tr.mk.; index. circ. 62,169. **Document type:** consumer publication.
   Formerly (until 1967): Deutsches Waffen-Journal (ISSN 0012-138X)

DATA EXTRACT. see *COMMUNICATIONS* — Television And Cable

790.13   US
DECALCOMANIA. 1982. 10/yr. $9. DecalcoMania Club, Box 126, Lincroft, NJ 07738. TEL 908-591-2522. FAX 908-576-4429. E-mail: 72212.441@ compuserve.com. Ed. Phil Bytheway. adv. contact: Paul Richards. bk.rev. circ. 100. **Document type:** newsletter.
   Description: Covers the collection of radio paraphernalia and promotional items, such as stickers and "aircheckers."

745.5   JA   ISSN 0289-2847
DECORATIVE DESIGN. (Text in Japanese) 1982. q. 8800 Yen. Gakken Co., Ltd., 40-5, 4 chome, Kamiikedai, Ohta-ku, Tokyo 145, Japan. Ed. Jiro Takeuchi. **Document type:** trade publication.

790.13   US   ISSN 1055-0364
SK335
DECOY MAGAZINE. 1980. bi-m. $36 (Canada $40, elsewhere $70) (effective 1996). Joe Engers, Ed. & Pub., Box 277, Burtonsville, MD 20866.
TEL 301-890-0262. adv.: B&W page $495, color page $695; trim 8 1/2 x 11. bk.rev.; circ. 3,000 (paid). **Document type:** consumer publication.
   Description: Serves the needs and interests of decoy collectors worldwide. Contains auction coverage, calendar, and general articles on decoys.

790.13   GW
DEUTSCHER KLEINTIER ZUCHTER: AUSGABE GEFLUGEL. bi-m. DM.109.20. Oertel & Spoerer, Burgstr. 1-7, 72764 Reutlingen, Germany.
TEL 49-7121-302555. FAX 49-7121-302512. Ed. Ermo Lehari. R&P contact: Ermo Lehari. adv. contact: Eva Masche. index. circ. 11,500. (back issues avail.) **Document type:** consumer publication.

RESOURCE DIRECTORY
On-the-Shelf Resources

Wall Street Journal Index

Publisher: UMI Co.
P.O. Box 1346, Ann Arbor, MI 48106
800-521-0600
800-864-0019 fax

Type of information available:

Monthly digest of articles appearing in the *Wall Street Journal*. For a more definitive listing, this resource is also available online through many colleges and universities.

How to use it:

Find *Wall Street Journal* articles relating to your industry.

For example:

Penny is considering buying a jewelry store franchise. Everything about the business seems good, but she has heard that being part of a chain could be a dead-end undertaking, with no way to get out. Penny's husband, Tom, is wondering about the rights of the franchisee and the stability of the franchise market as a whole. Checking out the *Wall Street Journal Index,* Penny finds several articles on the safety of franchising, and even a few articles on how franchisees bought out their franchisors. She and Tom will discuss these articles and weigh the alternatives, then make a decision about whether to go forward.

Availability: University and business libraries;
$25 per month (minimum) for transactional accounts, Internet, or local dial-in;
$2,730, full-text CD-ROM;
$5,800, entire subscription (per year)

RESOURCE DIRECTORY
On-the-Shelf Resources

FRANCHISING

Joining a chain will not always rescue a troubled business, as Shelee Howard learned when she tried to revive a troubled bagel shop in Queens NY by converting it to a Manhattan Bagel outlet. Franchiser Manhattan Bagel Co financed a makeover for the store and became its supplier, but the conversion did not pay off for Howard, and the store closed in Jan 1997 after she failed to meet all her obligations to the franchiser. (S)F 4 - B, 2:4

The prospects for golf-related franchises are discussed. Among the opportunities for new franchisees are MacBirdie Golf Gifts Inc, a novelty retailer, Nevada Bob's Pro Shop Inc, a sports equipment retailer, TeamGolf Corp, which arranges golf-related corporate meetings and incentive programs and Lomma Enterprises Inc, which operates miniature-g...

McDona...
wiches for ...
lating US t...
said its fra...
pating in t...
from top m...

In a set...
signaled th...
disclosures...
the FTC re...
properly su...
needed to ...
misleading...

Franchise...
eral court i...
Internationa...
Inc. Accor...
has collecte...

FRAUD

see also Corruption in Government; Pyramid Operations

A bogus company is sending out $189 invoices made to look like a US EPA notice. The Feds are investigating and the National Restaurant Association warns members not to pay the bill. (S)Ja 2 - A, 1:5

Horizon/CMS Healthcare Corp. battered by legal and regulatory troubles, said it paid the federal government $5.8 million to resolve a potentially devastating investigation into alleged Medicare and Medicaid billing fraud. (M)Ja 2 - A, 3:1

Federal auditors are cracking down on hospices that seek Medicare payments for treating the terminally ill when the patients are not on the brink of death...

The Justice Dept said Marty Allison, a former vice president of Archer-Daniels-Midland Co. pleaded guilty in federal court on Feb 25, 1997 to conspiring to defraud the grain-processing company of more than $300,000. Allison was a subordinate of Mark E. Whitacre, who was charged with stealing more than $9 million from ADM through a phony invoice scheme. (S)F 27 - B, 2:5

The US Attorney's office is conducting a criminal investigation of alleged wrongdoing in connection with HUD's multibillion-dollar mortgage-auction program. The probe covers allegations of widespread fraud, insider dealing and contracting abuses within the agency. (S)F 28 - B, 15:3

In a twist to the bitter commercial war over dig-...

FOUNDATION FOR NEW ERA PHILANTHROPY

John G. Bennett Jr, the founder of the Foundation for New Era Philanthropy, reversed course and pleaded no contest to federal charges of defrauding hundreds of charities, churches, colleges and philanthropists of $135 million; illus. (M)Mr 27 - A, 3:4

FOUNDATIONS

Hundreds of corporate executives and entrepreneurs holding loads of appreciated stock are sprinting to take advantage of one of the sweetest deals around: private charitable foundations. Buried in 1996's small-business legislation was a gift to the nation's wealthy: the return of private charitable foundations. (S)Ja 27 - A, 1:1

The Better Hong Kong Foundation, a group of Hong Kong billionaires dedicated to downplaying rumors that Chinese takeover of the colony will be bad for business, has quietly begun to underwrite congressional trips to Hong Kong and China that normally are hosted by creditable Washington foreign-policy groups. And it has taken other steps to insinuate itself into the Washington foreign-policy community; photo. (L)Mr 3 - A, 20:1

FOVEAUX, JESSIE LEE BROWN

"The Life of Jessie Lee Brown from Birth Up to 80 Years," a memoir written by Jessie Lee Brown Foveaux, is discussed. The book tells the story of Foveaux's life from an idyllic childhood to a troubled marriage; illus. (L)Mr 7 - A, 1:1

Jessie Lee Brown Foveaux of Manhattan KS has become an overnight sensation following a front-page story about her in the Wall Street Journal. A bidding war has erupted among publishers following the Journal's article about the 98-year-old woman's memoir, which recounted her life raising eight children and struggling with an alcoholic husband. (L)Mr 14 - A, 1:4

1997 against rebel forces in the eastern part of the country, and the recent mass migration in the region, are further signs that France's neoimperial construction is coming to an end; map. (L)Ja 24 - A, 14:4

Bouygues SA of France, a construction and telecommunications group, said it expects to post earnings of Ffr650 million ($116.9 million) for 1996, swinging from a loss of Ffr2.91 billion in 1995. Sales fell an estimated 1% to Ffr81.2 billion. (S)Ja 29 - A, 7:1

Cie. de Suez shares jumped 5% and Lyonnaise des Eaux SA stock soared 6.9% in Paris on a Le Figaro report that the French companies had revived their 1995 proposal for a merger. But Suez, a holding company, and Lyonnaise, a water distribution, building and communications giant, denied such a move was imminent. (S)Ja 29 - A, 7:2

Total SA, a French petroleum giant, said its 1996 net income jumped 50% to FFr5.6 billion ($1.01 billion) from 1995, meeting expectations. (S)Ja 30 - A, 8:1

Rhone-Poulenc SA of France, a pharmaceutical and chemical group, posted 1996 profit that grew 28% to FFr2.7 billion ($486.8 million) from a year earlier, slightly topping expectations. It said the increase stemmed primarily from its drug and animal and plant health lines. (S)Ja 31 - A, 14:2

LMVH Moet Hennessy Louis Vuitton SA of France, a wine, spirits and luxury goods concern, said 1996's sales rose 4.6% to FFr31.14 billion ($5.61 billion) from 1995. Sales were restrained slightly by increased competition and negative effects of foreign-currency fluctuations. (S)Ja 31 - A, 14:3

The unemployment rate in France was unchanged in Dec 1996 at 12.7%, according to the French National Employment Agency and the labor ministry. The number of job-seekers fell by 29,000 during the month, reversing a rise of 20,700 in the previous month. (S)F 3 - B, 6A:3

France the week of Mar 31, 1997 will alter rules to make corporate takeovers slightly more difficult by giving targets more time to defend themselves. Holders will have 25 business days, up from 10-13 days now, to tender their shares to a bidder. (S)Mr 31 - A, 11:4

French industrial production fell 1.2% in Jan 1997 from Dec 1996 but increased 1.6% from a year earlier, statistics institute Insee said. Excluding energy, industrial production was down 1% in January from December, but up 1.1% from Jan 1996. (S)Mr 31 - A, 9A:3

France's unemployment rate hit a record 12.8% in Feb 1997 after having held steady at 12.7% since Nov 1996, according to the French National Employment Agency and the labor ministry. The number of job seekers in February fell by 7,500, to 3.1 million. (S)Mr 31 - A, 9E:3

FRANCESCHINI, DONALD J

Sara Lee Corp named as president 50-year-old C. Steven McMillan, who has been one of two executive vice presidents at the company. The consumer products and food company named Donald J. Franceschini, 60, the company's other executive vice president, to the post of vice chairman. (S)Mr 28 - B, 5:5

FRANCHISING

More franchisers are creating alternative deals for prospective franchisees who cannot afford the usual terms. US Franchise Systems Inc, the franchiser of Microtel inns, says purchasers ordinarily need $600,000 in cash toward a $2.2 million investment, but some entrants now can put $150,000 into an escrow account and agree to lease with an option to buy. Deals offered by SRA International Inc, International Franchise Systems Inc and Gourmet Cup of America Inc are also noted. (S)F 4 - B, 2:3

ASSOCIATION RESOURCES

TRADE ASSOCIATIONS

Trade associations are potentially rich sources of information for both start-ups and those already in business. Tens of thousands of trade associations serve almost every kind of business. Whatever your industry, there is likely to be a trade association that can provide you with industry information, consumer demographics, publications, networking opportunities, and listings of trade shows, as well as other information.

With so many different trade associations, how can you find one that serves your interests? The Internet has become a powerful tool for locating organizations eager to assist you. There are also reference books listing hundreds of associations, and several major trade associations cover the retail industry in general.

HOW TO FIND A "VERTICAL" TRADE ASSOCIATION

Using the Internet:

Perhaps the largest resource of them all is the Internet. In the few short years the Net has been widely available to home and business computer users, it has grown exponentially to include billions of documents on millions of topics. Because of the sheer size of the Net, you need an efficient and reliable way to filter through the information. Several software programs can help you accomplish this otherwise daunting task. These programs (called "search engines") manage the tidal wave of data by allowing you to submit limiting search criteria. Some of the major search engines are: Yahoo, Lycos, WebCrawler, InfoSeek, Excite, HotBot, and Altavista.

For example, say you would like to find general information about trade associations that service the giftware industry. Using a computer to access an online service, you can use the HotBot search engine, asking it to do a "keyword search" with the words "gift trade association." Depending on the specificity of your search criteria, the search engine may return from zero to several million hits matching your request. Most search engines list the results 10 or 20 at a time, in order of confidence (how closely the result matches what the search engine thinks you were really looking for). You may choose to limit your search further with other terms or Boolean modifiers (AND, OR, NEAR), or widen your search with a new set of keywords. In any case, you will undoubtedly find a wealth of information on whatever topic you choose.

There are also several "on-the-shelf" directories that list many of the trade associations in existence, including their size, services provided, political initiatives, and membership requirements.

Resource books that list Trade Associations and other industry organizations:

Directory of Business Information Resources

1995 Edition
Grey House Publishing
Pocket Knife Square
Lakeville, CT 06039
Ph: 860-435-0868
Fax: 860-435-0867

A guide to the print media, electronic media, and trade shows for 93 industry groups.

Encyclopedia of Associations

29th Edition 1995
Volume 1: National Organizations of the
  United States
Gale Research Inc.
835 Penobscot Building
Detroit, MI 48226-4094

A guide to more than 22,000 national and international organizations including: trade, business, and commercial; legal, governmental, public administration, and military; educational; athletic and sports; labor unions, associations, and federations.

Encyclopedia of Business Information Sources

1995/1996
10th Edition
Gale Research Inc.
835 Penobscot Building
Detroit, MI 48226-4094

A bibliographic guide to more than 26,000 citations covering more than 1,100 subjects of interest to business personnel. Includes: abstracting and indexing services, almanacs and yearbooks, bibliographies, CD-ROM databases, financial ratios, price sources, trade associations, and professional societies.

Major trade associations serving the retail industry:

American Franchisee Association (AFA)

53 W. Jackson Blvd., Suite 205
Chicago, IL 60604
Ph: 312-431-0545 or
        800-334-4232
E-Mail: afa@infonews.com
Internet: http://infonews.com/franchise/afa

The American Franchisee Association (AFA) is the nation's oldest and largest trade organization for small business franchisees. AFA represents franchisees in all industries in the development of franchising; educates franchisees, potential franchisees, the government, the business community, and the public as to the needs and requirements of franchisees; improves and promotes the business conditions for franchising generally; and protects and enhances franchisees' economic investment.
Source: AFA Web site

American Association of Franchisees and Dealers (AAFD)

P.O. Box 81887
San Diego, CA 92138-1887
Ph: 619-235-2556 or
        800-733-9858
Fax: 619-235-2565
E-mail: aafd@aol.com
Internet: http://www.gateads.com/aafd/index.htm

The American Association of Franchisees and Dealers was formed in May 1992 for the purposes of bringing fairness to franchising. The AAFD is a national nonprofit trade association representing the rights and interests of franchisees and independent dealers throughout the United States. Since its formation the Association has grown to represent thousands of franchised businesses throughout the United States. It currently has members in 50 states and represents more than 250 different franchise systems.

The AAFD provides a broad range of member services designed to help franchisees build market power, create legislative support of interest to fran-

chisees, provide legal and financial support, and provide a wide range of general member benefits.
Source: AAFD Web site

Direct Marketing Association (DMA)

1120 Avenue of the Americas
New York, NY 10036-6700
Ph: 212-768-7277
Fax: 212-719-1946
E-mail: dma@the_dma.org

The Direct Marketing Association (DMA), founded in 1917, is the largest trade association for businesses interested in database marketing, with more than 3,600 member companies from the United States and 47 foreign nations. Its members include direct marketers from every business segment, including the nonprofit and public sectors. Included are catalogers, financial services, book and magazine publishers, book and music clubs, retail stores, industrial manufacturers, and a host of other vertical segments, including the service industries that support them.
Source: DMA Web site

International Franchise Association (IFA)

1350 New York Avenue NW, Suite 900
Washington, DC 20005-4709
Ph: 202-628-8000
Fax: 202-628-0812
Fax-on-Demand Information Line:
        202-628-3 IFA (3432)
E-mail: ifa@franchise.org
Internet: http://www.franchise.org

The mission of the International Franchise Association, founded in 1960, is to enhance and to safeguard the business environment for franchisees and franchisors worldwide. IFA serves as a resource center for current and prospective franchisees and franchisors, the media, and the government. IFA has been instrumental in developing legislation that safeguards franchising from abuse by fraudulent operators. The Association has testified on behalf of programs that expand opportunities for women and minorities in franchising.
Source: IFA Web site

National Federation of Independent Businesses (NFIB)

NFIB Public Policy Headquarters
Suite 700
600 Maryland Avenue SW
Washington, DC 20024
Ph: 202-554-9000

NFIB Membership Support Headquarters
Suite 300
53 Century Boulevard
Nashville, TN 37214
Ph: 615-872-5800

The National Federation of Independent Businesses is the nation's largest advocacy organization representing small and independent businesses. With an audited membership of more than 600,000 business owners, NFIB is a melting pot of commercial enterprise: high-tech manufacturers, family farmers, neighborhood retailers, and service companies.

Founded in 1943, NFIB was created to give small and independent business a voice in governmental decision making. Today, it remains true to its charter of advancing the concerns of small-business owners among state and federal legislators and regulators.
Source: NFIB Web site

National Retail Federation (NRF)

Liberty Place
325 7th Street NW
Suite 1000
Washington, DC 20004
Ph: 860-783-7971
Fax: 860-626-8145
Internet: http://www.nrf.com

The nation's largest retail trade association, the National Retail Federation (NRF) has members from the leading department, specialty, discount, mass merchandise, and independent stores, as well as 31 national and 49 state retail associations— more than 1.4 million U.S. retail establishments, $2.2 trillion in 1994 sales, and a workforce of more than 20 million people, or one in five Americans. These firms, together with international members that operate stores in more than 50 nations, create a powerful voice for retailing. The NRF supports more than 30 operational committees that deal with subjects ranging from product safety, logistics, and loss prevention to government and legal affairs.

The NRF also maintains several publications including *STORES* magazine, *Retail Sales Outlook, Retail Technology*, and *The Standard Color and Size Code Handbook.*
Source: The National Retail Federation

GENERAL
RESOURCES

GENERAL

Here are some organizations that can assist you with the development of your business plan. Many of their services are free and can provide invaluable advice and information on recruiting and hiring, staffing, organization, motivation, compensation, training, finance, and other factors related to business planning.

❑ Small Business Development Centers (SBDC)

❑ National SBDC Research Network

❑ State Economic Development Agencies

❑ Service Corps of Retired Executives (SCORE)

❑ Occupational Safety and Health Administration (OSHA)

❑ Chambers of Commerce

❑ U.S. Business Advisor

Small Business Development Centers (SBDC)

A Small Business Development Center counsels, conducts research, and trains businesspeople in a wide variety of business topics. It also provides comprehensive information services and access to experts in many fields. Each SBDC encourages unique local efforts, region to region, state to state, and community to community, to meet small-business needs in its area. SBDCs develop and maintain partnerships among community organizations and local, state, and federal agencies, providing a focal point for broad networks of public and private resources at the community level. SBDC partnership programs and activities serving small businesses have contributed significantly to economic growth in each state.

Following is a list of SBDCs for each state plus the District of Columbia, Puerto Rico, and the Virgin Islands.

State Headquarters	Phone/Fax/Internet
ALABAMA	
Alabama SBDC Consortium	205-934-7260
Medical Towers Building	205-934-7645 (fax)
1717 11th Avenue South, Suite 419	
Birmingham, AL 35294	http://www.cba.ua.edu /~cba/sbdc.html
ALASKA	
Alaska SBDC	907-274-7232
University of Alaska, SBDC	907-274-9524 (fax)
430 West Seventh Avenue, Suite 110	
Anchorage, AK 99501	http://www.ptialaska.net /~jedc/sbdc.htm
ARIZONA	
Arizona SBDC Network	602-731-8720
2411 West 14th Street	602-731-8850 (fax)
Tempe, AZ 85281-6941	http://www.dist.maricopa.edu /sbdc
ARKANSAS	
Arkansas SBDC	501-324-9043
University of Arkansas at Little Rock	501-324-9049 (fax)
100 South Main, Suite 401	
Little Rock, AR 72201	http://www.ualr.edu/~sbdcdept
CALIFORNIA	
California SBDC Program	916-324-5068
Department of Commerce	916-322-5084 (fax)
801 K Street, Suite 1700	
Sacramento, CA 95814	http://www.commerce.ca.gov /business/small/starting

State Headquarters	Phone/Fax/Internet
COLORADO	
Colorado SBDC	303-892-3809
Colorado Office of Business Development	303-892-3848 (fax)
1625 Broadway, Suite 1710	
Denver, CO 80202	http://www.state.co.us /gov_dir/obd/sbdc.htm
CONNECTICUT	
Connecticut SBDC	860-486-4135
University of Connecticut	860-486-1576 (fax)
2 Bourn Place, U-94	
Storrs, CT 06269-5094	http://www.sbdc.uconn.edu
DELAWARE	
Delaware SBDC	302-831-2747
005 Purnell Hall	302-831-1423 (fax)
University of Delaware	
Newark, DE 19716-2701	http://www.be.udel.edu/sbdc
WASHINGTON DC	
District of Columbia SBDC	202-806-1550
Howard University	202-806-1777 (fax)
2600 6th Street NW, Room 125	
Washington, DC 20059	http://www.cldc.howard.edu /~husbdc
FLORIDA	
Florida SBDC Network	904-444-2060
19 West Garden Street, Suite 300	904-444-2070 (fax)
Pensacola, FL 32501	http://www.cob.uwf.edu/~fsbdc
GEORGIA	
Georgia SBDC	706-542-7436
University of Georgia	706-542-6803 (fax)
Chicopee Complex, 1180 East Broad Street	
Athens, GA 30602-5412	http://coles.kennesaw.edu /pages/sbdc

State Headquarters	Phone/Fax/Internet

HAWAII
Hawaii SBDC Network
University of Hawaii at Hilo
SBDC State Office
200 West Kawili
Hilo, HI 96720-4091

808-974-7515
808-974-7683 (fax)

http://www.maui.com/~sbdc/hilo.html

IDAHO
Idaho SBDC
Boise State University
1910 University Drive
Boise, ID 83725

208-385-1640
208-385-3877 (fax)

http://www.idbsu.edu/isbdc

ILLINOIS
Illinois SBDC
620 East Adams Street
Springfield, IL 62701

217-524-5856
217-524-0171 (fax)

http://www.ilcommerce.com/DCCA/Menus/BusinessAssistance/SBDCMap.htm

INDIANA
Indiana SBDC
One North Capitol Avenue
Suite 420
Indianapolis, IN 46204

317-264-6871
317-264-3102 (fax)

http://www.in.net/iupui

IOWA
Iowa State University SBDC
2501 North Loop Drive
Building No. 1, Room 615
Ames, IA 50010

515-296-7828
515-296-6714 (fax)

http://www.iowasbdc.org

KANSAS
Kansas SBDC
Wichita State University
1845 Fairmount
Wichita, KS 67260-0148

316-978-3193
316-978-3647 (fax)

http://twsuvm.uc.twsu.edu/~sbdcwww/
http://www.pittstate.edu/bti/sbdc.htm

KENTUCKY
Kentucky SBDC
University of Kentucky
Center for Entrepreneurship
225 Gatton Business & Economics Building
Lexington, KY 40506-0034

606-257-7668
606-323-1907 (fax)

http://128.163.26.168/KentuckyBusiness/ksbdc/ksbdc.htm

LOUISIANA
Louisiana SBDC
Northeast Louisiana University
Administration Building 2-57
Monroe, LA 71209

318-342-5506
318-342-5510 (fax)

http://leap.nlu.edu/lsbdc.htm

MAINE
Maine SBDC
University of Southern Maine
96 Falmouth Street
P.O. Box 9300
Portland, ME 04104-9300

207-780-4420
207-780-4810 (fax)

http://www.usm.maine.edu/~sbdc

MARYLAND
Maryland SBDC
Department of Economic and
Employment Development
7100 Baltimore Avenue, Suite 401
College Park, MD 20740-3627

301-403-8300
301-403-8303 (fax)

http://www.eaglenet.com/tree1/SBDC/SB.Top.html

MASSACHUSETTS
Massachusetts SBDC
University of Massachusetts-Amherst
Room 205, School of Management
Amherst, MA 01003

413-545-6301
413-545-1273 (fax)

http://www.umassp.edu/msbdc

MICHIGAN
Michigan SBDC
2727 Second Avenue
Detroit, MI 48201

313-964-1798
313-964-3648 (fax)
http://bizserve.com/sbdc

MISSISSIPPI
Mississippi SBDC
University of Mississippi
Old Chemistry Building
University, MS 38677

601-232-5001
601-232-5650 (fax)

http://www.olemiss.edu/depts/mssbdc

MISSOURI
Missouri SBDC
University of Missouri
300 University Place
Columbia, MO 65211

573-882-0344
573-884-4297 (fax)

http://www.missouri.edu/~sbdwww

MONTANA
Montana SBDC
Montana Department of Commerce
1424 9th Avenue
Helena, MT 59620

406-444-4780
406-444-1872 (fax)

NEBRASKA
Nebraska SBDC
University of Nebraska at Omaha
College of Business, Room 407
Omaha, NE 68182

402-554-2521
402-554-3473 (fax)

http://nbdc.unomaha.edu

State Headquarters	Phone/Fax/Internet

NEVADA
Nevada SBDC
University of Nevada, Reno
College of Business Administration 032
Reno, NV 89557-0100
702-784-1717
702-784-4337 (fax)
http://www.scs.unr.edu/nsbdc

NEW HAMPSHIRE
New Hampshire SBDC
108 McConnell Hall
University of New Hampshire
Durham, NH 03824
603-862-2200
603-862-4876 (fax)
http://www.crminc.com/sbdc
/index.htm

NEW JERSEY
New Jersey SBDC
180 University Avenue, 3rd Floor
Ackerson Hall-University Heights
Newark, NJ 07102
201-648-5950
201-648-1175 (fax)
http://www.nj.com/njsbdc

NEW MEXICO
New Mexico SBDC
Santa Fe Community College
P.O. Box 4187
Santa Fe, NM 87502-4187
505-438-1362
505-438-1237 (fax)
http://www.nmsu.edu
/~dabcc/sbdc

NEW YORK
New York State SBDC
State University of New York
SUNY Central Plaza, S-523
Albany, NY 12246
518-443-5398
518-465-4992 (fax)
http://www.smallbiz.sunycentral.edu/nysbdc.htm

NORTH CAROLINA
North Carolina SBDC
SBTDC
333 Fayetteville Street Mall
Suite 1150
Raleigh, NC 27601-1742
919-715-7272
919-715-7777 (fax)
http://www.commerce
state.nc.us/commerce/sbtdc/sbtdchom.html

NORTH DAKOTA
North Dakota SBDC
University of North Dakota
UND Box 7308
Grand Forks, ND 58202
701-777-3700
701-777-3225 (fax)

OHIO
Ohio Department of Development
SBDC
77 South High Street, 28th Floor
Columbus, OH 43215
614-466-2711
614-466-0829 (fax)
http://www.seorf.ohiou.edu
/~xx002

OKLAHOMA
Oklahoma SBDC
Southeastern Oklahoma State University
Station A, P.O. Box 2584
Durant, OK 74701
405-924-0277
405-920-7471 (fax)
http://www.chickasaw.com
/~osbdcecu

OREGON
Oregon SB Network
44 West Broadway, Suite 501
Eugene, OR 97401-3021
541-726-2250
541-345-6006 (fax)
http://www.i2m.org
/alliances.html

PENNSYLVANIA
Pennsylvania SBDC
3733 Spruce Street
Vance Hall, 4th Floor
Philadelphia, PA 19104-6374
215-898-1219
215-573-2135 (fax)
http://www.libertynet.org
/pasbdc

PUERTO RICO
Puerto Rico SBDC
University of Puerto Rico
P.O. Box 5100
San German, PR 00683
787-264-1912 x7717
787-892-6350 (fax)

RHODE ISLAND
Rhode Island SBDC
Bryant College
1150 Douglas Pike
Smithfield, RI 02917
401-232-6111
401-232-6933 (fax)
http://www.ri-sbdc.com

SOUTH CAROLINA
The Frank L. Roddey SBDC
College of Business Administration
University of South Carolina
Columbia, SC 29208
803-777-4907
803-777-4403 (fax)
http://sbdcweb.badm.sc.edu

SOUTH DAKOTA
South Dakota SBDC
University of South Dakota
414 East Clark Street
Vermillion, SD 57069
605-677-5498
605-677-5272 (fax)

TENNESSEE
Tennessee SBDC
University of Memphis
Building 1, South Campus
Memphis, TN 38152
901-678-2500
901-678-4072 (fax)
http://www.tsbdc.memphis.edu
/tsbdc.htm

State Headquarters	Phone/Fax/Internet

TEXAS (DALLAS)
North Texas-Dallas SBDC   214-565-5831
Bill J. Priest Institute   214-748-5774 (fax)
for Economic Development
1402 Corinth Street, P.O. Box 420451
Dallas, TX 75342-0451   http://www.dcccd.edu
/bjp/bjpied.htm

TEXAS (HOUSTON)
University of Houston SBDC   713-752-8444
1100 Louisiana Street, Suite 500   713-756-1500 (fax)
Houston, TX 77002   http://smbizsolutions.uh.edu

TEXAS (LUBBOCK)
Northwest Texas SBDC   806-745-3973
Texas Tech University   806-745-6207 (fax)
2579 South Loop 289, Suite 210
Lubbock, TX 79423   http://nwtsbdc.ttu.edu

TEXAS (SAN ANTONIO)
UTSA South Texas Border SBDC   210-458-2450
1222 North Main Street, Suite 450   210-458-2464 (fax)
San Antonio, TX 78212   http://lot49.tristero.com
/sa/sbdc

UTAH
Utah SBDC   801-957-3480
Salt Lake Community College   801-957-3489 (fax)
1623 South State Street
Salt Lake City, UT 84115   http://sol.slcc.edu/utahsbdc

VERMONT
Vermont SBDC   802-728-9101
Vermont Technical College   802-728-3026 (fax)
P.O. Box 422
Randolph, VT 05060   http://www.vtsbdc.org

VIRGIN ISLANDS
UVI SBDC   809-776-3206
8000 Misky Centre, Suite 202   809-775-3756 (fax)
Charlotte Amalie, VI 00802

VIRGINIA
Virginia SBDC   804-371-8253
Department of Business Assistance   804-225-3384 (fax)
P.O. Box 466
Richmond, VA 23218-0446   http://www.richcom.com
/casbdc/home.htm

WASHINGTON
Washington SBDC   509-335-1576
Washington State University   509-335-0949 (fax)
P.O. Box 644851
Pullman, WA 99164-4851   http://www.sbdc.wsu.edu

State Headquarters	Phone/Fax/Internet

WEST VIRGINIA
West Virginia SBDC   304-558-2960
950 Kanawha Boulevard East   304-558-0127 (fax)
Suite 200
Charleston, WV 25301   http://www.state.wv.us
/wvdev/sbdc/sb_main.htm

WISCONSIN
Wisconsin SBDC   608-263-7794
University of Wisconsin-Extension   608-263-7830 (fax)
432 North Lake Street, Room 425
Madison, WI 53706
http://www.uwex.edu/sbdc/wsbdc4.html

WYOMING
WSBDC at the University of Wyoming   307-766-3505
P.O. Box 3922   307-766-3406 (fax)
Laramie, WY 82071-3922
http://www.uwyo.edu/om/research/sbdc/wsbdc1.htm

National SBDC Research Network

The National SBDC Research Network provides research support to the over 900 Small Business Development Centers throughout the United States. The Research Network is funded by the Small Business Administration and administered by the State University of New York.

A rich source of information and materials for entrepreneurs, the Network and its research may be accessed only through your local SBDC and its counselors. The counselor may determine that the research services of the Network would be useful to a client and will request that the Network provide such services. The Network has a home page on the World Wide Web (http://www.smallbiz.suny.edu) that provides computer links to numerous other sources of information for entrepreneurs.

State Economic Development Agencies

Every state has some form of economic development agency that provides services ranging from management assistance to financing. The types of services provided vary from state to state. As you develop your business plan, it is important to contact your state economic development agency to determine what types of help may be available. Following is a list of contact information for each state.

State Headquarters	Phone/Fax
ALABAMA	
Development Office, State of Alabama 401 Adams Avenue Montgomery, AL 36130	334-242-0400 334-242-5669 (fax)
ALASKA	
Alaska Department of Commerce & Economic Development P.O. Box 110800 Juneau, AK 99811-0800	907-465-2500 907-465-3767 (fax)
ARIZONA	
Arizona Department of Commerce 3800 North Central, Suite 1500 Phoenix, AZ 85012	602-280-1300 602-280-1305 (fax)
ARKANSAS	
Arkansas Industrial Development Commission One Capitol Mall, 4C-300 Little Rock, AR 72201	501-682-2052 501-682-7394 (fax)
CALIFORNIA	
California Trade & Commerce Agency 801 K Street, Suite 1700 Sacramento, CA 95814	916-322-1394 916-322-3524 (fax)
COLORADO	
Colorado Office of Business Development 1625 Broadway, Suite 1710 Denver, CO 80202	303-892-3840 303-892-3725 (fax)
CONNECTICUT	
Connecticut Department of Economic Development 865 Brook Street Rocky Hill, CT 06067	860-258-4200 860-721-7650 (fax)
DELAWARE	
Delaware Economic Development Office 99 Kings Highway P.O. Box 1401 Dover, DE 19903	302-739-4271 302-739-5749 (fax)

State Headquarters	Phone/Fax
FLORIDA	
Enterprise Florida 390 North Orange Avenue Suite 1300 Orlando, FL 32801	407-316-4600 407-316-4599 (fax)
GEORGIA	
Georgia Department of Industry, Trade & Tourism 285 Peachtree Center Avenue NE P.O. Box 1776 Atlanta, GA 30301	404-656-3545 404-656-3567 (fax)
HAWAII	
State of Hawaii Department of Business, Economic Development & Tourism P.O. Box 2359 Honolulu, HI 96804	808-586-2433 808-586-2452 (fax)
IDAHO	
Idaho Department of Commerce Division of Economic Development 700 West State Street P.O. Box 83720 Boise, ID 83720-0093	208-334-2470 208-334-2631 (fax)
ILLINOIS	
Illinois Department of Commerce & Community Affairs 620 East Adams Street Springfield, IL 62701	217-782-7500 217-785-6328 (fax)
INDIANA	
Indiana Department of Commerce One North Capitol Avenue Suite 700 Indianapolis, IN 46204-2288	317-232-8800 317-232-4146 (fax)
IOWA	
Iowa Department of Economic Development 200 East Grand Avenue Des Moines, IA 50309	515-242-4817 515-242-4749 (fax)

State Headquarters	Phone/Fax
KANSAS	
Kansas Department of Commerce & Housing	**800-2KANSAS**
	913-296-6988 (fax)
700 Southwest Harrison Street, Suite 1300	
Topeka, KS 66603-3712	
KENTUCKY	
Kentucky Cabinet for Economic Development	**502-564-7670**
	502-564-3256 (fax)
2400 Capital Plaza Tower	
Frankfort, KY 40601	
LOUISIANA	
Louisiana Department of Economic Development	**504-342-3000**
	504-342-5349 (fax)
One Maritime Plaza	
P.O. Box 94185	
Baton Rouge, LA 70804-9185	
MAINE	
Department of Economic and Community Development	**207-287-2656**
	207-287-5701 (fax)
59 State House Station	
Augusta, ME 04333	
MARYLAND	
Maryland Department of Economic & Employment Development	**410-767-6300**
	410-333-6911 (fax)
217 East Redwood Street	
Baltimore, MD 21202	
MASSACHUSETTS	
Massachusetts Department of Economic Development	**617-727-8380**
	617-727-8797 (fax)
One Ashburton Place, Room 2101	
Boston, MA 02108	
MINNESOTA	
Minnesota Department of Trade & Economic Development	**612-297-1291**
	612-296-5287 (fax)
121 East 7th Place, 500 Metro Square	
St. Paul, MN 55101-2146	
MISSISSIPPI	
Mississippi Department of Economic & Community Development	**601-359-3449**
	601-359-2832 (fax)
1200 Walter Sillers Building	
550 High Street	
P.O. Box 849	
Jackson, MS 39205-0849	

State Headquarters	Phone/Fax
MISSOURI	
Missouri Department of Economic Development	**573-751-3946**
	573-751-7700 (fax)
P.O. Box 1157	
Jefferson City, MO 65102	
MONTANA	
Montana Department of Commerce	**406-444-3494**
	406-444-2903 (fax)
1424 Ninth Avenue	
P.O. Box 200501	
Helena, MT 59620	
NEBRASKA	
Nebraska Department of Economic Development	**402-471-3111**
	402-471-3778 (fax)
301 Centennial Mall South, 4th Floor	
P.O. Box 94666	
Lincoln, NE 68509	
NEVADA	
Nevada Commission on Economic Development	**702-687-4325**
	702-687-4450 (fax)
Capitol Complex	
Carson City, NV 89710	
NEW HAMPSHIRE	
New Hampshire Division of Economic Development	**603-271-2341**
	603-271-6784 (fax)
172 Pembroke Road	
P.O. Box 1856	
Concord, NH 03302-1856	
NEW JERSEY	
New Jersey Department of Commerce and Economic Development	**609-292-2444**
	609-777-4097 (fax)
20 West State Street, 4th Floor-CN820	
Trenton, NJ 08625	
NEW MEXICO	
New Mexico Economic Development Department	**505-827-0300**
	505-827-0328 (fax)
Joseph Montoya Building	
1100 St. Francis Drive	
P.O. Box 20003	
Santa Fe, NM 87504-0003	
NEW YORK	
New York State Department of Economic Development	**518-474-5669**
	518-486-6604 (fax)
One Commerce Plaza	
Albany, NY 12245	

RESOURCE DIRECTORY
General Resources

State Headquarters	Phone/Fax
NORTH CAROLINA	
North Carolina Department of Commerce	**919-733-4962**
	919-733-8356 (fax)
301 North Wilmington	
4th Floor, Education Building	
Raleigh, NC 27626	
NORTH DAKOTA	
North Dakota Department of	**701-328-5300**
Economic Development & Finance	**701-328-5320 (fax)**
1833 East Bismarck Expressway	
Bismarck, ND 58504	
OHIO	
Ohio Department of Development	**614-466-3379**
77 South High Street	**614-644-0745 (fax)**
P.O. Box 1001	
Columbus, OH 43266-1001	
OKLAHOMA	
Oklahoma Department of Commerce	**405-815-6552**
6601 Broadway Extension	**405-815-5199 (fax)**
P.O. Box 26980	
Oklahoma City, OK 73126-0980	
OREGON	
Oregon Economic Development	**503-986-0123**
Department	**503-581-5115 (fax)**
775 Summer Street Northeast	
Salem, OR 97310	
PENNSYLVANIA	
Pennsylvania Commerce Department	**717-787-3003**
Community and Economic	**717-234-4560 (fax)**
Development	
433 Forum Building	
Harrisburg, PA 17120	
RHODE ISLAND	
Rhode Island Economic	**401-277-2601**
Development Corporation	**401-277-2102 (fax)**
1 West Exchange Street	
Providence, RI 02903	
SOUTH CAROLINA	
South Carolina Department of	**803-737-0400**
Commerce	**803-737-0418 (fax)**
1201 Main Street, P.O. Box 927	
Columbia, SC 29202	
SOUTH DAKOTA	
Governor's Office of Economic	**605-773-5032**
Development	**605-773-3256 (fax)**
Capitol Lake Plaza	
711 East Wells Avenue	
Pierre, SD 57501-3369	

State Headquarters	Phone/Fax
TENNESSEE	
Tennessee Department of Economic	**615-741-1888**
and Community Development	**615-741-7306 (fax)**
320 6th Avenue North, 8th Floor	
Nashville, TN 37243-0405	
TEXAS	
Texas Department of Commerce	**512-936-0100**
1700 North Congress	**512-936-0093 (fax)**
P.O. Box 12728	
Austin, TX 78711-2728	
UTAH	
Department of Community	**801-538-8700**
& Economic Development	**801-538-8889 (fax)**
324 South State Street, Suite 500	
Salt Lake City, UT 84111	
VERMONT	
Vermont Department of Economic	**802-828-3211**
Development	**802-828-3258 (fax)**
109 State Street	
Montpelier, VT 05609-0501	
VIRGINIA	
Virginia Economic Development	**804-371-8150**
Partnership	**804-371-8112 (fax)**
901 East Byrd, P.O. Box 798	
Richmond, VA 23218	
WASHINGTON	
Washington State Department of	**206-753-7426**
Trade & Economic Development	**206-586-3582 (fax)**
906 Columbia Street SW, P.O. Box 48300	
101 General Administration Building	
Olympia, WA 98504-8300	
WEST VIRGINIA	
West Virginia Development Office	**304-558-0350**
State Capitol Complex	**304-558-0449 (fax)**
Building 6, Room 553	
Charleston, WV 25305-0311	
WISCONSIN	
Wisconsin Department of	**608-266-9467**
Commerce	**608-266-5551 (fax)**
123 West Washington Avenue	
P.O. Box 7970	
Madison, WI 53707-7970	
WYOMING	
Wyoming Department of Commerce	**307-777-7285**
Division of Economic & Community	**307-777-5840 (fax)**
Development	
6101 Yellowstone Road, 4th Floor	
Cheyenne, WY 82002	

RESOURCE DIRECTORY
General Resources

Service Corps of Retired Executives (SCORE)

SCORE, an organization sponsored by the U.S. Small Business Administration (SBA), is a non-profit association with over 13,000 retired and active business executives who provide free counseling on a wide variety of small business topics. They assist in the analysis and definitions of your problems, and help you find solutions based on their experiences with similar situations.

There is no limit on the length of time you may utilize SCORE resources. All information about your business is kept strictly confidential and is not released to anyone outside of SCORE. In addition, SCORE also conducts seminars and workshops focused on small-business needs.

SCORE has 400 chapters with counselors in all 50 states, Puerto Rico, Guam, the Virgin Islands, and the District of Columbia. Contact the SBA at 800-827-5722 or the National SCORE Office at 202-653-6279 to locate the SCORE office nearest you.

OSHA

The mission of the Occupational Safety and Health Administration (OSHA) is to save lives, prevent injuries, and protect the health of America's workers. To accomplish this, federal and state governments must work in partnership with more than 100 million working people and their six and a half million employers, who are covered by the Occupational Safety and Health Act of 1970.

OSHA and its state partners have approximately 2,100 inspectors, plus complaint discrimination investigators, engineers, physicians, educators, standards writers, and other technical and support personnel spread over more than 200 offices throughout the country. This staff establishes protective standards, enforces those standards, and reaches out to employers and employees through technical assistance and consultation programs.

Nearly every working man and woman in the nation comes under OSHA's jurisdiction (with some exceptions such as miners, transportation workers, many public employees, and the self-employed). Other users and recipients of OSHA services include occupational safety and health professionals, the academic community, lawyers, journalists, and personnel of other government entities.

Source: OSHA Web site

Chambers of Commerce

The U.S. Chambers of Commerce
1615 H Street NW
Washington, DC 20062
Ph: 202-659-6000 or
800-638-6582 (Membership Services)

Almost every city and state has a chamber of commerce, a nonprofit association that caters to the business community. Many chambers of commerce have small-business sections that help their members and the community in general by conducting seminars, publishing educational and informational books and tapes, acting as advocates to government agencies, and providing advice and information on entrepreneurship.

Often, membership has other benefits for the small-business person. It enables members to obtain group rates on medical, dental, and life insurance, as well as other programs. The main headquarters can give you a list of chambers in your area and a catalog of books and tapes offered. Your local chamber should also be listed in your phone book and with Directory Assistance. Find out what services your local chamber offers.

Many chambers have sections that deal with the particular needs of minorities, women, and ethnic groups. Contact the national chamber or your local chamber and ask for the person who serves your special interest group, or ask for a referral to chambers that deal specifically with its issues. American chambers located in foreign countries can provide information about other countries, help make business contacts, and assist in a variety of other ways. Contact the national headquarters listed above to get lists of overseas chambers.

Additionally, other foreign countries and cities have branches of their chambers of commerce here in America. Many foreign chambers are located in Washington, D.C., and in major cities in the United States (look in phone books or call the U.S. State Department or the U.S. Chamber of Commerce to find them). Chambers from other countries can be invaluable sources of information on those markets and can help arrange introductions to businesspeople in their countries.

The U.S. Business Advisor

Internet: http://www.business.gov

This is a one-stop electronic link to government for business. The U.S. Business Advisor exists to provide business with access to federal government information, services, and transactions. Its goal is to make the relationship between business and government more productive. You can get information from the U.S. Business Advisor in five ways:

❑ **Common Questions**

Gives answers to questions that businesspeople frequently ask the government. If you have a question, check here first to see if it has been answered.

❑ **How To...**

Contains expert tools, step-by-step guides, and transactions.

❑ **Search**

Helps you find online resources and regulations for specific topics of interest to you. If you can't find what you're looking for in other areas, this is the best place to find out if the *U.S. Business Advisor* has a resource that can help you.

❑ **Browse**

Contains information and services arranged by category.

❑ **News**

Gives current items of interest to the general business community.

Source: U.S. Business Advisor Web site

FINANCIAL RESOURCES

Several potential sources of financing for your business are described here. The best place to start your search is at your local bank(s). Explain your business plan and financing requirements, and obtain loan information. Find out what subsidies or other assistance may be available to small businesses.

❑ The U.S. Small Business Administration (SBA)
❑ Small Business Investment Companies (SBIC)
❑ Export-Import Bank
❑ Venture Capital

U.S. SMALL BUSINESS ADMINISTRATION

Main Office
1441 L Street NW
Washington, DC 20416
800-827-5722   Answer Desk
202-205-7717   General questions and answers
800-697-4636   Computer access (9600 baud)

The U.S. Small Business Administration (SBA) has a variety of loan programs. A description of these programs follows, along with eligibility requirements and terms. Most of these programs are administered at the local level. Therefore, the best place to start is at your SBA district office. The SBA also maintains a "Small Business Answer Desk" (800-827-5722) that can provide you with information relative to their various programs as well as the telephone numbers and addresses of the district SBA offices.

What you should know about SBA loans

All SBA lending consists of loan guarantees, except for direct SBA loans to handicapped business owners.

SBA-guaranteed loans are generally administered through commercial lending organizations (i.e., banks). While most banks and other lending institutions can make SBA-guaranteed loans, certain ones, called certified and preferred lenders, have special relationships with the SBA, which enable the institutions to expedite loans to creditworthy small businesses. Contact your local SBA office for a list of certified and preferred lenders.

To obtain an SBA-guaranteed loan, you must demonstrate the ability to repay the loan from the cash flow and profits from your business.

SBA-guaranteed loans can be used only to finance the start-up, operation, or expansion of a business. The proceeds may not be used to repay other debts, be reinvested in financial instruments, or be used for speculative purposes.

How to obtain an SBA-guaranteed loan

1. Attempt to obtain a loan from at least one commercial lender. If you are turned down for reasons other than your ability to repay the loan, ask if the lender would be willing to make the loan if it were guaranteed by the SBA. Reasons for rejection may include the amount of the loan, the period of repayment, or the length of time the business has been in operation.

2. The bank will contact the SBA to determine if the loan can be guaranteed by the SBA. If the loan meets SBA criteria, the determination of whether to make the loan rests solely with the bank. The bank will make all necessary arrangements to secure the guarantee with the SBA. If a bank refuses to make a guaranteed loan, the borrower may try another bank.

3. Borrowers must be prepared to pay closing costs on SBA-guaranteed loans. While closing costs depend on many factors, total closing costs between 3% and 5% of the loan amount are common.

Type of Loan	Lender	Amount	Maturity
BASIC 7(A)	Banks	Up to $750,000 guaranteed portion	Working Capital – 7 yrs. Equipment – 10 yrs. Real Estate – 25 yrs.
CAPLINE PROGRAMS	Banks	Up to $750,000 guaranteed portion	Up to 5 yrs.
STANDARD-ASSET BASED	Banks with an asset-based department	Guaranty up to $750,000	Up to 5 yrs.
SMALL-ASSET BASED	Banks	Up to $200,000	Up to 5 yrs.
SEASONAL LINE OF CREDIT	Banks	Up to $750,000 guaranteed portion	12 months to 5 yrs., renewed annually
SMALL LOAN PROGRAM	Banks	Up to $50,000 total loan amount	Working capital – 7 yrs. Machinery and equipment – 10 yrs. Real estate – 25 yrs.
EXPORT WORKING CAPITAL (pilot program)	Banks	Up to $750,000 guaranteed portion	Maturities match a single transaction cycle with a term of up to 18 months or a support line of credit of up to 12 months
FA$TRAK (pilot program)	Banks (selected)	Up to $100,000 total loan amount	Working capital – 7 yrs. Equipment – 10 yrs. Real estate – 25 yrs.
MICROLOAN	Designated microlenders	Up to $25,000 total loan amount	Up to 6 yrs.
504 PROGRAM	Banks and Certified Development Companies (CDC)	Up to $750,000 SBA priced out debenture amount	Debenture of 10 of 20 yrs.
WOMEN'S PREQUALIFICATION (pilot program)	Banks do lending, SBA does prequalifying	Up to $250,000 total loan amount	Working Capital – 7 yrs. Equipment – 10 yrs. Real Estate – 25 yrs.
LOWDOC	Banks	$100,000 or less total loan amount	Working Capital – 7 yrs. Equipment – 10 yrs. Real Estate – 25 yrs.

Source: U.S. Small Business Administration

Interest Rate	Collateral Guarantees	SBA % Guaranty	Comments
Maturity less than 7 yrs., max. is 2.25% over Wall Street prime. Maturity greater than or equal to 7 yrs., max. is 2.75% over prime.	Personal guarantees Pledge of assets	$100,000 or less: 80% Over $100,000: 75%	Owners must have sufficient equity injection, meet SBA size standards and eligibility requirements. Must be for-profit business. Former Veterans program now folded in here.
Up to 2.25% over Wall Street prime	Personal guarantees Pledge of assets Anticipated inventory	$100,000 or less: 80% Over $100,000: 75%	Financing for short-term cyclical working capital
2.25% over Wall Street prime	Accounts receivable Inventory	$100,000 or less: 80% Over $100,000: 75%	
2.25% over Wall Street prime	Accounts receivable Inventory	$100,000 or less: 80% Over $100,000: 75%	Must cash flow over 7–yr. term.
Maximum 2.25% over Wall Street prime	Personal guarantees Pledge of assets	$100,000 or less: 80% Over $100,000: 75%	Must be in business one year. Structured to be repaid from seasonal cash flow. 30-day payout. Only one per season.
Maturity less than 7 yrs., max. is 4.25% over Wall Street prime for loans less than $25,000. Maturity greater than or equal to 7 yrs., max. is 4.75% over Wall Street prime for loans up to $25,000 and 3.75% over prime for loans $25,000 to $50,000	Personal guarantees Pledge of assets	Up to 80%	This program is particularly valuable for service firms
May be fixed or variable with no minimum	Personal guarantees Pledge of export inventory, foreign receivables, contract and L/C proceeds	$100,000 or less: 80% Over $100,000: 75%	Provides short-term financing to small businesses for export-related transactions. Proceeds from the export sales are the primary source of repayment.
Maturity less than 7 yrs., max. is 2.25% over Wall Street prime. Maturity greater than or equal to 7 yrs., max. is 2.75% over prime.	Personal guarantees Pledge of assets	Up to 50%	Lenders approve loans without SBA review. Reviewed every 2 yrs.
Up to 4% over Wall Street prime	Personal guarantees Pledge of assets	None	Funding for this program provided by the SBA
Fixed	Personal guarantees Pledge of assets	Up to 40% of project, up to $1 million.	Private lender puts up 50%, CDC 40%, equity 10%. Long-term fixed rate financing for fixed assets
Maturity less than 7 yrs., max. is 2.25% over Wall Street prime. Maturity 7 yrs. or more, max. is 2.75% over prime	Pledge of personal and business assets Personal guarantees	$100,000 or less: 80% Over $100,000: 75%	Businesses must be at least 51% owned and operated by women. SBA does prequalifying, intermediaries assist applicants in preparing a business plan.
Same as in 7(a) above except loans under $50,000 may be higher (see SBA for more detail)	Personal guarantees Pledge of assets	Up to 80%	Focuses on character, credit, and experience. One-page application. Lenders use normal credit analysis. SBA responds quickly (2 to 3 days).

New SBA Loan Initiatives

The Small Business Administration introduced several new programs last year. The **Precertification Program,** developed in cooperation with the Minority Business Development Agency, is designed to make it quicker and easier for minority and women business owners to obtain loans up to $50,000. The **FastTrack** loan program will give certain preferred lenders the opportunity to make loans up to $100,000 to creditworthy businesses. Loans can be made very quickly, and the SBA can guarantee up to 50% of the loan.

Small Business Investment Companies

Small Business Investment Companies (SBICs) are privately capitalized, owned, and managed investment firms licensed by the SBA that provide equity capital, long-term financing, and management assistance to small businesses. For more information on SBICs, contact the nearest SBA office. A directory of SBICs is available by sending $10 to:

**National Association
of Small Business Investment Companies**
NASBIC Directory
P.O. Box 4039
Merrifield, VA 22116
Source: Small Business Resource Directory

Export-Import Bank (EXIMBANK)

811 Vermont Avenue NW
Washington, DC 20571
800-565-3946

EXIMBANK is an independent government agency that provides export financing to large and small businesses and to potential exporters that have had difficulty obtaining working-capital loans from commercial lenders. For more information about specific EXIMBANK programs, call the EXIMBANK Financing Hotline at 800-565-3946.

Venture Capital

Venture capital companies are different from other sources of financing in that the venture capitalist takes part-ownership of the company in return for the funding. Sources of venture capital include individual investors, partnerships, and investment companies seeking to invest in fast-growing small businesses and start-ups with excellent growth potential. The following associations and organizations can help growing businesses find potential sources of venture capital:

The Capital Network	**512-794-9398**
National Association of Small Business Investment Companies	**703-683-1601**
National Venture Capital Association	**703-351-5269**
Seed Capital Network	**615-573-4655**

The National Venture Capital Association sells a directory listing more than 150 venture capital firms. Price: $25. Order by calling 703-351-5269.
Source: Small Business Resource Directory

Section VI

Appendices

APPENDICES

Sample Corporate Charter

Articles of Incorporation, or "corporate charters," are governed by each individual state. That is, each state will have its own laws, requirements, restrictions, and forms for the different types of corporation. What follows are Articles of Incorporation for the state of Maine. Contact your secretary of state for the forms required.

BUSINESS CORPORATION

STATE OF MAINE

ARTICLES OF INCORPORATION

_____
Deputy Secretary of State

True Copy When Attested By Signature

_____
Deputy Secretary of State

(Check box only if applicable)
❑ This is a professional service corporation formed pursuant to 13 MRSA Chapter 22.

Pursuant to 13-A MRSA 403, the undersigned, acting as incorporator(s) of a corporation, adopt(s) the following Articles of Incorporation:

FIRST: The name of the corporation is _____

and its principal place of business location in Maine is
_____

_____

(physical location - street (not P.O. Box), city, state, and zip code)

SECOND: The name of its Clerk, who must be a Maine resident, and the registered office shall be:

_____

(name)

_____

(physical location - street (not P.O. Box), city, state, and zip code)

_____

(mailing address if different from above)

THIRD: ("X" one box only)

❑   A. 1. The number of directors constituting the initial board of directors of the corporation is _____ (See Section 703.1.A.)
2. If the initial directors have been selected, the names and addresses of the persons who are to serve as directors until the first annual meeting of the shareholders or until their successors are elected and shall qualify are:

Sample Corporate Charter *(continued)*

NAME   ADDRESS

_____   _____

_____   _____

_____   _____

3. The board of directors ❑ is ❑ is not authorized to increase or decrease the number of directors.

4. If the board is so authorized, the minimum number, if any, shall be _____ directors (see Section 703.1.A.), and the maximum number, if any, shall be _____ directors.

❑ B. There shall be no directors initially; the shares of the corporation will not be sold to more than twenty (20) persons; the business of the corporation will be managed by the shareholders. (See Section 701.2.)

FOURTH: ("X" one box only)

❑ There will only be one class of shares (title of class) _____

   Par value of each share (if none, so state) _____ Number of shares authorized: _____

❑ There will be two or more classes of shares. The information required by Section 403 concerning each such class is set out in Exhibit _____ attached hereto and made a part hereof.

SUMMARY

The aggregate par value of all authorized shares (of all classes) **having a par value is** $_____

The total number of authorized shares (of all classes) **without par value** is $_____

FIFTH: ("X" one box only) Meetings of shareholders ❑ may ❑ may not be held outside of the State of Maine.

SIXTH: ("X" if applicable) ❑ There are no preemptive rights.

SEVENTH: Other provisions of these articles, if any, including provisions for the regulation of the internal affairs of the corporation, are set out in Exhibit _____ attached hereto and made a part hereof.

_____

INCORPORATORS   DATED _____

_____   _____
(signature)   (residence address)

_____   _____
(type or print name)   (city, state, and zip code)

Sample Corporate Charter *(continued)*

_____   _____
(signature)   (residence address)

_____   _____
(type or print name)   (city, state, and zip code)

_____   _____
(signature)   (residence address)

_____   _____
(type or print name)   (city, state, and zip code)

For Corporate Incorporators*

Name of Corporate Incorporator _____

By _____   _____
        (signature of officer)   (principal business location)

_____   _____
(type or print name and capacity)   (city, state, and zip code)

_____

* Articles are to be executed as follows:

If a corporation is an incorporator (Section 402), the name of the corporation should be typed and signed on its behalf by an officer of the corporation. The articles of incorporation must be accompanied by a certificate of an appropriate officer of the corporation certifying that the person executing the articles on behalf of the corporation was duly authorized to do so.

Sample Partnership Agreement

1.   **Introduction.** Agreement to form a partnership (Partnership) made on [date], between [name], residing at [address], and [name], residing at [address].

2.   **Partnership Purpose and Name.** The parties agree to form Partnership on the terms set out below to engage in the business of [nature of business]. Partnership's name shall be [name], and its principal office shall be at [address].

3.   **Duration of Partnership.** Partnership will begin on [date] and will continue until it terminates in accordance with the provisions of this Agreement.

[Alternative Paragraph]

3.   **Duration of Partnership.** Partnership will begin on [date] and end on [date].

4.   **Partners' Capital Contributions.** The Partnership capital shall be contributed by the Partners, partly in cash and partly in personal property. The cash contributions shall be:

[schedule of Partners' names and cash amounts]

The contributions of personal property and the values to be placed upon them shall be:

[schedule of Partners' names, descriptions of property, and values of property]

5.   **Partners' Capital Accounts.** Partnership shall maintain a separate capital account for each Partner. Neither Partner may withdraw any part of the Partner's contributed capital without the other's consent. If a Partner's capital account falls below the amount of the Partner's contributed capital because of losses or permitted withdrawals, the Partner's share of profits will be credited to the Partner's capital account until the capital contribution has been restored, and before any profits can be credited to the Partner's income account.

6.   **Division of Profits and Losses.** The net profits and losses of Partnership will be equally divided between the Partners.

[Alternative Paragraph A]

6.   **Division of Profits and Losses.** The net profits and losses of Partnership will be divided in

accordance with the proportion that the amount of each Partner's contributed capital bears to Partnership's total contributed capital.

[Alternative Paragraph B]

6. **Division of Profits and Losses.** The net profits and losses of Partnership will be divided or charged to the Partners in the following proportions:

[schedule of Partners' names and percentages of profit or loss allotted]

7. **Partners' Income Accounts.** Partnership shall maintain a separate income account for each Partner to which each Partner's share of Partnership's income or losses shall be credited or charged. If there is no credit balance in a Partner's income account, losses shall be charged to the Partner's capital account.

8. **Partners' Right to Salary and Drawings.** Neither Partner shall receive any salary for the Partner's services to Partnership. Each Partner may withdraw any credit balance in the Partner's income account at any time. Neither Partner shall be entitled to an additional share of profits solely because the Partner's capital account exceeds that of the other, except as otherwise provided in this Agreement.

[Alternative Paragraph]

8. **Partner's Right to Salary and Drawings.** Partner [name] shall draw a salary of _____ dollars ($_____) weekly, and Partner [name] shall draw a salary of _____ dollars ($_____) weekly. The Partners' salaries shall not be charged to their capital or income accounts but shall be charges for the purposes of determining Partnership's net income. Withdrawals of credit balances from the Partners' income accounts shall be made only at the times and in the amounts that the Partners agree upon from time to time.

9. **No Interest on Capital.** No interest will be paid on any balances in the Partners' capital accounts.

10. **Management of the Partnership.** Each Partner shall have an equal voice in the management of Partnership, and each shall be devoted full time to the conduct of its business. Without the other's written consent, no Partner shall, on Partnership's behalf:

   a. Borrow or lend money;

      b. Make, deliver, or accept commercial paper;

      c. Execute any mortgage, security agreement, bond, or lease; or

      d. Buy or execute a purchase agreement, or sell or execute a sales agreement for any property other than that bought or sold in the regular course of Partnership's business.

11. **Sale of, Assignment of, or Granting Lien on Partnership Interest.** Without the other's written consent, no Partner shall:

      a. Assign, mortgage, give a security interest in, or sell the Partner's Partnership interest;

      b. Agree with a party not privy to this Agreement that such party will have an interest in Partnership; or

      c. Do anything that would be detrimental to Partnership's ability to conduct its business.

12. **Partnership Bank Account.** All Partnership funds shall be deposited in its name in an account with the [name of bank] located at [address], or such other bank or banks as the Partners may agree upon from time to time. All withdrawals from these accounts shall be by check signed by either Partner.

13. **Partnership Books and Records.** Partnership books of account will be kept in accordance with generally accepted accounting principles. The books and supporting records will be maintained at Partnership's principal office and will be examined by Partnership's certified public accountants at least [frequency]. Partnership's fiscal year shall start on [month and day] and close on [month and day]. Partnership's certified public accountants shall prepare an income statement and balance sheet for each fiscal year within [number] months after the end of the fiscal year. These financial statements shall be binding upon the Partners as to income or losses and the balances in the Partners' income and capital accounts.

14. **Voluntary Dissolution of Partnership.** The Partners may agree to dissolve Partnership at any time. Should the Partners so agree, they will liquidate Partnership in an orderly fashion. The proceeds derived from the sale of Partnership's property, including its name and goodwill, shall be applied in the following order:

a. Discharge all Partnership liabilities and pay the costs of liquidation;

b. Bring the Partners' income accounts into balance;

c. Pay the balance shown in each Partner's income account to that Partner;

d. Bring the Partners' capital accounts into balance; and

e. Pay the balance shown in each Partner's capital account to that Partner.

15. **Effect of Partner's Retirement.** A Partner may retire from Partnership at the end of any Partnership fiscal year by serving written notice of his or her intention to retire upon the other Partner no later than [number] months before the end of the fiscal year. The remaining Partner may elect either to purchase the retiring Partner's interest or to terminate and liquidate Partnership together with the retiring Partner. Written notice of the remaining Partner's election shall be served on the retiring Partner no later than [number] months after receipt of the notice of intention to retire.

    If the remaining Partner elects to purchase the retiring Partner's interest, the purchase price and terms of payment shall be those set out in Paragraph 17.

    If the remaining Partner elects to terminate and liquidate Partnership together with the retiring Partner, the termination and liquidation shall be carried out in the manner described in Paragraph 14.

16. **Effect of Partner's Death.** If one of the Partners dies, the survivor may either purchase the deceased Partner's interest or terminate and liquidate Partnership.

17. **Election to Purchase the Deceased Partner's Interest in the Partnership.**

    a. *Notice of Election.* If the surviving Partner elects to purchase the deceased Partner's interest, the Partner shall serve written notice of this election within [number] months after the Partner's death upon the executor or administrator of the decedent if one has been appointed and qualified or, if none has qualified, upon the decedent's heirs at their last known addresses.

    b. *Purchase Price.* The purchase price will be an amount equal to the balance in the decedent's capital account as of the date of the decedent's death, plus or minus the balance in the decedent's income account at the end of the fiscal year immediately pre-ceding the Partner's death, increased or decreased by the decedent's share of Partnership profits or losses for the period beginning with the start of the fiscal year in which the Partner died and ending the last day of the month in which death occurred, reduced by any withdrawals from the deceased Partner's income account during the same period. The purchase price will not include any separate amounts for goodwill, trade name, patents, or other intangible assets. The surviving Partner will be entitled to use Partnership trade name. The purchase price will be paid without interest in [num-ber] equal monthly payments commencing [number] months after the month in which the decedent died.

[Alternative Paragraph]

b. *Purchase Price.* The purchase price will be an amount equal to the balance in the deceased Partner's capital account together with a sum equal to [number] times the average net income earned by Partnership in the [number] fiscal years immediately prior to the deceased Partner's death. If the deceased Partner's death occurs in the last six months of any fiscal year, that fiscal year shall be one of the [number] fiscal years included for the computation of average net income. The determination by Partnership's certified public accountants of Partnership's average net income shall be conclusive upon all parties.

18. **Election to Liquidate Partnership.** If the surviving Partner elects to liquidate Partnership, the liquidation will proceed as quickly as possible, following the procedure described in Paragraph 14 of this Agreement. In addition to its share of the proceeds from the liquidation, the deceased Partner's estate shall be entitled to any profits that have not been withdrawn and that have been earned up to and including the date of the deceased Partner's death. If there have been losses up to and including the date of the deceased Partner's death that have not been charged to the Partner's income account, they shall be so charged before any distribution is made to the deceased Partner's estate.

19. **Arbitration of Disputes.** Any controversy concerning this Agreement will be settled by arbi-tration according to the rules of the American Arbitration Association, and judgment upon the award may be entered and enforced in any court.

[signatures]

Partners

Source: Basic Legal Forms
   © *Warren, Gorham, & Lamont*

ARTICLES OF ORGANIZATION FOR LIMITED LIABILITY COMPANY
GENERALIZED FORM

ARTICLES OF ORGANIZATION
OF
[name of limited liability company]

The undersigned hereby execute and acknowledge the following Articles of Organization for the purpose of forming a limited liability company under the [specify state statute].

1. The name of the limited liability company is _____, LLC.

    NOTE: The name of each limited liability company must contain the words "limited liability company," "limited company," or an appropriate abbreviation such as LLC or LC.

2. The street address of the registered office in [state of organization] is [address].

3. a. The name of the registered agent for service of process in [state of organization] is _____.

    b. The address of the registered agent for service of process is [address]

    c. The registered agent is [mark appropriate box]:

    ❏ An individual resident of [state of organization]

    ❏ A domestic corporation

    ❏ A foreign corporation authorized to do business within [state of organization]

    ❏ A domestic limited liability company

    ❏ A foreign limited liability company authorized to do business within [state of organization].

4. The [appropriate state official] is hereby appointed the agent of [name of LLC] for service of process if the registered agent has resigned, the registered agent's authority has been revoked, or the agent cannot be found or served with the exercise of reasonable diligence. The address within [state of organization] to which the [appropriate state official] shall mail a copy of any process against [name of LLC] is _____

5. The name and business address of each organizer is: [list name and address of each organizer].

6. The latest date on which the limited liability company is to be dissolved [and its affairs wound up] is [date].

    NOTE: Some states set a thirty-year ceiling on the life of an LLC. The trend, however, is to leave the precise period open, since the setting of a specific term will not necessarily negate the corporate attribute of "continuity of life." Ordinarily, state law or the operating agreement will specify events such as the bankruptcy, retirement, or death of a member that will interrupt the existence of the LLC, unless all (or a majority of) the remaining members vote to continue it.

[Alternative Clause]

6.   The period of duration of [name of LLC] is from [date articles are filed] to [date of final dissolution].

7.   The management of [name of LLC] shall be vested pursuant to the Operating Agreement in a manager/managers, who shall be appointed by the members and who shall have the exclusive right to control and manage [name of LLC]. The members shall not take part in the management and control of [name of LLC] and shall have no power to bind [name of LLC].

   NOTE: Some states provide that management of the LLC will be vested in the members in proportion to their membership interests, unless the articles provide otherwise.

[Alternative Clause]

7.   The management of [name of LLC] shall be vested pursuant to an operating agreement in the following managers, who shall be appointed by the members. The names and street addresses of the managers are: [names and addresses of managers].

[Alternative Clause]

7.   The management of [name of LLC] shall be vested in the members. The names and street addresses of the members are: [names and addresses of members].

8.   [name of LLC] has been formed for the following purposes: [specify purposes], and to conduct or promote any lawful business or purpose permitted by the laws of [state of organization].

9.   In the event of the death, retirement, resignation, expulsion, bankruptcy, or dissolution of a member or the occurrence of any other event that terminates the continued membership of a member in [name of LLC], the remaining members have the right [under the operating agreement] to continue the business of [name of LLC].

10.   [Name of LLC] is intended to be treated as a partnership [or corporation] for purposes of federal income taxation.

11.   A member's interest in [name of LLC] may be evidenced by a certificate of membership interest signed by [person or persons with signing authority], which may be assigned or transferred. The right to assign or transfer a member's interest in [name of LLC] is limited by the provisions of Article _____, Paragraph _____ of the Operating Agreement.

Source: Basic Legal Forms
   © *Warren, Gorham, and Lamont*

Income Statement from a Restaurant Business

Yesteryear Bar and Grill
STATEMENT OF INCOME
Year Ended August 31, 1996

Sales	Amount	% of Sales
	$544,576	100%
Cost of Sales:		
Cost of Food	161,194	29.6
Cost of Paper	18,516	3.4
Salaries and Wages	115,450	21.2
Payroll Taxes	19,060	3.5
	314,220	57.7
Gross Profit	230,356	42.3
Operating Expenses	208,573	38.3
Gross Margin on Operations	21,783	4
General Administrative Expenses	11,980	2.2
Operating Income	9,803	1.8
Other Income (expense)	8,168	
Income before income taxes	$17,971	

Source: Macdonald, Page & Co.

Safeguarding Your Business

Trademark. . . *To protect your name*

A trademark, or service mark, in the service industry, is defined as a word, name, symbol, device, design, slogan, distinctive sound, or any combination thereof that distinguishes your merchandise and service(s) from those of your competitors. Prior to choosing a name for your business, you should check with your secretary of state's office to be sure that name is not already reserved and if not, complete the paperwork to register it. If you intend to provide services out-of-state (let's say you own a landscaping business in eastern Kentucky and plan to conduct business in West Virginia), you might want to register your name in both states. If, on the other hand, you plan to do business nationwide, as in the case of a newsletter, you would want to register your trademark through the U.S. Patent and Trademark Office, at the following address:

> U.S. Patent and Trademark Office
> 2121 Crystal Drive
> Arlington, VA 22202
> 703-305-8341
> 800-786-9199

Copyright. . . *To protect your writings*

A copyright, as the term implies, protects an author against someone copying his or her works. To be copyrighted, a work must be original. The Copyright Act of 1976 gives several rights to copyright owners, including: the rights of reproduction, adaptation, distribution, performance, and display. These rights can be sold to others in the form of licenses. Copyrights are registered at the copyright office at the Library of Congress. Information can be obtained by calling 202-707-3000 or 202-707-9100 for applications. You can also write to the address below. Your original work is considered copyrighted as soon as it is created. You are not required to register it with the Register of Copyrights. However, once your work has been registered, the symbol ©, the year of first publication, and the name of the copyright owner should be displayed on your work. There is a $10 fee for registration of copyright which lasts for the life of the creator plus 50 years.

> Register of Copyrights
> Information and Publication Section, LM-455
> Library of Congress
> Washington, DC 20559

Patents. . . *To protect your inventions*

A patent is the registered, exclusive right to make, use, and sell an invention. A patent is granted by the government through the Patent and Trademark Office. The process for obtaining a patent is complicated, time consuming, and expensive. A copy of the "General Information Concerning Patents" can be obtained from the U.S. Patent and Trademark Office, at the address listed above. If you are considering conducting a patent search or filing for a patent, a patent attorney or agent should be consulted.

The U.S. Patent and Trademark Office now offers a great deal of useful information about patents, trademarks, and copyrights via the Internet (http://www.uspto.gov).

Ratio Analysis

A **ratio analysis** is a simple mathematical comparison that examines the relationship between certain income statement and balance sheet items. Once a ratio analysis has been completed for your business, the results can then be compared to industry averages. Ratio analysis is important in ongoing financial analysis for a business that's up and running or in the analysis of a business you are considering purchasing. It can also be useful to test some of the assumptions you have made on pro forma statements for a start-up. In addition, bankers use comparative ratios as they analyze financial statements in response to loan requests.

TYPES OF RATIOS

Ratios are grouped into four categories: Liquidity Ratios, Activity Ratios, Leverage Ratios, and Profitability Ratios. Following is an example of a commonly used ratio from each category. The numbers shown are for illustrative purposes only. More information about ratios and ratio analysis is readily available in most business finance texts or a publication such as *Financial Studies of the Small Business*.

Liquidity Ratio — *Current ratio*

Liquidity is an indication of the ability of a business to cover its current liabilities on a day-to-day basis. Liquidity analysis focuses on balance sheet asset and liability relationships that indicate how well a firm's assets cover its debts. In other words, the analyst (or user of this data) wants to know if the debts could actually be liquidated (paid off). The *current ratio* is one such measure. It is calculated by dividing Current Assets by Current Liabilities.

$$\frac{\text{Current Assets}}{\text{Current Liabilities}} = \text{Current ratio} \qquad \frac{\$125,000}{\$100,000} = 1.25$$

A current ratio of 1.25 means that there is $1.25 in current assets (including cash, receivables, and inventory) for every $1.00 in current liabilities (such as accounts payable, notes payable, and accrued expenses). In general, to assure liquidity the current ratio should be between 1 and 2. The actual figure depends on the type of firm, the volatility of economic conditions, and the quality of current assets.

Activity Ratios — *Average collection period*

Activity ratios focus on the speed with which receivables are collected, inventory is sold (turned over), or payables are being paid. This analysis allows you to determine whether common operating activities are being handled efficiently. The average number of days it takes to collect receivables is calculated in two steps:

$$\frac{\text{Net sales}}{\text{Average receivables}} = \text{Receivables turnover} \qquad \frac{\$290,000}{\$29,500} = 9.8$$

$$\frac{\text{Business days in a year}}{\text{Receivables turnover}} = \text{Average collection period} \qquad \frac{360}{9.8} = 36.7 \text{ days}$$

Ratio Analysis *(continued)*

Ideally, only a monthly average of receivables and sales on credit is used in the sales figure. (For simplicity's sake, in this example all sales have been assumed to be on credit.)

Leverage Ratio — *Times interest earned*

Long-term investors and creditors of a firm want to know whether a firm's income is adequate to allow for promised returns to them, as well as to allow for reinvestment toward future growth. For example, the *times interest earned* ratio provides long-term creditors with a measure of how well the interest on their debt can be covered by income.

In another sense, *times interest earned* indicates the extent to which earnings can decline before the firm is unable to meet its annual interest costs. Banks use this measure to assess the firm's ability to meet interest obligations. It is calculated by dividing *net operating income* by total *interest expense*.

$$\frac{\text{Net operating income}}{\text{Interest expense}} = \text{Times interest earned} \qquad \frac{\$23{,}707}{\$2{,}800} = 8.5$$

This is considered to be an indication of general financial strength. The appropriate level varies from industry to industry. A ratio of 5.0 or better would be considered to be a strong position in many industries, but in the utilities industry, for example, a *times interest earned* ratio of 3.0 is considered adequate.

Profitability Ratio — *Return on owner's equity*

Profitability is the assessment of a company's bottom line (profit) in relation to the size of its sales, assets, debts, or owner's equity. Profitability measures can show how effectively a business controls its expenses or utilizes its assets and investments. *Return on owner's equity* is calculated by dividing *net income* by *total owner's equity*.

$$\frac{\text{Net income}}{\text{Owner's equity}} = \text{Return on owner's equity} \qquad \frac{\$17{,}771}{\$209{,}900} = 8.5\%$$

The *return on owner's equity* ratio provides a measure of the earnings on the owner's investment in the business, which, at the very least, can be compared to the rate of return on current money market investments. In general, investors want to know whether the return on their investment is remaining stable over time, and whether or not it exceeds the rate of return on other balance sheet factors like *total assets* and *total debt*.

Once you have calculated your ratios, compare them to those of similar businesses. This information can be found in the publications of Robert Morris Associates, Dun & Bradstreet, Prentice Hall Publishing, and FRA's *Financial Studies of the Small Business*. Each of these publications lists ratios by industry types, and some of them break them down further by size of business. You can get copies of them from your banker, who uses them to compare your company to others, or try your local or state library.

Remember, the ratios presented in the publications cited above are industry averages. Some companies produce better, some worse. To remain viable, your target ratio should be above the average. Also, your business will probably be smaller than the industry average. *Financial Studies of the Small Business* includes smaller sales categories, making it a particularly good reference for start-ups.

Bibliography

Accounting, Bookkeeping, and Taxes

Accounting and Financial Fundamentals for Nonfinancial Executives, by Robert Rachlin and Allen Sweeney (AMACOM, 1996, 256 pages; $18.95; 800-262-9699).

Bottom Line Basics: Understand and Control Business Finances, by Robert J. Low (Oasis Press, 1995, 304 pages; $19.95; 800-228-2275).

Budgeting for a Small Business, by Terry Dickey (Crisp Publications, 1994, 200 pages; $15.95; 800-442-7477).

The Ernst & Young Tax Guide: 1997 (John Wiley & Sons, updated annually, 752 pages; $14.95; 800-225-5945).

The Ernst & Young Tax Saver's Guide: 1997 (John Wiley & Sons, updated annually, 280 pages; $10.95; 800-225-5945).

Financial Basics of Small Business, by James O. Gill (Crisp Publications, 1994, 250 pages; $15.95; 800-442-7477).

Banking, Financing, Cash and Capital Resources

Banking Smarter: How to Save Money in Your Business Banking Relationship, by Dennis M. Suchocki and Andrew M. Smith, BCS & Associates (Traci Rae Publishing, 1994, 120 pages; $39.95; 800-644-8384).

Free Money for Small Businesses and Entrepreneurs, by Laurie Blum (John Wiley & Sons, 4th ed., 1995, 293 pages; $14.95; 800-225-5945).

How to Finance a Growing Business: An Insider's Guide to Negotiating the Capital Markets, by Royce Diener (Merritt Professional Publishing, 4th ed., 1995, 328 pages; $24.95; 800-638-7597).

Practical Merchandising Math, by Leo Gafney (John Wiley & Sons, National Retail Federation series; 1996; 300 pages; $45; 800-225-5945).

Pratt's Guide to Venture Capital Sources, Edited by Daniel Bokser and Ted Weissberg, (Securities Data Publishing, 19th ed., 1997, 740 pages; $325; 800-455-5844).

Business Valuation, Buying a Business

Business Analysis & Valuation Using Financial Statements: Text and Cases, by Krishna G. Palepu, Victor L. Bernard, and Paul M. Healy (South-Western College Publishing, 1996, 896 pages; $93.95; 800-354-9706).

Business Valuation: Theory and Practice, by Dr. Joseph Vinso (J & H Publishing, 1996, updated annually, 550 pages; $95; 406-542-1213).

Guide to Business Valuations, by Jay Fishman, Shannon Pratt, Clifford Griffith, and Keith Wilson (Practitioners Publishing, 7th ed., 1997, updated annually, 3 volumes, average 400 pages each; $172; 800-323-8724).

Handbook of Small Business Valuation Formulas and Rules of Thumb, by Glenn Desmond (Valuation Press, 3rd ed., 1993, 372 pages; $79.95; 800-421-8042).

Valuation: Measuring and Managing the Value of Companies, by Tom Copeland, Tom Koller, and Jack Murrin, McKinsey & Co. (John Wiley & Sons, 2nd ed., 1995, 576 pages; $64.71; book and disk, $139.95; 212-859-5000).

Computers and Other Office Equipment

Business Consumer Guide (Beacon Research Group, bimonthly, 40 to 50 pages per issue, $119 for a 2-year subscription (12 issues); back issues, $25; 800-938-0088).

. . . For Dummies Series, by various authors (IDG Books Worldwide, many updated annually, 200 to 700 pages; $16.95 to $34.95; 888-438-6643).

Direct Marketing

Beyond 2000, The Future of Direct Marketing, by Jerry I. Reitman (NTC Business Books, 1994, 288 pages; $34.95; 800-323-4900).

Direct Marketing Rules of Thumb, by Nat G. Bodian (McGraw-Hill, 1995, 448 pages; $59.95; 800-722-4726).

Direct Marketing, Strategy, Planning, and Execution, by Edward Nash
(McGraw-Hill, 3rd ed., 1995, 512 pages; $44.95; 800-722-4726).

Profitable Retailing Using Relationship and Database Marketing, Deloitte & Touche LLP
(Commissioned by the Direct Marketing Association, 1994, 144 pages;
$125; 212-768-7277).

*The New Direct Marketing: How to Implement a Profit-Driven Database
Marketing Strategy*, by David Shepard Associates (Irwin Professional
Publishing, 2nd ed., 1994, 493 pages; $60; 800-634-3966).

Successful Direct Marketing Methods, by Bob Stone (NTC Business Books,
6th ed., 1997, 560 pages; $49.95; 800-323-4900).

Electronic Commerce, Internet/Web

101 Businesses You Can Start on the Internet, by Daniel S. Janal (Van Nostrand Reinhold, 1996,
506 pages; $24.95; 800-842-3636).

Build a Web Site: The Programmer's Guide to Creating, Building, and Maintaining a Web Presence,
by net.Genesis, edited by Devra Hall (Prima Publishing, 1995, 656 pages; $34.95; 800-632-8676).

Business Development: Doing More Business on the Internet, by Mary Cronin (Van Nostrand
Reinhold, 2nd ed., 1995, 368 pages; $29.95; 800-842-3636).

Software Directory for Retailers, Coopers & Lybrand (John Wiley & Sons,
5th ed., 1995, 733 pages; $125; 800-225-5945).

World Wide Web Bible, by Bryan Pfaffenberger (MIS Press, 2nd ed., 1996,
688 pages; $29.95; 800 488-5233).

World Wide Web Marketing: Integrating the Internet into Your Marketing Strategy, by
Jim Sterne (John Wiley & Sons, 1995, 352 pages; $24.95; 800-225-5945).

Forms of Ownership and Organization

Basic Legal Forms, by Marvin Hyman (Warren, Gorham & Lamont, 2nd. ed.,
1995, updated annually, 864 pages; $145; 800-431-9025).

The Essential Limited Liability Company Handbook, by Corporate Agents, Inc.
(Oasis Press, 1995, 260 pages; $19.95; 800-228-2275).

The Essential Corporation Handbook, by Carl R.J. Sniffen (Oasis Press, 2nd ed.,
1995, 244 pages; $19.95; 800-228-2275).

Franchising

Franchise Bible, How to Buy a Franchise or Franchise Your Own Business, by Erwin J. Keup
(Oasis Press, 3rd ed., 1995, 310 pages; $19.95; 800-228-2275).

Tips and Traps When Buying a Franchise, by Mary E. Tomzack (McGraw-Hill,
1994, 224 pages; $14.95; 800-722-4726).

The Franchise Kit, A Nuts and Bolts Guide to Owning and Running a Franchise Business, by Kirk Shivell
and Kent Banning (McGraw-Hill, 2nd ed., 1995, 304 pages; $14.95; 800-722-4726).

Human Resources, Managing People

CompControl: The Secrets of Reducing Workers' Compensation Costs, by
Edward J. Priz (Oasis Press, 1995, 155 pages; $19.95; 800-228-2275).

How to Really Recruit, Motivate, & Lead Your Team: Managing People, edited by Ruth G. Newman and
Bradford W. Ketchum, Jr. (*Inc.* magazine, 1994, 260 pages; $15.95; 800-468-0800).

Managing Human Resources in Small & Mid-Sized Companies, by Diane Arthur
(AMACOM, 2nd ed., 1995, 352 pages; $59.95; 800-262-9699).

Insurance

Dictionary of Insurance, by Lewis E. Davids (Roman & Littlefield, 7th ed., 1990,
504 pages; $17.95; 800-462-6420).

Understanding Insurance Law, by Robert H. Jerry II (Matthew Bender, 2nd ed.,
1996, 1022 pages; $30; 212-967-7707).

BIBLIOGRAPHY

Legal Issues, Agreements, and Contracts

A Legal Guide for Small Business, by Charles P. Lickson (Crisp Publications, 1994, 210 pages; $15.95; 800-442-7477).

Basic Legal Forms, by Marvin Hyman (Warren, Gorham & Lamont, 2nd. ed., 1995, updated annually, 864 pages; $145; 800-431-9025).

Law & Advertising, by Dean Keith Fueroghne (The Copy Workshop, 1995, 505 pages; $37.50; 800-651-3133, ext. 1179).

Location Analysis

Location, Location, Location: How to Select the Site for Your Business, by Luigi Salvaneschi (Oasis Press, 1996, 250 pages; $19.95; 800-228-2275).

Management and Planning

301 Great Management Ideas, edited by Leslie Brokaw (*Inc.* magazine, revised ed., 1995, 360 pages; $14.95, 800-468-0800).

How to Really Start Your Own Business, by David E. Gumpert (*Inc.* magazine, 2nd ed., 1994, 238 pages; $19.95; 800-468-0800).

Masterminding the Store, Advertising, Sales Promotion, and the New Marketing Reality, by Don Ziccardi with David Moin (John Wiley & Sons, National Retail Federation Series, 1996, 336 pages; $27.95; 800-225-5945).

The Mission Statement Book, by Jeffrey Abrahams (Ten Speed Press, 1995, 640 pages; $21.95; 800-841-2665).

Specialty Shop Retailing, How to Run Your Own Store, by Carol L. Schroeder (John Wiley & Sons, National Retail Federation series, 1997, 352 pages; $29.95; 800-225-5945).

Marketing and Market Research (Advertising, Customer Service, and Pricing)

Advertising Campaign Planning, by Jim Avery (The Copy Workshop, 3rd ed., 1997, 222 pages; $24.95; 800-651-3133, ext. 1179).

Customer Service for Dummies, by Karen Leland and Keith Bailey (IDG Books Worldwide, 1995, 346 pages; $19.99; 888-438-6643).

How to Really Create a Successful Marketing Plan, by David E. Gumpert (*Inc.* magazine, revised and updated 2nd ed., 1994, 280 pages; $19.95; 800-468-0800).

How to Really Deliver Superior Customer Service, edited by John R. Halbrooks (*Inc.* magazine, 1994, 268 pages; $15.95; 800-468-0800).

The Strategy and Tactics of Pricing, by Thomas Nagle (Prentice Hall, 2nd ed., 1994, 432 pages; $55; 800-947-7700).

Merchandising

Management of Retail Buying, by R. Patrick Cash, Joseph S. Friedlander, and John W. Wingate (John Wiley & Sons, 3rd ed., 1995, 424 pages; $80; 800-225-5945).

Standard Color & Size Code Handbook, (National Retail Federation, updated annually, approx. 400 pages; $235; 202-626-8177).

Visual Merchandising and Store Design's Buying Guide, Visual Merchandising and Store Design (ST Publications, annual update, approx. 200 pages; $25; 800-925-1110).

Patents, Copyrights, and Trademarks

Patent It Yourself, by David Pressman (Nolo Press, 6th ed., 1997, 300 pages; $44.95; 800-992-6656).

Licensing Intellectual Property, by Diane E. Cornish (Carswell, 1995, 110 pages; $38.00; 800-387-5164).

Store Survival

Small Store Survival, Success Strategies for Retailers, Arthur Andersen LLP (John Wiley & Sons, National Retail Federation Series, 1997, 386 pages; $34.95; 800-225-5645).

Competing with the Retail Giants, How to Survive in the New Retail Landscape, by Kenneth E. Stone (John Wiley & Sons, National Retail Federation Series, 1995, 272 pages; $17.95; 800-225-5945).

Glossary

Acid-test ratio, quick ratio

An informal indication of a business's ability to meet its financial obligations. The formula focuses on liquid assets by excluding inventory and is determined by dividing current liabilities by current assets.

Action devices

Techniques used in direct mail to encourage consumer response (e.g., trial packages, coupons).

Advisory board

A group of business peers willing to help you make major business decisions.

AIDA

A popular formula for laying out direct mail copy. The acronym stands for (get) Attention, (arouse) Interest, (stimulate) Desire, (ask for) Action.

Anchor

The primary tenant in a shopping mall, usually a department or discount store that occupies more than 50,000 square feet. It serves as a major draw for foot traffic to the mall.

Asset

Any item owned that has cash value, such as real estate, equipment, stocks, or licenses, that can be used to satisfy debts.

Bait and switch

An illegal advertising tactic in which customers are lured into the store by an advertised low-priced offer and are intentionally directed toward more expensive products.

Blue laws

State laws designed to regulate or eliminate retail sales on Sunday. Most states have repealed their blue laws.

Book inventory

A system that enables retailers to know the dollar value of inventory on hand. This system saves time and labor, since it does not require taking a physical inventory.

Bottom line

The profit or loss line on the income statement. It is the last line on the statement.

Browser

A software program that allows the user to view the World Wide Web.

Buying group

Several small, independent stores that combine orders for merchandise into one large order to get better prices and terms.

Carrying cost

The expense of having funds tied up in inventory and the cost of storage space. Carrying costs increase over time if units remain unsold.

Cherry pick

Carefully selecting specific items in a broad line of products to provide your customers with the best merchandise available.

Coding

A cryptic code of letters and numbers used to categorize customers on a database list. The code can be deciphered to determine customer demographics, geographic markets, and the effectiveness of various marketing methods.

Compiled list
Names and addresses collected from directories, subscription lists, public records, customer databases, trade show guest lists, and the like to identify target audiences.

Computer personalization
Merging of letters or other promotional pieces with database information by a computer. This allows the sender to tailor the mailing to a specific individual by name, address, and other information.

Consignment
Goods available for sale in the store, but not owned as inventory by the store. The ownership of consignment goods passes directly from the owner/ manufacturer of the goods (not the retailer) to the consumer.

Cooperative direct marketing
A group of businesses sharing a single mailing (usually via a direct marketing firm) to promote their products or services, thereby lowering their promotional costs.

Cost of goods sold (COGS)
The total cost of merchandise that has been sold, including manufacturing overhead, administration costs, carrying costs, shipping costs, and markdowns.

CPM
The cost for a specific advertising medium divided by the number of hits it generates. For example, if a radio ad costs $300, and it reaches 10,000 people, it has a CPM of (300/10,000) 3¢.

Deep and narrow
Selling a small selection of items, but in large quantities. The opposite is *shallow and wide*, which is a broad selection of items with only a few of each in stock. Most major discount stores have a shallow and wide inventory, while specialty shops are usually deep and narrow.

Demographics
Statistics for various socioeconomic variables such as age, race, income, etc. Often used to determine target market.

Depreciation
For tax reporting and accounting purposes, the reduction in value of property (asset) over its useful life.

Discount
Selling merchandise at a price lower than standard retail price.

Discounts and allowances
Reduction in price of services or merchandise to customers based on classification of customer (i.e., commercial versus individual) and/or volume of sales activity. Allowances are typically offered to the retailer by the manufacturer, as in the case of retail display allowances.

Distribution center
A central node, usually a warehouse, that receives inventory from several vendors and distributes it to several stores.

Distribution channel An interconnected chain of businesses that move products via air, land, or sea from the point of production to the point of sale.

Download/upload To use a computer to retrieve or send electronic files to another computer or disk.

Economic order quantity

The order quantity, based on the fixed costs of placing an order and the associated inventory carrying costs, that minimizes the total cost for an item.

Electronic commerce Methods for ordering and selling goods over the Internet, which can involve various payment methods, including credit cards and automatic bank transfers.

Electronic Data Interchange (EDI)

The exchange of business data (e.g., orders) from supplier to retailer and vice versa by computer.

Equity Ownership interest in a business in the form of stock, paid-in capital, and/or retained earnings.

Exclusive territory The sole right to sell specific products in a particular area as determined by the supplier. Franchisors often allocate exclusive territories for their franchisees.

Extended warranty Optional warranties purchased by the consumer separate from the product. These warranties continue for a period of time beyond the duration of a standard, or "express," warranty.

Fair Debt Collection Practices Act

A 1978 law designed to protect the consumer from harassment and unfair collection procedures.

Federal Trade Commission (FTC)

An independent agency responsible for enforcing antitrust laws. The FTC regulates methods of competition and prosecutes violators for unfair competitive practices.

File transfer protocol (FTP)

A method for retrieving files from the Internet.

Firewall A security measure used to protect computers on a local area network from outside access.

Footprint The layout of a business location to scale.

Goodwill Intangible but valuable asset (i.e., reputation) of a business that is developed from the sale and/or distribution of quality services or merchandise. Also, community involvement by the business to promote the public good.

Home page An electronic "billboard" on the World Wide Web used for advertising a business. A home page can include a listing of services offered, pictures of products, E-mail addresses, hours of operation, and other helpful information.

Hypertext	A system that directly links documents scattered across many sites.
Hypertext markup language (HTML)	
	The standard format for documents on the World Wide Web.
Income	A highly important demographic selection factor, which can be found on consumer databases. Divisions exist for incomes in $1,000 increments and can be cross-matched with other demographic data to define a target audience.
Internet (the Net)	A global information network created by the interconnection of millions of computers worldwide. The Net makes it possible to obtain information from resources ranging from the New York Public Library and U.S. Congress to your local school board and hundreds of colleges and universities. It can also be used to send electronic mail (E-mail) messages to anyone across the globe who has a computer and telephone.
Inventory turns	A ratio of sales to inventory. An inventory "turn" equals sales divided by inventory value. The greater the number of turns, the more efficiently the store's inventory dollars are being used.
Java	A programming language for the World Wide Web that allows developers to create mini-programs, or "applets," that can be easily transferred over the Internet and run on any computer regardless of operating system.
Leverage	Borrowing money for a business venture to produce an expected return higher than the cost of the borrowed funds.
Licensed product	Products for which a licensing fee has been paid to the individual or company owning the rights to the image. For example, the cost of a Budweiser T-shirt featuring the beer's logo includes a licensing fee to Anheuser-Busch, the owner of the rights to the logo.
Links (hyperlinks)	A connection between two locations on the Web. A link can be used to direct a person from a particular home page to a resource containing more in-depth information on a particular subject or to an E-mail address.
Margin	The difference between the total cost of an item (including all overhead costs) and its retail price.
Middleman	An agent or broker that handles merchandise from one or more suppliers and sells it on their behalf to a distributor or retailer. The middleman retains a fee (usually based on the profits from the sale) for handling the goods.
Mission statement	Outline of business purpose that includes long-term organizational objectives, management philosophy, and community outreach goals.
Net worth	The amount by which a business's assets exceed its liabilities.

Niche
A particular segment of the market in which a business specializes. By focusing efforts on a discrete sector, a company can help ensure efficient use of its marketing efforts.

Off-price retailing
The practice of purchasing merchandise such as end-lots, closeouts, and seconds at lower-than-usual wholesale prices, to sell the goods at below-average retail prices.

Operating expenses
Amounts paid to maintain and/or operate property, such as the cost of utilities, supplies, taxes, depreciation, and insurance.

Organizational chart
A tree chart diagramming the structure of responsibility and authority within an organization.

Owner equity
The amount of capital investment by the owner(s) after retained earnings, dividends, and other financial obligations.

Positioning
Your company image, in the eyes of your customers, in relation to that of your competitors. For example, you may position your company as a low-priced alternative to a premium-priced competitor.

Product life cycle
The cycle of market development for a given product or service through introduction, market saturation, and decline.

Pull promotions
Promotions that retailers target to consumers. They are designed to "pull" the customer into the store.

Push money
Money spent by suppliers to provide bonuses to salespeople to encourage the sale of selected merchandise. This tactic is designed to encourage the existing sales force to "push" the product on the consumer.

Push promotions
Promotions that vendors target at retailers. These promotions often take the form of in-house challenges and rewards for the most units sold or for the greatest percentage of sales.

Rate card
Printed card issued by the publishers and directors of journals, newspapers, and other media outlets detailing costs for advertising and advertisement sizes and frequency.

Revenue
The gross amount of money received for services rendered or merchandise sold.

Search engine
Applications on the World Wide Web that allow the user to enter key words and search for documents on the Internet.

Service provider
A company that provides connections to the Internet.

SKU (stock keeping unit)
Inventory products of the same style, color, and size.

Small Business Development Center (SBDC)

A small-business assistance center that provides counseling, training, and other services—in most cases at no charge. Partially funded by the U.S. Small Business Administration, SBDCs are located in all 50 states, plus the District of Columbia, Puerto Rico, and the U.S. Virgin Islands (see directory on pages 264-267).

SOHO   Acronym for Small Office/Home Office.

Target market   Specific group(s) of persons with common demographic characteristics who have significant potential for buying a particular product or service.

Teaser   Advertisement designed to create curiosity about a coming advertisement or promotion.

Telecommunications   Transmission of information by telephone, wire, or computer.

Telemarketing   Use of the telephone for promotion or sales.

Trademark   A nationally registered insignia or logo that distinguishes one manufacturer's products from all others. A trademark could be a picture, design, company or personal name, or other unique symbol.

Uniform resource locator (URL)

A type of address that points to a specific document on the World Wide Web (e.g., *Inc.* magazine's URL is http//www.inc.com).

U. S. Small Business Administration (SBA)

A division of the federal government dedicated to promoting small business by providing management and technical assistance and loan guarantees through various programs such as the Service Corps of Retired Executives (SCORE), Small Business Development Centers (SBDCs), and Business Information Centers (BICs).

Venture capital   Source of financing for start-up or emerging businesses that present greater than average investment risk for the short term, but will potentially produce greater returns in the long run. Typically used by high-tech or emerging-technology companies.

Visual merchandising   Encouraging purchases by displaying merchandise in an attractive manner.

Web site   See below; see also Home page.

World Wide Web   A service of the Internet, the Web is a connection of millions of computers forming a supernetwork of electronic information. It allows users to retrieve hypertext and graphics from various Internet sites.

Index

R

S

T

U

V

W